英语专业博雅教育课程系列教材

英语文学翻译教程
小说与散文

陈伯雨 编著

TRANSLATION OF ENGLISH LITERATURE FICTION AND ESSAY

清华大学出版社
北京

内 容 简 介

本教材充分整合与翻译实践相关的各学科理论，涉及普通语言学、语义学、语用学、修辞学、文体学、翻译学、认知语言学、篇章语言学和系统功能语言学等知识，按照难易程度划分为初级理论（语言功能、语境意识、意义类型、修辞手段和连贯意识）、中级理论（预设意识、文体变异、隐喻翻译和合作原则）及高级理论（语篇功能、人际功能和概念功能）三大板块，同时辅以详实的例子和基于理论的解释，让翻译学习者真正掌握品鱼和打鱼的方法。翻译练习部分精选了多部英语名著的片段和完整章节，以及十篇妙趣横生的散文。

鉴于教材篇幅有限，另外一部分练习和全部参考译文放在ftp://ftp.tup.tsinghua.edu.cn/上供大家下载。

版权所有，侵权必究。举报：010-62782989，beiqinquan@tup.tsinghua.edu.cn。

图书在版编目（CIP）数据

英语文学翻译教程：小说与散文 / 陈伯雨编著. —北京：清华大学出版社，2021.2（2024.3重印）
英语专业博雅教育课程系列教材
ISBN 978-7-302-53105-0

Ⅰ.①英… Ⅱ.①陈… Ⅲ.①英语文学—文学翻译—高等学校—教材 Ⅳ.①H315.9 ②I046

中国版本图书馆CIP数据核字（2019）第101118号

责任编辑：钱屹芝
封面设计：子 一
责任校对：王凤芝
责任印制：宋 林

出版发行：清华大学出版社
网　　址：https://www.tup.com.cn, https://www.wqxuetang.com
地　　址：北京清华大学学研大厦A座　邮　　编：100084
社 总 机：010-83470000　　　　　　　邮　　购：010-62786544
投稿与读者服务：010-62776969, c-service@tup.tsinghua.edu.cn
质量反馈：010-62772015, zhiliang@tup.tsinghua.edu.cn

印 装 者：三河市龙大印装有限公司
经　　销：全国新华书店
开　　本：185mm×260mm　　印　张：19.25　字　数：421千字
版　　次：2021年2月第1版　　　　　印　次：2024年3月第4次印刷
定　　价：79.00元

产品编号：072131-01

前　言

- **时代背景**

　　根据 2019 年"第四届全国高等学校外语教育改革与发展高端论坛"公布的数据，开设外语类本科专业的高校占全国本科高校数量的 82.4%。英语专业在外语专业中地位重要，而"英汉笔译"又是英语专业中的必修课，再加之全国高校和科研院所翻译本科和翻译硕士点数量较多，而这些专业也必然会有各种类型的英汉笔译课，另外研究生全国统考英语试卷中有英语长句翻译一项，因此不难推断，需要学习翻译的学生来自英语专业、翻译专业以及其他所有专业，英汉笔译学习已俨然成为大学生和研究生的刚性需求。

- **预期读者**

　　本教材最初针对的是英语专业学生和翻译专业学生。后来笔者也在大学英语选修课上使用过本教材，发现效果都很不错。很多非英语专业的学生纷纷表示，通过学习教材内容，他们不仅提高了自身的英汉笔译能力，也大大提高了英语理解和鉴赏能力，同时一定程度上提升了英语写作能力。所以，本教材的预期读者包括英语专业、翻译专业在内的所有大学生，所有预期读者都可以从本教材中找到对自身学习有用的方法。

- **编写目的**

　　本教材编写的目的是通过引入普通语言学、语义学、语用学、修辞学、文体学、翻译学、认知语言学、篇章语言学和系统功能语言学的相关理论，帮助学习者较为深刻地认识到文学翻译活动的复杂性和规律性，初步理解并掌握文学翻译的原理、策略和技巧，切实提高学习者的文学语篇理解、鉴赏和翻译的能力，为学习者日后能够从事文学翻译及非文学翻译实践，或从事相关学术研究打下坚实的基础。

● **教材特点**

（一）理论讲解系统全面、通俗易懂、例证翔实、注重分析、实操性强

教材的理论以普通语言学对语言交际功能的划分发端，继而循序渐进地引入了贯穿于所有领域的语境理论、语义学中对意义类型划分的理论、英语修辞学中常用的 25 种修辞手段、篇章语言学中的连贯理论、翻译学中的预设理论、文体学中的变异理论、认知语言学中的概念隐喻理论、语用学中的合作原则、系统功能语言学的三大元功能（语篇功能、人际功能和概念功能）理论。教材语言表达通俗易懂，引用的概念和观点符合学术规范，例子丰富而典型、分析过程详尽，必要时又辅以语料库的论证，易于理解，而且实操性强，能帮助学习者触类旁通，举一反三。

（二）翻译练习精挑细选、内容有趣、风格多样、题量丰富、译文精良

笔者在选材时可谓煞费苦心。书中所有例子和练习都在教学中使用过，文章有一定积极性和趣味性。所选材料整体上呈现出多样化的特点：散文部分篇幅合适，风格多样；小说部分既有篇幅不长的短篇小说，也有风格各异的长篇小说完整章节节选，更有从长篇小说中精选出的"对话类""记叙类"和"描写类"段落。整本教材练习量达到四万四千多词，课堂教学足够使用三个学期，教师和学生可以有较大选择余地。另外，所有译文都是在"翻译工作坊"模式下形成，其中的部分译文还多次经过课堂检验，因此参考译文基本拥有较高质量，对教学和自学会有很大帮助。

● **使用建议**

鉴于翻译是一项涉及众多变量的语言转换活动，因此本教材并未在每章结束后设置相应的单项练习题，但这并不妨碍使用者选择书后面合适的练习题，在练习时重点理解和应用该章所讲理论。每章学习模式都是如此，这是"盲人摸象式"学习法，也是"滚雪球式"学习法。本教材内容丰富，可以使用一个学年（4 学分），也可以使用一个学期（2 学分），或者一个半学期（3 学分）。如果使用一个学年，教师可以采用讲授书上全部理论内容并指导学生练习的方式，也可以采用翻转课堂等教学模式来增加对翻译练习的指导；如果只有一个学期的课时，那么可以考虑舍弃第九、十一和十二章；如果有一个半学期可用，那么除了第十二章，其他章节都应讲授。不管是教师布置的作业，还是学生自选的练习，都建议使用者先独立完成译文，经过两三次认真修改后再对照参考译文，并与老师和同学交流，想

前　言

一想自己的译文为什么要这样表达，是否有相应的翻译理论作为支撑，是否与参考译文存在本质的不同。如果很不一样，到底是自己的译文更好，还是参考译文更好，然后再想想好在哪里，或差在哪里，这样就会慢慢积累起自己对于翻译的宝贵经验。

★笔者的心路历程

笔者也曾像很多莘莘学子一样，从各种笔译教材那里开始翻译实践，也曾像许多翻译教师那样，从使用他人编写的教材开始教授翻译课程。这种寻常的经历当然很重要，是翻译初学者成长必然要经历的过程。不过，正如笔者曾体会过的那样，一些教材作者虽然将自己的翻译经验倾囊相授，但是缺乏理论的支撑，或者虽然讲了一些理论，但那些理论往往是他人经验的总结，或是那些理论缺乏系统性，因而难以成为学习者可以自觉运用的有效理论。后来，笔者主动去寻求向翻译家和研究者当面学习的机会，例如曾四次参加中国翻译协会举办的翻译师资培训，不断提高自己的翻译能力和教学能力。再后来，笔者努力寻找各种翻译出版的机会，不仅翻译文学名著，而且翻译非文学书籍，极大地提高了自己的翻译能力，同时为翻译教学积累了丰富的一手素材，而曾经学习的翻译理论则在翻译实践中不断被加深理解。

经过多年来翻译实践、翻译教学和翻译理论学习之间的有机互动，笔者认识到：翻译教学和学习绝对不能仅凭他人经验或自己经验的积累，必须在理论指导下开始；这些理论应该清晰易懂而又很成体系，这样才容易建构出一个有益于实践的内化理论；课堂翻译练习必须注重质量，但数量也不可缺少，因为翻译能力的大幅提升只有靠质与量结合在一起才能做到；对于翻译教师而言，自身翻译能力必须要很强，自身必须有翻译实践经历，而且是多多益善，同时自身必须要有体系化的理论作为教学和实践的指导，只有教师本人有了理论意识，学生才可能有理论意识，才能在实践时知其然并知其所以然，才能对自己或他人完成的译文给出比较客观的质量评估。正是在上述经历和观念的影响下，笔者最终对自己多年来的翻译实践、教学和理论学习的成果做了一个较为系统的梳理。

本教材的理论和实践内容并非凭空产生，笔者这里首先要感谢中国翻译协会组织的各种理论和实践研讨班，还要感谢曾经以直接或间接方式向自己传道、授业、解惑的各位学者，尤其是感谢曹明伦教授、陈世丹教授、叶子南教授、王东风教授、黄国文教授和何伟教授，这些学者对笔者的翻译理念和治学态度的形成产生了很大的影响。同时，笔者对于资助本教材的中央财经大学外国语学院表示感谢！对于清华大学出版社为本教材出版所做的努力表示感谢！最后，笔者还要感谢家人的支持，尤其要感谢妻子曹丹和女儿一铭，感谢你们多年来默默的奉献！

  限于个人水平有限，书中不足之处在所难免。恳请各位专家和广大读者批评指正。

陈伯雨
2020 年 12 月
于中财骋望楼

目 录

翻译理论：上编

第一章　语言功能·· 2
第二章　语境意识·· 12
第三章　意义类型·· 20
第四章　修辞手段·· 34
第五章　连贯意识·· 53

翻译理论：中编

第六章　预设意识·· 68
第七章　文体变异·· 82
第八章　隐喻翻译·· 104
第九章　合作原则·· 123

翻译理论：下编

第十章　语篇功能·· 138
第十一章　人际功能·· 176
第十二章　概念功能·· 207

翻译实践

小说翻译···243
散文翻译···280

参考文献···295
附　　录···299

翻译理论：上编

本编首先从语言功能切入，引导译者树立语言交际功能的对等转换意识，注意语境对意义解读的影响，提高对词语意义类型的感知，同时关注修辞手段的对等转换，并且在语言和文化两方面都建立起连贯意识。

第一章 语言功能 Language Functions

本章的核心观点是译者必须具备语言功能的识别与转化意识。本章由两个部分构成：一、语言学家对语言功能的划分；二、翻译中的五种语言功能。其中第二部分是重点，它又可分为五个小部分：（一）信息功能；（二）指示功能；（三）表情功能；（四）美学功能；（五）酬应功能。

一、语言学家对语言功能的划分

在正式学习翻译理论和进行翻译实践之前，首先应该知道语言具有不同的功能。也就是说，我们可以使用语言来做各种类型的事情。不同的语言学家对语言功能有不同的划分（胡壮麟等，2001：10-11）。

俄国语言学家雅各布逊把语言划分为所指功能（即传递信息和消息）、诗学功能（即满足于对语言自身的兴趣）、表情功能（即表达态度、感受与情感）、意动功能（即借助命令与恳求的方式来说服和影响他人）、寒暄功能（即确定与他人进行交流的关系）和元语言功能（即阐释说话者的意图和语言的意义）。

英国语言学家韩礼德在早期著作中通过对儿童语言发展的观察，提出语言具有七个功能范畴，即工具功能、控制功能、表达功能、交互功能、自指功能、启发功能和想象功能。

另一位英国语言学家利奇也对语言功能提出了自己的划分。他从语义学视角出发，把语言在交际中的功能划分为五种：信息功能、指示功能、表情功能、美学功能和酬应功能。

鉴于翻译是一种跨文化交际行为，而利奇对语言功能的划分简单、明确，并且与翻译实践直接相关，因此我们的翻译研究和翻译实践将采用利奇的理论视角，这有利于翻译初学者了解语言的交际功能，直观地把握翻译实践。

二、翻译中的五种语言功能

（一）信息功能（Informational Function）

语言的信息功能就是指语言可用来传递信息和消息。通常来说，任何言语表达都含有这个功能，这也是语言最基本、最常用的功能。当然，除了传递一般信息外，有时还会传递文化信息。总之，当某些言语的功能主要体现为传播信息时，译者就应做好信息功能的翻译。

第一章 语言功能

【例1】

原　文：I'm sitting at my mother's desk, a mahogany *secretary*[1] with a writing leaf that folds down to reveal rows of cubbyholes and tiny drawers—even a sliding secret compartment. (*My Mother's Desk*)

译　文：我坐在母亲的书桌前，这是一张红木做的**带书架的写字桌**，上面有个可活动的桌面，桌面向下折叠后便露出几排小格子和几个小抽屉，里面还有一个可以拉动的暗格。

讲　评：翻译初学者通常都会把 secretary 翻译成"书桌"或"写字台"，也有翻译成"办公桌"或"课桌"的，甚至有人翻译为"秘书桌"。可是英英词典里对 secretary 的解释为 a large cabinet with a fold-down desktop, usually with drawers below and an enclosed bookcase above。定义中的解释基本上可以说明，这种类型的桌子在中国人的日常生活中比较罕见。因此，secretary 不应该是上面提到的那些翻译表达，而应译成"带书架的写字桌"，这样才会传递出这个词应该含有的信息，才不会误导读者。

【例2】

原　文：When at last I brought the desk down, it was dusty from months of storage. Lovingly, I polished the drawers and cubbyholes. Pulling out the secret compartment, I found papers inside. A photograph of my father. Family *wedding announcements*. And a one-page letter, folded and refolded many times. (*My Mother's Desk*)

译　文：最后当我把书桌从阁楼上搬下来时，由于数月的搁置，它已是尘埃满身了。我小心翼翼、倍加珍惜地擦干净小抽屉和小格子，然后抽出暗格，结果发现里面有几样东西：一张父亲的照片、几份亲人送来的**结婚喜帖**、还有一封只有一页却反反复复折叠了许多次的书信。

讲　评：没有经验的译者往往会把 wedding announcements 译成"结婚声明""结婚公告"等。这种翻译令人不知所云，因为从古至今，中国人在结婚时似乎并无这种以正式公开的形式告之于众的传统，所以会难以理解，甚至会产生错误联想。那么，wedding announcements 到底应该翻译成什么？wedding announcements 译成"结婚喜帖"比较合适[2]。

---

[1] 本书对某些词语所做的下划线、斜体或加粗处理，都是为了方便读者阅读。如果没有特别说明，都是编者所为，并非原文作者所加。

[2] 结婚喜帖（wedding announcements）：在婚礼仪式后发送结婚喜帖给亲朋好友，正式表明婚姻生活已经开始，并同时邀请亲朋好友参加定于稍晚些时候的结婚答谢宴会，表示对他们的感谢，这是西方结婚仪式的一种必不可少的传统。结婚喜帖上往往会印上新郎、新娘的名字和照片、双方父母的名字、结婚仪式的日期和地点、新人的住址，以及婚后新娘的新的姓氏。

（二）指示功能（Directive Function）

指示功能是指通过命令或请求来说服、影响他人，以便实现某种目的。其实，指示功能也包含着信息功能，只不过这时指示的意图更加凸显罢了。当译者识别出言语表达的主要功能为指示时，就应在译文中努力营造这种效果。

【例3】
原　文：　"You *want* a brooch," said Mrs. Fairfax. (Chapter 13, *Jane Eyre*)
译　文：　"你**还缺**一枚胸针。"费尔法克斯太太说道。
讲　评：　这句话的语境是罗切斯特先生回到府宅后要求简·爱过去见他。管家费尔法克斯太太提醒简·爱务必穿得正式。引号中的句子比较直白地表达了指示功能，强调胸针必须佩戴，因此应译为"你还缺一枚胸针。"

【例4】
原　文：　"Madam, I *should* like some tea," was the sole rejoinder she got. She hastened to ring the bell; and when the tray came, she proceeded to arrange the cups, spoons, etc., with assiduous celerity. I and Adèle went to the table; but the master did not leave his couch. (Chapter 13, *Jane Eyre*)
译　文：　"太太，我**想**喝茶。"罗切斯特先生这样做了回应，这是她所得到的唯一的回答。费尔法克斯太太急忙按铃，召唤仆人前来。待托盘端来后，她又殷勤麻利地摆好了茶杯和茶匙等东西。我和阿黛勒走到桌前，可罗切斯特先生却在沙发上一动未动。
讲　评：　虽然罗切斯特先生是桑菲尔德府的主人，费尔法克斯太太是他的管家，但是两人毕竟有亲属关系，而且费尔法克斯太太又上了年纪，所以罗切斯特先生使用 should 来表达委婉和请求。但即便如此，这个句子主要还是在表达指示功能。

（三）表情功能（Expressive Function）

表情功能指语言用以表达看法、态度、情感或情绪。如果言语表达体现出来的主要是表情功能，那么该表达中的其他功能就会退居次要地位，这时译者就要在译文中凸显出表情功能了。对于表情功能的把握，词义和语境的理解是关键。

【例5】
原　文：　Years later, during her final illness, Mother reserved various items for my sister and brother. *"But the desk,"* she'd repeat, *"is for Elizabeth."* I sensed Mother communicating with this gift, a communication I'd craved for 50 years. (*My Mother's Desk*)

译　　文：多年以后，母亲在弥留之际给我的兄弟姐妹留下了各种各样的家什。**"那个书桌，"她反复叮嘱说，"一定一定要留给伊丽莎白。"**我能感觉到母亲正通过这份礼物与我交流，而这种感觉我已经朝思暮想了整整五十年。

讲　　评：原文中的"But the desk," she'd repeat, "is for Elizabeth." 就明显具有表情功能。这个句子前面和后面的句子提供了较为充分的语境，尤其是前面的"during her final illness"，还有后面的"had craved for 50 years"。通常说来，人在弥留之际，都不会再掩饰自己内心的情感，所以母亲一定会向女儿显露真情，而我"朝思暮想了整整五十年"的表述也从侧面回应了母亲的情感，说明母亲的那句遗言确实反映了她的心声，也确实是作者极为期待的。另外，But 用于句首，常常用来表达强调，这种情况在文学语言中更为常见。'd（would）表示的意思是 used to，之所以使用这个情态动词，说明母亲当时确实说了不止一遍，这也体现了母亲对女儿的殷切期盼。同时，这个句子也含有指示功能，不过这时候指示功能已经退居到次要地位，所以译者这时要努力再现原文的情感功能。正因为如此，这个句子要译为"那个书桌，"她反复叮嘱说，"一定一定要留给伊丽莎白。"

【例6】

原　　文："Oh! single, my dear, to be sure! A single man of large fortune; four or five thousand a year. What a fine thing for our girls!" (Chapter 1, *Pride and Prejudice*)

译　　文："他还是单身呢！亲爱的，千真万确！一个拥有巨额财产的单身汉，每年的收入有四五千镑。我们女儿真是好福气啊！"

讲　　评：这一段承接的是贝内特先生的提问"Is he married or single?"本来，对于一般疑问句，只需要回答是 A 选项或 B 选项，但是贝内特太太明显兴奋异常，后面说了好几句，还都跟钱有关，而且以感叹句结尾，似乎某个女儿嫁给有钱的宾利先生那一幕肯定要发生。这样的句子明显具有表情功能，因此译出说话人的语气和口吻非常重要，这样才能译出对话应有的味道，才能把握住人物的情感。

（四）美学功能（Aesthetic Function）

美学功能就是指语言可以使人沉浸在语言的美感之中。语言的美学功能也称为审美功能，或诗学功能，在所有体裁的文章中都可以或多或少地见到，尤其以文学语言最为密集。因此，译者在翻译文学作品时必须有足够的审美能力，必须能够识别出各种修辞手法，然后再想方设法地在译文中还原这种功能。

利奇和肖特在《小说中的文体》（*Style in Fiction: A Linguistic Introduction to English Fictional Prose*）一书中写道：

Two pieces of language can be seen as alternative ways of saying the same thing: that is, there can be stylistic variants with different stylistic values. By comparing a writer's choices against other choices with the same sense, "what the writer might have said but didn't", one has a greater control over the notion of stylistic value.

(Leech & Short, 1981:34)

　　文体学认为，同样一件事可以有两种不同的说法，也就是说，存在着不同的文体变体（stylistic variant）；而这些文体变体具有不同的文体价值（stylistic value）。在语义不变的情况下，将作者的某些选择与其他选择加以比较，想一想"作者当时也许还可以怎么说，而却没有那么说"，这样就会对文体价值有更深刻的理解了。

　　对于"具有价值的文体变体"这种现象，还有一些学者进行了研究。例如，杰里米·芒迪（2012：96）使用"标记"来表述：

　　Markedness relates to a choice or patterns of choices that stand out as unusual and may come to the reader's attention... The key is to look for the reason behind the markedness.

　　"*标记（性言语）*"能引起读者注意到与众不同的言语选择，或多种选择的组合……研究"标记"这一特征的关键，就是要找出使其产生的真正原因。

　　在各种类型的文学作品中，作家之所以使用"具有文体价值的言语"或"标记性言语"，可能是想要突出语言之美，或者使语言显得特别，或者凸显要表达的意思，以期吸引读者，从而打破语言运用的俗套，也就是创造出"不走寻常路"的表达方式。理论上说，具有美学价值的新奇表达，可以体现在书写、搭配、语用、逻辑等所有领域。

【例 7】

原　文：When at last I brought the desk down, it was dusty from months of storage. *Lovingly,* I polished the drawers and cubbyholes. Pulling out the secret compartment, I found papers inside. A photograph of my father. Family wedding announcements. And a one-page letter, folded and refolded many times. (*My Mother's Desk*)

译　文：最后当我把书桌从阁楼上搬下来时，由于数月的搁置，它已是尘埃满身了。我**小心翼翼、倍加珍惜地**擦干净小抽屉和小格子，然后抽出暗格，竟发现里面有几样东西：一张父亲的照片、几份亲人送来的结婚喜帖，还有一封只有一页却反反复复折叠了许多次的书信。

讲　评：在这个句子中，缺乏经验的译者通常会忽视 lovingly 这个词的位置所具有的意义。通过查询 COCA（美国当代英语语料库），我们发现，当严格限定条件——让 lovingly 出现在句首，同时后面紧跟逗号时（图 1-1　COCA 语料库截图），即与原文中 lovingly 的使用具备相同条件，会查到该词出现在句首的 MI 值（Mutual Information）仅为 0.12（图 1-2　COCA 语料库截图），虽然 COCA 语料库中有 11 个例子（图 1-3　COCA 语料库截图），但这明显低于常见搭配所需要的 3 这一标准值，说明 lovingly 通常不出现在句首，也很少后面紧跟逗号。lovingly 通常跟谁相伴出现呢？我们只要重新设置一下查询条件（图 1-4　COCA 语料库截图），就可以看到与 lovingly 这个副词经常搭配的四种词类——名词、形容词、动词和副词（图 1-5　COCA 语料库截图）。

这里以 lovingly 与形容词搭配为例，做一个简单的解释：最左边一列数字代表语料库中出现相应搭配的例子数量，左边第二列代表 MI 值，这列数值越高，代表 lovingly 与该词的搭配越容易出现。所以，我们可以看到，crafted 最容易出现在 lovingly 后面，其次是 restored 等其他形容词。即便我们不考虑 lovingly 出现在句首这个条件，而只让该词后面出现逗号（图 1-6 COCA 语料库截图），即 lovingly 后面紧跟逗号，可以出现在句中的任何位置，这种情况下可以查到的 MI 值也仅仅是 0.43，比起限定在句首的 0.12 并没有提高多少，虽然有 170 个例子出现（图 1-7 COCA 语料库截图），依然明显低于 3 这个标准值。部分具体的例句，大家可以自行阅读（图 1-8 COCA 语料库截图）。

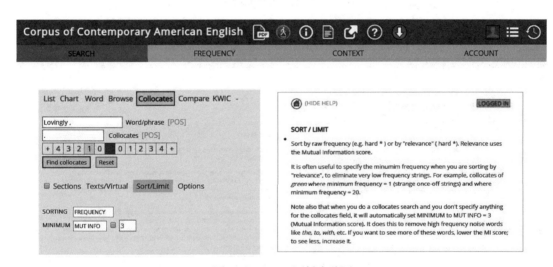

图 1-1 COCA 语料库截图

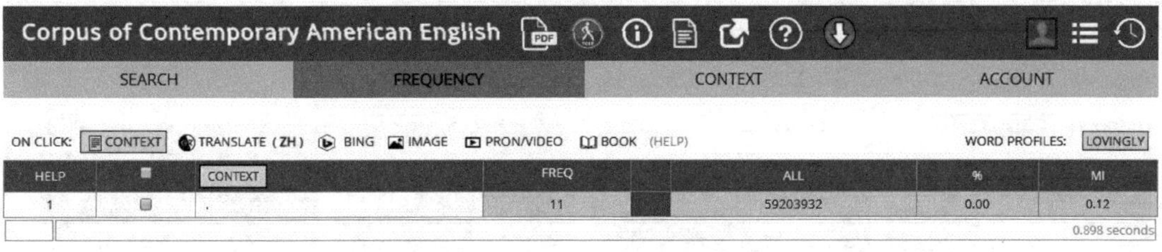

图 1-2 COCA 语料库截图

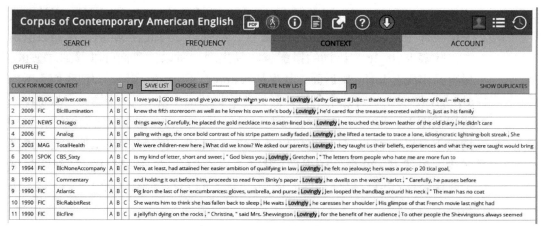

图 1-3　COCA 语料库截图

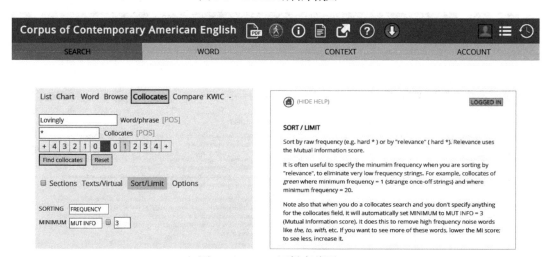

图 1-4　COCA 语料库截图

图 1-5　COCA 语料库截图

第一章 语言功能

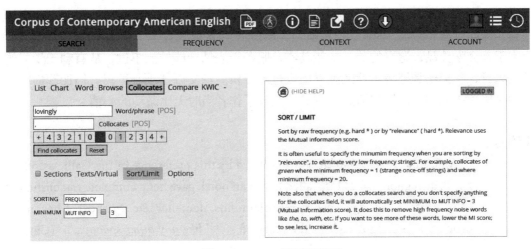

图 1-6　COCA 语料库截图

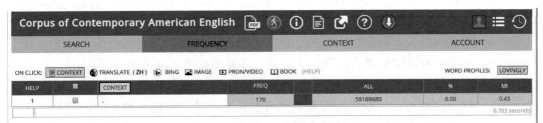

图 1-7　COCA 语料库截图

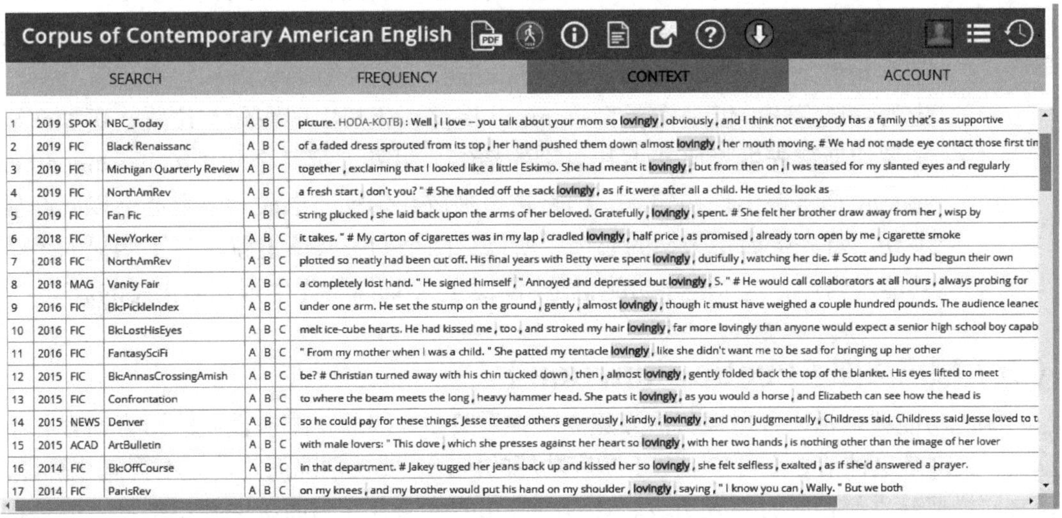

图 1-8　COCA 语料库截图

这些翔实的语料足以说明，lovingly 放在句首比较罕见，即该词在这段文章中具有典型的美学功能。结合语境再继续分析，我们会发现，作者渴望了五十年的母女交流，尤其是亲密无间的那种，始终未能实现。而在母亲去世后，作者伊丽莎白才得知，母亲把书桌特别留给了自己,这明显体现出母亲对女儿的殷切期盼,也很好地说明了作者为何会无比地欣喜和激动。因此,结论就是,lovingly在这里既有美学功能,又有表情功能。但由于是文学作品,这里的美学功能其实是服务于表情功能的。不过,从有利于学习的角度来看,我们还是把美学功能独立出来进行分析。译文以"小心翼翼、倍加珍惜"两个四字格短语来加重语气和情感,有效地凸显了作者当时无比激动的心情。

【例8】

原　文："And, Miss Eyre, *so much was I flattered* by this preference of the Gallic sylph for her British gnome, *that* I installed her in an hotel; gave her a complete establishment of servants, a carriage, cashmeres, diamonds, dentelles, &c. In short, I began the process of ruining myself in the received style, *like any other spoony*..." (Chapter 15, *Jane Eyre*)

译　文："爱小姐,那位高挑的法国美女竟爱上了我这个英国侏儒,**受宠若惊都不足以形容我当时激动的心情。于是,**我把她安顿在一家公馆中,还给她配了一整套的仆人、马车、山羊绒、钻石、蕾丝花边等享受之物。简而言之,我走上了一条司空见惯的自我毁灭之路,**跟其他痴情汉没有半点区别。**"

讲　评：这个情节出现在《简·爱》第15章。当时,简在桑菲尔德府做家庭教师已有一段时间,与罗切斯特先生也有过几次交谈。根据小说后面的叙述,这个时候罗切斯特先生已经爱上了简。趁着一次机会,罗切斯特先生向简讲述起自己与法国歌女赛莉纳·瓦伦的恋爱故事。当然,罗切斯特先生是以自嘲的口吻讲述这段爱情的,毕竟这段经历对他的伤害很深很大。英文第一句的基本句型是 I was so much flattered... that...,这种结果状语从句本来就具有一定的强调意味,但是作者将 so much 提前,让其出现在句首位置,更加凸显了罗切斯特先生无比悲愤和自嘲的情绪。另外,第二个句子的 like any other spoony 通常都出现在句首,但是这里被放在句尾,形成句末重心,以此凸显罗切斯特先生悔不当初的心情。所以,两个句子整体上就具有了明显的美学功能。当然,这个美学功能也是用来表达罗切斯特先生强烈的情感的。

(五)酬应功能(Phatic Function)

　　酬应功能就是指语言用来与他人建立或维系关系。因此,酬应性质的语言内容并不重要,关键是这种话必不可少。至于酬应功能的翻译,要视情况而定。但不管怎么翻译,译文同样要建立起相应的酬应功能。具有酬应功能的语言在书面语中并不常见,但是在口语中却非常普遍,毕竟人们就是靠这类语言来维系彼此关系的。例如:中国人路上相遇总会打招呼。路人甲说:"去哪儿啊?"路人乙回答:"去办点事。"如果是用英语来表达,其实就是: A 说:Hi。B 回答:Hi。不过,很多酬应语言在英汉中是一致的,比如:你好(Hello),再见(Byebye),早上好(Good Morning)等等。

　　另外,有些酬应语言已经成为某些场合的习惯性说法。例如,通过大量的数据统计,我们发现，美国前总统奥巴马在演讲结束时通常会说"God Bless you"和"God Bless the United States of America"。这两句话简直就是奥巴马结束演讲时的标配语言。这种表达就含有酬应功能，具有团结美国民众的作用。对于这样的语言，如果可以直译，中文读者可以轻松接受的话，那就直译好了。否则，我们就要好好考虑一下，译成什么表达才能具有同等的酬应功能。

本章小结

对于文学翻译而言，情感功能基本占据核心地位，毕竟人物的情感和作者的观点贯穿文学作品的始终。信息功能、指示功能、美学功能和酬应功能往往服务情感功能。总的来说，言语表达往往体现了多种功能的混合，不过会凸显某种功能，而一个句子、一个语篇到底以哪种交际功能为主，不能单凭主观的感觉，要靠事实说话，而首先要考虑的事实就是语境这个因素。

第二章 语境意识
Context Awareness

本章的核心观点是：译者应该始终具有语境识别和转化意识。本章一共分为三个部分：一、语境的定义；二、语境的分类；三、实例分析。第二部分具体包括：（一）文本语境；（二）情景语境；（三）文化语境。

一、语境的定义

朗文词典对 context 的解释如下：① the words that come just before and after a word or sentence and that help you to understand its meaning；② the situation, events or information that are related to something and that help you to understand it. 第一个意思就是言语表达，这种表达会出现在需要理解的词语的前面或后面，有助于读者理解该词。第二个意思就是指情景、事件或信息，而这些内容与当前词语有关，并且有助于读者理解该词。

柯林斯词典对 context 的解释如下：① The context of a word, sentence, or text consists of the words, sentences, or text before and after it which help to make its meaning clear；② The context of an idea or event is the general situation that relates to it, and which helps it to be understood. 第一个定义说明一个单词、句子或语篇的语境是由之前和之后的言语表达构成，这些表达有助于意义变得明了。第二个定义说明一种思想或一个事件的语境是与之有关的概况，这个概况有助于人们理解。对于第一个释义中的"语篇"概念，需要在这里插入明确的解释，因为这个概念与语境关系极为密切。《朗文语言教学与应用语言学词典》中对 text（语篇或篇章）的定义如下：A piece of spoken or written language. A text may be considered from the point of view of its structure and/or its functions, e.g. warning, instructing, carrying out a transaction. A text may consist of just one word, e.g. DANGER on a warning sign, or it may be of considerable length, e.g. a sermon, a novel, or a debate. A full understanding of a text is often impossible without reference to the context in which it occurs. 译文：语篇指口语或书面语的一个单位，语篇可以从结构和 / 或功用的角度来考虑，如警告、指示或完成一笔交易。语篇可能只有一个单词，如警告牌上写的【危险】，也可能是相当长的一段话，如一次布道、一篇小说或一场辩论。语篇的意义通常要参照语境才能全面理解。

通过分析上述 context 和 text 的定义，可知：语境的准确定位对于言语意义的理解至关重要。

二、语境的分类

早在1923年,英国伦敦经济学院人类学教授马林诺夫斯基就首先提出了语境理论。他将语境分为三种类型:文本语境、情景语境和文化语境。

(一)文本语境(Context of Utterance)

文本语境即微观语境,也可以通俗地称为"上下文",即某一语言单位前面或后面的字、词、句、段或语篇。由于一词多义是语言的普遍现象,而关注上下文则有助于确定该词在本语境中的具体意义。

例如,appreciate 一词在不同的上下文中具有不同的意义:

① He can appreciate modern music.(欣赏)

② I do not appreciate fully what he means.(理解)

③ I appreciate the regard you have for me, but I'm not qualified to take on the job.(感谢)

有时,某一词语在原文不同语境中的意义基本一致,但因为译入语的搭配关系,译文表述上会出现一些变化。例如,下面句子中 work 的意思都是 to be active in the proper way:

① I think your suggestion will work.

我看你的建议行得通。

② The new rules are working well.

新规定执行得很顺利。

③ The treatment works like magic.

这种疗法功效神奇。

(二)情景语境(Context of Situation)

马林诺夫斯基的学生、语言学家弗斯接受并发展了恩师的情景语境理论。他指出:情景语境不仅包括说出来的话语,而且还包括说话人的面部表情、手势、身体姿态以及所有参与交谈的人和这些人所处的环境。例如:

A: That's the phone.

B: I'm in the bath.

A: OK.

这个语篇的语境很可能是:B在洗澡,或者在浴室中忙着什么,不方便出来,A告诉对方有电话打来。A的身份难以确定,有可能是B的家人,也可能是B的朋友,但不太可能是对方的至亲关系。根据生活经验,我们大概能想象出电话打来时的情境:A坐在客厅的沙发上,悠闲地看着电视,B躺在浴缸里,舒舒服服地泡澡,此时客厅的电话铃声响起,A快步走到浴室门口,冲里面大喊"That's the phone",可是B只能无奈地回答"I'm in the bath",于是A只好说"OK",这时A有两个选择,任由电话铃继续响下去，或者替 B 接一下电话。上述情境很容易出现在我们的脑海中，我们甚至还能想象出 A 和 B 说话时各自的神态、语气和手势，乃至浴室和客厅内的摆放和陈设。毫无疑问，这些情景语境也很重要，对于我们真正理解语篇意义不可或缺。

（三）文化语境（Context of Culture）

1935 年，马林诺夫斯基在《珊瑚园及其魔力》（*Coral Gardens and Their Magic*）一书中提出了文化语境的概念，他认为情景语境之外存在着一个"可以称为文化语境的东西""词语的定义在某种程度上取决于其文化语境"（Malinowski, 1935: 58）。后来，韩礼德在基于自身所命名的系统功能语法中提出，语篇产生于社会文化环境（sociocultural environment）之中，而社会文化环境包括了政治、历史、法律、社会和文化等因素，这些因素共同居于韩礼德语言模式的最高层次，对语篇的意义产生了间接或直接的影响。因此，文化语境可以看成最宏大的语境，是语义理解的最外围环境，这个环境会或多或少影响处于其中的话语或文本。例如，《傲慢与偏见》中有这样一句："Indeed you must go, for it will be impossible for us to visit him, if you do not." 这是贝内特太太在央求自己的丈夫尽快去拜访新搬来的邻居宾利先生。参考译文如下："你一定得去，你要是不去，我们母女就没法登门了。"如果单纯看语言表达，理解上没有任何障碍，但是仔细想一下，就难以理解了。为什么贝内特先生必须要先去拜访邻居呢？贝内特太太和女儿们自己就可以去了嘛。问题恰恰就出在这里，因为按照英国 18 世纪的习俗，一个地方搬来了新的住户，家中的男主人要先去拜访之后，女主人和孩子才能登门与对方往来。所以，这里语义的理解必须要考虑到文化语境，这是超出文本之外的因素在发挥重要作用。

综上所述，语境指影响言语交际的各种主客观因素。主观因素包括言语使用者和理解者的目的、性格、经历、职业、性别、心情、处境等。客观因素大至历史、文化、社会、自然，小至时间、地点、场合、对象以及上下文等。

三、实例分析

（一）文本语境实例（Case Analysis to Utterance Context）

【例 9】

原　文：Why did Earl run to rescue that little boy? Why did I support his decision, instead of stopping him? The greatest *instinct*, I believe, is to help a child in need. (*A Valentine to One Who Cared Too Much*)

译　文：为什么厄尔要跑去救那个小男孩？为什么我支持他去而没有阻止他？人类最伟大的<u>天性</u>，我相信，就在于救助危难中的孩子吧。

讲　评：对于 instinct，必应词典给出的英文定义是 a natural tendency for people and animals to behave in a particular way using the knowledge and abilities that they were born with rather than thought or training。对应的中文是"本能"或"天性"。翻译时到底选择哪一个更好呢？《现代汉语词典》对这两个词的解释如下。天性：指人先天具有的品质或性情。总体说来，这个词语具有中性含义，偏向于与人的关系。本能：1）人类和动物不学就会的本领，如初生婴儿会吃奶、蜂酿蜜都是本能的表现。2）有机体对外界刺激不知不觉地、无意识地做出反应，例如：他看见红光一闪，本能地闭上了眼睛。总体来说，"本能"这个词语具有中性的含义，但由于也常用来指动物或有机体的反应，因而变得不那么"高大上"了。所以，我们应该选择"天性"这个表达，毕竟跳到河里去救人并非是动物般本能的反应，而是人应具有的优秀品质。再看 instinct 前面的 greatest 这个褒义形容词，也就是近处的文本语境，这更加证明 instinct 应该翻译成"天性"。

【例 10】

原　文：He therefore still kept up a familiar intercourse with him, daily receiving the old physician in his study, or visiting the laboratory, and, for recreation's sake, watching the processes by which <u>weeds</u> were converted into <u>drugs of potency</u>. (Chapter 10, *The Scarlet Letter*)

To such a professional body Roger Chillingworth was a brilliant acquisition. He soon manifested his familiarity with the ponderous and imposing machinery of antique physic; in which every remedy contained a multitude of far-fetched and heterogeneous ingredients, as elaborately compounded as if the proposed result had been the <u>Elixir of Life</u>. In his Indian captivity, moreover, he had gained much knowledge of the properties of native <u>herbs and roots</u>; nor did he conceal from his patients that these simple medicines, Nature's boon to the untutored savage, had quite as large a share of his own confidence as the European Pharmacopoeia, which so many learned doctors had spent centuries in elaborating. (Chapter 9, *The Scarlet Letter*)

译　文：因此，他跟医生仍像平常一样密切来往，每天在书房中予以接待，或者去对方的实验室闲聊，看看人家如何把<u>草根树叶</u>变成<u>灵丹妙药</u>。（《红字》第十章）若与同行们相比，罗杰·齐灵渥斯就是卓越的医师了。他很快就展现出他对纷繁复杂、令人惊叹的古老医术的精通。每一个古方里都包含了无数多方搜寻来的各色成分，合成之精妙就好像配制的是<u>长生不老药</u>。此外，在被印第安人囚禁期间，他对当地<u>草药</u>有了很多了解。面对病人，他坦诚地表示，相比于许多欧洲名医几百年来精心研制的药剂，大自然赐予这些野蛮人的简单药物毫不逊色，完全能够取得他本人的信任。（《红字》第九章）

讲　评：《红字》第十章中的 weeds 在本段中的意思是"野草"，drugs of potency 是"有效力的药剂"。这两个表达之所以这样理解，是受到了前面出现的文本语境的影响。由于第九章中有 herbs and roots（草药）和 Elixir of Life（长生不老药）这两个短语，第十章中的 weeds 和 drugs of potency 就成了它们的近义词表达，即语义表达的词汇衔接（具体请参见高级理论的第一章）。出于前后语义连贯的考虑，第十章中的 weeds 由"野草"变成了"草根树叶"，drugs of potency 由"有效力的药剂"变成了"灵丹妙药"，这就是受远处文本语境影响的结果，也可以说是与远处的语境相呼应。

（二）情景语境实例（Case Analysis to Situation Context）

【例 11】

原　文：And I came out immediately, for I trembled at the idea of being dragged forth by the said Jack. "What do you want?" I asked, with awkward diffidence.
"Say, 'What do you want, Master Reed?'" was the answer. "I want you to come here;" and seating himself in an arm-chair, he intimated by a gesture that I was to approach and stand before him. (Chapter 1, *Jane Eyre*)

译　文：一想到要被杰克揪出来，我就禁不住全身颤抖，于是只好主动站了出来。"你要干什么？"我怯生生地说道。
"你应该说，'里德少爷，您要干什么？'"他答道，"我要你过来。"说着，他就在一把扶手椅里坐了下来，然后打了个手势，示意我站到他跟前。

讲　评：此处的对白发生在十岁的简·爱与十四岁的表哥之间，内容非常简单。不过要想真正理解其中的情感，需要换位思考，需要想象两个人的表情和肢体语言。这段对话发生之前，小简·爱躲在早餐室的窗帘后面，正在静静地看书，这时表哥闯进屋子，嘴里还骂骂咧咧，其实就是想要把简·爱找出来，然后欺辱对方。这种情况以前经常发生，因此简·爱对表哥非常厌恶，同时也非常害怕，对话之后还有很多更详尽的描写。因此，这里简·爱的语气是怯生生的，而表哥是趾高气扬的，甚至有一点小流氓的口吻。另外，简·爱在说话时有可能是紧靠着窗子，手里握着自己的衣襟，或者是双手紧张地握在一起，脸上满是惊恐之情，而表哥则很可能是不怀好意地微笑，说话的调门拔得很高，脑袋得意地晃着，身体斜躺在椅子里，连打出的手势都是轻蔑的。这很可能就是当时的情景语境，虽然作者并未写出来，但是根据上下文，再根据整部小说的语境，这是很可能的。因此，只有充分体会到情景语境，才有可能充分领悟到这里的人物情感。

（三）文化语境实例（Case Analysis to Culture Context）

【例12】

原　　文：He re-entered, pale and very gloomy. "I have found it all out," said he, setting his candle down on the *washstand*; "it is as I thought." (Chapter 15, *Jane Eyre*)

译　　文：他回来了，脸色苍白，神色非常阴郁。"我把一切都查清楚了，"他把烛台放在<u>脸盆架</u>上说道，"跟我猜想的一样。"

讲　　评：根据柯林斯词典的定义，washstand 的意思是 a piece of furniture designed to hold a bowl for washing your hands and face in, which was used in former times before washbasins had taps on them。请看下面这些图片：

这种东西没有固定的结构，样式很多。20世纪70、80年代的时候，人们平时洗漱都用，现在的年轻人应该很少见到过，不过由于现代洗手盆（请见下图）的普及，大家应该可以根据"脸盆架"的中文表达，在很大程度上猜测出来这是干什么用的，这样也就足够了。对于"washstand"这种文化语境，这种东西虽然现在不常见了，但是比较容易理解和想象，因此译者可以选择合适的表达，以求在字面上就能让读者基本看懂，而不必非要加上注释，更何况缺乏图片的文字注释效果也未必就好。

【例 13】

原　文：As conscientious parents, we strive to foster independence. But when it happens, you pause outside that door and look at the *blank panels*. It is always a little unsettling. (*A Room of His Own*)

译　文：作为有强烈责任心的父母，我们会努力培养孩子的独立能力。可是，一旦他们独立了，你却只能在**紧闭的门扉**外徘徊，这种情况总会让人有些担忧和不安。

讲　评：为什么要将 blank panels 译成紧闭的门扉呢？首先，根据柯林斯词典的定义，panel 的意思是 a flat rectangular piece of wood or other material that forms part of a larger object, such as a door。而 blank 的意思是 something that is blank has nothing on it。二者合在一起，就是光光的门扇。不过，父母们站在光光的门扇外面是什么意思呢？这个就不太好懂了。为了说明这个问题，我们需要引入另外一个单词以及相关的文化现象。根据必应词典的定义，noticeboard 是 a board which is usually attached to a wall in order to display notices giving information about something。这种东西在西方很常见，各种教学楼和企业办公楼都有，甚至连家里也有，超市中还有出售。有时候，noticeboard（提示板）也会挂在门上。但无论是挂在墙上，还是挂在门上，作用都只有一个，就是写一些提示性信息，让大家不要忘记该做的事情。如果放在公共场合，往往用于贴出通知，而放在家里则往往起到备忘录的作用，只不过这种东西现在国内仅限于学校和公司等场合，家里几乎看不到。文章中说到的就是这种情况，儿子在独立之前，卧室门外挂了一块 noticeboard，上面有各种信息，而母亲可以通过这些来了解儿子的动态和近况。可现在儿子显然把 noticeboard 挪进了屋内，于是母亲再也无法方便地了解儿子的情况。所以文章中才会说 pause outside that door and look at the blank panels。鉴于上面的分析，blank panels 当然不能翻译成对中国人来说不知所云的"光光的门扇"，而要译成"紧闭的门扉"，这样才能体现出儿子的独立倾向和母亲的失落情绪。因此，对于造成隔阂的文化语境，译者如果可以文内处理，也就是能够传递出作者的真实意图，就直接在文字上处理即可。

【例 14】

原　文：I returned to my book—*Bewick*'s *History of British Birds*: the letterpress thereof I cared little for, generally speaking; and yet there were certain introductory pages that, child as I was, I could not pass quite as a blank. They were those which treat of the haunts of sea-fowl; of "the solitary rocks and promontories" by them only inhabited; of the coast of Norway, studded with isles from its southern extremity, *the Lindeness*, or Naze, to *the North Cape*— (Chapter 1, *Jane Eyre*)

第二章 语境意识

译　文：我的注意力转回到书上，继续翻看***比尤伊克***[1]的《英国鸟类史》。一般说来，我这样小的孩子不会太在意文字，但是这本书中有几页导言，我却不愿把它们当作空白页随手翻过。那几页讲到了海鸟栖息之地，讲到了只有海鸟停留的"孤独的岩石和海岬"，还讲到了从最南边的***林讷角***[2]（即纳斯）直至最北边的***北角***[3]，周边岛屿星罗棋布的挪威海岸。

讲　评：不过，对于有些文化语境，单纯的正文文字表述是不足以阐释清楚的，这个时候就要给予必要的注释。至于何时给出注释，何时不必给出，这就要取决于译者的经验了（具体如何注释，请参见本书"预设意识"那一章）。因此，译者需要不断丰富自己的知识储备，提高自己的判断能力。

本章小结

译者对待语境应该秉持的态度是：
对待文本语境：始终瞻前顾后；
对待情景语境：需要换位思考；
对待文化语境：跨越文化障碍。

从前面的论述可知，全局性语境意识是把握言语交际功能的首要前提，而下面该考虑的事情就是对微观词语的理解了，这就需要接下来了解词语的意义类型。

---

[1] 比尤伊克（Thomas Bewick，1753-1828）：英国木刻家、画家。他的一些知名作品都是关于自然历史的插图书籍。他的《英国鸟类史》出版于1797年，书中的木刻插图是他创作的，文字部分是科茨（Cotes）所写。

[2] 林讷角（Lindeness）：挪威最南端的海角，也叫林讷斯内斯角，又称纳斯（Naze）。

[3] 北角（North Cape）：挪威北部马格吕岛北端，被认为是欧洲大陆最北端的岛屿。

第三章 意义类型
Meaning Types

> 本章的核心观点是：译者应始终具有意义类型识别和转换的意识。本章采用的是英国语言学家利奇对意义类型的划分理论，即意义分为七种类型：（一）概念意义；（二）内涵意义；（三）社会意义；（四）情感意义；（五）反射意义；（六）搭配意义；（七）主位意义。

学习翻译之所以要讲意义的分类，是因为翻译最核心的问题就是意义的理解与表达。虽然道理不难理解，但是学者们对意义的分类始终见仁见智。语言学家帕默（F. Plamer, 1981）从语言使用的角度把意义分成"句子意义"和"话语意义"；语言学家莱昂（Lyons）从语用学和社会学的视角，把意义分为"词汇意义""句子意义"和"话语意义"；而语言学家利奇（Leech）则主要从语义学和功能语言学的视角，把意义分解为七种类型，就是前面列出的那些分类。鉴于利奇把意义的类型分析得较为详尽，而这有利于我们对意义进行深刻理解，也有利于在翻译实践中对意义呈现的重点方面展开分析，因而我们这里采用利奇的意义七分理论。

按照利奇的解释，这七种意义类型又可以划分为三类，其中内涵意义、社会意义、情感意义、反射意义和搭配意义又可以统称为联想意义（associative meaning），它与概念意义合在一起，基本上就描述出词语或短语搭配后所产生的意义，而主位意义描述的是词语在经过有目的的组合后所产生的句义。

利奇在《语义学：意义研究》（*Semantics: The Study of Meaning*）第二章结尾将意义类型归结为如下表格：

Seven Types of Meaning	1. Conceptual Meaning or Sense		Logical, cognitive, or denotative content.
	Associative Meaning	2. Connotaitive Meaning	What is communicated by virtue of what language refers to.
		3. Social Meaning	What is communicated of the social circumstances of language use.
		4. Affective Meaning	What is communicated of the feelings and attitudes of the speaker/writer.
		5. Reflected Meaning	What is communicated through association with another sense of the same expression.
		6. Collocative Meaning	What is communicated through association with words which tend to occur in the environment of another word.

续表

7. Thematic Meaning	What is communicated by the way in which the message is organized in terms of order and emphasis.

(Leech, 1981: 23)

意义的七种类型	1. 概念意义（或含义）		内容具有逻辑性、认知性或指示性特征。
	联想意义	2. 内涵意义	由于指称而附加在概念意义上所形成的联想。
		3. 社会意义	由于展示出语言运用所处的社会环境而引发的联想。
		4. 情感意义	词语所体现出的说者或听者的情感或态度。
		5. 反射意义	人们在看到某表达的一个意义时同时联想到它的另一个意义。
		6. 搭配意义	由于联想到常出现在该语境中的另一个/些词语而形成的意义。
	7. 主位意义		通过词序、焦点或强调而凸显的句子意义。

（参考译文）

（一）概念意义（Conceptual Meaning）

概念意义，也被称为"词语本义""内容具有逻辑性、认知性或指示性特征"，往往是语言交流中最基础的成分，与语言的信息功能关系最为紧密。词语概念意义的获取当然是要首先仔细查阅词典，认真阅读单词的英语释义，同时参看英汉词典中的汉语表达，而那些汉语翻译也会反过来促进对英语释义的理解，然后再结合语境去做出正确判断，即该词的概念到底是什么，可以译成哪个或哪些汉语词汇。

【例15】

原　文：I'm sitting at my mother's desk, a mahogany *secretary* with a writing leaf that folds down to reveal rows of cubbyholes and tiny drawers—even a sliding secret compartment. (*My Mother's Desk*)

译　文：我坐在母亲的书桌旁，这是一个红木做的**带书架的写字桌**，上面有个可以折叠的活动桌面，桌面翻下来就可以看见几排小格子和一些小抽屉，里面还有一个可以拉动的暗格。

讲　评：secretary 的英文释义为 a large cabinet with a fold-down desktop, usually with drawers below and an enclosed bookcase above。结合原文语境，该词可以翻译为"带书架的写字桌"，这是一个比较准确的表达，体现出该词意义的主要方面就是传递有关桌子的概念。因此，正如意义七分法表格所描述的，该词的翻译体现出认知性和指示性，反映出语言的信息功能。

【例16】

原　文："Did you leave the *balcony*, sir," I asked, "when Mdlle. Varens entered?" (Chapter 15, *Jane Eyre*)

译　　文：　"瓦伦小姐进来的时候，您离开*阳台*了吗？"我问道。
讲　　评：　这是《简·爱》第 15 章中的一个情节，当时罗切斯特先生讲述了自己在瓦伦小姐的卧室中窥见了不曾预料到的一幕，而这句话就是简随之而来的发问。鉴于前文已经提及了"卧室"这个语境，再加上英语词典的帮助，我们发现 balcony 的意思应该是 a platform on the outside of a building, above ground level, with a wall or railing around it，也就是指普通住宅或宾馆的阳台。显然，该词体现出了纯粹的概念意义。
但是，如果换一个语境，还是这个词语，概念意义则可能有变化。

【例 17】

原　　文：　During the first group of dances, I sat up very high in the *balcony* with my family and the stage seemed too far away. (*The Ballet Dancer*)
译　　文：　第一组舞蹈上演时，我和家人一起坐在高高的*楼厅*里。
讲　　评：　句子的语境是一家人观看芭蕾舞演出，而地点是在高大的礼堂中。有了这个背景，balcony 就不可能是阳台了。考虑到语境，再查一下英英词典，就很容易发现，balcony 的意思是 the seats upstairs at theatre，也就是剧院中的楼上厅座，简称楼厅。

上述三个例子充分说明，概念意义具有逻辑的、认知的或指示的特征，在语境下往往比较容易辨认。不过，到底该译成哪个词语，有时候还是要费些思量的，毕竟有时词典中未必有完全对应的汉语表达。

（二）内涵意义（Connotative Meaning）

内涵意义，指"由于指称而附加在概念意义上所形成的联想"，体现出的是在纯粹概念意义之上的交际功能。换言之，内涵意义通常要比概念意义更加重要，所以译者要努力将其再现。内涵意义往往由比喻或引申而形成，比较形象生动，常常具有美学功能，因而也被称为比喻意义或引申意义。如果内涵意义是词语意义的焦点，那么译者务必要将其译出。较为理想的译法是既翻出了词语的概念意义，又凸显了其形象的内涵特征。

【例 18】

原　　文：　It was true that Jeff had graduated from college that past June and had flown from *the nest*. (*A Room of His Own*)
译　　文：　确实，杰夫在那一年六月就已大学毕业，并且飞离了他的*小窝*。
讲　　评：　词典上 nest 的概念意义是 a hollow place or structure that a bird makes or chooses for laying its eggs in and sheltering its young，也就是"鸟窝"。不过，由于 nest 还可以指 the home, thought of as the safe place where parents bring up their

children，于是 the nest 便产生了"家"或"家园"的内涵意义。在这个语境中，内涵意义"家"（即杰夫自己的房间）是主要的，概念意义"鸟窝"是次要的。不过，"鸟窝"是非常形象的概念，因此可以尽量保留。换句话说，我们可以把 the nest 看作"小家+鸟窝"的合体。因此翻译成"小窝"会更好。这样一来，人们可能还会因此联想到倦鸟归巢，那么在外工作的杰夫是否有再飞回小窝的那一天呢？另外，有一句俗语说得好：金窝银窝，不如自己的狗窝。因此，"窝"或者"巢"的说法形象生动，深入人心。

除了名词，隐喻性英语动词也具有内涵意义，它们常与比喻词 like 或 as 连用。

【例19】

原　文：Men wearing sky blue jackets leapt to girls whose dresses *ruffled like swans*. (*The Ballet Dancer*)

译　文：身穿连衣舞裙的姑娘们***像展翅欲起的天鹅***，身着天蓝色短装的小伙子们跃到姑娘们的身边。

讲　评：ruffle 的一个概念意义是：If a bird ruffles its feathers or if its feathers ruffle, they stand out on its body, for example when it is cleaning itself or when it is frightened. 由于 ruffle 后面出现了 like swans，这里女芭蕾舞演员明显被比喻成了鸟儿——天鹅。对于这样的内涵意义，译者通常要"照单全收"，全部翻译出来，这样就使得抽象的概念意义——芭蕾舞演员上下挥舞手臂的动作——具有了鲜活的形象，读者也更容易获得美的享受。

（三）社会意义（Social Meaning）

社会意义是指"由于展示出语言运用所处的社会环境而引发的联想"。一方面，我们可以通过语境，包括对口语中语音语调的感知，来识别说话人/写作人的社会身份；另一方面，我们也可以通过对自身所用语言的选择和编织，来完成对自我社会身份的建构和展示。利奇（Leech, 1981: 14-16）对"社会意义"这个概念做了不同维度的界定，它们是"方言"（展示了语言源于某一社会阶层或某一地区）、"时代"（比如该语言来自于14世纪或18世纪）、"使用领域"（比如该语言是"法律用语""科学用语"或"广告用语"等）、"使用情形"（比如该语言属于"礼貌用语""口语"或"俚语"等）、"使用形式"（比如该语言属于"外交备忘录用语""演讲用语"或"玩笑用语"等）和"个人风格"（比如该语言有"狄更斯的风格"或"海明威的风格"等）。言语的"社会意义"展示了话语使用者的社会身份，因此译者应对这一点给予足够重视，尽可能在词语层面或句式层面予以还原，以达到同样的社会效果。

【例20】

原　文：1. They chucked a stone at the cops and then did a bunk with the loot.

2. After casting a stone at the police, they absconded with the money.

（Leech, 1981:15）

译　　文：1. 他们朝条子扔了块石头，然后就带着抢来的钱溜之大吉了。
2. 他们朝警察投掷石块，后携款潜逃。

讲　　评：通过对比，我们发现，两个句子在词语和句式使用方面存在诸多不同：

词汇和句式对比	句1	句2
(1) chuck vs. cast	(informal,) to throw sth. carelessly or without much thought	(literary) to throw somebody/something somewhere, especially using force
(2) cop vs. police	(informal) a police officer	an official organization whose job is to make people obey the law and to prevent and solve the crime; the people who work for this organization
(3) did a bunk vs. absconded	(informal) to run away from a place without telling anyone	to leave secretly and take something with you, especially money, that does not belong to you
(4) loot vs. money	(informal) money and valuable objects that have been stolen by thieves	coins or paper notes
(5) 并列句 vs. 含有时间状语的简单句	"and"连接而成的并列句在儿童或文化程度较低者的语言中出现频率较高。[1]	该句子的主干虽然是简单句，但是前面的时间状语其实是简化版的时间状语从句，而主从复合句往往在正式语言中出现频率较高。

上述词义的解释都源于权威的牛津英语词典。通过对比分析，我们发现，句1的使用者很可能文化程度较低，甚至与罪犯有比较亲密的关系，而句2的使用者很可能是正在办案的警方，也可能是正在报道这个事件的官方。两个句子说的是"同一件事情"，但却充分暴露出语言使用者不同的身份和态度。

不过，有时候，"社会意义"在翻译过程中未必会体现在所有单个词语的对等转换上。在考虑语境之后，可以从整体上再现语篇的感染力，以达到一种近似于"功能对等"的效果。

【例 21】

原　　文："*Goodwives*," said a hard-featured dame of fifty, "I'll tell *ye* a piece of my mind.

---

[1] 此处观点出自这段英文："One of the hardest sentence patterns for Chinese learners of English to grasp, it seems to me, is subordination. Mature English writing is heavily subordinated in multiple layers; coordination is thought of as the sentence pattern of the child and the poorly educated"。（参见 A. Robins: *The Writer's Practical Rhetoric*, p. 147, U. S. A.: John Wiley & Sons, Inc., 1980.）

It would be greatly for the public behoof if we women, being of mature age and church-members in good repute, should have the handling of such malefactresses as this Hester Prynne. What think *ye, gossips*? If the *hussy* stood up for judgment before us five, that are now here in a knot together, would she come off with such a sentence as the worshipful magistrates have awarded? *Marry*, I *trow* not." (Chapter 2, *The Scarlet Letter*)

译　文：　"**各位婆娘**，我要说说我的想法。"一个五十岁上下、面相凶恶的女人说道，"对于我们这些上了一把年纪、名声良好的清教徒来说，要是能把海丝特·白兰这样的坏娘儿们给处理了，那倒是给大家办了件好事。**婆娘们**，你们怎么看呢？可敬的长官大人赏给那**贱货**一个仁慈的判决，可要是由我们五个姐们儿来宣判，她还能如此轻易地逃脱吗？**哼，反正我不信。**"

讲　评：　这段英文选自《红字》第二章，背景是海丝特·白兰首次从狱中走出来，到广场的刑台上示众。当下这个段落讲的是台子前面围了很多人，其中有五个妇女，这里是第一个妇人在发表看法。文中的"hard-featured"这个词非常关键，因为凶恶的面相影射着这人怀有"深深的恶意"，引语内容恰好验证了这一点。请看下面表格内的分析：

词语	"社会意义"
Goodwives	(*Scottish*) the woman in charge of a household or family, especially a married woman
ye	(*old use or dialect*) a word meaning "you", used when talking to more than one person
gossip	Someone who likes talking about other people's private lives—*used to show disapproval.*
hussy	(*old-fashioned, disapproving*) a girl or woman who behaves in a way that is considered shocking or morally wrong
Marry	(*interjection, Archaic*) used as an exclamation of surprise, astonishment, etc.
trow	(*Archaic*) to believe, think, or suppose

从表格可以看出，上述词语要么是古语或旧的用法，要么是方言，要么含有贬义。这些都显示出这个妇人的社会身份——属于社会底层，没有受过教育，苏格兰移民的后裔，等等。这些社会意义无法在词语层面一一对等体现，不过可以在语篇整体上尽可能再现说话者的社会身份。

（四）情感意义（Affective Meaning）

情感意义指"词语所体现出的说者或听者的情感或态度"。任何概念意义都有可能被言语使用者附上情感意义，也就是既可以褒扬也可以贬低，既可以喜欢也可以讨厌，等等。因此，情感意义总是体现语言的表情功能。一般来说，情感意义可以与其他任何意义类型交织在一起。在完成语篇翻译时，尤其是文学类语篇，译者要特别注意审视词语所处的语境，仔细揣摩其中的情感，然后在译文中尽力再现。

【例 22】

原　文：It was a pretty show at such a distance, but the dancers with their bright dots of costumes appeared as small and no more alive than *marionettes*. (*The Ballet Dancer*)

译　文：楼厅离舞台很远，远远望去，那场面倒也不错，只是身着亮片服装的演员们看上去太小，并不比**牵线木偶**活泼多少。

讲　评：marionettes 本来只具有概念意义，意思是 a puppet operated by means of strings attached to its hands, legs, head, and body，就像下面图片中所展示的玩偶那样。

本来，玩偶就是玩偶，一种给儿童看的常见表演，大多数时候很可能会为孩子们带来欢乐。可是，文章中的小女孩由于身处礼堂二楼的厅座，距离舞台太远，看不太清楚芭蕾舞演员的表演，心里不免产生了烦躁情绪，于是认为那些演员的表演很僵硬、很乏味。在这个语境下，牵线木偶就有了贬义色彩，只不过这种情感不能在词语翻译中直接体现，但却可以弥散于语境之中。

【例 23】

原　文：Suddenly, amid all the upheaval my throat caught. There, in a pile of assorted sketches, was a pencil drawing of T-Bird—Jeff's beagle, dead these many years—curled up asleep. Jeff's rendering was *so evocative* I could almost feel *the dear old dog's satiny warm ears*. And in that room, with Jeff's things heaped around me, I could almost touch the little boy I knew was gone forever. (*A Room of His Own*)

译　文：突然，就在整理忙碌之中，我一下子哽咽住了。在一摞各式各样的素描画里，一幅蜷缩着酣睡的小狗引起了我的注意，那画的是杰夫死去多年的小猎犬"雷鸟"。杰夫的描绘**如此生动传神**，以至于小狗看起来**可爱极了，那长长的耳朵光滑亮泽、柔软温暖**，似乎触手可及。就在这个房间里，到处都堆放着杰夫的东西，我几乎随手都可以触摸到我的小杰夫，但我知道他再也不会回来了。

讲　评：原文讲的是一位名叫杰夫的男孩大学毕业后去了远方，杰夫的母亲在整理儿子的房间时思绪联翩。由于多年来母子在这间屋中留下了许多美好记忆,于是就有了上面那一幕。作者除了使用 so evocative 来描绘杰夫的画作之外,还特别用了四个修饰语"dear old dog's satiny warm"来描述狗耳朵的样子,而这种多定语同时使用的现象并不多见。为什么会这样呢?毫无疑问,母亲对儿子杰夫的爱如此深沉,以至于儿子所做的一切都让她记在心里。现在,儿子开始了新的生活,而独留下母亲空自回忆。这种浓浓的母爱散播于字里行间,只要仔细体会,便可以感受得到,而感受到了之后,就要尽力再现这种情感。

不过,词语的情感意义并不是固定不变的,而是会随人的情感倾向的变化而变化,由原来的褒义变成现在的贬义,或者由原来的贬义变成现在的褒义。这种变化会因特定语境而经常发生。

【例 24】

原　文:"Why, look you, she may cover it with a brooch, or such like heathenish adornment, and so walk the streets *as brave as ever*." (Chapter 2, *The Scarlet Letter*)

译　文:"哼,你们走着瞧吧,她准会拿枚胸针或异教徒的装饰去遮住胸口,然后**恬不知耻地**走在大街上。"

讲　评:原文中的"as brave as ever"通常都是褒义表达,赞美人们勇敢依旧。围观海丝特受罚的五个女人没有半点同情心,其中第三个女人所用的"as brave as ever"充满了嘲讽的语气,这充分体现出她对海丝特的情感倾向——即道德上强烈批判,情感上完全唾弃。

(五)反射意义(Reflected Meaning)

反射意义指人们在看到某表达的一个意义时,同时联想到它的另一个意义。语言中有些词语,即当你读到或听到它们时,总会同时联想到与之相关的其他事物。在这种情况下,联想到的意义便是反射意义。反射意义较多出现在文学作品、日常会话和娱乐电视节目里,尤其是后者最为频繁。通常说来,反射意义的翻译难度较大,有些近乎于不可翻译。但是,反射意义的价值和味道就在于"反射"部分,因此译者还是要尽力去再现。如果真的无法将两重含义同时译出,那么至少要翻译出交际价值较大的那层意思,即或者表达原有含义,或者再现反射意义。

【例 25】

原　文:Let's say you are great at soccer, and you want to learn golf, but you don't have the time or money for clubs or lessons. What's an athlete to do? Well, check it.

Footgolf, as in foot golf. Same rules as golf, but with your feet and a bigger 21 inch diameter cup. Because you can't kick a soccer ball as far as you can hit a golf ball, the average footgolf hole is less than half the distance away as a traditional golf hole.

It's cheaper to play, too, so whether you *achieve the feet of victory* or feel the agony of defeat, it's not hard *to foot the bill*, and you are guaranteed *to get a kick out of it* without ever joining a club. We are going to find some more stories and puns *to tee up* for you tomorrow. Thanks for watching. (CNN Student News：2014-10-09)

译　　文：假如你很擅长踢足球，可还想学习高尔夫，但却没有时间和金钱去俱乐部受训或练习，这种情况下你能做些什么呢？好啦，来瞧瞧吧。

脚尔夫，是一种用脚来踢的高尔夫，规则与高尔夫相同，但用的却是你的脚和一个更大的（直径21英寸）杯状球洞。因为你踢出足球的飞行距离不可能有打出的高尔夫球飞得那么远，因此脚尔夫的平均洞距都只有传统高尔夫洞距的一半。这个游戏玩起来无需付出多大代价。无论是你感受到失败的痛苦，还是*品尝到"脚胜"的喜悦*，都可以轻松地*用脚来买单*。就算不加入高尔夫俱乐部，你肯定也能*踢出一脚高尔夫*。明天，我们会去寻找更多的段子和妙语来为你"*开球*"。感谢收看。

讲　　评：在这则短短的语篇中，共有五处反射意义，现在通过表格分析如下：

	原有含义	反射意义	参考翻译
1. footgolf	高尔夫（golf）	足球（football）	脚尔夫
2. achieve the feet of victory	赢得用脚比赛的胜利（achieve the victory with feet）	赢得足球比赛的胜利（achieve the football victory）	品尝到"脚胜"的喜悦
3. to foot the bill	用脚来完成游戏（to foot the bill）	（用钱来）买单（to pay the bill）	用脚来买单
4. to get a kick out of it	踢出一脚足球（to get a kick out of it）	打出一杆高尔夫（to get a hit out of it）	踢出一脚高尔夫
5. to tee up	把高尔夫球放在球座上，准备挥杆开球（to tee up）	把足球放在球场中线，裁判鸣哨后开球（to kick off）	开球

上述五个例子的反射意义都较好地翻译出来了，但有时译者只能译出最重要的一层含义，而将无法译出的另一层意义舍弃。

【例26】

原　　文：No longer an Olympic sport, but these folks sure put in an Olympic effort. All boat traffic on the Mississippi River stops in early August for the Great River Tug Fest. Why? So teams from Illinois and Iowa can grab hold of a 2700 foot rope and try to drag competitors they can't even see well toward the river. Including this year's event, Illinois leaves the overall tug tally with 17 wins to Iowa's 11. The two teams could actually *see each other* and *things could get tugly*. They could *get knotted up*, but it's just a friendly rivalry, after all, a river do it. Some of you will think our puns are kind of *in drag*, but they really help *pull our show together*. (CNN Student News: 2014-08-12)

译　文：拔河比赛不再是奥运会项目，但拔河参赛者依旧体现出了奥林匹克拼搏精神。八月初的"大拔河节"期间，密西西比河上的所有船只都要停运。为什么呢？因为这样一来，伊利诺伊州队与爱荷华州队就能利用这根 2700 英尺长的绳子进行较量了，就可以把河对岸他们甚至都看不清楚的对手拽到水里。包括今年的获胜在内，伊利诺伊州队目前以 17∶11 次的比分领先于爱荷华州队。两队其实彼此**心照不宣，拉拉扯扯就这样开始了**。他们**死死地纠缠在一起**，但那只是一场友好的较量，毕竟一条河隔在那里。一些人认为我们的妙语是**男扮女装**，但它们真的**有助于把我们拴在一起**。

讲　评：在这则语篇中，也有五处反射意义，现在通过表格分析如下：

	原有含义	反射意义	参考译文
1. see each other	看到彼此	想象出彼此	心照不宣 （倾向于反射意义）
2. things could get tugly	绳子拽来拽去	两队拽来拽去	拉拉扯扯就这样开始了
3. get knotted up	两队被绳子紧紧拴在一起	两队越使劲拽，比赛就越紧张	死死地纠缠在一起
4. in drag	男人穿戴女人的衣服	明明有弦外之音，却呈现表面意思	男扮女装 （倾向于原有含义）
5. pull our show together	把我们的节目拴在一起	把节目与电视观众拴在一起	有助于把我们拴在一起 （倾向于反射意义）

通过上面表格的分析，我们发现，第 2 例和第 3 例的译文基本上把原有含义和反射意义都翻译出来了，第 1 例和第 5 例的译文只能翻出反射意义，而第 4 例译文只翻出原有含义才比较合适。

所以，结论就是，反射意义的翻译要视情况而定：如果能同时译出两重含义，那样自然最好；如果不能，则翻译出交际价值较大的那层意义，或者保留原有含义，或者再现反射意义，而这一切都要以让读者看懂为底线。

（六）搭配意义（Collocative Meaning）

搭配意义指"由于联想到常出现在该语境中的另一个/些词语而形成的意义"。由于搭配不同，同一个词语就会呈现出不同的词性、不同的含义。因此，译者必须勤查词典，对那些与语境和逻辑并不匹配的语义要特别注意，绝不能马虎大意。

【例 27】

原　文： "Mercy on us, goodwife" exclaimed a man in the crowd, "is there no virtue in woman, *save* what springs from a wholesome fear of the gallows? That is the *hardest word* yet! Hush now, gossips, for the lock is turning in the prison-door, and here comes Mistress Prynne herself." (Chapter 2, *The Scarlet Letter*)

译　文： "各位太太，可怜可怜我们吧。"人群中有个男人喊道，"*除了*对绞刑心存敬畏*之外*，女人就再没有其他美德了吗？你们的话*说得太重*啦！嘘，小点儿声，各位，狱门的锁正转动着呢，海丝特本人就要出来了。"

讲　评： save 在人们脑海中很容易闪现的词性就是动词，意义大概是"节约""拯救"或者"保存"；而 hard 较常见的意思是"坚硬的""结实的"或者"困难的"。但由于语境和搭配的限制，save 在这里是介词，词义是"除了……之外"；hard 由于跟 word 搭配，于是产生了"苛刻的"或"冷酷的"含义。

【例 28】

原　文： A *card* of mine lay on the table; this being perceived, brought my name under discussion. Neither of them possessed *energy* or wit to belabour me *soundly*, but they insulted me as coarsely as they could in their little way: especially Céline, who even waxed rather *brilliant* on my personal defects—deformities she termed them. (Chapter 15, *Jane Eyre*)

译　文： 桌上放着一张我的*名片*，他们正好看到了，竟开始议论起我来。两人既无*能力*，也无智慧，却对我*大加*贬低，他们只会挑一些细枝末节的小地方来诋毁我，内容要多粗俗有多粗俗，尤其是赛莉纳，她将我外貌上的缺点*肆意*夸大，甚至还称之为残疾。

讲　评： 原文中 card 的含义通常是"贺卡""信用卡"或"卡片"，但是这里有 of mine 的搭配，因此就是"名片"的意思；energy 的含义通常是"能量""精力"或"活力"，但是这里前有 possessed，后有 wit 与之呼应，因此就变成了人所拥有的"能力"；soundly 的含义通常是"酣睡地"或"明智地"，可是该词前面有 belabour me，因此就变成了"完全地"或"彻底地"的含义；brilliant 通常用作褒义词，表示"卓越的""极好的""辉煌的"或"灿烂的"意思，但是这里由于后面存在 on my personal defects，因此就有了"肆意"这个贬义用法。由此可以看出，语篇中的词义往往不能由词语自身来决定，能决定它的是周围的词语。

（七）主位意义（Thematic Meaning）

主位意义指"通过词序、焦点或强调而凸显的句子意义"。具体说来，"主位"就是说话人/写作者在句子开头处所给出的话题或信息，往往表示听说双方都已知晓的内容，是句子后面叙述的起点，是整个句子得以叙述的基础。说话人/写作者以主位（Theme）

来组织句子，向听话人/阅读者传输有关信息。在一个句子中，还有另外一部分信息，与"主位"相对，被称之为"述位（Rheme）"。述位在句子的后面，是说话人/写作者对已给出话题或已知信息的叙述、描写、说明、扩展、引申或阐释。大多数时候，"述位"所传输的语义是句子的焦点，是整个句子信息结构的核心。

英语和汉语的主位和述位位置，既有一致的情况，也有不一致的情况。就英译汉而言，许多时候，译文主位与原文主位一致，译文述位与原文述位一致。

【例 29】

原　文：In January 1970 I got the form that you have to apply for black lung compensation. I wrote down everything on that form. Two months later we were all told that everyone who had applied for compensation would have to go to the town of Hazard and apply again.（《译学辞典》214 页）

译　文：1970 年 1 月，我拿到了一张申请领取黑肺病抚恤金的登记表。我在登记表上写明了一切情况。两个月后，我们接到了通知，说是要每一个申请领取抚恤金的人都得到哈扎镇再申请一次。

讲　评：原文与译文的主位述位对比：

主位（Theme）	述位（Rheme）
In January 1970 1970 年 1 月，	I got the form that you have to apply for black lung compensation. 我拿到了一张申请领取黑肺病抚恤金的登记表。
I 我	wrote down everything on that form. 在登记表上写明了一切情况。
Two months later 两个月后，	we were all told that everyone who had applied for compensation would have to go to the town of Hazard and apply again. 我们接到了通知，说是要每一个申请领取抚恤金的人都得到哈扎镇再申请一次。

从这个例子可以看出，说话人/写作者一般都会把话题，也就是旧信息或次要信息，放在主位的位置上，而把具体内容，也就是新信息或主要信息，放在述位的位置上。对于这类句子的主位，功能语言学家称之为"无标记主位"（unmarked theme）。多数时候，人们会用"无标记主位句"来传递各种信息，或进行情感交流。当然，这种类型的句子通常不会引发听话人/阅读者过多的关注。换言之，这些"无标记主位句"都是一些"普普通通的"句子。

不过，作者若想凸显某些信息的重要价值，往往会采用一些手段来重新设计语序，重新确定焦点，或者使原来并不重要的词语出现在被强调的位置上。如果这种现象发生在主位的位置上，那么这个新的主位就被称为"有标记主位"（marked theme），也就是说话人/写作者想要凸显的内容，这时该主位不再次要，而变成了全句的焦点。

【例 30】

原　　文：The door of the jail being flung open from within, there appeared, in the first place, *like a black shadow emerging into sunshine*, the grim and gristly presence of the town-beadle, with a sword by his side, and his staff of office in his hand. (Chapter 2, *The Scarlet Letter*)

译　　文：突然，狱门从里面打开了，一个狱卒首先出现在众人面前。他腰间佩了一把剑，手中握着权杖，<u>整个人就像是一个阴森可怖的黑影，慢慢地飘到了阳光下。</u>

讲　　评：

Theme（marked）	Rheme
The door of the jail being flung open from within, there appeared, in the first place, *like a black shadow emerging into sunshine*,	the grim and gristly presence of the town-beadle, with a sword by his side, and his staff of office in his hand.

原文中的状语 like a black shadow emerging into sunshine 貌似平常，其实非常重要。整个句子的结构是 There be 句型，而一般情况下 there be 后接的名词短语前不会插入其他句子成分。这样一来，前插的 like+ 名词短语就成了句子焦点，整个主位因为这个介词短语位置的前移而变得有标记，因而被强调的意味非常明显。而汉语句子的焦点通常都会放在句子末尾，所以就形成了上面的译文。读过之后，我们能够明确感受到，狱卒被描绘成了"鬼魅"的形象，被批判的意思十分明显，这也间接暗示了对即将走出监狱的海丝特的同情。

还有一些时候，句子的主位意义未必在一个"有标记主位"上体现，而是通过"不正常主位"的组合形式来凸显或强调某些信息。

【例 31】

原　　文：...*Strange*!" he exclaimed, suddenly starting again from the point. "*Strange* that I should choose you for the confidant of all this, young lady; *passing strange* that you should listen to me quietly, as if it were the most usual thing in the world for a man like me to tell stories of his opera-mistresses to a quaint, inexperienced girl like you!... (Chapter 15, *Jane Eyre*)

译　　文：……"*奇怪！真奇怪！*"他突然又一次岔开了话题，大声说道，"爱小姐，我竟然把一切都告诉了你。<u>更奇怪的是，</u>你<u>居然</u>还能那么安静地听我倾诉，就好像这些事情再正常不过一样，<u>可现实却是</u>，我在讲述自己与一个歌女的故事，而听众却是你这般古怪而又不谙世事的姑娘！……

第三章 意义类型

Theme(marked)	Rheme
Strange!"	he exclaimed, suddenly starting again from the point.
"*Strange*	that I should choose you for the confidant of all this, young lady;
passing strange	that you should listen to me quietly, as if it were the most usual thing in the world for a man like me to tell stories of his opera-mistresses to a quaint, inexperienced girl like you!

讲　评：原文选自《简·爱》第 15 章，故事背景是罗切斯特先生有一次与简长谈自己的情史，讲到了被瓦伦小姐深深伤害的那段往事。按理说，这些内容是不应该告诉一个家庭教师的。原文的 strange、strange 和 passing strange 形成了平行结构，语气越来越重。同时，这三个句子明显不正常，因为它们都不是完整的句子，都省略了形式主语 It 和系动词 be。之所以会有这种形式，是因为作者就是要特别加重 strange 后面内容的分量，使其变得更加沉重，由此突出罗切斯特先生当时特别矛盾的心情——他在情感上强烈地喜欢简，可是理智却告诉他应该放弃。于是，译文使用了"竟然""居然"和"可现实却是"与三个"奇怪"相配合，并兼顾汉语表达的连贯与气势，把第二个"奇怪"提前，与第一个"奇怪"形成"重复"修辞格，并加上一个"真"字来进一步强调。这样一来，原文独特的"有标记主位"就得到了凸显。

本章小结

　　总体说来，上述七种意义的翻译需要译者真正理解，不断反思，不断实践，不断强化意识，这样才有可能运用自如。七种意义类型彼此间的关系比较复杂，需要译者具体问题具体分析，这样才能识别出哪种或哪些意义类型在语境中占据主导地位，然后去努力地加以再现。至于其他不太重要的意义类型，译者顺便兼顾即可，如果无法兼顾，将其舍弃也是常理。简而言之，将词语和句子中最重要的那个或那些意义类型抓住，努力地加以再现，必然会把作者想表达的"意思"翻译得很好，也就自然地体现出了语篇应有的交际功能。语言交际功能的体现还经常与修辞手段的运用交织在一起，于是对修辞手段翻译的学习便成为我们接下来要解决的问题。

第四章 修辞手段 Rhetorical Devices

本章的核心观点是：译者须具有修辞手段识别与转化的意识。本章分为三个部分：一、修辞的定义；二、常见的25种英文修辞；三、修辞手段的翻译策略。

一、修辞的定义

柯林斯词典对 rhetoric 的解释如下：the skill or art of using language effectively。修辞是有效运用语言的艺术和技巧。也就是说，修辞中有审美，修辞能力是可以通过训练来提高的。

朗文词典对 rhetoric 的解释如下：the skill of using language in speech or writing in a special way that influences or entertains people。从定义可知，修辞在口语和书面语中都存在，这是一种特殊的语言运用方式，具有影响或娱乐他人的功能。

综合上述两个词典给出的定义，我们可知，修辞手段具有审美功能，可以影响他人，还可通过训练得以提高。那么在学习翻译时，我们当然要尽可能掌握，尤其是那些常用的修辞手段，并且思考它们在翻译时如何转换。

二、常见的25种英文修辞

（一）明喻（Simile）

A figure of speech in which one thing is likened to another, in such a way as to clarify and enhance an image. It is an explicit comparison (as opposed to the metaphor where the comparison is implicit) recognizable by the use of the word like or as. 明喻大概是我们最熟悉的修辞手段之一，作用在于表述清楚并且强调事物或意象，这是一种显而易见的比喻，因为句中会出现 like 或 as 这样表示"好像"的词汇。例如：

He bellowed *like* a bull seeking combat.

他<u>像</u>寻衅的公牛<u>一样</u>怒吼着。

In his dream he saw the tiny figure fall *as* a fly.

在梦中，他看见那小小的人影<u>像</u>苍蝇<u>一般</u>落了下去。

"like"和"as"翻译成中文是"好像""好似""犹如"等意思。个别词语有时还会以 like 作为后缀，也构成明喻。例如：

It does good to no woman to be flattered by her superior, who cannot possibly intend to marry her; and it is madness in all women to let a secret love kindle within them, which, if unreturned and unknown, must devour the life that feeds it; and, if discovered and responded to, must lead, *ignis-fatuus-like*, into miry wilds whence there is no extrication. (Chapter 16, *Jane Eyre*)

如果一个身份远高于自己的男人没有娶你的打算，那么被这样的人恭维可绝无好处。如若放任爱情之火在心中秘密燃烧，就只会有两种结局：那份爱意若是得不到回应或是不被人家知晓，则爱情之火势必会将自己的生命活活吞噬；而若是被对方发现并且得到了回应，却又要*像"鬼火"一样*，将两人一同引入沼泽而不得救赎。对于女人而言，无论是哪种情况，都是一样令人疯狂。

（二）隐喻（Metaphor）

A figure of speech in which one thing is described in terms of another. The basic figure in poetry. A comparison is usually implicit; whereas in simile it is explicit. 隐喻与明喻类似，但却是隐性比喻，也就是没有 as 或 like 这样的词语。隐喻是诗歌中的基本修辞手段。例如：

Habit is a cable; every day we weave thread, and soon we cannot break it.

习惯是缆索，每天我们都编上一条线，不久我们便扯不断了。

除了 A is B 这种结构，隐喻还可以通过动词来体现。

【例 32】

原　文：It does good to no woman to be flattered by her superior, who cannot possibly intend to marry her; and it is madness in all women *to let a secret love kindle within them*, which, if unreturned and unknown, *must devour the life that feeds it*; and, if discovered and responded to, must lead, ignis-fatuus-like, into miry wilds whence there is no extrication. (Chapter 16, *Jane Eyre*)

译　文：如果一个身份远高于自己的男人没有娶你的打算，那么被这样的人恭维可绝无好处。如若*放任爱情之火在心中秘密燃烧*，就只会有两种结局：那份爱意若是得不到回应或是不被人家知晓，则爱情之火*势必会将自己的生命活活吞噬*；而若是被对方发现并且得到了回应，却又要像"鬼火"一样，将两人一同引入沼泽而不得救赎。对于女人而言，无论是哪种情况，都是一样令人疯狂。

讲　评："to let a secret love kindle within them"指放任爱情之火在心中秘密燃烧，"must devour the life that feeds it"译为势必会将自己的生命活活吞噬。在这组隐喻中，前面的句子将爱情比喻成一团火，所以后面才会有将生命活活吞噬的说法。

（三）拟人（Personification）

A figure of speech in which a thing, quality, or idea is represented as a person. 拟人，就是将某个事物、某种品质或某个思想比喻成一个人，也就是该事物具有了人的思想、行为或情感。

【例33】

原　文：My little horse must *think it queer*
　　　　　To stop without a farmhouse near
　　　　　Between the woods and frozen lake
　　　　　The darkest evening of the year.
　　　　　　　　　　（"Stopping by Woods on a Snowy Evening", by Robert Frost）

译　文：我的小马准**抱着个疑团**：
　　　　　干嘛停在这儿，不见人烟，
　　　　　在一年中最黑的晚上，
　　　　　停在树林和冰湖之间。

讲　评："Stopping by Woods on a Snowy Evening"是20世纪美国著名诗人罗伯特·弗罗斯特的代表作。原文是think it queer，译文却说"抱着个疑团"，这里马儿明显被比喻成了人。

【例34】

原　文：*Money talks; money prints; money broadcasts; money reigns*; and kings and labor leaders alike have to register its decrees, and even, by a staggering paradox, to finance its enterprises and guarantee its profits.

译　文：**说话的是钱，印书出版的是钱，在无线电广播的是钱，统治着国家的是钱，**而国王们和共党领袖们同样必须听命于钱，而且最为矛盾，叫人目瞪口呆的是：他们还必须出钱去维持富人们所办的企业，保证他们的利益。

讲　评：在"Money talks; money prints; money broadcasts; money reigns;"这些句子中，钱（money）的谓语是talk、prints、broadcast以及reign，这些都是人才能做的动作。毫无疑问，money被比喻成了人，作者由此说出了它的特性。

（四）拟物（Plantification）

A figure of speech in which a human or thing is given plant-like characters. "人"或"物"具有了某种植物的特征，因此，"拟物"也是一种常见的比喻。例如：

The moon hung above *like a golden mango*.
悬在我们头上的月亮**像一只金黄色的芒果**。
Her body swayed while she danced, *as a plant sways in the water*.

她跳舞时身姿摇曳，<u>犹如水中绿草随波摇荡</u>。

有时，一组词语都是围绕同一个拟物展开。

【例 35】

原　文：My Spring is gone, however, but it has left me *that French floweret* on my hands, which, in some moods, I would fain be rid of. Not valuing now *the root* whence it *sprang*; having found that it was of a sort which nothing but *gold dust* could *manure*, I have but half a liking to *the blossom*, especially when it looks so artificial as just now. (Chapter 14, *Jane Eyre*)

译　文：可是，我的春天早已逝去，我的手中只剩下了<u>这朵法国小花</u>。心情不佳的时候，我真想把它扔掉。暂且不论它是从哪个<u>根</u>上<u>发芽的</u>，就看它完完全全需要<u>金土</u>才能<u>培育</u>这一点，我就很不喜欢，尤其像刚才那样，显得那么不自然。

讲　评：原文中的 that French floweret、the root、sprang、gold dust、manure，以及 the blossom 都是围绕同一个拟物修辞展开，即 Adèle is a floweret，阿黛勒是一朵小花。

（五）借代（Metonymy）

A figure of speech that consists in using the name of one thing for that of something else with which it is associated. 借代是用一个事物的名字来指代与之相关联的另一个事物。例如：

Have you ever read <u>Jack London</u>?

你读过<u>杰克·伦敦的作品</u>吗？

Sometimes *the pen* may be mightier than *the sword*.

有时<u>文人</u>比<u>武士</u>更有力量。

在这里，Jack London 指代他所写的作品，the pen 指代文人，the sword 指代武夫。有时候，指代的用法跟文化和文学关系密切。

【例 36】

原　文：I thought sometimes I saw beyond its wild waters a shore, sweet as *the hills of Beulah*; and now and then a freshening gale, wakened by hope, bore my spirit triumphantly towards the bourne: but I could not reach it, even in fancy—a counteracting breeze blew off land, and continually drove me back. (Chapter 15, *Jane Eyre*)

译　文：有时，我的目光会越过汹涌澎湃的波涛，遥望海那边甜美如<u>比乌拉山地</u>一样的海岸。"希望"时不时刮起一阵强风，把我的心顺利吹抵目的地，但我却始终无法靠岸，甚至在幻想中都不能。总有一股逆风从陆地上袭来，不断强迫我打道回府。

讲　评：原文中的"the hills of Beulah"翻译为比乌拉山地，该表达出自英国作家班扬的《天路历程》一书，指与天国之城相邻的一片乐土。

（六）委婉（Euphemism）

　　As a figure of speech, a euphemism is a polite word or expression that is used to refer to things which people may find upsetting or embarrassing to talk about, for example sex, the human body, or death. 委婉是人们在谈论令人烦恼或尴尬的事情时，所使用的一种礼貌的表达方式。比如当谈论"性""人体某些器官"或者"死亡"时，我们就要委婉一些。例如：

　　"I lived long ago with mama; but she is *gone to the Holy Virgin*." (Chapter 11, *Jane Eyre*)
　　"那个时候，我和妈妈一起住，但她已经<u>去圣母玛利亚那儿了</u>。"
　　阿黛勒在谈及自己母亲死亡的事实时，故意使用了"去圣母玛利亚那儿"的委婉说法。

【例37】

原　文："I used to think I was poor," she wrote. "Then they told me I wasn't poor; I was <u>needy</u>. Then they said it was self-defeating to think of myself as needy, that I was <u>culturally deprived</u>. Then they told me deprived was a bad image, that I was <u>underprivileged</u>. Then they told me that underprivileged was overused, that I was <u>disadvantaged</u>. I still don't have a dime—but I have a great vocabulary!" (William & Mary Morris, *Harper Dictionary of Contemporary Usage*. 1975. New York: Harper & Row, Publishers. P229.)

译　文："我以前总认为自己穷，"她写道，"后来他们告诉我说，我并非'穷'，而是'<u>匮乏</u>'；而后他们说，认为自己'匮乏'未免自我拆台，而说'<u>丧失了文化教育权利</u>'；而后他们又说'丧失'二字形象不佳，应该说'<u>享有权益较少</u>'；而后他们又说，这个说法已经用腻了，现在该说'<u>处于不利地位</u>'。到头来我还是一文不名，可词儿却有了一大堆！"

讲　评：政客们为了维护面子，不直说 poor（贫穷），而是委婉地说 needy、culturally deprived、underprivileged、disadvantaged，从这些委婉语的频繁使用可以看出，某些政客有多么虚伪。

（七）双关（Pun）

　　As a figure of speech, a pun is a clever and amusing use of a word or phrase with two meanings, or of words with the same sound but different meanings. 双关是同一个词语或短语机智而有趣的言语使用方式。为什么会有这种情况呢？因为该表达具有两个完全不相关的意思。还有另外一种情况，就是两个词语发音完全相同，拼写可能不同，语义完全不同，这也是一种有趣的双关现象。

【例 38】

原　文：A professor tapped on his desk and shouted: "Gentlemen—*order*!"
The entire class yelled: "*Beer*!"

译　文：一位教授敲着桌子喊道："先生们，**安静**！"
全班一致回答："**啤酒**！"

讲　评：在这个例子中，order 之所以会产生双关，就是由于 order 是法庭等正式场合的用语，表示命令在场人员保持安静，但是该词也可以表达点餐的意思，全体同学故意选择了餐馆这个语境，于是回答说 Beer，意思是说我们要啤酒，这样便产生了顽皮的效果。不过翻译成中文后，这种双关效果很难还原，除非加注释说明。

【例 39】

原　文：*Rue* and *thyme* grow both in one garden.

译　文：**芸香**和**百里香**共园生长，**悔恨**和**时间**同长。

讲　评：rue 和 thyme 是两种欧洲常见的植物，往往相伴而生。而 rue 还同时具有悔恨的意思，thyme 的发音与 time（时间）的发音完全相同。这句谚语是在告诫人们，有些错误不能犯，否则随之而来的悔恨会伴随终生，就像芸香和百里香共园生长那样。与前一个例子相似，这个双关中国读者也不好理解。总而言之，双关修辞格的翻译比较难，译者只能在翻译意思的基础上尽力而为，翻译出或注释出应有的双关含义。

（八）夸张（Hyperbole）

A hyperbole is a figure of speech which greatly exaggerates the truth. 夸张就是一种言过其实的表达，与事实明显不符。

【例 40】

原　文：His eloquence *would split rocks*.

译　文：他的雄辩口才**能开岩裂石**。

讲　评：再雄辩的口才也不可能像炸药一样，这明显是夸张了。

【例 41】

原　文：When a woman loves a man, her body *has the odor of a thousand apple trees in blossom*.

译　文：当一个女人爱上一个男人时，她身上**会散发出一千棵苹果树开花的香气**。

讲　评：常吃苹果的人都会知道，这种水果容易散发出馥郁的芬芳。苹果树的花香更是迷人，而一千棵苹果树开花的香气是难以想象的。所以，以此来比喻恋爱中的女人的芳香明显是夸张了。

（九）反语（Irony）

As a figure of speech, irony is a method of humorous or subtly sarcastic expression in which the intended meaning of the words used is the direct opposite of their usual sense. 反语的使用会使得词语的真实意义变为正常含义的反面，这是一种幽默的或者巧妙的讽刺。

【例42】

原　　文：What a noble illustration of the tender laws of his favored country!——they let the paupers go to sleep.

译　　文：他亲爱的祖国有着多么温柔体贴的法律，其高尚仁慈的例证就是他们让穷人睡觉。

讲　　评：睡觉不是人人都应该有的最基本的生理需求吗？怎么让穷人睡觉就成了他们高尚仁慈的例证呢？这当然是反语，是在讽刺。有时，反语是以整个段落来体现的。

【例43】

原　　文："You," I said, "a favourite with Mr. Rochester? You gifted with the power of pleasing him? You of importance to him in any way? Go! your folly sickens me. And you have derived pleasure from occasional tokens of preference——equivocal tokens shown by a gentleman of family and a man of the world to a dependent and a novice. How dared you? Poor stupid dupe!" (Chapter 16, *Jane Eyre*)

译　　文："你是罗切斯特先生的意中人吗？"我对自己说道，"你有让他开心的天赋吗？你有哪一点对人家来说举足轻重吗？滚远一点儿吧！你愚蠢得让我恶心。人家偶然一次小示青睐，就让你高兴得不行，殊不知那不过是一个出身名门的绅士、一个精通世故的长者对一个下人、一个涉世未深的少女所做的暧昧表示罢了。你也真敢痴心妄想！让人家骗成那个样子，你是多么可怜，多么愚昧！"

讲　　评：故事背景是头天晚上，罗切斯特先生的卧室着了火，简·爱发现后奋力将火扑灭，罗切斯特先生获救后紧紧握住了简·爱的手，情不自禁地表露了自己的爱意。可是第二天一早，罗切斯特先生却不辞而别。到了晚饭时间，简·爱才从费尔法克斯太太那里得知，罗切斯特先生是去里斯见一些贵族朋友，而且要很久才能回来，于是简·爱开始心神不宁，自怨自艾之情越发不可遏制。上面的那一段独白就是在这样的背景下发生的。由此，我们明白了，这一大段其实都是简·爱的反语。

（十）轭式搭配（Zeugma）

As a figure of speech, zeugma makes one word refer to two items when it properly refers to only one of items. 轭式搭配指的是一个词与另外两个词汇可以同时搭配，而通常都是只能与其中一个搭配。

【例44】

原　文：When commemorating the great soul, the friends of his went to the graveyard *with weeping eyes and hearts*.

译　文：他的朋友怀念着他伟大的灵魂，<u>眼里流着泪，心中悲泣着</u>前往他的墓地。

讲　评：我们知道，weeping 与 eyes 在一起搭配是合情合理的，而通常情况下与 hearts 不能搭配。现在由于 weeping eyes 的存在，hearts 也能附加在后面了。于是，eyes 和 hearts 与前面的 weeping 之间的关系，就很像车轭。换言之，weeping 就是放在两头牛或两匹马脖子上的那根曲木，而 eyes 与 hearts 就是那两头牛或两匹马。

【例45】

原　文：She *was dressed in a maid's cap, a pinafore, and a bright smile*.

译　文：<u>她戴一顶少女帽，穿着一件无袖连衣裙，面露灿烂的微笑</u>。

讲　评：我们知道，be dressed in 后面通常都是搭配帽子和衣服之类的东西，从来不会搭配 smile，但由于这里是轭式搭配，于是就出现了"was dressed in a maid's cap, a pinafore, and a bright smile"这样新奇的表达，不过汉语却不适于那样说，翻译时要考虑词语搭配。

（十一）对语 / 对句（Antithesis）

As a figure of speech, antithesis refers to the use of words or phrases that contrast with each other to create a balanced and opposing effect. 对语指一对词语或短语，及所在的句子在意义上截然对立，并形成一种比较平衡和对称的结构。

【例46】

原　文：Any man or State who fights on against Nazism will have *our aid*. Any man or State who marches with Hitler is *our foe*.

译　文：任何与纳粹进行战斗的个人或国家都会获得<u>我们的帮助</u>，任何与纳粹同流合污的个人或国家都在<u>与我们为敌</u>。

讲　评：显而易见的是，在这个例子中，our aid 和 our foe 形成了 Antithesis，即对语的关系，而两个句子因为结构相同，语义相反，也形成了 Antithesis，即对句的关系。

【例47】

原　文：*Knowledge* makes *humble*, *ignorance* makes *proud*.

译　　文：*知识使人谦虚，无知使人骄傲*。

讲　　评：在这个例子中，knowledge 与 ignorance 形成对语的关系，humble 与 proud 也形成对语的关系，两个句子又成了对句的关系。

（十二）移就/通感（Hypallage）

　　Also known as transferred epithet. A figure of speech in which the epithet is transferred from the appropriate noun to modify another to which it does not really belong. 移就或通感，又被称为修饰语的转移，即某个修饰语本来是修饰一些正常的词语，现在被用来去修饰一些通常不会修饰的词语。

【例 48】

原　　文：The old man lay all night on *the sleepless bed*.

译　　文：*老人躺在床上，彻夜未眠*。

讲　　评：sleepless 一词本来属于感觉的范畴，用来修饰人的，比如 That night, he was sleepless. 或者用来修饰 night，形成 sleepless night 这个最常见的搭配，可是这里用来修饰的是 bed，这是明显的触觉和视觉，于是感觉发生了转移，以此来强调这位老人辗转反侧，整夜无眠。

【例 49】

原　　文：He crashed down *a protesting chair*.

译　　文：*他哗啦一声坐在一把椅子上，以示抗议*。

讲　　评：protesting 一词本来属于听觉的范畴，后面常接人来担任宾语，比如 He was surrounded by protesting players. 也常接宾语从句或者是介词短语等，可是现在接的是 chair 这个非常罕见的宾语，听觉由此转移到了触觉。可以看出，这个人非常不满，于是通过肢体语言来发泄自己的情绪。

（十三）矛盾修辞（Oxymoron）

　　Oxymoron is a figure of speech that combines two usually contradictory terms in a compressed paradox. 矛盾修辞指一对矛盾的词语共存于一个短语之中，用来修饰同一个中心语。

【例 50】

原　　文：Barbara may be *the most famous unknown figure* on the planet.

译　　文：芭芭拉可能是当今*最著名的不为人知的人物*。

讲　　评：Barbara 是芭比娃娃的创始人，正因为如此，她是 the most famous figure。但同时她也是一个普通人，普通到没人知道她是谁，所以是 the most unknown figure。二者合为一体，于是就形成了矛盾修辞格。

第四章 修辞手段

【例 51】
原　文：Till morning dawned I was tossed on *a buoyant but unquiet sea*, where *billows of trouble* rolled under *surges of joy*. (Chapter 15, *Jane Eyre*)
译　文：直到清晨，我都在**愉悦却不安的海洋**中颠簸。我能体验到，那**欢乐的大潮**之下隐藏着**烦恼的巨浪**。
讲　评：这是《简·爱》第 15 章结尾的段落，如前所述，简·爱被罗切斯特先生握住手后一直心绪难平，既欣喜又恐惧，所以感觉自己在愉悦却不安的海洋中颠簸，也就是体会到那欢乐的大潮之下所隐藏的烦恼的巨浪。简而言之，简·爱是在欢喜之中惴惴不安。于是，我们可以看到，两个对立词语表面矛盾，但其实互为补充，和谐统一。

（十四）戏仿（Parody）

As a figure of speech, a parody is a humorous piece of writing which imitates the style of a well-known person or represents a familiar situation in an exaggerated way. 戏仿是一种幽默的写作方式，目的是模仿某位名人的风格，或者是用夸张的方式来表达熟悉的情景。

【例 52】
原　文：A friend in need is *a friend to be avoided*.
译　文：患难中的朋友是**要躲避的朋友**。
讲　评：这句话是在戏仿一句英语谚语，那句话是我们都很熟悉的"A friend in need is a friend indeed."患难见真知。

【例 53】
原　文：—It's said Jane has *fallen in love* with Jack.
　　　　—Yes, but she says she had hesitated for a long time before she finally *walked into love*.
译　文：—据说简与杰克**堕入了情网**。
　　　　—是的，不过她说她曾经犹豫了很长的一段时间，最后才**步入情网**。
讲　评：在这组对话中，fall in love 是正常搭配，表示迅速进入爱情状态，这大概是年轻人所期待的，而 walk into love 是戏仿，明显带有无可奈何的意味。步入情网说明两人是缺乏爱的激情的，而恋爱初期缺乏激情似乎不是好兆头。
　　　下面，第 15~24 个修辞手段中所举例子都来自美国前总统奥巴马的演讲。

（十五）层进（Climax）

As a figure of speech, climax is a rhetorical series of ideas, images, etc. arranged progressively so that the most forceful is last. 层进指一系列的观点、意象等以渐进的方式排列，最有力量的在最后出现。例如，奥巴马在谈论自己的竞选之旅时，就使用了这个修辞格。

【例 54】

原　文：I was never the likeliest candidate for this office. We didn't start with much money or many endorsements. *Our campaign was not hatched in* the halls of Washington. *It began in* the backyards of Des Moines, and the living rooms of Concord, and the front porches of Charleston. *It was built by* working men and women who dug into what little savings they had to give $5 and $10 and $20 to the cause. *It grew strength from* the young people, who rejected the myth of their generation's apathy, who left their homes and their families for jobs that offered little pay and less sleep. *It drew strength from* the not-so-young people, who braved the bitter cold and scorching heat to knock on doors of perfect strangers, *and from* the millions of Americans who volunteered and organized and proved that more than two centuries later a government of the people, by the people, and for the people has not perished from the Earth. This is your victory.

译　文：我一直都不是最有希望的候选人。开始，我们没有太多资金，也没有太多人支持。*我们的竞选活动并非始于*华盛顿的豪门府邸。*而是始于*小城德梅因的民宅小院，小镇康科德的民居客厅，小市查尔斯顿的廊前檐下。*我们的成功源于*辛勤劳作的民众，他们积蓄虽微，但却慷慨解囊，捐出一笔又一笔 5 美元，10 美元，20 美元。*竞选活动声势浩大*，青年民众积极参与，他们用行动回击了人们对其漠不关心社会的指责。他们离开家门，远离亲人，从事报酬微薄，披星戴月的工作。*竞选活动如火如荼*，已经不再年轻的民众也积极加入，他们冒着严寒酷暑，敲开陌生人的家门热情宣传。*我们的成功更源于*亿万国民的支持，他们主动组织参与。所有这些都证明了在两个世纪之后，这个民有、民治、民享的政府将会永世长存。*这是你们的胜利！*

讲　评：奥巴马使用了 our campaign was not hatched in、it began in、in was built by、it grew strength from、it drew strength from，最后是一句总结性的陈述，"This is your victory."全场的气氛由此被点燃。

（十六）头韵（Alliteration）

As a figure of speech, alliteration is the use in speech or writing of several words close together which all begin with the same letter or sound. 头韵在口语和书面语中都存在，是距离较近的单词都以相同的字母或声音开头。

【例 55】

原　文：And, above all, I will ask you to join in the work of remaking this nation, the only way it's been done in America for 221 years—*block by block, brick by brick, calloused hand by calloused hand.*

译　文：最重要的是，我会邀请你们加入进来，重建这个国家，以美国建国 221 年来从未改变的方式：_一砖一瓦，一梁一木，同舟共济，同心协力_。

讲　评：原文中的 block block、brick brick、calloused calloused、hand hand 是典型的头韵修辞格，译文也同样使用了头韵法"一砖一瓦，一梁一木，同舟共济，同心协力"。

（十七）平行结构（Parallelism）

As a figure of speech, parallelism means giving two or more parts of one or more sentences a similar form to create a definite pattern, a concept and method closely related to the grammatical idea of parallel construction or structure. 平行结构在一个句子内部和几个句子之间都可以存在，体现为两个或两个以上的成分，在结构上相同或相近，以此形成一种明确的模式、概念或方法。

【例56】

原　文：There's _new energy to harness, new jobs to be created, new schools to build, and threats to meet, alliances to repair._

译　文：我们亟待_开发新的能源，创造新的就业机会，修建新的学校，应对众多威胁，修复与盟国的关系_。

讲　评：该句子前面是"new+ 名词 + 不定式"所形成的第一个平行结构，后面是"名词复数 + 不定式"所形成的第二个平行结构。总体说来，这是在短语层面的平行结构。下面再看一个句子层面的平行结构和词汇层面的平行结构。

【例57】

原　文：And _to all those_ watching tonight from beyond our shores, from parliaments and palaces, _to those who_ are huddled around radios in the forgotten corners of the world, our stories are singular, but our destiny is shared, and a new dawn of American leadership is at hand. _To those who_ would tear the world down: we will defeat you. _To those who_ seek peace and security: we support you. _And to all those who_ have wondered if America's beacon still burns as bright: tonight we proved once more that the true strength of our nation comes not from the might of our arms or the scale of our wealth, but from the enduring power of our ideals: _democracy, liberty, opportunity and unyielding hope._

译　文：_那些关注我们今晚集会的海外人士_，无论你是国会的上下议员，皇宫的王室贵族，还是被遗忘的世界里聚在收音机旁收听的庶民，我们的经历各不相同，但是，我们的命运紧密相连，新的美国领袖将为世界带来新的曙光。_那些想要颠覆这个世界的人_：我们必将击败你们。_那些追求和平和安全的人_：我们一定支持你们。_那些怀疑美国这座灯塔能否继续引领世界的人_：今晚我们将再次向你们证明，美利坚的真正力量并非来自我们武力的强大或者财富的规模，而是来自我们信念中永恒的力量：**民主、自由、机会和希望**。

讲　评：原文中的 to all those、to those who、to those who、to those who、and to all those who 这些表达都是在小句和句子层面的平行结构，目的是引起听众关注，明白接下来的话语都是对谁讲的。本段最后的四个名词 democracy、liberty、opportunity and unyielding hope 则是在词语层面上形成的平行结构。请注意，英文的平行结构并不要求像汉语对联那样工整，所以最后一个名词前面会出现 unyielding 一词，不过译成中文还是工整一些更好，因此可以译成"民主、自由、机会和希望"。

（十八）典故（Allusion）

As a figure of speech, allusion is something said or written that mentions a subject, person etc. either directly or implied. 典故是以间接或直接的方式来提及某个主题、某个人物、某个事件，等等。

【例 58】

原　文：She was there for *the buses in Montgomery*, *the hoses in Birmingham*, *a bridge in Selma*, and a preacher from Atlanta who told a people that "*We Shall Overcome*."

译　文：库柏看到了"**蒙哥马利市的乘车斗争**""**伯明翰市的抗议活动**""**塞尔马市的示威游行**"，来自亚特兰大的修道士马丁·路德·金告诉人们"**我们终将成功**"。

讲　评：原句中的四个事件——the buses in Montgomery, the hoses in Birmingham, a bridge in Selma, and a preacher from Atlanta who told a people that "We Shall Overcome."——是美国黑人在 20 世纪为争取民主和人权所做的和平的或流血的抗争。美国人对这些事件非常熟悉，尤其是美国黑人。因此，典故修辞通过言简意赅的短语或小句，便达到了"言有尽而意无穷"的效果。虽然中国人不熟悉这些典故，但基本不妨碍对其意义的理解。不过，如果该译文是正式出版的译文，目的是为相关人士提供政策咨询或文化研究，这时必须要加上注释。

（十九）反复（Rhetorical Repetition）

As a figure of speech, repetition means using the same words again. 反复就是把同一个表达，重复表达，无论是单词还是短语，以达到某种特定的效果。

【例 59】

原　文：This election had many firsts and many stories that will be told for generations. But one that's on my mind tonight's about a woman who cast her ballot in Atlanta. She's a lot like the millions of others who stood in line to make their voice heard in this election except for one thing: Ann Nixon Cooper is 106 years old.

第四章 修辞手段

She was born just a generation past slavery, a time when there were no cars on the road or planes in the sky, when someone like her couldn't vote for two reasons—because she was a woman and because of the color of her skin. And tonight, I think about all that she's seen throughout her century in America: the heartache and the hope, the struggle and the progress, the times we were told that we can't, and the people who pressed on with that American creed, *yes we can*.

At a time when women's voices were silenced and their hopes dismissed, she lived to see them stand up and speak out and reach for the ballot. *Yes we can*.

When there was despair in the Dust Bowl and depression across the land, she saw a nation conquer fear itself with a New Deal, new jobs, a new sense of common purpose. *Yes we can*.

When the bombs fell on our harbor and tyranny threatened the world, she was there to witness a generation rise to greatness and a democracy was saved. *Yes we can*.

She was there for the buses in Montgomery, the hoses in Birmingham, a bridge in Selma, and a preacher from Atlanta who told a people that "We Shall Overcome."
Yes we can.

A man touched down on the moon, a wall came down in Berlin, a world was connected by our own science and imagination. And this year, in this election, she touched her finger to a screen, and cast her vote, because after 106 years in America, through the best of times and the darkest of hours, she knows how America can change.
Yes we can.

America, we have come so far. We have seen so much. But there is so much more to do. So tonight, let us ask ourselves—if our children should live to see the next century, if my daughters should be so lucky to live as long as Ann Nixon Cooper, what change will they see, what progress will we have made?

This is our chance to answer that call. This is our moment. This is our time, to put our people back to work and open doors of opportunity for our kids; to restore prosperity and promote the cause of peace; to reclaim the American dream and reaffirm that fundamental truth—that out of many, we are one; that while we breathe, we hope, and where we are met with cynicism, and doubt, and those who tell us that we can't, we will respond with that timeless creed that sums up the spirit of a people: *yes we can*.

译　文：这次大选创造了很多"第一次"和许多动人的故事，它们必将世代流传。然而我今晚想起的却是在亚特兰大投票的一位女士。她和其他成百上千万排队投票的选民没有什么两样，除了一点：安·尼克松·库柏已是106岁的高龄。她出生在奴隶制度刚刚废除的年代，那时路上没有汽车，天上也没有飞机。像她这样的人不能投票只有两个原因：一是她的性别；二是她的肤色。今晚，我想到了她在过去一百年间所亲历的一切：心痛和希望，挣扎与进步，那些被告知"我们不行"的年代，以及那些在逆境中前行的美国勇士，他们的信念就是"*是的，我们行*"。

曾几何时，妇女的声音被压制，希望被剥夺，然而今天，库柏看到妇女们站起来了，可以发表意见了，可以自由投票了。*是的，我们行*。

当20世纪30年代的沙尘暴和大萧条席卷美国，库柏看到了罗斯福新政战胜了恐慌，人们有了新的工作，生活有了新的目标。*是的，我们行*。

当炸弹袭击我们的海港，独裁专制威胁这个世界，库柏见证了美国民众的伟大崛起，见证了美国民主再度新生。*是的，我们行*。

库柏看到了"蒙哥马利市的乘车斗争""伯明翰市的抗议活动""塞尔马市的示威游行"，来自亚特兰大的修道士马丁·路德·金告诉人们"我们终将成功"。*是的，我们行*。

人类登上了月球，柏林墙最终倒下，世界因为我们的科学和想象而被联系在一起。今年，就在这次大选中，库柏用手指轻触屏幕，投出了她自己的一票，因为在美国生活了106年之后，在经历了最黑暗的时代和最美好的时光之后，她知道美国能够变革。

是的，我们行。

美利坚，我们与你一路走来。一起经历了许许多多。但是我们仍有很多事情要做。今晚，让我们问自己这样一个问题：如果我们的孩子能够活到下个世纪，如果我们的儿女能有幸像库柏一样长寿，他们将会看到怎样的改变，看到我们取得怎样的进步？

现在，我们获得了回答这个问题的机会。这是我们的时刻。这是我们的时代：让人们重新就业，为孩子打开机遇之门；重塑繁荣，推进和平；让"美国梦"重放光芒；让我们再次证明这个事实——我们是相亲相爱的一家人。只要一息尚存，我们就还有希望。倘若我们遭遇嘲讽和怀疑，倘若还有人说我们不行，我们就用这个凝聚了民族精神的永恒信念来回应：*是的，我们行*。

讲　评：在上面这个例子中，"Yes we can、Yes we can、Yes we can、Yes we can."本来是一句普通的表达，但是通过修辞性反复，竟然达到了惊人的感染效果。具体效果可以参看奥巴马演讲视频。

（二十）例证（Exemplification）

As a figure of speech, exemplification means giving a typical example. 例证要求给出一个典型的例子。正如上面反复修辞格中给出的 Ann Nixon Cooper 这个例子，奥巴马想通过这个例子来说明这次大选投票是多么深入人心，就连106岁的黑人老太太都来参与了。

（二十一）呼告（Apostrophe）

As a figure of speech, apostrophe is a digression from a discourse, esp. an address to an imaginary or absent person or a personification. 呼告是在一篇演讲或话语中对一个虚幻的或不在场的人物的呼唤。例如反复修辞格例子中的"America"，就是奥巴马在演讲中经常呼唤的对象，类似于我们在诗歌或演讲中也会使用的"祖国啊，你是我伟大的母亲"。

（二十二）修辞问句（Rhetorical Question）

As a figure of speech, rhetorical question is a question that you ask as a way of making a statement, without expecting an answer. 修辞问句就是你提出一个问题，作为一种陈述，并不期待别人的回答，这等同于中文中的反问或设问。例如上面反复修辞格中给出的一个例子"what change will they see, what progress will we have made?"奥马巴紧接着做了回答："This is our chance. This is our moment. This is our time."

（二十三）对照（Contrast）

As a figure of speech, a contrast is a great difference between two or more things which is clear when you compare them. 对照是在两个或两个以上事物间所做的清晰而有力的对比。例如，奥巴马在 2009 年就职演讲中就使用了对比。

【例 60】

原　文：*Our journey has never been* one of short-cuts or settling for less. *It has not been* the path for the faint-hearted—for those who prefer leisure over work, or seek only the pleasures of riches and fame. *Rather, it has been* the risk-takers, the doers, the makers of things—some celebrated but more often men and women obscure in their labor, who have carried us up the long, rugged path towards prosperity and freedom.

译　文：我们的国家一路走来，征途中从未有过捷径，也不屈服妥协。**这条路不是为**懒惰怯懦者准备的旅程，**也不属于**好逸恶劳和贪图名利之人。**这条路属于**探险者、实干者、创造者。他们有些人声名显赫，但大多数默默无闻，他们带领我们走过漫长崎岖的征程，走向繁荣与自由。

讲　评：在这个例子中，Our journey has never been、It has not been、Rather, it has been 构成了对比修辞，其中前两个小句与第三个小句语义对立，凸显了美国之所以伟大，是因为探险者、实干者和创造者的共同努力。

（二十四）引用（Quotation）

As a figure of speech, a quotation is a sentence or phrase taken from a book, poem, or play, which is repeated by someone else. 引用是一个短语或一个句子，它来自于某本书、某首诗、

某出剧，是由他人所讲或所写的。例如，奥巴马在2009年总统就职演讲中就有一处引用。

【例61】

原　文：So let us mark this day with remembrance, of who we are and how far we have traveled. In the year of America's birth, in the coldest of months, a small band of patriots huddled by dying campfires on the shores of an icy river. The capital was abandoned. The enemy was advancing. The snow was stained with blood. At a moment when the outcome of our revolution was most in doubt, *the father of our nation ordered these words be read to the people*:

"*Let it be told to the future world...that in the depth of winter, when nothing but hope and virtue could survive...that the city and the country, alarmed at one common danger, came forth to meet* [*it*]."

译　文：为此，让我们铭记这一天，铭记我们的身份和所走过的旅程。在美利坚诞生的岁月，在那些最寒冷的日子，为数不多的爱国志士聚集在冰河的岸边，身旁的篝火即将熄灭。他们撤离了首都，敌人还在进军，雪地上沾满了鲜血。在我们的革命何去何从，结局最难预料的时刻，*我国的开国元勋托马斯·潘恩这样告诉我们*：

"*让我们昭示世界的未来。在这个酷寒的冬季，万物萧索，只有希望和美德可以生机勃勃。城市和乡村，面对共同的危难，挺身而出，奋起迎战。*"

讲　评：从这例子可以看出，说话人在引用他人语言时，未必会说出是谁说的，因为引用的话语对于那些听众或读者是不言自明的，可是译入语读者往往就不行了，必须予以说明。

（二十五）尾韵（Rhyming）

As a figure of speech, rhyming has an ending that sounds similar to the ending of another word or line of poetry, or has endings that sound similar. 尾韵是诗歌中常用的手法，就是一行结尾的发音与另一行结尾的发音相同或相近，以此形成节奏感和朗朗上口的感觉。

【例62】

原　文：Shall I compare thee to a summer's day?
　　　　Thou art more lovely and more temperate.
　　　　Rough winds do shake the darling buds of May,
　　　　And summer's lease hath all too short a date.
　　　　Sometime too hot the eye of heaven shines,
　　　　And often is his gold complexion dimmed,
　　　　And every fair from fair sometime declines,
　　　　By chance or nature's changing course untrimmed:

But thy eternal summer shall not fade
　　　Nor lose possession of that fair thou ow'st,
　　　Nor shall Death brag thou wand'rest in his shade,
　　　When in eternal lines to time thou grow'st.
　　　So long as men can breathe or eyes can see,
　　　So long lives this, and this gives life to thee.

译　文：阁下比春孰短长？
　　　君更可爱更温良。
　　　阳春期限叹苦短，
　　　娇花五月落风狂。
　　　天眼如炬有时热，
　　　金面或暗暂无光。
　　　人间万美难恒健，
　　　零落随机道无常。
　　　君有韶华不消褪，
　　　总葆朱颜独自芳。
　　　阎罗无奈由尔去，
　　　尔命永寄在诗行。
　　　但有人气人眼亮，
　　　君凭我赋万年康。
　　　　　　　　　　　　　　　　　　　　　　（辜正坤译）

讲　评：莎士比亚十四行诗的每一个诗节（quatrain）的押韵模式是A-B-A-B，整首诗的押韵模式是A-B-A-B-C-D-C-D-E-F-E-F-G-G。具体说来，第一个诗节中的day与May押韵，temperate与date押韵；第二个诗节中的shines与declines押韵，dimmed与untrimmed押韵；第三个诗节中的fade与shade押韵，ow'st与grow'st押韵；最后一组对句（couplet）中的see与thee押韵。参考译文使用了汉语近体诗绝句和律诗的押韵模式，即每个诗节的一二四句或二四句押韵，整首诗一韵到底。具体说来，"长、良、狂、光、常、芳、行、亮、康"押了平水韵中的七阳韵。

【例63】

原　文：I sat next the Duchess at tea.
　　　It was just as I feared it would be.
　　　Her rumblings abdominal
　　　Were simply abominable,
　　　Everyone thought it was me.

译　文：公爵夫人坐身旁，
　　　害我一阵心发慌。

她腹鸣如鼓，
我仓皇四顾，
那屁并非出自我的胃肠。

讲　评：英文诗歌的押韵并非都像莎翁的十四行诗那样，一三句押韵，二四句押韵。还有其他多种押韵格式，例如，有时是一二五句，就像上面这首英文打油诗。原文的"tea""be"和"me"押韵。"abdominal"与"abominable"则是三四句押韵。译文也实现了一二五句押韵，和三四句押韵。

三、修辞手段的翻译策略

鉴于修辞格是美学功能的典型体现，因此能保留的修辞格尽量保留，不能保留的也要尽可能保留相等的语言功能。因此，修辞手段的翻译策略应该是：

以相同修辞格对应翻译（首选）；
以其他修辞格替代翻译（补充）；
以直白语言取代修辞格（慎用）。

本章小结

修辞手段犹如菜肴中的各种佐料，可以使得语言表达变得有滋有味。翻译时当然要尽可能再现原文的口味，这不仅是体现了原文的交际功能，而且是在还原作者的写作风格。因此，理论上讲，修辞格翻译应该尽可能原样复现，至少是用具有类似功能的修辞格替换原文中不好翻译的修辞格，而删除修辞格则是下下策。当然，单单处理好语言功能和修辞手段还是不够的，语言连贯意识的建立也同样重要。

第五章 连贯意识
Coherence Awareness

　　本章的核心观点是：译者应该始终具有连贯意识。本章分为三个部分：一、连贯的定义；二、连贯的分类；三、连贯的翻译策略。其中，第二部分具体包括：（一）语言连贯；（二）文化连贯。

一、连贯的定义

　　朗文词典对 coherence 的解释是 when something such as a piece of writing is easy to understand because its parts are connected in a clear and reasonable way。连贯的意思就是某个语篇之所以容易理解，是因为该语篇的各个部分是以一种清晰易懂而又合情合理的方式组织在一起的。

　　柯林斯词典对 coherence 的解释是 a state or situation in which all the parts or ideas fit together well so that they form a united whole。连贯是一种状态或情境，处于这种情况下的语篇的各个部分或其中的思想有机地组织在一起，形成了一个整体。

　　《朗文语言教学与应用语言学词典》对 coherence 定义如下：Coherence refers to the relationships which link the meanings of utterances in a discourse or of the sentences in a text. These links may be based on the speakers' shared knowledge. For example

　　A: Could you give me a lift home?
　　B: Sorry, I'm visiting my sister.

　　There is no grammatical or lexical link between A's question and B's reply but the exchange has coherence because both A and B know that B's sister lives in the opposite direction to A's home.

　　Generally a paragraph has coherence if it is a series of sentences that develop a main idea (i.e. with a topic sentence and supporting sentences which relate to it).

　　连贯指的是各种关系，这些关系将交谈中话语的意义，或者语篇中句子的意义连接在一起。这些关系可能建立在言语交际者的共有知识基础之上。例如：

　　A：能让我搭你的车回家吗？
　　B：不好意思，我要去看我姐姐。

　　A 的提问和 B 的回答之间没有任何语法或词汇联系，也就是不存在衔接手段，但 A 和 B 都知道 B 的姐姐的住处与 A 的家的方向相反，因而该对话具有连贯性。

　　一般说来，如果一段话的各个句子都围绕中心大意展开（即有明确的主题句，还有与之相关的论证的句子），那么这段话就具有连贯性。

从上述三部词典的定义，我们可以得出有关连贯的重要推论：

1）连贯意味着语篇中的各级成分（单词、短语、小句和句子）构成了一个和谐相生的整体。

2）连贯意味着语篇意义清晰，容易理解，合乎逻辑。

3）连贯意味着言语交际双方拥有共同的知识，意味着译者必须透彻了解原文背后的内容，必须为译文读者提供足以保证理解的"信息"和"文化"。

因此，连贯是意义产生、意义解读和意义再现的必要条件。所以，无论是翻译、校译还是校对，连贯意识都起着十分关键的作用。

二、连贯的分类

任何语篇都是词语搭配与词语选择的写作，也是特定社会文化背景的反映。因此，语篇是否通顺、连贯，必定会与语言、文化存在互动关系。有鉴于此，连贯可在宏观上分为语言连贯与文化连贯。一般来说，语言连贯与文化连贯相辅相成，互为支撑。

（一）语言连贯（Language Coherence）

现代语言学奠基人索绪尔1916年在《普通语言学教程》（*Course in General Linguistics*）一书第五章的开篇即言："在语言状态下, 一切都要依靠关系"，并在接下来的论述中, 将这种关系归结为两种类型, 即句法关系（syntagmatic relations）和联想关系（associative relations），也称为组合关系（syntagmatic relations）与聚合关系（paradigmatic relations）。

出于研究的方便，后来的研究者大都使用"组合关系"和"聚合关系"这种通俗易懂的说法。下面，请看《朗文语言教学及应用语言学辞典》给出的解释：

Syntagmatic relations refers to the relationship that linguistic units (e.g. words, clauses) have with other units because they may occur together in a sequence. For example, a word may be said to have syntagmatic relations with the other words which occur in the sentence in which it appears, but paradigmatic relations with words that could be substituted for it in the sentence. For example

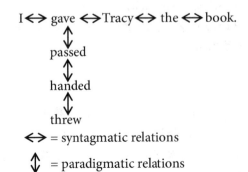

第五章 连贯意识

组合关系指语言单位（例如词语、小句）与其他语言单位因为共同出现在同一序列中而具有的语言关系。例如，可以说一个词语与同一句中的其他词语具有组合关系，但是与句中可以取代它的词语具有聚合关系。例如：

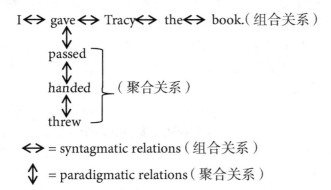

↔ = syntagmatic relations（组合关系）

↕ = paradigmatic relations（聚合关系）

索绪尔提出的这组概念道出了写作的真相，也就是说，言语表达就是在符合语法搭配和用词得体的基础上，表达自己想要说的意思。因此，翻译中语言连贯的本质就是原文的组合关系与聚合关系在译文中被"等值"重构。

具体来说，所谓组合关系的重构，是指译文的词语组合或搭配符合译入语的语法规范，同时还能体现出原文的语言功能和语用意义。所谓聚合关系的重构，是指译文在组合关系重构成功的基础上，充分考虑语境和语域，在译入语中选择具有同等语境效果的较好词语的过程。组合关系与聚合关系的"等值"重构是翻译成功的必要条件。

【例64】

原　文：I looked at the room around me and, in my heart, I let it go. To hold on would be, as Jeff said, selfish. Now it was time for John, shouldering through the door with an armload of his things his eyes bright with the promise of independence, to disappear behind the door. (*A Room of His Own*)

译　文：此时，环顾着这间屋子，我觉得我真的应该放手了。正如杰夫所说，始终占有是自私的。现在，该轮到约翰了。他双眼闪耀着独立的喜悦，双手满抱着自己的东西，用肩膀将门倚开，然后消失在门后。

讲　评：这是一个较好的语言连贯的例子。译文理解很准确，读着很舒服，总而言之，质量很高。究其原因，就是因为译文的词语搭配符合语法规定，用词语义清晰，句式自然流畅，同时也把作者的思想和情感表达得非常充分。

【例65】

原　文：Has a girl of fourteen a heart large enough, vigorous enough, to hold the swelling spring of pure, full, fervid eloquence? Such was the characteristic of Helen's discourse on that, to me, memorable evening; her spirit seemed hastening to live within a very brief span as much as many lives during a protracted existence. (Chapter 8, *Jane Eyre*)

译　文：一个十四岁的女孩有这样活跃、这样宽大的胸怀，装得下这纯洁、充盈、炽热的雄辩之泉吗？这就是那个使我难以忘怀的夜晚海伦谈话的特色。她的心灵仿佛急于要在短暂的片刻中，过得与众多长期苟活的人一样充实。

讲　评：这是一个欠佳的语言连贯的例子。仔细读过这个译文之后，我们大概可以理解译者想要说些什么，可是总感觉不太对劲。到底哪里出了问题呢？我们来看一下本段的三个句子：

第一个地方："一个十四岁的女孩有这样活跃、这样宽大的胸怀，装得下这纯洁、充盈、炽热的雄辩之泉吗？"这个表达主要存在两个问题，一个就是句式上的，通常我们会说"一个十四岁的女孩会有这样活跃、这样宽大的胸怀吗？"或者是"一个十四岁的女孩能装得下这纯洁、充盈、炽热的雄辩之泉吗？"，而不会将两个句子合二为一。用韩礼德的系统功能语法来分析（详见本书下编），这是在及物性系统的运用上出现了问题，因为"有"表达的是"关系过程"，而"装"或者说"装得下"表达的是"动作过程"，二者是不适合放在一个句子之中的，所以有读来怪怪的感觉。这个句子还有另一个问题，就是"雄辩之泉"这个搭配也让人难以接受，作者本来想说海伦·彭斯，这个十四岁的小姑娘，说起话来滔滔不绝，犹如汩汩流淌的泉水一样，一发不可收拾，这个意思我们都懂，但要是简缩成"装得下雄辩之泉"，就让人有些不好接受了，毕竟"雄辩"与"泉水"是不能直接搭配的。

第二个地方："这就是那个使我难以忘怀的夜晚海伦谈话的特色。"这个句子读起来也不舒服，因为后面的核心表达"那个特色"之前加入了太多的修饰语，如果说成"这就是那个使我难以忘怀的谈话特色"或者"这就是那个夜晚海伦的谈话特色"，两者都可以接受，但语义又会有一定程度的丢失，所以需要进一步修改表达。

第三个地方："她的心灵仿佛急于要在短暂的片刻中，过得与众多长期苟活的人一样充实。"这个句子存在两个明显的问题。第一个就是"短暂"与"片刻"的搭配问题，片刻本身就包含了"短暂"的意思，所以这个短语中有冗余存在。第二个就是"过得与众多长期苟活的人一样充实"，这里面有语义冲突，本来过得与某人一样充实，表达的是褒义概念，那个某人自然也是值得效仿的对象，可是译文里说的是"长期苟活的人"，这样的人也值得学习吗？很值得怀疑。看看原文就明白了，这里译者出现了明显的失误。"many lives during a protracted existence"指代的是那些过普通生活的人们，也就是通常可以活到六七十岁，甚至七八十岁的人们，这里并没有明显的褒贬，是中性的表达，可是这个"长期苟活"具有非常强烈的贬义色彩，所以译者在这里犯了严重的错误，毫无疑问必须修改。

简而言之，这段译文犯了如下错误：（1）词语搭配不当；（2）修饰词语过长；

（3）不同句式杂糅；（4）词语情感色彩失调。换言之，就是语言连贯中的组合关系与聚合关系都出现了问题。

那么应该如何处理这些问题呢，请看参考译文：难道十四岁的小姑娘就能如此胸怀宽广，如此旁征博引，如此才思泉涌吗？在那个让我难以忘怀的夜晚，海伦证明了她就具有此等才华。她的灵魂仿佛要急于利用这短暂的时光，把别人在漫长一生中所过的生活都充分体验一番。

总之，组合关系与聚合关系就犹如织品的经纬。其中组合关系提供的是语法正确的表达，而聚合关系则要为语义的精准表达保驾护航。两种关系和谐共处，才能编织出语言连贯的语篇。北宋著名译僧释赞宁在《（宋）高僧传》中提出过这样一个观点[1]，特别值得我们关注。他说："翻也者，如翻锦绮，背面俱花，但其花有左右不同耳。"意思是说，翻译就犹如织锦，原文就是背上的花，而译文就是面上的花，二者虽然同处于一个块锦绮之上，但是其花却左右不同。这就提醒我们，虽然认识清楚了原文的组合关系与聚合关系，但是不等于一定要照搬到译文中，而应该在保证原文功能、意义和情感基本不变的前提下，使译文表达符合自身的组合关系和聚合关系的和谐共生。这就是所谓"翻也者，如翻锦绮，背面俱花，但其花有左右不同耳"的真实含义。

根据前面讲过的标记理论，语言连贯也可以分成有标记和无标记两种。无标记语言连贯就是通常所说的很顺的表达，反映的是语义清晰、逻辑流畅、用词得体的语篇关系；有标记语言连贯则是指不合语法、搭配混乱、甚至没有逻辑，但实际上却能反映出作者真实意图的语篇关系。无标记语言连贯就是常规的语言连贯，而有标记语言连贯则是变异的语言连贯，是作者故意使用的一种诗学手段。有标记语言连贯在后现代文学作品中出现得非常频繁。因此，在翻译这类文学作品时，我们不能将其还原成正常的组合关系和聚合关系，而应该在译文中尽量保留原文的有标记语言连贯。

福克纳的名作《喧嚣与骚动》(*The Sound and the Fury*)就是典型的有标记连贯文本，请看第一部分头两段：

【例66】

原　文：April 7, 1928

Through the fence, between the curling flower spaces, I could see them hitting. They were coming toward where the flag was and I went along the fence. Luster was hunting in the grass by the flower tree. They took the flag out, and they were hitting. Then they put the flag back and they went to the table, and he hit and the other hit. Then they went on, and I went along the fence. Luster came away from the flower tree and we went along the fence and they stopped and we stopped and I looked through the fence while Luster was hunting in the grass.

---

[1] 详见中华书局1987年出版的《（宋）高僧传（上）》第52页。

"Here, caddie." They went away across the pasture. I held to the fence and watched them going away.

译　文：一九二八年四月七日 [1]

透过栅栏，穿过盘绕的花枝的空当，我看见他们在打球。他们朝插着小旗的地方走过来，我顺着栅栏朝前走。勒斯特在那棵开花的树旁草地里找东西。他们把小旗拔出来，打球了。接着他们又把小旗插回去，来到高地[2]上，这人打了一下，另外那人也打了一下。他们接着朝前走，我也顺着栅栏朝前走。勒斯特离开了那棵开花的树，我们沿着栅栏一起走，这时候他们站住了，我们也站住了。我透过栅栏张望，勒斯特在草丛里找东西。

"球在这儿，开弟[3]。"那人打了一下。他们穿过草地往远处走去。我贴紧栅栏，瞧着他们走开。

讲　评：这个版本译文通俗易懂，语言流畅，再加上有脚注，似乎没有问题。不过，我们非常有必要了解一下这部作品的写作风格。《喧嚣与骚动》的第一个写作特点就是多视角的叙述方法。该小说一共有四个部分，在前三部分，福克纳让班吉、昆丁与杰生三兄弟各自讲一遍自己的故事，在第四部分，作者又用"全能角度"，即以迪尔西为主线，讲剩下的故事。上面的例子就是以班吉，一个智商非常低下的白痴，来叙述自己的所见、所感和所思。《喧嚣与骚动》的第二个写作特点就是在第一、二、三部分都采用意识流的写作手法。那么，什么是意识流呢？简单地说，意识流的写作特点可以归纳为：1）人物的心理活动不会冠以"他想""他思忖"之类的引导语，而是仿佛从人物的头脑里直接涌流而出，直接被作者记录下来；2）人物的思想活动具有跳跃性，不必有逻辑，也不必按照时间或空间顺序展开；3）除了正常的思想活动之外，人物还会有潜意识、下意识这一类的意识活动。当然，本书还有一些其他的写作特征，但是因为与本部分翻译无关，就不再赘述。

仔细阅读这个例子，我们可以找到一些"奇怪"的表达方式，现列举并分析如下：

1　这一章是班吉明（班吉）的独白。这一天是他33岁生日。他在叙述中常常回想到过去不同时期的事。下文中译者将一一加以说明。

2　指高尔夫球的发球处。

3　"开弟"，原文为caddie，本应译为"球童"，但此词在原文中与班吉姐姐的名字"凯蒂"（Caddy）恰好同音。班吉每次听到别人叫球童，便会想起心爱的姐姐，哼叫起来。

第五章 连贯意识

（1）对及物性系统的破坏 ① I could see them hitting. ② and they were hitting. ③ and he hit and the other hit.	文中的 4 个 hit 都被用作了不及物动词，也就是不带宾语。根据文中语境，hit 在这里只有"打球"这个意思。根据系统功能语法中的及物性系统理论（详见本书下编），hit 是一个表示动作过程的动词，它的出现应该有两个参与者角色同时出现，而现在只有一个，即 hit 之前的名词或代词，作者以此来表明主人公班吉，也就是文中出现了 5 次的"I"，智商低下，因为他已经 33 岁，可是连 hit 在表示打球时要后接宾语这一点都不清楚。作者明显是故意这样写的，因此翻译时要充分考虑到这一点，译文也要形成断裂感，这样才能表现出这是作者故意造成的语言层面的"有标记"连贯。
（2）代词使用混乱 ① They were coming toward where the flag was... ② Luster was hunting in the grass by the flower tree. ③ They took the flag out, and they were hitting. ④ Then they put the flag back and they went to the table, and he hit and the other hit. ⑤ Luster came away from the flower tree and we went along the fence and they stopped and we stopped and I looked through the fence while Luster was hunting in the grass.	文中的第三人称代词的使用也给人混乱的感觉，直接出现的"They"和"them"让人不知指代的是谁。另外，Luster 的突然出现也多少有点莫名其妙。再有，两个"we"的使用，也使得读者搞不清楚 Luster 与"I"当时到底处于一种什么样的位置关系，也就是说，两个人都在栅栏外，还是一个在里面一个在外面？从原文看，根本就得不出明确的答案。总体来说，作者在使用这些代词和人名时，故意造成混乱，目的就是想从班吉这个弱智的角度来呈现对现实的感知。因此，我们在翻译时必须要考虑这一点，也就是如何在译文中营造一种茫茫然不知所措的感觉。
（3）句法使用错误 Luster came away from the flower tree and we went along the fence and they stopped and we stopped and I looked through the fence while Luster was hunting in the grass.	第一段结尾处的长句明显有句法错误，这一连串的 and 就是明证，因为正常的写作都是 A，B，C，D，and E，这样才符合语言运用中的经济原则。作者试图通过错误的句法来证明这是一个弱智者在叙述他眼中的世界。另外，根据语言学家的研究，在儿童的语言中，and 所引导的并列句出现频率很高，而这个句子中的 and 引导的不是结构清晰的并列句，而是一连串的"并列句"，当然是句法错误。这也是译者应尽力再现的地方。
（4）双关的误译 "Here, caddie."	直接引语中的句子是打高尔夫球的人在喊球童去捡球，或者是喊球童走过去。但是，这里隐含着一个"双关"，就是主人公班吉的姐姐名叫 Caddy。因为班吉的姐姐凯蒂（Caddy）对班吉非常关爱，而班吉一直对此念念不忘，虽然姐姐早已出嫁，他也好久没有看到姐姐，但是当听到有人喊 Caddie 时，便以为是有人在叫自己的姐姐，所以他才会嘴里一直高兴地哼唱。小说的第一部分一直是班吉在做第一人称自述，描绘他的所感和所知，因此这里的"Caddie"应该被译成"凯蒂"，而不是"球童"。

另外，原文给出注释的行为也值得商榷。作者在这里故意营造出一种朦胧和混乱的感觉，故意从一个虽然已经 33 岁但却只有 3 岁儿童智商的弱智者视角呈现这个世界，也就是让读者跟随傻傻的却纯真的班吉去认识这个他所感知到的现实环境。可是，译者却一开始就通过注释让我们的读者看得清清楚楚，这完全有悖于作者的初衷。《喧哗与骚动》虽然很有名，但是阅读受众却并不像《傲慢与偏见》那样广泛，毕竟这是后现代作品，采用了多视角和意识流的写作手法，而且第一部分是模仿一个痴呆者的思维，因此至少在一开篇是不宜加上注释的。如果读者因此而不喜欢阅读此书，那也没关系，毕竟这不是传统经典小说，读者不要指望一遍就能看得明明白白。鉴于以上分析，请看参考译文：

一九二八年，四月七日

透过栅栏，在花枝卷曲的空隙间，我看到他们在击打。他们正朝着插旗子的地方走，我沿着栅栏跟随。勒斯特正在一棵开花树旁的草丛里找东西。他们把旗子拔出来，接着击打，然后又把旗子插回去。他们登上一个台子，他击打完了另一个人击打。然后，他们往前走，我沿着栅栏也往前去。勒斯特离开了那棵开花的树，还有我们也沿着栅栏跟着走，还有他们停下来，还有我们也停下来，还有我透过篱笆张望，还有勒斯特在草丛里找东西。

"在这儿，凯蒂。"他们走过草场，去了那边。我紧抓住栅栏，看着他们离开。

阅读文学译作时，我们有可能会发现一些怪现象，就是某个词语或句子完全读不通，这个时候大家要小心了，可能这里并非是什么有标记语言连贯，而是伪有标记语言连贯，也就是说，译者完全理解错了，翻译错了。

【例 67】

原　文：...Through the hall of the Buchanans' house blew a faint wind, carrying the sound of the telephone bell out to Gatsby and me as we waited at the door.

"<u>The master's body!</u>" roared the butler into the mouthpiece. "I'm sorry, Madame, but we can't furnish it—it's far too hot to touch this noon!"

What he really said was: "Yes...Yes...I'll see."

He set down the receiver and came toward us, glistening slightly, to take our stiff straw hats. (Chapter 7, *The Great Gatsby*)

译　文：……盖茨比和我在门口等开门的时候，一阵微风吹过布坎南住宅的前厅，传来电话铃的声音。

"<u>主人的尸体！</u>"男管家大声向话筒里嚷道，"对不起，太太，可是我们不能提供——今天中午太热了，没法碰！"

实际上他讲的是："是……是……我去瞧瞧。"

他放下了话筒，朝我们走过来，头上冒着汗珠，接过我们的硬壳草帽。

讲　评：除了上面的译法，还有已经出版的译著将"The master's body!"译为"要老爷的身体？"可不管是哪种译法，都无法说通。这里的语境是布坎南家的管家正在接一个电话，虽然我们暂时不知道电话是谁打来的，但是仔细想想，作者会随意安排一个管家接电话的场景吗？会让管家说出"主人的尸体"这样惊悚的言语吗？这里的主人当然就是指"布坎南"，可无论是译成"尸体"还是"身体"，都会产生非常可怕的联想。小说后面的内容告诉我们，布坎南很快就去接了电话，并且撂下电话后就在自己家的客厅里接待了到访的盖茨比和尼克。作者写出"The master's body!"，难道是别有深意吗？当然不是，这里既不是作者匠心独运的表达，也不是什么诗学用法，而是因为译者想当然地以为"body"就是常见的"尸体"或"身体"的意思，同时认为管家接电话只是偶然事件，并不重要，也无深意。可是，仔细查一下词典，就能发现，"body"在这里就是指汽车的车体，也就是汽车的车壳。再加上后面的"it's far too hot to touch this noon!"和"glistening slightly"这两个文本语境的提示，我们便明白了，在这样的大夏天，车子被太阳暴晒之后，当然会热得没法触碰，那个管家当然也就会头上冒出汗珠了。另外，小说的第七章开头也在多处交代了当时正值盛夏，气温很高这个事实。有鉴于此，请看参考译文：

……此时，我和盖茨比正站在布坎南家门厅外等候，一丝微风从门厅吹过，屋内传出打电话的声音。

"我家主人的汽车！"管家似乎在对着话筒大声嚷嚷，"很抱歉，太太，我们无法装饰——今天中午太热了，车子根本不能碰！"

最后，那个管家又说道："好的……好的……我去瞧瞧。"

管家挂了电话，然后满头是汗地朝我们走来，把我们的硬草帽接了过去。

在文学作品中，常常会出现一些作者刻意造成的语言连贯变异的情况，译者必须能够识别出作者这样表达的意图。当确认这是有标记语言连贯之后，也就是确认这是有价值的变异表达，那么就要在译文中以合适的形式努力再现，以便反映原文潜在的诗学价值和作者的真实情感。简而言之，对于语言连贯，通常以无标记对无标记，有标记对有标记。但是，对于"伪有标记语言连贯"，译者需要高度警惕。

（二）文化连贯（Culture Coherence）

如前所述，语言连贯对于翻译非常重要，但隐含在语言之中的文化连贯也同样重要。好的译文中的文化连贯不仅可以有效传递作者要表达的信息，而且还可以对译文读者起到传播知识的作用。

【例68】

原　文：Well has *Solomon* said—"Better is a dinner of herbs where love is, than a stalled ox and hatred therewith."

I would not now have exchanged Lowood with all its privations for Gateshead and its daily luxuries. (Chapter 8, *Jane Eyre*)

译　文：*所罗门*¹说得好："吃素餐而彼此相爱，好过吃肥牛而彼此相恨。"
现在，要是让我用罗沃德的匮乏去换取盖茨黑德的奢华，我是绝不愿意的。

讲　评：参考译文对"所罗门"加了注释，因为绝大部分中国人都不知道所罗门是谁。通过注释，我们得知，所罗门智慧超群，因此小简·爱这里引用他说的——吃素餐而彼此相爱，好过吃肥牛而彼此相恨——就是想表明，宁可在罗沃德学校里吃得很差，也不愿意再回到里德舅妈和表哥表姐们身边。小简·爱通过引用西方智者的名言，表示自己的想法是合情合理的，同时也再次表达了对盖茨黑德府的厌恶。这就是好的文化连贯，因为注释内容与正文内容存在着密切的关联。

【例 69】

原　文：Sunday morning while church bells rang in the villages along shore the world and its mistress returned to Gatsby's house and twinkled hilariously on his lawn.
"He's a bootlegger," said the young ladies, moving somewhere between his cocktails and his flowers. "One time he killed a man who had found out that he was nephew to von Hindenburg and *second cousin to the devil*. Reach me a rose, honey, and pour me a last drop into that there crystal glass." (Chapter 4, *The Great Gatsby*)

译文 1：星期日上午，当教堂的钟声响彻海边的村子时，时髦社会里的男男女女来到了盖茨比的别墅，在草坪上寻欢作乐。
"他是个贩卖私酒的，"年轻的女宾们在花园里来回走动，随性闲聊，边喝着鸡尾酒，边观赏着奇花异草。"有一回他杀了一个人，因为那人发现他是兴登堡²的侄子，*恶魔的表兄弟*。递给我一朵玫瑰花，宝贝，再给我那只水晶杯里斟上一点儿酒。"

译文 2：星期天早上，教堂的钟声回荡在长岛沿岸的每一个地方。这个时候，上流社会的男男女女又来到盖茨比的府邸，在他的花园里纵情狂欢。
"他是个私酒贩子，"年轻的女宾们在花园里信步闲聊，一边喝着鸡尾酒，一边观赏奇花异草，"他曾经杀过一个人，就因为那人发现他既是兴登堡³的

---

1 所罗门（Solomon，公元前 973—前 931）：传说是古代犹太王国的国王，以贤明著称，也是一位有名的诗人，写过一千多首诗歌，相传《圣经》中的《雅歌》和《箴言》为其所作。所罗门当政时期是以色列与犹太联合王国最强盛的时期，军队强大，商业繁荣。《旧约·列王纪》称他有超人的智慧，现在人们称赞一个人具有非凡的聪明才智时，常用"所罗门的智慧"这句话来形容。
2 兴登堡（1847—1934）：德国元帅，第一次世界大战期间任德军总司令。
3 兴登堡（Hindenburg, 1847—1934）：全名为保罗·冯·兴登堡（Paul von Hindenburg），德国陆军元帅，政治家。"一战"爆发后，他在东线坦能堡会战中击败俄国军队后晋升为陆军元帅。但是德国在"一战"中最终是以失败而告终，兴登堡作为战败国代表参与谈判。因此，兴登堡在协约国眼中是典型的战犯。在那些人看来，臭名昭著的战犯的侄子当然不可能是好人。

第五章 连贯意识

侄子，又是*德皇威廉二世*[1]的表兄弟。递给我一枝玫瑰吧，亲爱的，再往我的水晶杯里添点酒。"

讲　评：原文是《了不起的盖茨比》的第四章开头的两段。译文1虽然对兴登堡做了简单的脚注，但是这个注释并未给出与语境有足够关联性的信息。另外，"恶魔的表兄弟"是非常令人困惑的表达，相信不明历史真相的人都会有晕头转向的感觉。恶魔到底是谁呢？根据大多数人一知半解的理解，也许人们会认为是希特勒，毕竟这人是个十恶不赦的大坏蛋。但是《了不起的盖茨比》出版于1925年，那时候的希特勒尚未崭露头角，尚未引起人们的注意。也许一些饱学之士会认为"恶魔"是指《圣经》中的魔鬼撒旦，但是那也不能成立，毕竟那是虚构的神话人物。因此，对于不懂历史的读者来说，"兴登堡的侄子，恶魔的表兄弟"，还有其他译本的"魔鬼的表兄弟"，简直犹如天书翻译，没有起到传播文化的作用，文化连贯自然也就没有建构起来。那么，真正的文化连贯应该怎样呢？请看译文2及注释。由此一来，我们明白了，来到盖茨比府邸的那些宾客们不仅在这里白吃白喝，而且还缺乏一颗感恩的心，其中一些人甚至把盖茨比污蔑成兴登堡和威廉二世的亲戚，以此来贬低他的形象。

【例70】

原　文："He has to telephone," said Mr. Wolfshiem, following him with his eyes. "Fine fellow, isn't he? Handsome to look at and a perfect gentleman."

"Yes."

"He's an *Oggsford* man."

"Oh!"

"He went to *Oggsford College* in England. You know Oggsford College?"

"I've heard of it."

"It's one of the most famous colleges in the world." (Chapter 4, *The Great Gatsby*)

译　文："他有个电话要打，"沃尔夫山姆先生一边目送他出去，一边跟我解释，"他人不错，是吧？英俊潇洒，风度翩翩。"

"是的。"

---

[1] 德皇威廉二世（Kaiser Wilhelm II，1888—1918年在位）：威廉二世是一位狂热的军国主义者，其政治野心就是称霸世界。1895年，他宣称德意志帝国要成为世界帝国，即建立起所谓的"大德意志帝国"。1914年6月28日，震惊世界的萨拉热窝事件发生后，威廉二世欣喜若狂，极力鼓动奥匈帝国发动战争。在他的煽动下，第一次世界大战爆发了。但与他预期的相反，战争最终以德国的惨败告终。1918年，愤怒不已的德国民众发动了十一月革命，迫使威廉二世于11月9日宣布退位，并于次日逃亡荷兰。在以英美为代表的西方国家中，威廉二世有魔鬼之称。小说原文此处用"second cousin to the devil"是指盖茨比与恶魔有关系，而这个恶魔就是指威廉二世。

"他是*羊津*¹ 毕业的。"

"哦！"

"他上过英国的*羊津大学*。你知道羊津大学吗？"

"听说过。"

"那是全世界最著名的一所大学呢。"

讲　评：某个译本对"Oggsford man"处理为"狗津人"，对"Oggsford College"处理为"狗津大学"，然后还加上了注释，说原文为 Oggsford，系"Oxford"（牛津）的讹读，"oggs"音近"dogs"，此处译为"狗津"。另外，还有一些译本把"Oggsford"处理为"扭津"或"牛劲"，并分别给出了简单的注释。这些译文的处理方式无疑是正确的。作者就是要表现出沃尔夫山姆先生没有文化，素质低下的形象。这位先生是纽约当时的黑社会老大，做了很多坏事，包括教唆盖茨比去做一些违法的事情。作者故意使用了有标记的文化连贯策略，把世人皆知的牛津大学"Oxford University"改称为"Oggsford College"，这是明显的文化连贯变异现象。为了忠实再现作者意图，各译本的处理手法都很成功，换言之，只要不还原成"牛津大学"，基本就成功了一半，剩下的工作只要贴近发音，或者贴近"牛津大学"的联想表达，比如参考译文就译成"羊津大学"。毕竟在中国人的脑海中，牛和羊是很容易联想到一起的。最后，再加上注释做必要的说明，就会取得有标记文化连贯翻译的成功。

还有一些文化连贯的翻译，稍微细想一下，就会让人心生好奇，感觉就像是在读有标记文化连贯。读了之后好像明白了，但其实没明白。

【例 71】

原　文：There was dancing now on the canvas in the garden, old men pushing young girls backward in eternal graceless circles, superior couples holding each other tortuously, fashionably and keeping in the corners—and a great number of single girls dancing individualistically or relieving the orchestra for a moment of the burden of the banjo or the traps. By midnight the hilarity had increased. A celebrated tenor had sung in Italian and a notorious contralto had sung in jazz and between the numbers people were doing "stunts" all over the garden, while happy vacuous bursts of laughter rose toward the summer sky. A pair of stage "twins"—who turned out to be the girls in yellow—did a baby act in costume and champagne was served in glasses bigger than finger bowls. The moon had risen higher, and floating in the Sound was *a triangle of silver scales*, trembling a little to the stiff, tinny drip of the banjoes on the lawn. (Chapter 3, *The Great Gatsby*)

---

1 原文为 Oggsford，是沃尔夫山姆先生"Oxford"【牛津】的讹读，这里译为"羊津"，表现沃尔夫山姆先生没有文化，素质低下的形象。

第五章 连贯意识

译　文：这时，不少人在花园中铺着篷布的台子上跳起舞来。有老男人推着妙龄女郎蹩脚地转来转去，舞姿不甚雅观；也有自视甚高的男女抱在一起，踩着流行节奏在舞池的角落里扭来扭去；还有好些单身姑娘在跳独舞，或者在乐队中帮班卓琴手[1]弹一弹，帮打击乐手打一打，好让他们休息一下。到了午夜，狂欢的气氛更加浓厚。先是一位著名的男高音歌手用意大利语放声高歌，接着一位声名狼藉的女低音歌手唱起了爵士歌曲，表演期间还有一些宾客纷纷展示自己的"绝活"，引得一阵阵放浪形骸的欢笑响彻了夏日夜空。舞台上还有一对"双胞胎"演员，后来发现就是那两个穿黄裙子的姑娘，她们表演了一出扮装儿童剧。仆人们往来穿梭，一杯杯香槟酒被源源不断地端到宾客面前，盛酒的杯子比洗指碗[2]还大。月亮升得更高了，海湾上空浮现出<u>一架三角形模样的银色天平</u>[3]，正应和着花园中班卓琴的铿锵旋律轻轻颤动。

讲　评：这个段落的大半部分都是在描绘盖茨比府宅中夜宴狂欢的景象，读者可以清晰地看到宾客们都纷纷陶醉在那浪漫又刺激的夏夜放纵之中。由于酒喝多了的缘故，宾客们觉得天空中的那个三角形样式的银色天平都在随着音乐的伴奏而轻轻颤动。已经出版的绝大部分译本都把原文的"a triangle of silver scales"翻译为"三角形天平样的银色星座"，或者是类似的表达，某些译本还加上一个注释，说这个银色天平就是指天秤座星斗。这些译文的语言表达很连贯，文化连贯似乎也说得过去。可是，宾客们真醉得把天空中的某些星星看成一个三角形星座，抑或是看出那是天秤座星斗吗？

通过阅读前面完整的参考译文和脚注，我们就可以知道，醉酒的宾客们看到的只是位于天空中央的三颗非常明亮的星星，它们俗称"夏夜大三角"或"夏季大三角"，但它们并不构成任何星座。

在文学作品中，文化连贯与语言连贯总是交织在一起，译者有责任将语言中的文化信息表达清楚，有责任把文化连贯与作者意图建立起关联，以确保读者可以理解。通常

1　班卓琴（banjo）：一种西洋乐器，上部形状像吉他，下部形状像铃鼓，有四根弦或者五根弦，用手指或拨子弹奏。历史相传，班卓琴起源于西非，后来传入美国，从南方的种植园渐渐传至美国北方各州。

2　洗指碗（finger bowls）：洗指碗曾是高级西餐厅或高级餐馆中的一种餐具，现在已经很少使用了。它一般是一个玻璃小碗，尺寸大小不一，通常跟饭碗的尺寸差不多。里面往往会盛有碗容量3/4的温水，有时还有一些花瓣或柠檬片作为装饰点缀其中，碗下通常会垫一块亚麻布或细棉布制成并镶有花边的精美垫布，放在甜点盘子的中央。洗指碗往往伴随着海鲜、甜点、烧烤等需要用手拿的食物出现。使用时应将单手手指第二关节以下部位浸入水中，稍稍清洗，然后用餐巾擦干。动作不要太大，要从容优雅。

3　三角形模样的银色天平（a triangle of silver scales）：读者看到这个说法，可能会以为是指天秤座，可是天秤座的四颗主星构成的是平行四边形，而且该星座只能在南半球看到，而小说的背景是北半球的美国纽约。其实，这个三角形银色天平指的是著名的"夏夜大三角"，即在北半球夏季的东南方高空里由天琴座的织女星（白色0等星）、天鹅座的天津四（白色1等星）以及天鹰座的牛郎星（白色1等星）组成的三角形。即使在大城市里，只要避开强烈的灯光干扰，也能看到这个明显的三角形。

说来，文化连贯对于译文读者具有很大的交际价值，因为它事关对作者意图的把握，事关译文的连贯，同时还可能有一定的诗学价值。对于文化连贯，通常要做显性化处理，即让读者意识到异域文化的存在，尤其是有标记文化连贯的翻译，一定要体现出作者意图。但是，对于"伪有标记文化连贯"，需要高度警惕。

三、连贯的翻译策略

综合上述论证，连贯的翻译策略可以概括为如下四点：
1）连贯的翻译通常意味着词语搭配合理，小句语义明确，句子之间的逻辑清晰。
2）连贯的翻译通常意味着译者在保证语言连贯的同时也要保证文化连贯。
3）有标记连贯的翻译需要紧抓作者意图，在此基础上再尽可能使译语表达遵守规范。
4）伪有标记连贯的解决之道是多方求证，以求最大限度地杜绝此类错误。

本章小结

一般来说，文学翻译首先要遵循的就是语言连贯原则，也就是保证译文阅读的流畅性。但对于有标记语言连贯，则要在译文中以合适形式再现，以便凸显原文的美学功能和作者的真实意图。鉴于语言连贯常与文化连贯交织在一起，因此译者有责任同时保证文化连贯，以便译文读者了解异域文化。简而言之，对于语言连贯和文化连贯，通常以无标记对无标记，有标记对有标记，但要谨防"伪有标记连贯"现象出现。

翻译理论：中编

本编是上编的延伸和升级，文学译者对此应该通晓。在掌握好初级理论的基础上，译者应该具备预设意识，知道何时使用注释，并且知道怎样注释。同时，译者应该具备识别文体变异的能力，知道如何对等转换变异表达。对于隐喻翻译，译者必须能识别出隐喻价值的大小，知道如何做好不同文体中的隐喻翻译。另外，译者应遵从合作原则，较为客观地完成译文，并能对译文质量做出较为理性的分析。

第六章 预设意识
Presupposition Awareness

本章的核心观点是：译者应该始终具有处理预设的意识。本章分为三个部分：一、预设的定义；二、预设的分类；三、预设的翻译策略。第二部分包括普遍预设、特殊预设，其中特殊预设是学习的重点和难点。

正如我们在上一章所讲到的，连贯不仅与语言表述有关，还与知识共享有关，前者是小句主位信息结构和衔接手段（详见下编第一章）的直接体现，后者则视"听众或读者对世界的预期和经验"而定（Baker, 2011: 232）。显而易见，由于时代和文化的不同，对于世界的预期和经验，作者和读者所共享的内容跟译者和译文读者所共享的内容是不可能完全一样的。这种不一致的情况特别需要译者以合适的方式处理，这样才有可能跨越文化的障碍。这里所谈到的作者与读者所共享的内容，就是我们要谈论的话题——预设（presupposition）。

一、预设的定义

《朗文语言教学及应用语言学词典》给出的 presupposition 定义是：what a speaker or writer assumes that the receiver of the message already knows. For example:

Speaker A: *What about inviting Simon tonight?*

Speaker B: *What a good idea; then he can give Monica a lift.*

Here, the presuppositions are, amongst others, that speakers A and B know who Simon and Monica are, that Simon has a vehicle, most probably a car, and that Monica has no vehicle at the moment. Children often presuppose too much. They may say:

…and he said "let's go" and we went there.

Even if their hearers do not know who *he is* and where *there is*.

预设：指说话者或写作者假定对方已知晓的信息。例如：

说话人 A：*今晚邀请西蒙怎么样？*

说话人 B：*好主意，那他还可以让莫妮卡搭个车。*

这里有一些预设，其中有：A 和 B 都知道西蒙和莫妮卡是谁，西蒙有交通工具，很可能是一辆小汽车，而莫妮卡目前没有交通工具。小孩子常常会预设太多的事情，他们会说：

> *……他说"我们走吧"，我们就去了那儿。*

可是听话者并不知道<u>*"他"*</u>指谁，<u>*"那儿"*</u>指哪儿。

德国学者诺德（Nord，2005: 105-110）认为，预设与原文读者和译文读者各自的背景知识有关，也与特定文化习俗和特定语篇体裁有关。英国学者芒迪（Munday，2016: 154）认为，预设与语言知识和言外知识相关，是发言者假设听众为了解读发言者的信息，应该具备或有必要具备的知识。但是，当译文受众不具备原文受众同样的背景知识时，或由于文化差异，也或由于篇章的翻译时间较为久远，以致原始信息无法追溯，译者在翻译时就要解决预设这个问题。

基于上述定义和论述，我们可知，文学翻译中的预设（也可称为文化预设，cultural presupposition）是交际双方在交际过程中对共有知识、背景信息和时代文化的省略，其目的是为了提高交际效率。预设成分虽然不在文学语篇中直接出现，但是因为共享同一语境，于是因预设而留下的语义真空就会被读者记忆中的各类"知识"填充，从而完成对语义连贯的建构。

由前面的理论，我们可以得出关于预设的重要推论：

1）预设是交际双方对共有知识的省略，目的是提高交际效率。
2）原文中的预设体现了作者与原文读者之间的和谐关系，折射出那个时代诸如社会、历史、文学、文化和习俗等知识。
3）随着时代的发展和文化的交流，原文中的某些预设也可能成为译文中的预设。
4）总体而言，预设翻译往往需要加注释解决，而语境还原是基本策略。

二、预设的分类

随着文化交流日益频繁，原文中的一些预设也渐渐为译文读者所熟知。但由于很多事情发生年代过于久远，或由于民族之间的生活习俗差距过大，又或由于彼此间的文化交流还不够充分，结果就是原文中的预设依然是译者必须要跨越的障碍。有鉴于此，预设可以大致分成普遍预设和特殊预设两种：前者的语境具有普遍性，因此基本上人人皆知，无须注释；后者的语境具有特殊性，只存在于源语文化之中，通常需要加注释说明。

（一）普遍预设（Universal Presupposition）

普遍预设可以指世人皆知的知识，它们自从诞生的那一天起，就为全人类所共享；也可以用来指曾经只存在于作者与原文读者之间的知识，它们对于同时代的外国读者可能是难以理解的障碍，但是随着文化交流越来越深入，现在几乎已成为人尽皆知的内容。上述两种知识就是普遍预设，往往直译即可。

【例 72】

原　　文："What do we talk of marks and brands, whether on the bodice of her gown or the flesh of her forehead?" cried another female, the ugliest as well as the most pitiless of these self-constituted judges. "This woman has brought shame upon us all, and ought to die; Is there not law for it? Truly there is, both in *the Scripture* and the statute-book. Then let the magistrates, who have made it of no effect, thank themselves if their own wives and daughters go astray." (Chapter 2, *The Scarlet Letter*)

译　　文："我们瞎扯什么记号、烙印呀，管它是贴在胸口上，还是印在额头上呢！"在这群自诩为法官的妇人当中，一个最丑陋也最没同情心的人嚷道，"这个女人让我们所有人蒙羞，所以她应该去死。难道就没有管用的法律吗？事实上，*《圣经》* 和法典里写得清清楚楚啊！然而这些地方长官却让法律形同虚设，要是他们的妻子和女儿也干了这种勾当，那才叫自作自受呢。"

讲　　评：原文中的 the Scripture 对于同时代的中国人来说，基本上还是比较陌生的，毕竟小说 *The Scarlet Letter*（《红字》）出版于 1850 年。尽管我们对《圣经》中有关女人因通奸而被惩戒的故事未必清楚，但是结合这一段后半部分文本语境，我们知道，按照当时的社会习俗来说，小说中的这个女人海丝特·白兰应该去死，而且应该是被众人羞辱后死去。理解到这个程度就够了，因为跨文化交际的目的已经实现。

【例 73】

原　　文：Nor could I pass unnoticed the suggestion of the bleak shores of Lapland, *Siberia*, Spitzbergen, Nova Zembla, *Iceland*, *Greenland*, with "the vast sweep of the Arctic Zone, and those forlorn regions of dreary space—that reservoir of frost and snow, where firm fields of ice, the accumulation of centuries of winters, glazed in Alpine heights above heights, surround the pole, and concentre the multiplied rigours of extreme cold." (Chapter 1, *Jane Eyre*)

译　　文：书里也讲到了拉普兰、*西伯利亚*、斯匹次卑尔根岛、新地岛、*冰岛* 和 *格陵兰岛* 的荒凉海岸，读到这些地方我自然会多看几眼："广阔无垠的北极地区和阴郁凄凉的不毛之地宛若严霜与冰雪的储存库。硬如磐石的坚冰，经过数个世纪的累积，犹如阿尔卑斯山耸立的高峰，晶莹耀眼，围绕北极造就了无比的酷寒。"

讲　　评：原文提到了 Siberia、Iceland 和 Greenland（西伯利亚、冰岛和格陵兰岛），相信中国人对这些地名并不陌生。每到冬天，我们就常听到"西伯利亚又来寒流"的报道，而凡是上过初中的人，也必然知道冰岛和格陵兰岛，毕竟这是中学地理课上讲过的内容，而且也很容易在地图上找到它们。

简而言之，对于原文读者和译文读者都熟悉的预设，只需要直译即可。当然，译名必须规范，也就是要使用约定俗成的表达，这样才能达成有效交际的目的。

（二）特殊预设（Special Presupposition）

特殊预设是指那些基本上只存在于作者与原文读者之间的预设，而且至今其内容依然不被大部分中国人了解。特殊预设在翻译时较复杂，大致有六种情况。

1. 可文内处理的文化预设（Adopting Free Translation in the Text）

有些特殊预设内容丰富，但与语境只有简单的关联，因此只要抓住关联点，就可以在正文中以意译的方式来处理。

【例 74】

原　文：In fact, this scaffold constituted a portion of a penal machine, which now, for two or three generations past, has been merely historical and traditionary among us, but was held, in the old time, to be as effectual an agent, in the promotion of good citizenship, as ever was the guillotine among *the terrorists of France*. (Chapter 2, *The Scarlet Letter*)

译　文：事实上，这座刑台是整个惩罚机器的一部分。它距离现在有两三代人之久，对我们不过是历史和传统的象征，**而在当时它就像法国大革命时期的断头台那样恐怖**，被认为是教人从善如流的有效工具。

讲　评：原文中的"the terrorists of France"指 18 世纪末期法国大革命中的革命派，代表力量有吉伦特派、雅各宾派、热月党人等。他们将一大批法国封建贵族送上了断头台，其中就有国王路易十六和王后玛丽·安托瓦内特，因而在欧洲掀起了革命风暴。在外部封建势力和国内保王党人的联合镇压下，法国大革命以失败而告终。这一段历史也是我国中学历史课上讲过的内容，大家比较熟悉，所以只需要在文内简单意译即可。

【例 75】

原　文：It was 1960, and I was glued to my AM radio, listening to *Del Shannon* and *Chubby Checker*. Accordions were nowhere in my hit parade. (*My Father's Music*)

译　文：当时是 1960 年，我迷上了调频广播，喜欢听**戴尔·夏侬和恰比·切克的摇滚乐**，手风琴在我这里根本排不上号。

讲　评：原文中的 Del Shannon 和 Chubby Checker 对中国人来说相当陌生。查询之后，我们知道，他们是当时美国流行乐坛非常有名的摇滚歌手。但这个信息只要在文内意译，就能起到跨文化交际的作用。

从上面两个例子可以看出，当特殊预设内容简单，无须注释就能达到跨文化交际的效果时，可以采用文内意译的方式。

2. 只需要简单注释的文化预设（Giving a Simple Footnote）

有些预设虽然能被读者猜出来大概是什么，但总还是有点懵懂的感觉，这时译者有义务让译文读者获得对该事物最基本的了解。

【例 76】

原　　文：Though Darcy could never receive him at Pemberley, yet, for Elizabeth's sake, he assisted him farther in his profession. Lydia was occasionally a visitor there, when her husband was gone to enjoy himself in London or *Bath*; and with the Bingleys they both of them frequently staid so long, that even Bingley's good humour was overcome, and he proceeded so far as to talk of giving them a hint to be gone. (Chapter 61, *Pride and Prejudice*)

译　　文：达西尽管始终不让威克姆到家里来做客，但看在夫人的面子上，还是帮威克姆谋了份差事。威克姆有时会跑到伦敦或是*巴斯*[1]寻欢作乐，在这段空闲时间，莉迪娅会到彭伯里做客，但也只是偶尔为之。不过，对于宾利家，威克姆夫妇倒是常去做客，而且一住就是很长时间，结果连宾利这样好脾气的人都忍受不住了，不得不说一些话，暗示他们赶快离开。

讲　　评：文中的 London（伦敦）可以说是人尽皆知的大城市。通过文本语境，我们可以猜出，Bath（巴斯）一定也是个地名，至于具体位置在哪里，是城市还是乡村，可能不少中国人还很陌生。具体内容请见脚注。

【例 77】

原　　文："But Reed left children?—you must have cousins? Sir George Lynn was talking of a Reed of Gateshead yesterday, who, he said, was one of the veriest rascals on town; and Ingram was mentioning a Georgiana Reed of the same place, who was much admired for her beauty a *season* or two ago in London." (Chapter 21, *Jane Eyre*)

译　　文："那么里德先生肯定留下孩子了吧？你肯定有表兄妹吧？昨天乔治·林恩爵士还提到了盖茨黑德府的约翰·里德，说他是伦敦城里最有名的无赖。布兰奇小姐也提到了此事，说那儿还有一位乔治亚娜·里德小姐，长得非常漂亮，前一两个*社交季*[2]大受男人倾慕。"

1　巴斯（Bath）：位于英格兰埃文郡东部，是一个被田园风光包围着的古典优雅的小城。它的典雅来自乔治亚时期的房屋建筑风格，它的美丽来自于绮丽的乡村风光。

2　社交季（season）：英文全称为"the social season"。从 17 世纪开始，英国的社会精英阶层会在固定时期内云集伦敦，举办舞会、晚餐会、大型慈善会等各类活动。经过二百年的发展演变，该传统在 19 世纪达到顶峰。在社交季里，各个地区的贵族名流会迁入伦敦城中的宅邸居住，以便参加各种活动。社交季在圣诞节之后正式开始，在盛夏结束。社交季在英国政治生活中扮演了重要角色，几乎上议院和下议院所有成员都会参加社交季的各种活动。上流社会达到适婚年龄的男女也会在这个时期正式露面，展开交际活动。传统上，社交季会在 8 月 12 日，即狩猎季节开始时结束。贵族绅士们会回到乡下，在秋季打鸟，在冬季猎狐，最终在圣诞节前再返回伦敦。

第六章 预设意识

讲　评：译文中的"社交季"已经翻译得很好，因为可以大概知道是一个时期内的社交活动，可是这种理解依然非常模糊。肯定会有不少读者想了解一下社交季到底是怎样的活动。具体内容请见脚注。

从这两个例子可以看出，当特殊预设的翻译给读者呈现出似懂非懂的状态时，就需要进行注释了。译者只要能说明该预设具有怎样的特点，就可以达到跨文化交际的目的。也就是说，这类特殊预设的翻译策略是"直译 + 简单型注释"。

3. 简单注释基础上有所拓展的文化预设（Based on the Simple Footnote, Giving an Extended Introduction）

有时候，译者不仅要在注释中对文化预设进行简单的说明，还要给出拓展性的介绍，这样才能满足读者的好奇心和求知欲。

【例 78】

原　文："Not as you represent it. Had she merely dined with him, she might only have discovered whether he had a good appetite; but you must remember that four evenings have been also spent together—and four evenings may do a great deal."

"Yes; these four evenings have enabled them to ascertain that they both like *Vingt-un* better than *Commerce*; but with respect to any other leading characteristic, I do not imagine that much has been unfolded." (Chapter 6, *Pride and Prejudice*)

译　文："事情可没你说的这么简单。要是简只跟他吃过四次晚饭，那也许只能知道对方胃口如何，但是你可别忘了，他们俩还共度过四个晚上。要知道，四个晚上的作用可了不得。"

"没错，这四个晚上让他们找到了一些共同点，那就是，他们都喜欢玩'<u>*二十一点*</u>'[1]，不太喜欢玩'<u>*康梅司*</u>'[2]。至于对方的主要性格特点，他们还没有太多了解。"

讲　评：对于"二十一点"和"康梅司"，已经出版的很多译本要么不做注释；要么只做最简单的注释，例如，有的解释为"康默斯是一种法国牌戏"；要么注释读过之后不明所以，比如，"科默斯，一种法国牌戏。每人发牌三张，可互换，直至换到有人赢牌为止"。毫无疑问，这样简单的注释不够妥当。具体如何解释，请看脚注。

【例 79】

原　文：Beholding it, Hester was constrained to rush towards the child—to pursue the little

---

1　二十一点（vingt-et-un）：一种纸牌游戏，又名黑杰克（BlackJack），起源于法国，历史悠久，现已流传到世界各地。该游戏可由 2~6 个人玩，使用除大小王之外的 52 张牌，游戏者的目标是使手中牌的点数之和不超过 21 点且尽量大，最接近者获胜。

2　康梅司（commerce）：19 世纪的法国牌戏，下注后每人发牌三张，其中一张可根据玩牌者的需要在牌堆中换掉，直到换妥为止，通常三张相同者最大，同花顺次之。

elf in the flight which she invariably began—to snatch her to her bosom with a close pressure and earnest kisses—not so much from overflowing love as to assure herself that Pearl was flesh and blood, and not utterly delusive. (Chapter 6, *The Scarlet Letter*)

译　　文：每当这种情形出现，海丝特总会情不自禁地去追赶那展翅欲飞的小*精灵*[1]，捉到之后便紧紧搂在怀里，然后给予热切的亲吻。这样做并非是因为过于溺爱，而是要让自己确信这孩子是血肉之躯，并非虚幻之物。

讲　　评：原文中的 elf 被译为"精灵"，这个名词呈现出的语义比较朦胧。中国人虽然已经看过很多西方电影，但对于什么是 elf，恐怕还说不清楚，而且还容易与西方文化中的"仙子"或"哥布林"产生混淆。具体解释请见脚注。

　　从这两个例子可以看出，当特殊预设的翻译只提供基本信息时，读者很可能做不到真正理解，这时就需要对注释进行一些必要的拓展，做些说明或比较之类的工作。也就是说，这种注释还是在解释"是什么"这类问题，只是解释得比较明白而已。因此，这类特殊预设的翻译策略是"直译+拓展型注释"。

　　4. 简单注释基础上做必要解释的文化预设（Based on the Simple Footnote, Giving a Necessary Explanation）

　　有时候，译者不仅要对文化预设进行简单的说明，即回答"是什么"，还要给出必要的解释，也就是回答"为什么"，这样的注释才能建立起有效的关联。

【例 80】

原　　文："We have not quite determined how far it shall carry us," said Mrs. Gardiner, "but perhaps to *the Lakes*."

No scheme could have been more agreeable to Elizabeth, and her acceptance of the invitation was most ready and grateful. "My dear, dear aunt," she rapturously cried, "what delight! what felicity! You give me fresh life and vigour. Adieu to disappointment and spleen. What are men to rocks and mountains? Oh! what hours of transport we shall spend! And when we do return, it shall not be like other travellers, without being able to give one accurate idea of any thing. We will know where we have gone—we will recollect what we have seen. Lakes, mountains, and rivers, shall not be jumbled together in our imaginations; nor, when we attempt to describe any particular scene, will we begin quarrelling about its relative situation. Let our first effusions be less insupportable than those of the generality of travellers." (Chapter 27, *Pride and Prejudice*)

---

[1] 精灵（elf）：是一种日耳曼神话中所出现的生物，他们往往被描绘成拥有稍长的尖耳、手持弓箭、金发碧眼、高大且与人类体型相似的日耳曼人的形象。精灵美丽无比，居住在森林的最深处。其他容易与精灵相混淆的生物还有仙子（fairy）和哥布林（goblin）等。总的来说，精灵没有翅膀，而仙子则带有翅膀（蜻蜓的束翅或是蛾蝶的鳞翅），且体型较小，便于飞行。哥布林则往往会被描绘成身材较为矮小、头戴尖帽（有时带有铃铛）、脚穿尖鞋的模样。

第六章 预设意识

译　文：   "要去哪里旅行，我们还没商量好呢！"加德纳太太说道，"也许会去*湖区*[1]。"对伊丽莎白而言，没有什么比这个邀请更令人满意了。她非常感激，毫不犹豫地答应下来。"亲爱的舅妈，"伊丽莎白欣喜若狂地大叫起来，"我好开心！好幸福！你给我的生命注入了新的活力。再见了，失望与消沉。比起高山大海来，人又算得了什么？哦！我们将度过多么快乐的旅行时光！我们回来的时候，一定不会像其他游人一样，什么都记不清。我们一定知道去过什么地方，一定记得看到过什么，大山、河流、湖泊，绝不会在我们脑海里混成一团。我们谈到某一处景色时，绝不会由于搞不清位置而争论不休。但愿我们回来畅谈旅行经历时，不会像大多数旅行者那样枯燥乏味。"

讲　评：   很多出版社的译文都对"湖区"做了貌似清楚，实则令人困惑的注释。例如，有的出版社这样写道："湖区指英格兰西北部著名旅游胜地，风景优美。'湖畔诗人'华兹华斯、柯尔律治等曾生活在此地。"但是作者为什么后面要写"脑子里混成一团"呢，为什么要说"搞不清位置而争论不休"呢？说到英国的湖区，可能很多中国人会联想到在西湖或太湖游览的经历，觉得游览过后脑子竟然会混乱，这实在是无法理解。那么问题出在哪里呢？问题就出在注释没有说清楚。具体内容请见脚注。

【例 81】

原　文：   "My dearest child," she cried, "I can think of nothing else! Ten thousand a year, and very likely more!' Tis as good as a Lord! And a *special licence*. You must and shall be married by a special licence. But my dearest love, tell me what dish Mr. Darcy is particularly fond of, that I may have it tomorrow." (Chapter 59, *Pride and Prejudice*)

译　文：   "我的心肝宝贝啊，"贝内特太太叫道，"现在我满脑子都是这件事啦！一年一万镑的收入啊，甚至还会更多！岂不是阔绰得要像王公大臣一样了！而且还可以有*特许结婚证*[2]。你当然要用特许结婚证结婚啦！我的宝贝，快点告诉我，达西先生喜欢吃什么，明天我就做给他。"

讲　评：   读者都明白什么是"结婚证"，可是伊丽莎白与达西先生为什么要用"特许结婚证"呢？这个证件又是怎么一回事呢？具体内容请见脚注。

1　湖区（the Lakes）：位于英格兰西北海岸，风景十分优美。19世纪英国浪漫主义诗歌奠基人华兹华斯就长居此地。现在是英国最美丽的国家公园，面积2300平方千米，这里湖泊山川纵横交错，有大大小小的湖泊16个，湖畔的道路蜿蜒曲折，游人到了这里，往往难以分清方向。故而说不清楚记忆中的各种美景到底在哪里出现。

2　特许结婚证（special license）：19世纪的英国存在四种结婚方式：公告结婚、登记结婚、特许结婚证结婚和平民许可证结婚，其中取得特许结婚证是最昂贵的结婚方式。特许结婚证可以使结婚人在任何时候、任何地点结婚，但是这个证书只可以从坎特伯雷大主教处取得，并且费用很高，19世纪中期时曾达到28基尼（=29.4英镑=588先令）。同时特许结婚证只会颁给出身名门的人，并且是大主教慎重决定后才会颁发。显然，贝内特太太唯恐凯瑟琳夫人反对，于是便建议伊丽莎白要求达西先生领取特许结婚证，这样他们的婚礼便无人再能阻拦。

从这两个例子可以看出，当特殊预设的翻译只回答"是什么"的时候，读者有时无法将注释与正文建立起有效的语义关联。也就是说，这时还要解释"为什么"。因此，这类特殊预设的翻译策略可称为"直译＋解释型注释"。

5. 直译后做语义明晰化注释的文化预设（Based on the Literal Translation, Giving a Clarifying Explanation in the Footnote）

阅读译文时，读者往往会用已有经验理解原文，但有时就会产生误解。这种情况下，译者必须要给出注释，哪怕原文似乎没有注释的必要。译者需要对原文中的预设高度敏感，这样才能给出让人意想不到却又是读者所需的注释。

【例 82】

原　文："I am afraid you do not like your *pen*. Let me mend it for you. I mend pens remarkably well."

"Thank you—but I always mend my own." (Chapter 10, *Pride and Prejudice*)

译　文："恐怕你不太喜欢那支**笔**[1]吧。我来替你修一修，修笔我很在行呢。"

"先谢过你了，但我一直都是自己修理。"

讲　评：译文将 pen 译为"笔"是正确的。可能有很多人会想，译成"钢笔"才是最准确的嘛。可是为什么不能这么解释呢？请看脚注。

那么，译成"羽毛笔"行不行呢？好像也不行，因为宾利小姐不可能对达西先生说"我不喜欢你那支羽毛笔"，这样说等于在暗示那个时代还有其他一些笔。现实情况是，那个时代人们写字用的笔就是羽毛笔。其实，这里是在强调 pen 的功能，而不是强调它的类型。所以，用模糊的方式译为"笔"即可，但要给出注释。

【例 83】

原　文：The dinner was exceedingly handsome, and there were all the servants, and all the articles of plate which Mr. Collins had promised; and, as he had likewise foretold, <u>he took his seat at the bottom of the table, by her ladyship's desire, and looked as if he felt that life could furnish nothing greater</u>. —He carved, and ate, and praised with delighted alacrity; and every dish was commended, first by him, and then by Sir William, who was now enough recovered to echo whatever his son in law said, in a manner which Elizabeth wondered Lady Catherine could bear. But Lady Catherine seemed gratified by their excessive admiration, and gave most gracious smiles, especially when any dish on the table proved a novelty to them. (Chapter 29, *Pride and Prejudice*)

译　文：接下来的宴会果真气派不凡，一旁服侍的仆人和满桌昂贵的器皿，真如柯林

---

[1] 笔（pen）：18 世纪的英国，人们使用的笔都是鹅毛笔，并非 20 世纪流行于全球的钢笔，钢笔最早发明于 19 世纪初期，而小说的背景是 18 世纪，那时钢笔还没有出现。

斯先生所预言的那样，的确是名不虚传。柯林斯先生所说的另一个预言也实现了，**凯瑟琳夫人果然请他坐在了末席，这简直是他人生最大的荣耀**[1]。他边切边吃，始终赞不绝口。每上一道菜，都是先由柯林斯先生夸赞一番，再由威廉爵士恭维一遍。看来威廉爵士已从震惊中缓过神来，女婿在那边一唱，他就在这边一和。伊丽莎白颇感纳闷，这样的恭维，凯瑟琳夫人怎么能受得了。然而令人意想不到的是，夫人对这种言过其实的赞赏十分满意，脸上总挂着亲切和蔼的微笑，尤其在发现有些佳肴是客人们从未见过的时候，便越发得意起来。

讲　评：稍微细想一下，我们就会非常困惑：为什么凯瑟琳夫人请柯林斯先生坐在餐桌末席，柯林斯先生还会感到"这简直是他人生最大的荣耀"呢？具体原因请见脚注。

看过注释之后，我们恍然大悟，原来这是地位高贵并且非常有钱的凯瑟琳夫人看得起柯林斯先生，所以才让他坐在那里。

从这两个例子可以看出，有时特殊预设会悄无声息地隐藏在文本所处的文化之中。译者若不能多问几个"为什么"，很可能就要带领读者囫囵吞枣式阅读了。也就是说，译者翻译时必须有批判精神，这样才可能发现深层文化预设。因此，这类特殊预设的翻译策略可称为"直译+明晰型注释"。

6. 直译后结合语境做研究性注释的文化预设（Based on the Literal Translation and Context, Giving an Investigative Footnote）

注释中最难的情况就是，译文读来非常流畅，似乎没有任何不明白的地方，但是这里面却存在着我们不知道的文化预设。当然，对这类特殊预设进行注释可不是一件容易的事情，因为它需要译者非常耐心地查证，毕竟这种知识是不会出现在百度百科里而任由我们复制粘贴的。

【例84】

原　文："The marriage cannot go on: I declare the existence of an impediment."

The clergyman looked up at the speaker and stood mute; the clerk did the same; Mr. Rochester moved slightly, as if an earthquake had rolled under his feet: taking a firmer footing, and not turning his head or eyes, he said, "Proceed."

Profound silence fell when he had uttered that word, with deep but low intonation. Presently Mr. Wood said—

"I cannot proceed without some investigation into what has been asserted, and

---

1　西方餐桌通常为长方形，两侧为宾客席位，两端为男女主人就座。来宾当中有地位、身份、年纪高于主人的，在排定位次时，要紧靠主人就座。男主人坐主位，右手是第一重要客人的夫人，左手是第二重要客人的夫人。女主人坐在男主人的对面，即餐桌末席，她的两边是最重要的第一、第二位男客人。小说中凯瑟琳夫人坐在男主人的位置，让柯林斯先生坐在末席，表明把柯林斯先生视为自家人，这也是餐桌上第二重要的位置，因此柯林斯先生才会感到"人生最大的荣耀"。

evidence of its truth or falsehood."

"The ceremony is quite broken off," subjoined the voice behind us. "I am in a condition to prove my allegation: *an insuperable impediment to this marriage exists*."

(Chapter 26, *Jane Eyre*)

译　　文：就在此刻，近处传来了一个清晰的声音："婚礼不能继续进行，我声明存在障碍！"

牧师抬头看了一眼说话人，惊得已无法言语，教堂执事也被吓得目瞪口呆。罗切斯特先生的身体稍微晃了一下，就好像脚下发生了地震一样。他重新站稳脚步，头也不回地说道："继续！"

他语气低沉地吐出那两个字之后，全场陷入一片沉寂。沃德牧师很快说道："如果不对刚才的反对意见进行一番调查，不能证明是真是假，恕我无法继续进行。"

"婚礼可以彻底结束了。"说话的那个人补充道，"我能够证明我的话都是真的，**这桩婚事确实存在着不可逾越的障碍**[1]。"

讲　　评：当读到最后一句时，相信几乎不会有人对此做任何质疑。这个不可逾越的障碍还用说么？当然是因为罗切斯特先生有妻子啦，所以才不可逾越。可是问题来了，罗切斯特先生离婚不就可以了嘛。这么容易就能想到的解决方案，作者会想不到吗？当然不可能想不到。具体解释请见脚注。

看过注释之后，我们终于明白了，罗切斯特先生为什么要骗婚简·爱，因为他是无法离婚的。对于这一点，那个时代的人都知道，而我们不知道。由此，我们对罗切斯特先生充满了同情，对他与简·爱的伟大爱情充满了敬意。

【例 85】

原　　文："Listen, Diana," said one of the absorbed students; "Franz and old Daniel are together in the night-time, and Franz is telling a dream from which he has awakened in terror—listen!" And in a low voice she read something, of which not

---

[1] 罗切斯特先生无法离婚，因为存在两个障碍：第一是宗教观念，第二是法律规定。基督教三大分支，无论是天主教、东正教，还是新教，都对离婚持反对态度。天主教禁止离婚，只有在极少数情况下，允许取消两人结合；东正教允许离婚和再婚，但需要满足一定条件，且要比通常民法规定的要求更加严苛；新教规定除非迫不得已，否则不鼓励离婚。所以，从宗教信仰角度来说，罗切斯特先生想要离婚很难。1857 年以前的英国，丈夫想要离婚需要经过如下流程：他要先指控妻子与他人通奸，等待教会做出两人分居的判决，然后再等待议会许可两人正式离婚。在 1857 年颁布的婚姻法（Matrimonial Causes Act, 1857）中，加入了虐待（cruelty）和遗弃（desertion）两个判定离婚的条件。其后在 1973 年的婚姻法（Matrimonial Causes Act, 1973）中，规定只有确认两人婚姻无回旋余地，才可判定两人离婚。判定无回旋余地的要素为五条，分别是通奸（adultery）、过激行为（unreasonable behaviour）、遗弃两年（desertion, two years）、两年分居协议离婚（separation, agreed divorce, two years）和五年分居争议离婚（separation, contested divorce, five years）。本小说创作于 1847 年，根据上述离婚规定，罗切斯特先生无法以妻子疯病作为借口离婚，因此从法律角度来看，罗切斯特先生想离婚再娶的可能性根本不存在，这就是"不可逾越的障碍"，同时也是他痛苦的根源所在。

one word was intelligible to me; for it was in an unknown tongue—neither French nor Latin. Whether it were Greek or German I could not tell.

"That is strong," she said, when she had finished: "I relish it." The other girl, who had lifted her head to listen to her sister, repeated, while she gazed at the fire, a line of what had been read. At a later day, I knew the language and the book; therefore, I will here quote the line: though, when I first heard it, it was only like a stroke on sounding brass to me—conveying no meaning:—

"'*Da trat hervor Einer, anzusehen wie die Sternen Nacht.*' Good! good!" she exclaimed, while her dark and deep eye sparkled. "There you have a dim and mighty archangel fitly set before you! The line is worth a hundred pages of fustian. *Ich wage die Gedanken in der Schale meines Zornes und die Werke mit dem Gewichte meines Grimms.*' I like it!"

Both were again silent. (Chapter 28, *Jane Eyre*)

译　文：　"听着，黛安娜，"其中一位专心致志的学生说道，"弗朗茨整晚都和老丹尼尔待在一起，弗朗茨正在讲他刚做的一个梦，那个梦把他吓醒了。听着！"接着，她低声读起了什么东西，可我一个字也没听懂。那是一种我不懂的语言，既不是法语，也不是拉丁语。至于是希腊语还是德语，我就说不清楚了。

"这语言写得真有力量，"她念完后说道，"我很喜欢。"另一个姑娘抬起头，一边盯着炉火，一边重复着刚才那姑娘念过的句子。尽管我初次听到时感觉那些话语毫无意义，就像是拿起铜管乐器胡乱敲打似的。后来，我知道了这门语言和这本书，因此我在这里引用一下这段文字：

"'这时走出来一个神明，看上去就像繁星满天的夜晚' 很好！很好！"她大声称赞。在烛光的映照下，她乌黑而深邃的眼睛熠熠闪光。"一个伟大的天使好像站在了你面前。刚才那一句话能抵上一百页空洞无味的语言了！'*我在我愤怒的秤盘里称重你们的思想，用我愤怒的砝码称重你们的所作所为。*'[1] 这几句话我真的很喜欢！"

1　本段单引号中的两个句子原文均为德语，引自席勒的名剧《强盗》。该剧是德国作家席勒的一部反封建、反专制独裁的杰出戏剧，完成于1780年。1782年1月13日在曼海姆公演，引起强烈反响。该剧讲述了卡尔·莫尔的故事，他是穆尔伯爵的长子，酷爱民主自由，富有正义感；次子弗朗茨秉性阴险狠毒，为了独吞父业，对卡尔进行造谣中伤，挑拨父亲和兄长的关系。莫尔伯爵听信了弗朗茨的谗言，与卡尔断绝了父子关系。出于对个人生活和时代的不满，卡尔与一群青年愤而遁入波希米亚森林为盗，并被选为首领，他试图以杀富济贫、除暴安良的侠义行动来对不公正的社会进行报复，以此改造社会。本段中的两句引用都为弗朗茨的对白，他在弑父未遂之后，与仆人老丹尼尔展开对话，讲述了他的梦中所见——他在梦境里遭到了严厉的制裁。该幕（第五幕）的后半段也表现了弗朗茨对于宗教和祷告的轻视，可在面临生命危险的时候，他又不得不向上帝祈祷，但最终自刎而死。本章前面有大量笔墨描写简·爱的祷告场景，与弗朗茨形成强烈反差，一方面传达出恶有恶报的含义；另一方面却也表明，简·爱之所以能够得助，要仰赖于她对上帝的虔诚信仰。

说到这里，两人又都沉默了。

讲　评：原文中的两个画线句子是德语，作者在这里用德语写作是什么目的呢？要弄清楚这个问题，我们得先回顾一下当时的语境。简·爱发现自己被骗婚后，便毅然决然地离开了罗切斯特先生的桑菲尔德府。可由于逃走时过于匆忙，简·爱把随身携带的包裹落在了驿站马车上。因为近乎身无分文，简·爱在旅途中经历了很多困难，她的身体因此变得越来越羸弱。就在她快要死去的时候，她强撑着来到一幢房子跟前。她发现那个房子有一扇矮窗，于是透过窗玻璃向里面张望，屋内有一位老妇人和两个年轻的姑娘。两位姑娘正在看书，她们很快就有了上面的那番对话。

对于德文部分，某个译本给出了这样的注释："原文为德语，引自德国诗人席勒的名剧《强盗》"。可是，这样的注释基本没什么价值。在简·爱最艰难的时刻，作者会让屋内的两位姑娘随意探讨一本书的内容吗？作者为什么不让她们讨论莎士比亚的戏剧或是弥尔顿的诗歌呢？这样想过之后，我们可以大胆地猜测：作者写那些德文对白，一定是有深意的。具体原因请见脚注。注释内容来源于对德国作家席勒的名剧《强盗》的仔细阅读，然后结合原文的文本语境，我们终于找到了作者让两位姑娘讨论弗朗茨与老丹尼尔对白的用意。

从这两个例子可以看出，有些特殊预设不仅会悄无声息地隐藏，而且还隐藏得极深，译者若不能多问几个"为什么"，若不能坚持批判式阅读，若不能非常耐心地研究原文，是不可能发现其中的深层文化预设的。因此，这类特殊预设的翻译策略可称为"直译＋研究型注释"。当然，这种注释比较耗时耗力，但会让译者豁然开朗，也会让译文读者收获满满。

总之，对于特殊预设，无论采用怎样的翻译策略，一定要实现跨文化交际，一定要让译文读者真正看懂作者的意图，体会到人物的真实情感。

三、预设的翻译策略

最后，我们将前面推导出的翻译策略总结如下：

预设类型	条件	翻译策略
普遍预设	文化因素具有普遍性	直译
特殊预设	文化因素具有特殊性	1. 文内意译 2. 直译＋简单型注释 3. 直译＋拓展型注释 4. 直译＋解释型注释 5. 直译＋明晰型注释 6. 直译＋研究型注释

第六章　预设意识

　　这里要特别说明一句，译者在翻译时不必刻意去思考自己所用的注释属于哪一种类型，而只需要想明白一点，就是如何把预设说得简洁而清楚，如何使预设翻译与语境建立起有效的关联。

本章小结

　　一般说来，是否具备预设意识往往是职业译者与业余译者的分水岭，而注释是否专业、是否能够解决问题，也是好的译文与差的译文的分界线之一。翻译其实只该有一种类型，就是真正满足读者需求的译文。正因为如此，译者必须具备预设意识，必须具备把原文中的预设成功翻译过来的能力。因此，文化预设七种翻译策略必须要牢牢掌握，并能熟练应用。当然，好的译者不仅要拥有做好注释的能力，还要有识别文体变异并在译文中成功再现的能力。

第七章 文体变异
Stylistic Deviation

本章的核心观点是：译者应该始终具有识别文体变异的意识。本章分为三个部分：一、文体变异的定义；二、文体变异的分类；三、文体变异的翻译策略。具体说来，其中第二部分又分为十个小部分：（一）主语位置变异；（二）宾语位置变异；（三）定语位置变异；（四）状语位置变异；（五）同位语位置变异；（六）句子成分省略变异；（七）语法规则变异；（八）修辞手段变异；（九）语种选择变异；（十）拼写或印刷变异。

一、文体变异的定义

文体变异是文体学研究的主要内容，同时也是翻译实践，尤其是文学翻译实践要解决的重要而具体的问题。在特定语境中，作者使用了较为特别的表达方式，这种新奇的表达方式被称为文体变异。在对作者意图理解充分的基础上，译者必须要对变异的文体表达进行合适的再现。下面请看几部词典对 deviation（文体变异）的定义：

柯林斯词典的解释如下：Deviation means doing something that is different from what people consider to be normal or acceptable.

朗文词典的解释如下：Deviation is a noticeable difference from what is expected or acceptable.

《文体学核心术语》的解释如下：Deviation refers to moves away from a norm on all linguistic levels (whether language is seen as a system or from a functional point of view).

从上述定义可知，文体变异存在于言语表达的一切层面。但凡有常规表达的地方，就有产生变异的可能。不过比较而言，文体变异的多发区是文学语言。文学语言的特点就是要偏离常规性表达，这就是为什么文体学的研究对象主要是文学语言，而文体学的研究重点就是文体变异。人们常说，文学是语言的艺术。那么到底"是什么使语言表达成为艺术的"呢？对于这个问题，俄国形式主义学者雅各布逊认为是诗学（poetics），即"语言艺术所具有的区别性特征（differentia specijica）"。他还指出："诗学关注的正是言语结构问题。"（1987: 63）

俄国另外一位著名的形式主义学者什克洛夫斯基在《作为技巧的艺术》一文中谈道："艺术之所以存在，就是为了恢复人对生活的感知；艺术之所以存在，就是为了使人感受事物，使石头具有石头的特性。艺术的目的就是要让人感觉到事物，而不是仅仅知道事物。艺术的技巧就是使要待表现的对象'陌生'，使表现形式难以理解，提高感觉的难度，增加感觉的时间，因为感觉过程本身就是审美目的，所以必须设法延长。艺术是对审美对象的艺术性进行体验的一种方式，而对象本身并不重要。"（Rivkin, et al.: 16）

在谈到文学语言时，什克洛夫斯基并未排斥日常语言的作用。他认为，"日常语言是文学语言的直接来源，文学语言是在日常语言基础上的一种升华。日常语言要成为文学语言，必须经过艺术家的扭曲、变形或陌生化。这样，陌生化就成了由日常语言向文学语言转化的必不可少的中间环节，或者说是中介。文学语言是陌生化之后的产物。"[1]

因此，陌生化语言必然要激起人们的惊奇感，使得作为审美主体的读者与审美对象之间存在着一定的张力。这种张力会吸引审美主体的关注，并使得他们在旧有阅读经验和新鲜表达范式的矛盾中获得快感。但我们同时要注意，这种冲突应该在一定限度之内。完全突破读者的已有阅读经验，会使得他们不能接受。而过于照顾读者原有的阅读习惯，则让他们无法完成审美过程。因此，陌生化的表达既要在意料之外，也要在情理之中。毕竟，对于读者而言，感觉之外没有艺术。

综上所述，文学之所以成为语言的艺术，就是因为具有雅各布逊所提出的"诗学特征"，也就是拥有什克洛夫斯基所认为的"陌生化表达"，那么该如何实现这一切呢？答案很清楚，那就是要使文学语言摆脱日常语言的束缚，使其在一定程度上成为变异表达。换言之，人们对文学语言的感知不再自动化，而是需要付出更多精力去感知和解读。当然，这种变异表达是泛泛而论，并不是指每一个文学作品中的每一个句子都是变异表达，而是指那些作者刻意强调的表达多多少少具有了不同寻常之处。

综上所述，我们可以得出关于文体变异的重要推论：

1）文学之所以成为文学，就是因为文学语言具有一些诗学特征，或者说拥有了不同于日常语言的一些陌生化表达；

2）一切常规的语言表达都有文体变异的可能，而文体一旦变异，陌生化的感觉就会出现，文学性因此也就打造完成；

3）文学中的变异表达不能随意为之，它必须要服务于作者的情感与观点；

4）文体变异的翻译既要充分考虑到作者意图，也要兼顾译文读者的接受能力。

二、文体变异的分类

雅各布逊和什克洛夫斯基等形式主义者之所以如此看重文学性的探讨，就是因为他们都认为，文学只有从形式分析入手，才能达到科学的高度。因为只有对原文表达从语言学视角来分析，得出的结论才是可靠而稳定的，毕竟艺术的表达形式是固定不变的，可以而且容易成为科学研究的对象。有鉴于此，下面将从十个常见的、可感的角度对文体变异展开探讨。

---

[1] 转引自朱立元《当代西方文艺理论（第三版）》，华东师范大学出版社，2014年，第35页。

（一）主语位置变异（Deviation of the Subject Position）

主语通常都是出现在句首或者是接近句首的位置，但是如果真正的主语出现在句尾或其他不常出现的位置，就会形成变异。这种现象通常出现在含有主语从句的句子中。这样句子焦点就落在了主语从句身上，结果形成句末重心。

【例 86】

原　　文：*It* is a truth universally acknowledged *that a single man in possession of a good fortune must be in want of a wife.* (Chapter 1, *Pride and Prejudice*)

译文 1：<u>有钱的单身汉总要娶位太太</u>，这是一条举世公认的真理。

译文 2：有一条举世公认的真理，<u>那就是，有钱的单身汉必会娶位太太</u>。

讲　　评：英文例句是《傲慢与偏见》的第一句话。这句话貌似寻常，但其真正的含义却未能为多数译者所把握。绝大多数译本都像译文 1 那样，将主语从句还原到了句首，也就是形成了中规中矩的"主系表"结构。然而，原句把 It 放在句首作形式主语，而把 that 引导的主语从句放在句尾，这并不仅仅是语法的规定，而且还凸显了句子的焦点信息。因为主语从句平移到句尾后不仅解决了句子头重脚轻的问题，而且后移的主语也得到了强调，同时也遵守了句末重心原则。另外，《傲慢与偏见》这部小说的风格是轻幽默和轻讽刺，而全书正是围绕第一句话展开的。译文 2 加上一句插入语"那就是"，延长了人们对"举世公认的真理"的期待，可但凡是"真理"，往往都是严肃话题，等看到句尾处"有钱的单身汉必会娶位太太"时，想必读者定会微微一笑，心中暗自思忖：这算哪门子真理？于是，通过第一句的主语位置变异，小说的轻幽默风格便奠定了基调。

【例 87】

原　　文："A wise sentence," remarked the stranger, gravely, bowing his head. "Thus she will be a living sermon against sin, until the ignominious letter be engraved upon her tombstone. *It* irks me, nevertheless, *that the partner of her iniquity should not at least, stand on the scaffold by her side....*" (Chapter 3, *The Scarlet Letter*)

译文 1："英明的裁决！"外乡人说着低下头沉思，"这样她将成为劝诫人们远离犯罪的活样本，直到这个耻辱的字母刻到她的墓石上。<u>不过，她的同犯居然没有站在她身旁一起示众，这着实让我不痛快。</u>……"

译文 2："真是绝妙的判决，"陌生男子郑重地点了点头说，"这样在那个可耻的字母刻到她的墓碑上之前，她永远都是让人引以为戒的鲜活例子。<u>不过，有件事让我很不舒服，就是共同作孽的那个家伙居然没有站在她身旁一起示众。</u>……"

讲　　评：这个例子来自《红字》第三章，主语位置变异情况与上一个例子完全一样，因此语法方面的分析不再赘述。文中的陌生男子是海丝特·白兰的丈夫——

第七章 文体变异

老齐灵渥斯医生，他刚从欧洲赶到马萨诸塞殖民地，就发现自己的妻子怀抱着私生子站在刑台上示众。他心中的怒火是不难想象的，绝对不是译文 1 所写的"着实不痛快"就能表达充分的，因此汉语译文的重心应该是不痛快的具体内容，即共同作孽的那个家伙居然没有站在她身旁一起示众。只有这样翻译，才能凸显句子的重心，才能表达出陌生男子无比的愤懑。所以，译文 2 才是较为合适的表达。

简而言之，主语一旦出现在句尾或其他不常出现的位置，就会形成主语位置变异，形成句末重心。对此，译者应调整好译文表达，以便牢牢抓住原文的焦点。

（二）宾语位置变异（Deviation of the Object Position）

宾语通常都出现在谓语动词后面，这是它应该占据的位置。但是如果宾语出现在动词前面或者其他什么罕见的位置，就会形成一定程度的变异现象，被强调的意味就会非常明显。

【例 88】

原　文：In an instant his bike was ripped from under him and he went sprawling on the river bank. Then he _made a choice_. He jumped into the water to get his bike and was carried rapidly downstream, a look of panic and horror registering on his young face. In an instant, we _had a choice to make_. (*A Valentine to One Who Cared Too Much*)

译　文：可是，河水的力量实在强大，一下子就把车子冲走了，而那孩子则摔坐在河岸上。这时，他_做出了一个选择_——跳进河里去捞车。他刚进入水中，就立刻被湍急的河水冲得顺流而下，而那一刻，他稚嫩的脸上写满了惊恐。刹那间，_我们需要做出一个抉择_。

讲　评：文章的语境是，一对刚刚订婚的未婚夫妇在情人节那天去洛杉矶河边散步。当时正好连下了十天雨，河水暴涨。几个小男孩在河岸边玩耍，其中一个男孩的自行车被河水卷走了，随后这个小男孩就做出了一个"选择"（made a choice），跳进河里去捞车。小男孩不知道河水的厉害，属于无知者无畏，因此可以轻松地做出一个选择，而故事的男女主人公都是成年人，他们深知贸然进入暴涨的河水会有多么大的危险。但是小男孩正被河水冲得顺流而下，所以在那一瞬间，他们需要立刻做出一个"救人还是不救"的生死决定。因此，这样的决定就不是普通的决定，而是生死抉择。原文此时使用的是"had a choice to make"，也就是将"make a choice"中的宾语提前，以此来凸显这个决定意义重大。文章的结局也验证了这一点，这个决定果然导致了男主人公的死亡。但是对于此种宾语变异，如果非要语序颠倒，译成"一个选择需要我们去做出"，反而会破坏汉语的阅读习惯，产生很奇怪的感觉。参考译文使用的是"我们需要做出一个抉择"，因为宾语变异也可以通过词语的选

85

择来体现，而不是非要通过宾语的位置来体现。译为"抉择"已经足以说明这个"choice"意义重大。

【例 89】

原　文：Thus the young and pure would be taught to look *at her*, with the scarlet letter flaming on her breast—*at her*, the child of honourable parents—*at her*, the mother of a babe that would hereafter be a woman—*at her*, who had once been innocent—as the figure, the body, the reality of sin. (Chapter 5, *The Scarlet Letter*)

译　文：他们教导纯洁的青年**好好看看这个**胸前佩戴红字的**女人**，**好好看看这个**有着受人尊敬的父母的**女人**，**好好看看这个**将来其女儿终究也会嫁为人妇的**女人**，**好好看看这个**原本纯洁无瑕，如今却被视为形象罪恶、肉体罪恶甚至存在也是罪恶的**女人**。

讲　评：有时候，宾语位置变异还有其他体现形式，比如将宾语不断重复，这样也能同样达到凸显宾语、表达情感的作用。原文中的 her 是介词 at 的宾语，在这个句中被使用了四次。作者以平行结构加同位语或非限制性定语从句的方式，使得 her 得到了最大限度的曝光。这是海丝特·白兰获得自由后第一次走出监牢，也是她第一次直面世人的嘲讽、指责和漫骂。世人给海丝特的道德谴责力度之强，从 her 被不断重复就可见一斑。充分理解之后，我们便可以使用"好好看看这个"来与"女人"相搭配，表达出世人对海丝特的强烈谴责之情。

简而言之，宾语一旦不在动词之后，译者就要仔细揣摩作者意图，然后尽力将变异的意义再现。

（三）定语位置变异（Deviation of the Attribute Position）

定语的作用就是要修饰后面紧跟的名词，它往往由形容词来担当，位置通常都在名词前面。如果定语的位置不在名词之前，例如成为同位语，这时往往就会造成变异现象。

【例 90】

原　文：For the last 15 years of her life we enjoyed a relationship on her terms—*light, affectionate, cheerful*. (*My Mother's Desk*)

译　文：在母亲生命的最后十五年里，我们按照她的心愿保持着那样一种关系：**彼此轻松愉快，同时满怀深情**。

讲　评：原文末尾的三个形容词本是用来修饰 relationship 这个词语，但是被放在了后面，成为 terms 的同位语，以此凸显出母亲想与女儿建立的关系到底是怎样的。不过，考虑到中文的表达习惯，三个英文形容词未必要译成对应的三个中文词语，可以考虑调整为两个短句"彼此轻松愉快，同时满怀深情"，这样也能起到强调的作用。

第七章 文体变异

【例 91】

原　文：This was a demoniac laugh—*low, suppressed, and deep*—uttered, as it seemed, at the very keyhole of my chamber door. (Chapter 15, *Jane Eyre*)

译　文：一阵魔鬼般的大笑传入我耳中，<u>低沉而压抑</u>，就像是从我房门的钥匙孔中发出来的一样。

讲　评：原文的三个形容词 low、suppressed、deep 原都被用来修饰 laugh，这里被故意后置，成为同位语。这样一来，定语的功能就得到了强调，参考译文的处理手法与上一例也很相似。

【例 92】

原　文：Wild was the wrestle which should be paramount; but another feeling rose and triumphed: *something hard and cynical: self-willed and resolute*: it settled his passion and petrified his countenance: ... (Chapter 15, *Jane Eyre*)

译　文：这场至关重要的战斗进行得无比激烈，可最后大获全胜的却是心中涌起的另一种感情。<u>那种情感冷酷而愤世嫉俗，任性却毅然决然</u>。他心中的激愤因此而慢慢平息下来，他的表情也变得越发木然……

讲　评：一些形容词会用作后置定语，修饰像 something、anything、nothing 之类的词语。在本句中，四个形容词两两组合，成为平行结构，共同修饰 something。由此可以看出，心中涌起的"某种情感"绝非寻常，一定是被强调的对象，因此定语就不应再译成定语，可以独立成具有主谓结构的句子，以示强调，如参考译文那样："那种情感冷酷而愤世嫉俗，任性却毅然决然。"

另外，还有一种定语位置变异现象也很普遍，就是非限制性定语从句。不管是关系代词引导，还是关系副词引导，也不管前面是否有介词加名词，非限制性定语从句部分通常要译成句子而非定语，这样才能凸显其重要性，因为这时定语从句只是表象，它已成为作者强调的对象。

【例 93】

原　文：This was probably because they considered me a "nice little girl," <u>*a point of view to which I had no objection*</u>. (*The Ballet Dancer*)

译　文：这很可能是因为大家都觉得我是个"可爱的小姑娘"吧，<u>这样的说法我倒是并不反对</u>。

讲　评：原文的语境是，在小姑娘观看芭蕾舞演出的幕间休息期间，家人的朋友来到礼堂的二楼楼厅，邀请她去一楼正厅第二排观看。再加之人家夸她一句"nice little girl"，于是她的得意之情更是溢于言表了。因此，非限制性定语从句根本不具有定语的功能，而应译成独立的句子，这样才能再现原文的语气和情感。

总之，对于定语位置变异问题，译者同样要高度警觉。只要定语并未处在前置定语应有的位置，或者出现连续多个前置定语，就应仔细揣摩作者用意。如果确信是作者有意为之，便要想方设法把变异定语的功能再现出来。

（四）状语位置变异（Deviation of the Adverbial Position）

英语中能够充当状语的句子成分非常多，小到单个形容词、副词，大到不定式短语、分词短语、各种词组，甚至是状语从句。但不管什么样的状语，只要出现在变异的位置上，即不常出现或不该出现的地方，就意味着被作者强调了，被用来表达特定的信息或情感，所以译者应该给予高度重视。

【例 94】

原　文： "John, are you moving furniture in there? *Again*?" I call. (*A Room of His Own*)

译　文： "约翰，你在挪家具吗？<u>怎么又挪了？</u>"我大声问道。

讲　评： 原文的语境是，母亲将大儿子杰夫的房间交给了二儿子约翰，因为杰夫大学毕业后远走他乡，再也不会回家居住，而且杰夫也同意母亲这样做。于是，约翰开始布置属于自己的房间。可是母亲对杰夫深厚的情感依然存在，所以对于约翰如此"破坏"那个屋子的摆设，多少有些不开心，因此才有了"Again"的单独发问。本来这个词可以放在前一个句子中的，也就是"Are you moving furniture in there again?"但是现在独立成句了，母亲不高兴的意味非常明显。

【例 95】

原　文： When at last I brought the desk down, it was dusty from months of storage. *Lovingly*, I polished the drawers and cubbyholes. Pulling out the secret compartment, I found papers inside. (*My Mother's Desk*)

译　文： 最后当我把书桌从阁楼上搬下来时，由于数月的搁置，它已经是尘埃满身了。我<u>小心翼翼、倍加珍惜地</u>擦干净小抽屉和小格子，然后把暗格抽了出来，发现里面有几张纸……

讲　评： 根据 BNC 语料库的查询，在含有 lovingly 的 283 个例句中，只有一个例句是将该词置于句首，其他都放在实义动词或过去分词前面，而唯一一个放在句首的那个在该词后面还没有加逗号，这充分说明本句的 lovingly 被给予了强调。结合语境再考察一下，就更容易懂了。作者渴求五十年不得的母女之情，在母亲去世之后终于得到了，获得的方式是继承了母亲非常珍爱的书桌。所以，作者在整理书桌时才会"小心翼翼、倍加珍惜"。我们通过这两个四字格词语的叠用，来营造强调的效果。[1]

【例 96】

原　文： Then he is driving a car, and we are falling asleep before he gets home, alert, *even in*

---

[1] 关于运用 COCA 语料库对该例子所做的解释，请参看上编第一章。

our dreams, to the sound of his motor gearing down. (*A Room of His Own*)

译　　文：现如今，他开上了车，于是在他每晚回家之前，我们一直不太敢睡，直到他回来后把车子熄火了方才睡去，*而有时在梦中还依旧惦念*。

讲　　评：本句说的是母亲一直在回忆杰夫成长的历程。母亲的关爱一路陪伴着杰夫，甚至在他学会开车之后也是这样。杰夫的父亲、母亲对儿子如此关注，已经到了听不见马达声熄灭就无法入眠的程度，甚至在他们的梦中还依旧惦念。原文把 even in our dreams 放在了短语 alert to 的中间，以此来强调 alert（屏息倾听），由此也就凸显了对儿子的格外关切。

【例 97】

原　　文：*In it* I taught him to read; we constructed architectural wonders out of blocks and set up elaborate desks. *It was where* Jeff perfected his artwork and struggled with college applications. *It was the place where* I told him a thousand stories *and where* we had a thousand talks. (*A Room of His Own*)

译　　文：*就在这里*，我教杰夫认字读书；*就在这里*，我们玩搭积木的游戏；*就在这里*，我们组装起精致的书桌；*就在这里*，杰夫修改他的插画作品，为申请上大学而煞费苦心；*就在这里*，我给杰夫讲过许许多多故事，并有过无数次倾心交谈。

讲　　评：作者使用了强调句式来突出地点状语，也就是这间屋子的重要意义。当然，英文的四个强调句式并不都是完整的那种，但是通过彼此参照，还是可以看出来的。另外，这四个强调句式同时形成了平行结构，作者的情感由此得到了进一步凸显。作为译者，理应对此有发现的意识和再现的能力。考虑到中文的排比习惯，我们要将其译为工整的表达"就在这里""就在这里""就在这里""就在这里""就在这里"，如此方能再现出母亲对儿子杰夫的深情。

　　最后，再说说状语从句位置变异的翻译。根据迪塞尔（Diessel）的研究（Diessel, 2001），英语为母语者使用状语从句时有一种较为显著的倾向，即主句在前而从句在后。迪塞尔使用语料库对书面故事、英语口语和科技论文进行统计，发现在 2034 个主状复合句中，有 1252 个语句是主句开头的，比例为 61.6%，其中在书面故事中的比例稍高一点，为 62.4%。相比之下，汉语的"偏正句"使用频率则更高一些。这里要解释一句，汉语的"偏正句"大体相当于英语的"主状复合句"，即汉语的偏句等于英语的状语从句，汉语的正句等于英语的主句。语料库研究证实（黎洪，2012），汉语偏正句有一些变异存在，即有相当数量的句子是"正句在前，偏句在后"，但总体上来说，汉语书面语中通常还是"偏句在前，正句在后"更多一些。不过当英语状语从句的位置出现变异之后，也就是使状语从句的交际价值成为全句的焦点，这时候与之对应的汉语偏正句就得做出相应的变化，也就是要制造出"正句在前，偏句在后"的变异表达。

【例 98】

原　　文：The old crone "nichered" a laugh under her bonnet and bandage; she then drew out a short black pipe, and lighting it began to smoke. Having indulged a while in this sedative, she raised her bent body, took the pipe from her lips, and while gazing steadily at the fire, said very deliberately—"You are cold; you are sick; and you are silly."

"Prove it," I rejoined.

"I will, in few words. You are cold, *because* you are alone: no contact strikes the fire from you that is in you. You are sick; *because* the best of feelings, the highest and the sweetest given to man, keeps far away from you. You are silly, *because*, suffer as you may, you will not beckon it to approach, nor will you stir one step to meet it where it waits you." (Chapter 19, *Jane Eyre*)

译　文：听到我如此回答，这个丑老太婆一阵大笑，声音犹如马嘶一般。随后，她掏出一只黑色短烟斗，点着后吸了起来。在烟雾缭绕中享受了一会儿之后，她直起腰，取出嘴里的烟斗，一边定睛凝视炉火，一边从容不迫地说道："你很冷，你有病，你愚蠢。"

"拿出证据来。"我答道。

"只消几句话，我就可以证明这一切。你很冷，**因为**你孑然一人，没有与人交往，无法激发出内心的火花；你有病，**因为**人所拥有的最美好、最崇高、最甜蜜的情感，都与你无缘；你愚蠢，**因为**你甘愿忍受痛苦，也不想主动召唤那种感情，连朝它迈出一步都不肯。"

讲　评：原文的语境是，罗切斯特先生装扮成女巫回到桑菲尔德府，以算命为借口来观察府宅上的年轻女宾，当然他主要是想考察简对自己的真情。例子的第一段结尾处，女巫直言不讳地说出"你很冷，你有病，你愚蠢"。根据系统功能语言学的说法，这是首次出现的新信息，值得读者关注。不过，当简·爱要求女巫证明这一点之后，这个观点就变成了旧信息，即成为新句子的"无标记主位"，然后其证明则成为述位，成为人们关注的焦点，也就是下面女巫所说的三个原因（three becauses）。一般说来，because 引导的原因状语从句仅仅提供次要信息，但是这个语境中出现了状语从句变异结构。因此，汉语也要做出相应的变异表达。如前面所述，汉语多数时候会把表示原因的偏句放在前面，把表示结果的正句放在后面，这是汉语偏正句的常态。但在这个句子中，汉语偏句需要放在后面，以此来凸显原因的重要性。

【例99】

原　文：I acknowledged no natural claim on Adèle's part to be supported by me, nor do I now acknowledge any, *for I am not her father*; but hearing that she was quite destitute, I e'en took the poor thing out of the slime and mud of Paris, and transplanted it here, to grow up clean in the wholesome soil of an English country garden. (Chapter 15, *Jane Eyre*)

第七章 文体变异

译　文：那时，我并未承认自己有抚养阿黛勒的义务，直到现在我也没有承认，**因为我不是她父亲**。可是，一听说这孩子生活艰难、孤苦伶仃，我就忍不住把她从巴黎的泥潭中解救出来，并把她栽到了英国乡村花园的沃土里，想让她在这里干干净净地长大成人。

讲　评：在这个例子中，for 引导的原因状语从句与 because 引导的从句情况相同，同样的语法分析就不再赘述。这里的语境是，瓦伦小姐先背叛了罗切斯特先生，然后又说阿黛勒是罗切斯特先生的女儿。当然，罗切斯特先生对此是拒绝接受的。再结合本段后半部分内容，便可知道前面需要"罗切斯特先生不是阿黛勒的父亲"这个原因存在，这样整个段落的逻辑才能流畅。于是，原因状语从句的变异促使汉语译文偏正句也得跟着变异。

总结上面六个例子，我们发现，状语位置变异的情况比较复杂，但不管什么情况，只要状语位置变异的情况能够被识别出来，语言功能再现就不再是难事。

（五）同位语位置变异（Deviation of the Appositive Position）

同位语的位置是在所修饰的核心词后面。一般说来，逗号后的同位语强调的意味并不明显，往往都是起补充说明的作用。

【例 100】

原　文：I remember when I was eleven years old and attended a ballet for the first time. It was held at the Memorial Auditorium, *a large building in the town where I lived*. (*The Ballet Dancer*)

译　文：记得十一岁时，我第一次观看芭蕾舞演出。演出在纪念礼堂举行，**那是我家镇上一幢高大的建筑**。

讲　评：在上面这个句子中，"a large building in the town where I lived" 只是对 "the Memorial Auditorium" 进行补充说明，并无强调的意味。

同位语要是出现在破折号之间，这时往往会有强调的意思。

【例 101】

原　文：Night comes, and the silence holds. There is a feeling about this season that is in no other — *a sense of snugness, security and solitude*. (*First Snow*)

译　文：夜幕悄然降临，天地间变得万籁俱寂。面对这样的季节，我心中油然生出一种独特的情感，**一种舒适、安宁而又孤独的情感**。

讲　评：对于破折号的处理方式，可以用逗号来取代，也可以保持不变。不过，建议大家使用逗号，毕竟破折号在汉语中并不是那么受欢迎，因为该符号对于前后内容逻辑关系的表述往往不容易看清楚。

【例 102】

原　文： After the concert Mom and Dad came backstage. The way they walked—*heads high, faces flushed*—I knew they were pleased. My mother gave me a big hug; Dad slipped an arm around me and held me close. (*My Father's Music*)

译　文： 演出结束后，父亲和母亲来到后台。瞧他们走路时的神气模样——**昂首挺胸，满面红光**——我就知道他们是为我而高兴。母亲把我抱得紧紧的，父亲也用一只手臂搂住了我的肩头。

讲　评： 同位语要是出现在两个破折号之间，这时强调的意味可能会更加明显。原文中两个破折号之间的"heads high, faces flushed"就是在对"The way they walked"进行强调，突出了父母对于"我"演出成功所表现出的喜悦，毕竟"我"曾经都想放弃练习手风琴了。

【例 103】

原　文： When the ballet was over and the dancers were bowing outside the curtain, I felt a terrible childish sadness, the kind that is felt only after the accidental pleasure. It is a puzzling sensation, the regret for the loss of that which one had not—*no, never*—even hoped for in the first place! (*The Ballet Dancer*)

译　文： 舞蹈结束了，演员们来到台前向观众谢幕。此时此刻，我感到一阵强烈而充满稚气的悲伤，一种只有经历了不期而遇的愉悦后才能感受到的悲伤。那是一种难以名状的感觉，是不曾希望**而且从未奢望**得到的东西在得到后却突然失去的痛惜之情。

讲　评： 原文中两个破折号中的"no, never"不仅是对"had not even hoped for in the first place"的补充说明，更是凸显了作者（即观看芭蕾舞演出的小姑娘）情感上出现了巨大落差。鉴于此处情感非常强烈，因此含有同位语的这个部分应用一个完整的小句翻译出来。这样句子变长之后，才能更好地加强情感。

　　一般说来，人们比较容易轻视同位语的价值。但是当它出现变异时，即出现在一个破折号后面，或是出现在两个破折号之间，我们就应努力再现它的功能和情感，尤其是两个破折号之间的这种。具体处理方法有三种：要么将同位语放在逗号或单破折号之后，要么使两个破折号之间的同位语融入原小句之中，要么使同位语独立成一个小句，并放在原小句后面。这样，就能起到强调的作用。

（六）句子成分省略变异（Deviation of Omitting Sentence Components）

　　除了上述五种句子成分的位置变异，句子成分省略也有可能造成变异。一般来说，省略句中剩下的内容就是句子的焦点，翻译时无须再将其恢复成正常句子的状态，只要保留原内容即可。

第七章 文体变异

【例 104】

原　文："Is he married or single?"

"Oh! single, my dear, to be sure! A single man of large fortune; four or five thousand a year. What a fine thing for our girls!" (Chapter 1, *Pride and Prejudice*)

译　文："成家了么？"

"还单身呢！亲爱的，千真万确！一个拥有巨额财产的单身汉，每年的收入有四五千镑。我们女儿真是好福气啊！"

讲　评：这里的语境是贝内特先生和贝内特太太在聊天。贝内特太太向丈夫提起了刚刚搬来的邻居宾利先生。由于事关女儿的终身大事，贝内特太太对于丈夫的问题异常兴奋，自言自语地说了一大堆话。再加之是对话，简洁性和凸显性非常重要，无关信息常常会被省略，剩下的都是说话人想要强调的内容。因此，译者不应该再根据语法，刻意将已被省略的信息再补充出来。翻译原则就是能省就省。

【例 105】

原　文：But none of these features by themselves gave the full effect. *The complete harmonious accord of the moment*—there was no way to explain it. (*The Ballet Dancer*)

译　文：然而，任何一次举手投足都无法单独展现出整体效果。**舞姿和谐唯美至如此境界**，竟已无法言传。

讲　评：原文的语境是，芭蕾舞演出到了最后时刻，那位男芭蕾舞演员的出色表演把小姑娘彻底征服了。于是本段的第二句就只剩下了主语，后面的句子成分全都消失了，这样便营造出想象的空间。小姑娘到底想说些什么？破折号之后的句子道出了关键。

总之，变异省略句中留下的成分都是精华，被省略的内容无须关注。翻译时只要能够突出其中的情感，就会达到很好的效果。不过，有一点需要注意，这里所说的省略句，是因为变异而造成的省略，与语法衔接而导致的省略句不同。那种省略句是为了交际的简洁和高效，这里的省略句是为了凸显某种情感或情绪。

（七）语法规则变异（Deviation of Using Grammar Rules）

有些时候，作者为了凸显某种情感，会违反某种语法规则，以此形成变异。最常见的就是把不该重复的词语一再重复。

【例 106】

原　文：The three days were, as she had foretold, busy enough. I had thought all the rooms at Thornfield beautifully clean and well arranged; but it appears I was mistaken. Three women were got to help; and *such* scrubbing, *such* brushing, *such* washing of paint and beating of carpets, *such* taking down and putting up of pictures, *such* polishing of mirrors and lustres, *such* lighting of fires in bedrooms, *such* airing of sheets and feather-beds on hearths, I never beheld, either before or since. (Chapter 17, *Jane Eyre*)

译文1： 果然被她说中了，这三天确实够忙的。我本以为桑菲尔德的所有房子都纤尘不染，收拾得很好。但看来我错了。他们雇了三个女人来帮忙。擦呀，刷呀，冲洗漆具呀，敲打地毯呀，把画拿下又挂上呀，擦拭镜子和枝形吊灯呀，在卧室生火呀，把床单和羽绒褥垫晾在炉边呀，这种情景无论是从前还是以后，我都没有见过。

译文2： 正如费尔法克斯太太所言，这三天真是忙得昏天黑地。我原以为庄园里所有房间早都收拾得干干净净，但是现在看来，我是大错特错了。费尔法克斯太太找了三个女人来帮忙，她们在家中到处洗*啊*，刷*啊*，擦*啊*，*把*油漆的器皿擦得闪闪发亮，*把*地毯掸得一尘不染，*把*挂画取下擦净后再重新挂上，*把*镜子和枝形吊灯擦得光洁如新。她们还在每一间卧室里生了火，*把*床单和羽绒床垫放到炉火边烘干。这样的场面我以前从未见过，后来也再没有见过。

讲　评： 原文的语境是简·爱得到费尔法克斯太太的通知，说是罗切斯特先生就要归来，命令府宅上下进行大清扫，准备迎接贵宾。于是，简·爱跟着府里的仆人和外请的三个帮工一起忙活起来。虽然很辛苦，简·爱却很开心，因为就要见到罗切斯特先生了。本段开头就交代了"busy enough"，然后把这种紧张又愉悦的情绪通过重复"such"来体现，可是按照语法，应该是"such A, B, C, D, E, F and G"，可是现实情况是，"such"被重复了七次。

读过译文1之后，我们可以比较肯定地说，译者感受到了作者的变异手法，但处理方式并不可取，因为不断重复的"呀"给人一种"嗲嗲"的感觉，可简·爱根本就不是那种说话"嗲嗲"，喜欢撒娇的女人。

译文2通过"洗啊，刷啊，擦啊"，以及五个"把"字句，较好地体现了桑菲尔德府当时的忙碌景象，也间接地体现出简·爱非常期待罗切斯特先生回家的心情。而同样是语气助词，"啊"就比"呀"显得更正式一些，同时使用数量也受到了限制，再加上比较正式的"把"字句，整体效果就好了很多。

【例107】

原　文： I had had no communication by letter, or message with the outer world. *School-rules*, *school-duties*, *school-habits and notions*, *and* voices, *and* faces, *and* phrases, *and* costumes, *and* preferences *and* antipathies—such as what I knew of existence. (Chapter 10, *Jane Eyre*)

译文1： 我与外部世界既没有书信往来，也不通消息。学校的规定、任务、习惯、观念、音容、语言、服饰、好恶，就是我所知道的生活内容。

译文2： 我和外面的世界既没有书信交流，也没有口信往来，<u>学校的规矩、学校的职责、</u>

第七章 文体变异

学校的习惯、学校的观念、学校的面貌、学校的用语、学校的着装、学校的偏爱、学校的憎恶，就是我所接触的全部生活。

译文3：　我和外面的世界既没有书信往来，也从不通消息。*学校的规定，学校的职责，学校的习惯和见解*，还有*那些个*声音、*那些个*面孔、*那些个*用语、*那些个*服饰和*那些个*好恶：这一切就是我所知道的生活。

讲　评：　原文的语境是简·爱在罗沃德学校待了整整八年，这里的生活艰苦而枯燥，可是她都默默地忍受了，因为这里有她喜爱的坦普尔小姐。可是有一天，坦普尔小姐嫁人了，并离开了这里，于是简·爱感到无比的失落。八年来，简·爱从未走出过罗沃德学校所在的山谷，也从未与外界有过任何联系，而盖茨黑德府也没有任何人来看望过简·爱，于是简·爱突然觉得这里讨厌极了。原文连续使用"school"和"and"，就是要通过违反语法规则中的经济性原则，来制造简·爱对罗沃德学校极度厌倦的情绪，并且在结尾还强调了一句"such as what I knew of existence"。

可以明显看出，译文1的译者完全没有意识到这里有变异存在，原文多次重复的"school"和"and"被消解了，译成了最符合语法规则的表达，结果就是简·爱不满的情绪大为降低。而不管是译文2还是译文3，都能够较好地表达出简·爱的厌恶情绪。

另外，大家要注意区分：词语重复变异并不等同于"重复"修辞格。修辞中的"重复"是符合语法规则的，而词语重复变异是违反语法规则的。特别提示：英语作家常常重复"and"来制造变异，翻译时需要留意。

一般说来，语法规则变异在后现代主义的作品中比较常见，福克纳的《喧哗与骚动》就很典型。小说的第一部分，就是弱智者班吉的自述部分，到处都是违反语法规则的表达。下面这个例子中有三处违反及物性系统使用的表达。

【例108】

原　文：　They were *hitting* little, across the pasture. I went back along the fence to where the flag was. It flapped on the bright grass and the trees.

...

It was red, flapping on the pasture. Then there was a bird slanting and tilting on it. Luster *threw*. The flag flapped on the bright grass and the trees. I *held to* the fence.
(*The Sound and the Fury*)

译　文：　他们在草坪那边*不打了*。我沿着篱笆回到插旗子的地方。旗子在鲜艳的绿草和树枝上方飘摆。

……

旗子是红的，在草坪上飘动。然后一只鸟斜飞过来落在上面。勒斯特*朝它扔了个东西*。旗子在鲜艳的绿草和树枝上面飘摆。我*紧抓过*篱笆。

讲　评：　第一处语法变异：动词hit表示动作过程，需要出现两个参与者角色，可是这里只有一个 They 出现，后面的 golf（高尔夫）消失了，却出现了 little 这个不合语法的副词；第二处语法变异：动词 threw 也表示动作过程，需要出现三个参与者角色，即 Luster threw a stone at the bird，可是后面的两个参与者角色"a stone"和"at the bird"都消失了；第三处语法变异：根据语境，动词过去式 held 此处表达"抓住"这个意思，需要两个参与者角色"I"和"the fence"出现，它们确实都出现了，可是 held 后面却多了一个不该出现的介词 to。通过破坏语法规则，作者成功地塑造出班吉这个弱智者形象。不过，译者在处理这三个地方时要适当兼顾读者的感受，不能使断裂感过大，不然读者很难接受，会认为翻译质量太差。

于是，参考译文通过"不打了"来省略后面的宾语；通过"朝它扔了个东西"使得照顾语法的同时，产生了语义不明的效果，毕竟到底是什么东西这里没有说清楚；通过"紧抓过"而不是"紧抓住"来产生搭配不和谐的效果。

另外，英文的句法也经常通过倒装来产生变异。

【例 109】

原　文：When I broke away from business it was against the advice of practically all my friends and family. *So conditioned are most of us* to the association of success with money *that* the thought of giving up a good salary for an idea seemed little short of insane. (*Life in a Violin Case*)

译　文：我毅然离开商界，几乎违背了所有亲友的劝告。我们大多数人都习惯把成功与金钱联系在一起，<u>结果就是</u>，那种为理想而放弃高薪的人<u>简直</u>会被认为是疯子。

讲　评：作者通过把"so conditioned"放到主语"most of us"前面，进一步强调为理想而坚持自己的梦想是一件多么难的事情。由于汉语没有英语那样的倒装手段，于是译文通过"结果就是"和"简直"配合使用，也起到了一定的强调效果。

总之，原文的语法规则变异通常都是作者刻意而为之，毕竟作家不太可能连基本的语法规则都掌握不好。所以，语法规则变异必定是在凸显某种情感，译者理应小心应对。

（八）修辞手段变异（Deviation of Using Rhetorical Devices）

一般说来，修辞格本身就是一种语言变异，但是由于一些修辞格过于常见，人们的感知渐渐变得麻木。不过，某些修辞格可能会被作者加重分量，这样就会形成修辞手段变异现象。

【例 110】

原　文：I say to you today, my friends, so even though we face the difficulties of today and tomorrow, <u>I still have a dream</u>. It is a dream deeply rooted in the American dream.
<u>I have a dream that</u> one day this nation will rise up, live up to the true meaning of its

第七章 文体变异

creed: "We hold these truths to be self-evident; that all men are created equal."

I have a dream that one day on the red hills of Georgia the sons of former slaves and the sons of former slave-owners will be able to sit down together at the table of brotherhood.

I have a dream that one day even the state of Mississippi, a state sweltering with the heat of injustice, sweltering with the heat of oppression, will be transformed into an oasis of freedom and justice.

I have a dream that my four children will one day live in a nation where they will not be judged by the color if their skin but by the content of their character.

I have a dream today.

I have a dream that one day down in Alabama with its governor having his lips dripping with the words of interposition and nullification, one day right down in Alabama little black boys and black girls will be able to join hands with little white boys and white girls as sisters and brothers.

I have a dream today.

I have a dream that one day every valley shall be exalted, every hill and mountain shall be made low, the rough places will be made plain, and the crooked places will be made straight, "and the glory of the Lord shall be revealed, and all flesh shall see it together." (*I Have a Dream*)

译　文：朋友们，今天我要对你们说，在此时此刻，我们虽然遭受种种困难和挫折，*我仍然有一个梦想。*这个梦是深深扎根于美国梦之中的。

*我梦想*有一天，这个国家会站立起来，真正实现其信条的真谛："我们认为这些真理不言而喻，那就是人人生而平等。"

*我梦想*有一天，在佐治亚州的红山上，昔日奴隶的儿子将能够和昔日奴隶主的儿子坐在一起，共叙兄弟情谊。

*我梦想*有一天，甚至连密西西比州这个正义匿迹，压迫成风，如同沙漠般的地方，也将变成自由和正义的绿洲。

*我梦想*有一天，我的四个孩子将在一个不是以他们的肤色，而是以他们的品格优劣来评判他们的国度里生活。

我今天有一个梦想。

*我梦想*有一天，阿拉巴马州能够有所转变，尽管该州州长现在仍然满口异议，反对联邦法令，但有朝一日，那里的黑人男孩女孩能与白人男孩女孩情同骨肉，携手并进。

我今天有一个梦想。

*我梦想*有一天，幽谷上升，高山下降，坎坷曲折之路成坦途，圣光披露，满照人间。

讲　评：马丁·路德·金在"I Have a Dream"这篇演讲中使用了很多反复修辞格，

同时将这些反复大部分融于平行结构之中，例如人们最熟悉的"I have a dream"，就使用了九次。对于这样的强调，译者理应使用同样的表达，同样的结构，这样才能有效传递出作者的感情。

【例 111】

原　文：From every mountainside, *let freedom ring*.

　　　　And if America is to be a great nation, this must become true. So *let freedom ring* from the prodigious hilltops of New Hampshire.

　　　　Let freedom ring from the mighty mountains of New York!

　　　　Let freedom ring from the heightening Alleghenies of Pennsylvania!

　　　　Let freedom ring from the snowcapped Rockies of Colorado!

　　　　Let freedom ring from the curvaceous slops of California!

　　　　But not only that; *let freedom ring* from Stone Mountain of Georgia!

　　　　Let freedom ring from Lookout Mountain of Tennessee!

　　　　Let freedom ring from every hill and molehill of Mississippi!

　　　　From every mountainside, *let freedom ring!*

　　　　When we *let freedom ring*, when we *let it ring* from every village and every hamlet, from every state and every city, we will be able to speed up that day when all of God's children, black men and white men, Jews and Gentiles, Protestants and Catholics, will be able to join hands and sing in the words of the old Negro spiritual, "Free at last! Free at last! Thank God almighty, we are free at last!" (*I Have a Dream*)

译　文：*让自由之声响彻*每个山冈。

　　　　如果美国要成为一个伟大的国家，这个梦想必须实现。

　　　　*让自由之声*从新罕布什尔州的巍峨峰巅*响起来*！

　　　　*让自由之声*从纽约州的崇山峻岭*响起来*！

　　　　*让自由之声*从宾夕法尼亚州阿勒格尼山的顶峰*响起来*！

　　　　*让自由之声*从科罗拉多州冰雪覆盖的落矶山*响起来*！

　　　　*让自由之声*从加利福尼亚州蜿蜒的群峰*响起来*！

　　　　不仅如此，还要*让自由之声*从佐治亚州的石岭*响起来*！

　　　　*让自由之声*从田纳西州的了望山*响起来*！

　　　　*让自由之声*从密西西比州的每一座丘陵*响起来*！

　　　　*让自由之声*从每一片山坡*响起来*。

　　　　当我们*让自由之声响起来*，*让自由之声*从每一个大小村庄、每一个州和每一个城市*响起来*时，我们将能够加速这一天的到来，那时，上帝的所有儿女，黑人和白人，犹太人和非犹太人，新教徒和天主教徒，都将手携手，合唱一首古老的黑人灵歌："终于自由啦！终于自由啦！感谢全能的上帝，我们终于

第七章 文体变异

自由啦！"

讲　评：上一个例子中，反复和平行结构连用九次已经非常罕见，但是马丁·路德·金在演讲的结尾又破纪录地使用了 12 次"Let freedom ring"，以如此强烈的反复形式，呼吁民众团结一心，为黑人的生存和未来而战斗。

除了反复，其他修辞格也有可能经过"加量"后变异。

【例 112】

原　文：Jane Eyre, who had been an ardent, expectant woman—almost a bride, was a cold, solitary girl again: her life was pale; her prospects were desolate. *A Christmas frost had come at midsummer; a white December storm had whirled over June; ice glazed the ripe apples, drifts crushed the blowing roses; on hayfield and cornfield lay a frozen shroud; lanes which last night blushed full of flowers, to-day were pathless with untrodden snow; and the woods, which twelve hours since waved leafy and flagrant as groves between the tropics, now spread, waste, wild, and white as pine-forests in wintry Norway.* (Chapter 26, *Jane Eyre*)

译　文：简·爱，一个曾经充满热情、充满期待的姑娘，差一点就当上了新娘，如今却再度变得郁郁寡欢、孤独无依。从今往后，她将变得前途惨淡，未来无望，*就好比仲夏时节出现了圣诞节的严寒，六月的天空降下了十二月的暴雪；好比成熟的苹果被裹上彻骨的冰凌，怒放的玫瑰被枝头的积雪压垮；好比牧场和田野突然被淋了一层冻雨，昨天还开满鲜花的小径今日就被大雪封锁了道路；又好比十二小时前还身处热带丛林之中，绿叶婆娑，芳香扑鼻，现在却置身于挪威严冬下的针叶林中，荒芜凄凉，白野茫茫。*

讲　评：原文的语境是就在简·爱即将嫁给罗切斯特先生之际，婚礼突然被人叫停，并被告知罗切斯特先生有妻子，而且就在桑菲尔德府居住。简·爱的精神完全崩溃了，她内心的苦闷和难过是难以用普通语言来表达的。那么，就用比喻来描述她此时的感受吧。可是，任何一个常规比喻的力度是远远不够的。作者也深知这一点，于是连用七个比喻，而且是非常规的比喻。

总之，修辞格经过扭曲或加重之后，就会形成变异，这更能有效地表达作者的强烈情感。译者要如法炮制，尽力将其效果译出。

（九）语种选择变异（Deviation of Language Selection）

作者在写作时，通常都会固定使用一种语言，一般都是自己的母语。不过，有时作者会突然使用另外一种语言的词语或句子，这很可能是想凸显某些情感。

【例 113】

原　文：This, *par parenthèse,* will be thought cool language by persons who entertain solemn doctrines about the angelic nature of children, and the duty of those charged with their education to conceive for them an idolatrous devotion: but I am not writing to flatter parental egotism, to echo cant, or prop up humbug; I am merely telling the truth. (Chapter 12, *Jane Eyre*)

译　　文：***特别提一句***，我的上述观点准会被某些人认为过于冷漠，因为他们心中怀有孩子就是天使这种神谕般的信条，并认为教育孩子应像崇拜偶像一样献身其中。可是，我之所以那样写，绝不是要去迎合父母自私的心理，也不想去附和伪善的言辞，更不愿意支持骗人的空话，我只不过是实话实说。

讲　　评：原文语境是，简·爱在表达自己对于阿黛勒的教育的看法时，突然抛出一句法语 "*par parenthèse*"，而且是斜体表达，而不是英文 "by the way"。这就明显是在表明，下面要说的观点绝对不是 "顺便说一下" 那么简单。为了凸显作者的强调意味，译文没有写成 "顺便说一句"，而是 "特别提一句"。再变成斜体并加粗，可以比较有效地表达作者的情感。

【例 114】

原　　文：He then said that she was the daughter of a French opera-dancer, Céline Varens, towards whom he had once cherished what he called a "grande passion". This passion Céline had professed to return with even superior ardour. He thought himself her idol, ugly as he was: he believed, as he said, that she preferred his "taille d'athlete" to the elegance of the Apollo Belvedere. (Chapter 15, *Jane Eyre*)

译　　文：罗切斯特先生告诉我，阿黛勒是法国歌剧舞蹈演员赛莉纳·瓦伦的女儿，而他曾对赛莉纳有过他所说的 "***伟大的爱情***"。对于他的爱情，赛莉纳曾声称要用更伟大的爱情来回报。罗切斯特先生并不英俊，却自认为是赛莉纳崇拜的偶像。他还坚信，用他的话说，比起贝尔维德尔的阿波罗优雅的体形，赛莉纳更喜欢他 "***运动员般的身材***"。

讲　　评：原文的语境是：有一次，罗切斯特先生向简·爱提起了自己的恋爱经历。他曾经深深地爱上了法国歌剧舞蹈演员赛莉纳·瓦伦，并给予对方丰富的物质条件。可是一个偶然的机会，罗切斯特先生发现瓦伦小姐背着自己找了一个情人，于是他勃然大怒，不仅用决斗的方式教训了那家伙，而且与瓦伦小姐彻底断绝了关系。可是，多年以后，罗切斯特先生在讲起这段往事时，依然非常愤懑，因为他突然使用了法语 "grande passion" 和 "taille d'athlete"，而不是英文 "grand passion" 和 "build of athlete"，这明显具有反讽的味道。罗切斯特先生使用法语有两个原因，一是这些表达都是瓦伦小姐当年对他说过的话；二是可以强烈地讽刺瓦伦小姐的虚伪，强烈地表达出他仍然对被骗一事耿耿于怀。读过小说后可知，罗切斯特先生身体健壮，但绝没有太阳神阿波罗那样优美的身材，因为他的个子比较矮，而身高对于男性往往比较重要。所以，罗切斯特先生也是在自嘲，后悔当年不该爱上瓦伦小姐。所以，对原文中的法语进行翻译时，处理成加粗并斜体会比较有效地体现强调和讽刺的作用。

总之，对于作者突然变换语种的行为，译者必须要当心，因为作者往往是想表达一些特殊的情感或观点。

（十）拼写或印刷变异（Deviation of Spelling or Printing）

还有一种变异现象，读者或译者容易忽视，那就是拼写或印刷有特殊之处。

【例 115】

原　文："Yaas, to be sure I do," drawled Lord Ingram; "and the poor old stick used to cry out 'Oh you villains childs!' —and then we sermonised her on the presumption of attempting to teach such clever blades as we were, when she was herself so ignorant." (Chapter 17, *Jane Eyre*)

译　文："*记——得*，我当然记得。"英格拉姆勋爵故意拖长声音说道，"这根可怜的老木头疙瘩总是喊什么'你们这些坏孩子'，然后我们就会训斥她，说她那么愚昧无知，还敢来教育我们这些聪明少年。"

讲　评：原文语境是，简·爱应罗切斯特先生的要求，坐在桑菲尔德府的客厅里听宾客们闲聊，可是其中一些客人根本看不起简·爱的家庭教师身份，甚至当面冷嘲热讽。其中布兰奇小姐问英格拉姆勋爵是否还记得当年捉弄家庭教师的那些事，英格拉姆勋爵得意洋洋地以重读的方式给予回应。于是，"Yes"变成了"Yaas"。译文通过加入一个破折号，使声音得以在视觉和听觉上延长，并辅以加粗和斜体，这样就生动地描绘出英格拉姆勋爵洋洋自得的丑陋嘴脸。

此外，有一类比较常见的印刷变异现象，就是某些英文表达使用了斜体。

【例 116】

原　文：In spite of the title, this article will really be on how *not* to grow old, which, at my time of life, is a much more important subject. My first advice would be to choose your ancestors carefully. (*How to Grow Old*)

译　文：题目虽然这样写，实际上本文要谈的却是人怎样才可以**<u>不老</u>**。这个问题非常重要，尤其是对像我这个年纪的人来说。我的头一条忠告就是，你可得要挑选好你的先人。

讲　评：作者生怕读者误会了文章的标题，于是用斜体来强调"not"。对于这类问题，译者也应该尽力在印刷体上给予再现，比如使用黑体，而非宋体，同时加粗，甚至再使用斜体，并加下划线。

另外，还有一种变异现象也较为常见，就是作家有时会使用一些能彰显某些人文化身份的语言，想以此表明这个人有很高或很低的文化水平，或者是用方言来凸显他们来自于哪里。

【例 117】

原　文：　"Thank you, John. Mr. Rochester told me to give you and Mary this." I put into his hand a five-pound note. Without waiting to hear more, I left the kitchen. In passing the door of that sanctum some time after, I caught the words—

"She'll happen do better for him nor ony o' t' grand ladies." And again, "If she ben't one o' th' handsomest, she's noan faal and varry good-natured; and i' his een she's fair beautiful, onybody may see that." (Chapter 38, *Jane Eyre*)

译　文：　"谢谢你，约翰。罗切斯特先生让我把这个给你们俩。"我往他手里塞了五英镑的钞票，不等他说话就离开了厨房。

没过多久，我再次从厨房门外经过，偶然听到了里面的谈话："也许她比任何富家小姐都更适合主人。虽然她长得不漂亮，但还算顺眼，而且性情还那么温和。更何况谁都看得出来，主人觉得她很漂亮。"

讲　评：　相信大家一眼就能看出，第二段文字中有很多不标准的单词拼写，甚至很多单词都难以辨认。这段文字是罗切斯特先生的仆人约翰和玛丽在背后谈论主人和简·爱的婚姻。约翰是罗切斯特先生的马车夫，玛丽是约翰的丈夫，也是罗切斯特先生的仆人，主要负责家里做饭之类的杂事。两人的文化水平都很低，甚至连字都认识不了几个。所以，他们说话常常发音不够标准，也有很多语法规则错误。作者用这些不规范的拼写来界定两人的社会身份，同时说明他们用的是哪种方言。对于这种变异，译者倒是不必担心，因为只需要译成较为标准的汉语即可。为什么可以这样做呢？因为若是译为俚语性质的汉语，或是我国某个地区的方言，读者就会感到很奇怪，毕竟他们会产生不必要的联想。如果说话人使用的是英格兰东北部地区的方言，难道我们要用东北方言来对应吗？这当然会很荒谬。用任何方言都不可以，那样只会产生诡异的效果。另外，两位仆人较为低微的语言其实并无深意，只是彰显了二人的社会身份而已，对于小说情节发展和人物情感理解基本没有影响。因此，对于这类问题，只需译为较为标准的汉语。

总之，由于编辑和校对人员的存在，作者不太可能犯下拼写错误，不小心印刷为斜体之类的错误似乎也不太可能。最有可能的是，作者是在制造文体变异，译者这时应该积极应对，翻出作者的真实意图。

三、文体变异的翻译策略

一般说来，文体变异的翻译主要分两个阶段。第一阶段是识别原文中的文体变异，即译者首先要确认原文的表达方式是常规还是变异，如果确实是变异，则必须对文体变异的意义做出解读，也就是解读出作者的真实意图。第二阶段是在译文中再现文体变异，即译者在译入语允许的一系列变体表达中选择文体价值相当的变异表达。如此一来，才

第七章 文体变异

能实现文体变异的等值翻译。总的说来，直译为主意译为辅是文体变异翻译的基本策略。至于变异的具体特点，需要结合语境具体分析。不过，有一点要特别提醒大家，文体变异不是到处都有。文体变异若成为普遍现象，就不叫文体变异了。当然，识别文体变异的意识必须具备。

本章小结

文体变异算得上翻译中的"深奥理论"，原因就在于读者往往愿意去读通顺流畅的语言，译者也概莫能外。于是，译者在做翻译实践时，容易自觉或不自觉地把译文表达得比较流畅，殊不知这样会抹杀掉作者苦心孤诣营造的文体变异。好在我们可以从语言学理论出发，有意识引导自己发现文本中那些独特的表达，尤其是在阅读和翻译文学作品的时候。正所谓"发现文体变异的意识有了，变异的再现还会遥远吗？"文学翻译中有不少重点和难点，文体变异只是其中之一，另一个同样值得我们必须了解和掌握的内容便是隐喻翻译。

第八章 隐喻翻译
Metaphor Translation

本章的核心观点是译者必须具备翻译隐喻的能力。本章分为三个部分：一、隐喻的定义；二、文本类型理论；三、文本类型理论视角下的隐喻翻译实践。第二部分主要介绍德国学者凯瑟琳娜·赖斯的文本类型理论和英国学者彼得·纽马克的文本类型理论；在第三部分，我们将学习：（一）信息型文本中的隐喻翻译；（二）感染型文本中的隐喻翻译；（三）表情型文本中的隐喻翻译。第三种类型最为重要，其中我们还将重点学习文学翻译中独特隐喻的特征，以及文学隐喻价值评估的工具——前景化。

一、隐喻的定义

说到隐喻，大家会想，我们不是在修辞手段那一讲中提到了么？不过是一种常见的修辞手段，怎么还要在这里专门研究一下呢？先看看英语词典和专业词典中的定义。

根据柯林斯词典的定义，A metaphor is an imaginative way of describing something by referring to something else which is the same in a particular way. For example, if you want to say that someone is very shy and frightened of things, you might say that they are a mouse.

根据朗文词典的定义，Metaphor is a way of describing something by referring to it as something different and suggesting that it has similar qualities to that thing → similie

根据《文体学核心术语》的定义，In rhetoric and other traditional approaches to figurative language, a metaphor is defined as a figure of speech, or trope, and is often seen as a kind of linguistic embellishment. In metaphor, a comparison of two distinctively different, yet similar, things is established by the claim that 'X is Y', as in 'my love is a rose'. Meaning is thereby transferred from the metaphorical term, 'a rose' to the subject, 'my love', and we may take the metaphor to imply that the speaker finds his/her love as beautiful as a rose (even if a rose also has thorns).

从上面三个定义可以看出，metaphor 传统上被视为一种修辞手段、比喻词语或象征性语言。这种理解真可谓由来已久，乔治·莱考夫和马克·约翰逊两位学者在《我们赖以生存的隐喻》（*Metaphors We Live By*）这本专著的第一章开头也做了类似的描述：

Metaphor is for most people a device of the poetic imagination and the rhetorical flourish—a matter of extraordinary rather than ordinary language. Moreover, metaphor is typically viewed as characteristic of language alone, a matter of words rather than thought or action. For this reason, most people think they can get along perfectly well without metaphor. (Lakoff, G. & Johnson, M., 2003: 3)

对于多数人来说，隐喻是一种充满诗意的想象和修辞学上的辞藻，经常出现在特殊场合，而非日常用语之中。再有，隐喻通常被视为仅仅是语言上的特征，只与言语有关，而与思想或行动无关。正因为如此，多数人认为，没有隐喻他们也能活得很好。

这可以称之为典型的 rhetorical view of metaphor，也就是隐喻的修辞观。如果对这段话再推演一下，大概就是：隐喻是一种诗学表达和修辞方式，所以它属于文学范畴；隐喻仅仅指言语，而非思想；隐喻是对词语有意识地或故意地使用，所以使用者必须有才华才能很好地应用；隐喻是一种修饰，那么没有隐喻也无所谓。上述想法基本反映了古今中外大部分人的内心，也体现在前面两个英文定义之中。

不过，metaphor 可没那么简单，莱考夫和约翰逊两位学者紧接着又说：

We have found, on the contrary, that metaphor is pervasive in everyday life, not just in language but in thought and action. Our ordinary conceptual system, in terms of which we both think and act, is fundamentally metaphorical in nature. (ibid.)

然而，我们发现，隐喻弥散于我们的日常生活之中，不仅仅存在于语言中，而且也存在于我们的思想和行动中。我们日常应用的概念系统，即指导我们思考与行动的这个系统，在本质上基本是隐喻性质的。

这种看法可以称之为 conceptual view of metaphor，也就是隐喻的认知观，或者说是隐喻的概念观。

说到这里，大家已经能够感觉到，metaphor 的理解变得复杂了。事实上它也确实复杂，这从研究隐喻的论文和专著汗牛充栋这一点就能看出来。因此，我们有必要先简单梳理一下西方学者对 metaphor 的认知演化史。

根据我国学者束定芳（2000）的划分，西方学者对 metaphor 的认知历经两千多年，大致经历了三个阶段：从古希腊的亚里士多德的"对比论"，认为隐喻是一个词语替代另一个词语来表达意义的语言手段，两个词语之间是对比关系；再到古罗马昆体良的"替代论"，认为隐喻实际上就是一个词去替代另一个词的修辞现象。这是隐喻研究的第一个阶段——修辞学研究阶段。20 世纪 30 年代，理查兹提出互动论，后又由布莱克做了发展，他们认为隐喻是一种新的意义的创造过程，是两个词语的词义相互作用的结果。直到 20 世纪 70 年代初期，一些学者从逻辑、哲学以及语言学视角，对隐喻的语义展开研究，这可以称为隐喻研究的第二个阶段——语义学研究阶段。从 20 世纪 70 年代至今，很多学者纷纷从认知心理学、哲学、语用学、符号学、现象学、阐释学等角度对隐喻展开研究，这其中尤其以 1980 年乔治·莱考夫和马克·约翰逊的认知学专著《我们赖以生存的隐喻》影响最大，从此人类对隐喻的认知进入了前所未有的新阶段，这可以称为隐喻研究的第三个阶段——多视角多层次阶段。本章就是从莱考夫和约翰逊的概念隐喻视角出发，探索隐喻到底该如何翻译。

1992 年，莱考夫又出版了专著《当代隐喻理论》（*The Contemporary Theory of Metaphor*），并在 Introduction 部分给出了 metaphor 的定义，请看：

The word metaphor has come to mean a cross-domain mapping in the conceptual system. The term metaphorical expression refers to a linguistic expression (a word, phrase, or sentence) that is the surface realization of such a cross-domain mapping.

隐喻是在概念系统中跨域映射。隐喻式表达指跨域映射在言语表达上的体现，比如具体表达为一个词语、一个短语，或者是一个句子。

另外，莱考夫在 Metaphors We Live By 一书中给出了大量的例子，从中我们可以得出概念隐喻的基本结构：A 是 B，例如，Life is a journey.（人生是一段旅程）。为了让大家有个直观印象，我们就以 Life is a journey 为例。

People might say that they try to give their children an education so they will *get a good start in life*. If their children act out, they hope that they are just *going through a stage* and that they will *get over it*. Parents hope that their children won't be *burdened with* financial worries or ill health and, if they face such difficulties, that they will be able to *overcome them*. Parents hope that their children will *have a long life span* and that they will *go far in life*. But they also know that their children, as all mortals, will *reach the end of the road*. (Metaphor: A Practical Introduction)

人们会说，他们要让孩子接受良好的教育，这样孩子就能**在生活中有良好的开端**。要是孩子出现逆反行为，他们希望这只是**成长中难免的阶段**，不久**就会过去**。父母希望孩子既没有经济上的**负担**，也没有健康上的**困扰**，但要是万一经济困难，或是健康不佳，孩子也能**渡过难关**。父母都希望自己的孩子**健康长寿**，**前程远大**。但是他们也知道，自己的孩子和常人无异，总会**走到生命的尽头**。

这个段落就是围绕 Life is a journey 这个概念隐喻展开的，请看原文中的这些短语和句子："get a good start in life、going through a stage、get over it、burdened with、overcome them、have a long life span、go far in life、reach the end of the road"。这些短语大部分都直接或间接地与旅程有关，只有 burdened with 需要稍微想一下，其实这个短语也与旅行有关系，毕竟谁出门不带行李呢，而行李当然是一种负担了。

我们发现，上述英文短语都有对应的汉语表达："在生活中有良好的开端、成长中难免的阶段、就会过去、负担、困扰、渡过难关、健康长寿、前程远大、走到生命的尽头"。这些汉语表达大部分跟旅程有关，只有"困扰"貌似没有关系，但其实也有关系，这种说法是翻译中换词的需要，也是出于语言连贯的考虑，或者通俗地解释为出于搭配正确的考虑，所以"困扰"本质上等同于"负担"。再有，"健康长寿"也指一段时间之旅，还是跟旅程有关。所以，通过这个例子，我们似乎可以说，中文的思维方式与英文的思维方式本质上都是隐喻性质的。

通读《我们赖以生存的隐喻》这部专著之后，莱考夫关于概念隐喻的观点可做如下小结：一个概念隐喻是由两个概念域组成，其中一个域（目标域 target domain）的理解要依靠对另一个域（源域 source domain）的理解来完成；一个域（源域）容易理解，而另一个域（目标域）难以理解；一个域（源域）是具体的，而另一个域（目标域）是抽象的；旅程、战争、建筑、食物、植物等比较容易理解，这些都是源域的例子；争辩、爱情、理论、思想、社会组织等比较难理解，这些都是目标域的例子。

下面，我们再从《我们赖以生存的隐喻》这本书中选取两个例子，让大家加深一下对概念隐喻的理解。

1) Argument is war. 争辩是战争。围绕这个概念隐喻，衍生出很多表达：

① Your claims are indefensible.

你的主张守不住（不堪一击）。

② He attacked every weak point in my argument.

他攻击我论辩中的每一个弱点。

③ His criticisms were right on target.

他的评论正中要害。

④ I demolished his argument.

我推翻了他的论证。

2) Ideas are plants. 思想是植物。围绕这个概念隐喻，也衍生出很多表达：

① His ideas have finally come to fruition.

他的想法终于结果了（意思就是实现了）。

② That idea died on the vine.

那想法死在藤上（意思就是中途夭折/失败）。

③ That's a budding theory.

那是个萌芽期的理论（意思就是早期的理论）。

④ It will take years for that idea to come to full flower.

那观念离盛开还有待时日（意思是尚未达到成熟）。

基于上述理论，我们对概念隐喻定义做一个小结：

· 隐喻不仅仅是言语表达，更是人类认知世界和交流思想的基本方式。

· 隐喻是一种常见修辞手段，其表达可以通过名词来实现，也可以通过动词，甚至是句子来实现。

· 隐喻是文学性的重要依托，尤其是"新鲜"隐喻。需要指出的是，"新鲜"隐喻既指从未出现过的，也可以指旧的隐喻焕发了新的生机，总之是能给人耳目一新的感觉，而且还能表达出作者想要凸显的情感和观点，这样的隐喻才"新鲜"，才有价值。

· 隐喻由相对抽象的目标域和比较具体的源域构成，人们通过容易理解的源域来认识不容易理解的目标域，所以源域一定会出现，而目标域未必出现。

· 隐喻往往是成系统的，一个基本隐喻会衍生出无数具体的隐喻表达，而同一个目标域可以由无数个源域来展示其不同方面的特征。

· 隐喻是以想象的方式将甲物等同于乙物，这种看法包含着使用者个人的情感因素和价值判断，因此隐喻意义并不固定，需要依靠语境才能正确判断。

二、文本类型理论

20 世纪 70 年代，德国学者凯瑟琳娜·赖斯对语篇翻译展开研究，讨论不同文本类型的翻译如何达成交际，实现对等。她借用了德国语言学家卡尔·布勒的语言功能三分理论，在 1971 年自己的著作《翻译批评：潜力与制约》（*Translation Criticism: The Potentials & Limitations*）一书中，将语言的功能与相应的语言特点、文本类型、交际情景联系起来，提出了文本类型理论，即文本可分为三种类型：Informative（信息型）、Expressive（表情型）和 Operative（感染型）。原表格（转引自 Munday, 2012: 112）及翻译如下：

Text type	Informative	Expressive	Operative
Language function	Informative (Representing objects and facts)	Expressive (Expressing sender's attitude)	Appellative (Making an appeal to the text receiver)
Language dimension	Logical	Aesthetic	Dialogic
Text focus	Content-focused	Form-focused	Appellative-focused
TT should	Transmit referential content	Transmit aesthetic form	Elicit desired response
Translation method	"Plain prose", explicitation as required	"Identifying" method, adopt perspective of ST author	"Adaptive", equivalent effect

文本类型	信息型	表情型	感染型
语言功能	传递信息（即表现事物与事实）	富于表情（即表达说话人的情感与态度）	旨在感染（即感染文本接受者）
语言特点	合乎逻辑	充满审美	常用对话
文本焦点	聚焦语篇内容	聚焦语言形式	聚焦感染效果
译文目的	传递原文指称的内容	表现原文的美学形式	引发预期的反应
翻译方法	"浅显的语言"，按要求使语言明晰化	"展示原作面目"，从原文作者视角出发	"采用编译"，以实现等效

后来，英国学者彼得·纽马克发展了文本类型理论，他在《翻译问题探讨》（*Approaches to Translation*）一书中提出了一个更加详尽的文本类型分类，他也将文本分为三种类型：Expressive（表情型）、Informative（信息型）和 Vocative（呼唤型）。请看下表（Newmark, 2001: 15）及对应翻译：

第八章 隐喻翻译

Text type	Expressive	Informative	Vocative
(1) Typical examples	Literature Authoritative texts	Scientific and technical reports and text books	Polemical writing, publicity, notices, laws and regulations, propaganda, popular literature
(2) "Ideal" style	Individual	Neutral, objective	Persuasive or imperative
(3) Text emphasis	Source language (SL)	Target language (TL)	Target language
(4) Focus	Writer (1st person)	Situation (3rd person)	Reader (2nd person)
(5) Method	"Literal" translation	Equivalent-effect translation	Equivalent-effect recreation
(6) Unit of translation 　Maximum 　Minimum	Small 　Collocation 　Word	Medium 　Sentence 　Collocation	Large 　Text 　Paragraph
(7) Type of language	Figurative	Factual	Compelling
(8) Loss of meaning	Considerable	Small	Dependent on cultural differences
(9) New words and meanings	Mandatory if in SL text	Not permitted unless reason given	Yes, except in formal texts
(10) Keywords (retain)	Leitmotifs Stylistic markers	Theme words	Token words
(11) Unusual metaphors	Reproduce	Give sense	Recreate
(12) Length in relation to original	Approximately the same	Slightly longer	No norm

文本类型	表情型	信息型	呼唤型
(1) 典型文本	文学和经典文本	科技报告和教材	广告、公告、辩论稿、宣传稿、法律法规、通俗文学
(2) "理想"语言风格	体现作者风格	中立，客观	劝导、命令
(3) 文本重点	对源语的理解	译语的表达	译语的表达
(4) 译文聚焦	作者（第一人称）	情景（第三人称）	读者（第二人称）
(5) 翻译方法	"直译"	等值翻译	创造等效
(6) 翻译单位 　最大单位 　最小单位	较小 　搭配 　词语	中等 　句子 　搭配	较大 　语篇 　段落
(7) 典型语言	形象性的	事实性的	说服性的
(8) 意义的损耗	很大	很小	取决于文化差异的大小

续表

文本类型	表情型	信息型	呼唤型
(9) 新词与新义在译文中的表达	只要原文中出现就必须表达	不被允许除非有理由	除正式语篇不保留外都要保留
(10) 要保留的关键词	反映主旨和文体特征的词语	有关话题的词语	标志性和象征性词语
(11) 独特隐喻	复现原文隐喻	译出意思	再造新的隐喻
(12) 与原文长度的对比	大体相等	稍微变长	没有定规

赖斯与纽马克所用的术语有些区别，对于信息型文本和表情型文本的描述，两人用词是一致的，对于第三类文本，赖斯使用了 operative，而纽马克使用了 vocative，但其内涵差不太多。当然，对于文本类型划分做过探讨的学者不止这两位，只是他们两位做出的贡献最大，也最有代表性，所以我们选择了他们所划分的表格。我们这里同时借用赖斯和纽马克的表格，是为了能够互相参照和补充，以便得出更科学的结论。不过，对于这三种文本类型，我们将它们放在本章第三部分，结合隐喻特点分开来学习。

三、文本类型理论视角下的隐喻翻译实践

从前面两位学者的研究可知，文学主要体现为表情型文本，但是这并不等于没有其他两种文本类型的特征。所以，我们这里将会全面探讨三种类型文本中隐喻的翻译。

（一）信息型文本中的隐喻翻译（Metaphor Translation in the Informative Text）

根据前面两个表格，可知赖斯的观点：信息型文本的语言功能是传递信息（即表现事物与事实）；语言特点是合乎逻辑，条理分明；文本焦点是聚焦语篇内容；译文目的是传递原文指称的内容；翻译方法要用"浅显的语言"，按要求使语言明晰化。纽马克的观点是：典型的信息型文本是科技报告和教材；理想语言风格是中立、客观；文本重点是译语表达；译文聚焦于情景，即从第三人称视角来说明事实；翻译方法为等值翻译，即追求译文信息与原文信息相等；翻译单位中等，即最大的翻译单位是句子，最小的翻译单位是搭配；典型语言是事实性的；意义在翻译过程中损耗很小；原文的新词或旧词新义通常在译文中不允许出现，除非有理由；需要保留的关键词是跟话题有关的词语；面对原文的独特隐喻，译出意思即可；与原文相比，译文稍微长一点。

基于上述观点，信息型文本中的隐喻翻译应该遵循的原则是：

1）译文聚焦在情景，方式应为等值。也就是情景不可偏值。
2）翻译单位中等，努力再现出事实。也就是事实不可胡编。
3）通用隐喻翻译时可保留以达等值。也就是通用隐喻可留。

第八章 隐喻翻译

4）原文不同寻常的隐喻往往被丢弃。也就是奇怪隐喻须弃。

下面，我们通过两篇典型的信息型文本来验证一下，看看是否真是这样。

【例 118】

原　文：Our economy *has just suffered a massive heart attack*, with over a trillion dollars of asset values destroyed in the past two weeks. Given the heightened risk of *a fatal recurrence*, things will never be the same. In the short run, we *need emergency measures* to calm the markets. Then we can use the crisis *to get ourselves on to a healthier path*. Only a fool ignores or denies such an experience; the wise will learn and *give up harmful habits*.[1]

译文 1：我们的经济**刚刚遭受了一场严重的心脏病**，价值逾万亿美元的资产毁于短短两周。鉴于**致命性疾病复发**的风险提高，情况将不会与过去一样。短期内，我们**需要急救措施**来平息市场。之后，要利用危机，**踏上健康发展的道路**。对于这次遭遇，无视或否定是愚蠢的；吸取教训、**改正恶习**才是明智之举。

译文 2：我们的经济刚刚遭受了一次打击，影响面甚广，价值上万亿的财产在过去两周化为乌有。由于致命性经济问题重现的风险提高了，荣景将难再光临。短期而论，我们需要采取紧急措施，使市场人心稳定。然后我们可以利用危机，**走上正轨**。只有愚者才会无视或者否认这样的经历，智者会吸取教训，**放弃不良习惯**。

讲　评：通过调查，我们发现，大部分人都愿意接受第二个译文，这很可能是跟原文的隐喻处理有直接关系。这个语篇从头至尾隐含着一个隐喻：Economy is a patient. 仔细看看，就能发现，原文中很多表达都在围绕这个隐喻展开，它们是 "has just suffered a massive heart attack、a fatal recurrence、need emergency measures、to get ourselves on to a healthier path、give up harmful habits"。

再看一下这两个译文，我们发现：译文 1 采用了直译的方式，也就是保留了全部隐喻，而译文 2 整体上倾向于意译，基本上放弃了隐喻，完整保留的有一个，"放弃不良习惯"，加以改动的有一个，"走上正轨"，它的原义应该是 "踏上健康发展的道路"，而其余三个难以理解或难以表达的隐喻都被舍弃了。

由此得出的结论就是：对于信息型语篇，译者大概只要说出隐喻意思即可，原隐喻可以舍弃，如能保留似乎更方便。

【例 119】

原　文：But it's also appropriate that we take the time to envision the future of medicine. We should ask tough questions, such as—Where do we *go from here*? And how do we *set a flight path to pilot the future* of the North Carolina Medical Society and

---

[1] https://www.douban.com/note/336161012/

American Medical Association? I'm convinced that we need to *start from the ground up*. We must *tear out the cracks and bumps in our runway*. And then we must *lay a new foundation* so that medicine can truly *take off* in the 21st century.[1]

译文 1：但是花些时间去前瞻一下医学的未来是恰当的。我们应该问一些困难的问题，例如，我们要*走向哪里*？我们如何*设定航程*，*引导*北卡医学会和美国医学会的*未来*？我确信，我们需要*从地面开始*。我们必须*清除跑道上的裂痕和路障*。然后我们必须*建立新的基础*，这样医学就能真正地在 21 世纪*起飞*。

译文 2：不过思考一下医学发展的未来是必要的。我们应该提出一些难题，比如，我们*走向哪里*？我们如何*设定航程*，以便为北卡医学会和美国医学会的未来*指出发展方向*？我确信，要从最基本的做起。我们必须*清扫*发展道路上的*障碍*，然后建立起新的发展基础，以便使医学在 21 世纪*起飞*。

讲　评：通过调查，我们发现，大家更愿意接受第二个译文，这很可能还是跟原文中的隐喻处理有关。这个语篇从头至尾隐含着一个隐喻：Future of medicine is a flight journey. 仔细看看，就能明白，原文中很多表达都在围绕这个隐喻展开，它们是"go from here、set a flight path to pilot the future、start from the ground up、tear out the cracks、bumps in our runway、lay a new foundation、take off"。再看看这两个译文，我们发现：译文 1 保留了全部隐喻，而译文 2 放弃了难理解的隐喻。

这里得出的结论就是：对于信息型语篇，译者似乎只要说出隐喻意思即可，隐喻能保留就保留，难理解的隐喻舍弃更方便。

通过这两个典型例子，信息型文本中的隐喻翻译策略可以概括为：

1）若通用隐喻可以顺其自然地移植到译文中，译者这时拥有较大的自由，即可以保留喻体，也可以只翻意思。

2）若独特且难懂的隐喻成为信息传递的障碍，译者须舍弃喻体，只翻意思。

可以看出，归纳出的翻译策略与前面理论推导出的结论完全一致。

（二）感染型文本中的隐喻翻译（Metaphor Translation in the Operative Text）

根据前面两个表格，可知赖斯的观点：感染型文本的语言功能是旨在感染（即感染文本接受者）；语言特点是常用对话；文本焦点是聚焦感染效果；译文目的是引发预期的反应；翻译方法采用编译，以实现等效。纽马克的观点是：感染型文本的代表是广告、公告、辩论稿、宣传稿、法律法规、通俗文学；理想语言风格是劝导或命令；文本重点是译语表达；译文聚焦于读者，即从第二人称视角来施加影响；翻译方法是要创造等效，即追求译文对读者产生尽可能大的影响；翻译单位最大，即最大的翻译单位是语篇，最小的翻译单位是段落，因此译者有较大的施展空间；典型语言是说服性的；意义在翻译

---

[1] 例子出自叶子南所著的《认知隐喻与翻译实用教程》第 150 页。

过程中的损耗取决于文化差异的大小，即文化差异大，意义损耗就大，文化差异小，意义损耗就小；除了正式语篇外，原文的新词和新义通常在译文中都要保留；须保留的关键词是标志性和象征性的词语；面对原文的独特隐喻，应该再造新的隐喻；与原文对比，译文的长度没有定规，即弹性很大。

基于上述观点，感染型文本中的隐喻翻译应该遵循的原则是：
1）译文聚焦在读者，方式追求等效。也就是等效不可抛弃。
2）翻译单位较大，重视语言说服力。也就是影响不可忘记。
3）通用隐喻翻译时可保留以便交际。也就是通用隐喻可留。
4）原文不同寻常的隐喻应该再创造。也就是重构独特隐喻。

下面，让我们通过三个典型的感染型文本（两个广告语和一个电影片名）的翻译来验证一下，看看是否真是这样。

【例 120】

原　文：Olympus: Focus on life.

译　文：奥林巴斯：瞄准生活。

讲　评：这是奥林巴斯相机的广告。这里的隐喻是通过动词短语"focus on"体现出来的，这可以让我们联想到透镜的使用。不过，"瞄准"一词很容易让我们想到射击，想到子弹射出后的血腥画面，不如改成"奥林巴斯：聚焦生活"，这样含义不变，可以让我们联想到经过透镜的聚焦后，事物看得更加清晰，或者是镁光灯聚焦下的美好事物。其实，无论是"瞄准"，还是"聚焦"，原隐喻都没改变，变化的只是译语的表达，这样只是为了语言更加连贯，并能唤起人们美好的联想。

由此得出的结论就是：对于感染型语篇，通用隐喻应该保留，但要注意语言连贯，也可考虑创造合适的新隐喻，以求意义等效。

【例 121】

原　文：Poetry in motion, dancing close to me.

译　文：动态的诗，向我舞近（丰田汽车）。

讲　评：这是丰田汽车曾经使用过的一则广告：这里的隐喻是把丰田汽车比喻成一首动态的诗，以跳舞的姿态向我靠近，目的是想说明丰田汽车风姿迷人。不过，这个隐喻中国人很难接受，因为它太抽象，我们很难理解丰田汽车跟诗歌有什么关系，又为什么能像诗歌一样跳起舞来。建议改成：梦幻之旅，尽在掌握（丰田汽车）。这样新广告语就用了一个新的隐喻——人在旅途，这也是大家都能接受的隐喻。当然，这个旅行并不普通，而是梦幻般的，而且尽在掌握，而掌握当然是指丰田汽车容易操控，易于驾驶。

由此得出的结论就是：对于感染型语篇，若是独特隐喻无法为读者所理解，那么必须用合适的隐喻更换，以求感受等效。

【例122】

原　文：这是一部电影片名的翻译。电影片名为 *Lolita*。

译　文：有1962年和1997年两个版本，其中1962年版本被译为《洛丽塔》。

讲　评：这部电影源自俄裔美国小说家、诗人、批评家和翻译家弗拉基米尔·纳博科夫的小说。故事的内容是这样的：一个叫亨伯特的中年男子从法国移民到美国，靠在大学里教授法语为生。亨伯特少年时期曾有过一段刻骨铭心的经历，当年的初恋女友不幸因病夭亡，令他此去经年依旧对那些充满青春气息的少女有着别样情感。因工作之需，亨伯特寻找住房，由此结识了寡妇夏洛特及其精灵一般的女儿洛丽塔。夏洛特喜欢上了儒雅庄重的亨伯特，一心与之交往；而亨伯特却迷恋上了夏洛特的女儿，青春逼人的洛丽塔。亨博特为了和洛丽塔长相厮守，甚至违心地与夏洛特结婚。他把对洛丽塔的情感全部写进了日记，锁入抽屉。直到某一天夏洛特打开抽屉，他们三人的命运就此改变。后续情节简单说就是夏洛特因为车祸而身亡，亨伯特开启了与洛丽塔的不伦之恋。当然，故事的结局以悲剧告终。亨伯特在狱中死于脑溢血，洛丽塔死于难产。自从这部小说出版后，Lolita 这个人名也成为了英语中的一个单词，指代吸引年长男性的早熟性感少女。

由此可见，1962年的电影译名完全是音译，是女主人公的名字，而1997年版电影被重新译为《一枝梨花压海棠》。《一枝梨花压海棠》是对苏东坡"一树梨花压海棠"这句诗的巧妙借用。"一树梨花压海棠"隐含着一个典故，出自苏东坡嘲笑好友张先的调侃之作。据说，北宋著名词人张先在80岁时娶了一个18岁的小妾，他兴奋之余作诗一首："我年八十卿十八，卿是红颜我白发。与卿颠倒本同庚，只隔中间一花甲。"苏东坡知道此事后便写诗调侃："十八新娘八十郎，苍苍白发对红妆。鸳鸯被里成双夜，一树梨花压海棠。"一树梨花指白发苍苍的丈夫，海棠指红颜娇羞的少妇，一个"压"字道尽无数未说之语！

《洛丽塔》这部小说刚出版时就被列为禁书，遭到许多人抵制，而这部同名电影也确实不适合青少年观看。新译名《一枝梨花压海棠》清晰而委婉地点出了故事主题，有利于观众对是否观看该影片做出正确的选择，而直译为《洛丽塔》就难以做到这一点，毕竟洛丽塔这个隐喻化的名字中国人并不买账。鉴于新译名能立刻使人想到老夫少妻的故事，同时也暗含着道德批评，堪称电影片名翻译的经典。

由此得出的结论就是：对于感染型语篇，若是某些表达或隐喻无法为读者所理解，那么必须创造新的表达或新的隐喻，以求传播及文化上的等效。

基于上述三个典型例子，感染型文本中的隐喻翻译策略可总结为：

1）通用隐喻或常见隐喻建议保留，也可以创造新的隐喻，以求意义等效。

2）若是独特隐喻无法为读者所理解，那么必须创造新的隐喻，以求传播及文化上的等效。

可以看出，归纳出的翻译策略与从理论推导出的结论完全一致。

（三）表情型文本中的隐喻翻译（Metaphor Translation in the Expressive Text）

根据前面两个表格，可知赖斯的观点：表情型文本的语言功能是富于表情（即表达说话人的情感与态度）；语言特点是充满审美；文本焦点是聚焦语言形式；译文目的是表现原文的美学形式；翻译方法应该展示原作的面目，即从原文作者视角出发。纽马克的观点是：表情型文本的代表是文学和经典文本；理想语言风格是体现作者风格；文本重点是对源语的理解；译文聚焦于作者，即从第一人称视角来把握作者的写作构思；翻译方法为"直译"，即尽可能再现原作的风格，但并不是按照原句顺序一点不改的生硬翻译；翻译单位较小，即最大翻译单位是搭配，最小翻译单位是词语；典型语言是形象性的；意义在翻译过程中的损耗很大；新词和旧词新义只要原文中出现就必须表达；要保留的关键词是反映主旨和文体特征的词语；面对原文中的独特隐喻，要将其复现；译文长度与原文长度大体相等。

基于上述观点，表情型文本中的隐喻翻译应该遵循的原则是：
1）译文聚焦在作者，方式常为直译。也就是直译不可轻弃。
2）翻译单位较小，重视语言形象性。也就是形象不可轻视。
3）通用隐喻翻译时要保留以便传情。也就是通用隐喻须留。
4）原文不同寻常的隐喻应准确再现。也就是复现独特隐喻。

下面，我们通过几个典型的表情型文本来验证一下，看看是否真是这样。

【例123】

原　文：There was music from my neighbor's house through the summer nights. In his blue gardens <u>*men and girls came and went like moths*</u> among the whisperings and the champagne and the stars. (Chapter 3, *The Great Gatsby*)

译文1：整个夏天的夜晚都有音乐声从我邻居家传过来。在他蔚蓝的花园里，<u>**男男女女像飞蛾一般**</u>在笑语、香槟和繁星中间来来往往。

译文2：这个夏天的每一个夜晚，我都能听到盖茨比家传来的音乐声。在他那个蓝色花园里，<u>**男男女女如飞蛾一般**</u>，在欢笑声、香槟酒和满天星光里流连忘返。

讲　评：原文画线部分含有一个隐喻：People are moths. 由于语境出现了"the summer nights"，因此这个隐喻就比较容易理解了。上面两个译文及其他已出版的译文都将 People 直接译成了"飞蛾"。飞蛾投火，不请自来，这个道理人人皆知。由此我们可知，那些赴宴的男男女女都是主动来的，而且是乐此不疲。

由此得出的结论就是：对于表情型语篇，通用或常见隐喻保留下来最合理，其他处理方式似乎并非最佳选择。

【例 124】

原　文： There are roughly three New Yorks. There is, first, the New York of the man or woman who was born here, who takes the city for granted and accepts its size and its turbulence as natural and inevitable. Second, there is the New York of the commuter—*the city that is devoured by locusts each day and spat out each night*. Third, there is the New York of the person who was born somewhere else and came to New York in quest of something. (*Here is New York*)

译文 1： 大致说来有三个纽约。第一个属于土生土长的纽约人。他们看惯了这座城市，它的巨大、它的混乱都是自然而然，不可避免的。第二个属于通勤者。*白天，他们涌进城里，夜晚再离开*。第三个纽约属于那些生在异乡、来此有所追求的人。

译文 2： 大致说来有三个纽约。第一个属于土生土长的纽约人。他们看惯了这座城市，它的巨大、它的混乱都是自然而然，不可避免的。第二个属于通勤者。*白天，整个城市被如飞蝗的人群吞噬，夜晚再被吐出来*。第三个纽约属于那些生在异乡、来此有所追求的人。

讲　评： 原文画线句子含有一个隐喻：The commuters are locusts. 我们特别把译文 2 的其他句子都改成了与译文 1 一模一样，以方便比较此处隐喻的翻译。通过调查，我们发现，多数人喜欢译文 2。译文 1 中的隐喻——人如潮水涌动实在是太平常了，甚至有点陈词滥调的感觉。译文 2 把人群比喻成蝗虫，进城犹如把城市吞噬，出城就是把吃进去的再吐出来，有一定的新意，但也不能算全新的隐喻，不过总要比译文 1 新鲜形象了很多。

　　由此结论就是：对于表情型语篇，一般性独特隐喻只要读者接受，保留下来更合理，换喻或释义不是最佳选择。

【例 125】

原　文： *A splendid Midsummer shone over England*: skies so pure, suns so radiant as were then seen in long succession, seldom favour even singly, our wave-girt land. *It was as if a band of Italian days had come from the South, like a flock of glorious passenger birds, and lighted to rest them on the cliffs of Albion.* (Chapter 23, *Jane Eyre*)

译文 1： *仲夏明媚的阳光普照英格兰。*当时那种一连几天日丽天清的天气甚至一天半天都难得惠顾我们这个波浪环绕的岛国。*仿佛持续的意大利天气从南方飘移过来，像一群色彩斑斓的候鸟，落在英格兰的悬崖上歇脚。*

译文 2： *明媚的仲夏闪耀在英格兰大地，*一连好几天都是天空澄澈，阳光灿烂，这样的好天气对我们这个波涛环绕的岛国来说真是难得一见，*就仿佛是意大利的天气化身为成群结队、五彩斑斓的候鸟，从南方迁徙而来，正在英格兰的悬崖上歇脚。*

讲　评： 原文中画线的两个句子各自含有一个隐喻：Midsummer is the sun（仲夏是太

阳）；Weather is a bird.（天气是鸟儿）。这两个隐喻毫无疑问非常独特，平时很难见到。相信大家觉得两个译文都很好，而第二个给人的感觉更流畅一些。如果单论隐喻部分的翻译，译文2的说法，"明媚的仲夏闪耀在英格兰大地"完全可以接受，不一定非要像译文1那样意译为"阳光普照英格兰"。对于第二个把天气比成美丽候鸟的隐喻，两个译文都保留了，看来译者们在此处的观点是一致的。这里，作者用这两个少见的隐喻突出了自己的意图，那就是表达出简·爱当时非常喜悦的心情，因为她从远方归来，终于又见到了自己的爱人罗切斯特先生。心情变好，天气就显得格外的好了。

  由此得出的结论就是：对于表情型语篇，若是独特隐喻表达了作者特殊意图，而且能被理解和接受，那么保留下来更合理，普通释义或更换比喻并不合适。

【例 126】

原　文：Would he arouse him with a throb of agony? The victim was for ever on the rack; it needed only to know *the spring that controlled the engine*: and the physician knew it well. (Chapter 11, *The Scarlet Letter*)

译文1：他要引起牧师一阵痛苦的悸动吗？那牺牲者反正永远处于遭受煎熬的状态；只消知道*控制引擎的弹簧*就成了，而医生对此恰恰了如指掌！

译文2：他打算让牧师感到一阵阵剧痛吗？牧师被永远绑在了刑具上，要做的只是按下*刑具的开关*，而医生对此是再熟悉不过了。

讲　评：原文画线部分含有一个隐喻：Torturing the victim is like triggering the spring that controlled the engine. 比较之后，相信多数人都喜欢第二个译文，因为第一个译文"控制引擎的弹簧"真的很难理解。对我们现代读者来说，作者使用了一个很独特的隐喻。其实，原文中 rack 这个单词是指旧时候折磨人的一种刑具，就是把人绑在刑具上之后，将人的四肢朝相反方向拉伸，类似于我国古代的车裂。根据原文的说法，我们可以猜测这种刑具在启动时，是通过弹簧这个设置来实现的。所以，英文短语 on the rack 意思就是倍感压力，痛苦不堪。不过，这样的解释实在是太麻烦，而且作者的意图也并不在于这个刑具中的弹簧本身，只是通过这个隐喻表达出医生想要折磨对方的恶毒心肠。于是，译文2中"被绑在刑具上，要做的只是按下刑具的开关"这个新隐喻就容易理解了，毕竟我们都知道开关是启动的意思。

  由此得出的结论就是：对于表情型语篇，独特隐喻虽然能表达作者的特殊意图，但若是很难为译文读者所理解，那么换成合适的隐喻就是不合理的合理选择了，或者也可以考虑舍弃隐喻而只翻意思。

【例 127】

原　文：We have spoken of Pearl's rich and luxuriant beauty—a beauty that shone with deep and vivid tints, a bright complexion, eyes possessing intensity both of depth and glow, and hair already of a deep, glossy brown, and which, in after years, would be nearly akin to black. *There was fire in her and throughout her: she seemed the unpremeditated offshoot of a passionate moment.* Her mother, in contriving the child's garb, had allowed the gorgeous tendencies of her imagination their full play, arraying her in a crimson velvet tunic of a peculiar cut, abundantly embroidered in fantasies and flourishes of gold thread. (Chapter 7, *The Scarlet Letter*)

译文 1： 我们已经讲过波儿丰盈而多姿多态的美；一种闪烁着浓厚而生动的色彩的美；一张鲜亮的小脸，一双含有浓烈底蕴和炙热光束的眼睛，一头已经变得熠熠发光的深棕色秀发，而且多年以后还会变得近乎黑发。*她从里到外都燃烧着烈火；她是激情勃发的瞬间意想不到的分蘖*。她的母亲，给孩子设计衣服费尽心思，让她想象中的奇异花哨的偏爱一一体现出来；她让孩子穿了一件大红天鹅绒紧身外衣，剪裁得别出心裁，还用金丝线刺绣出大量的华丽图案和花朵。

译文 2： 我们已经谈到过珀尔风华艳丽的美，一种熠熠生辉的美：富有光泽的皮肤，深邃明媚的双眸，润泽丰盈的棕发，再过几年就会变成亮丽的乌发。*她的周身上下犹如燃烧着一团火；像是激情迸发时不期而至的结晶*。母亲在设计孩子服装时，充分发挥了瑰丽的想象；为她缝制了这件深红的天鹅绒束身上衣，裁剪样式独特，还用金线绣满了奇巧精美的各式花样。

译文 3： 我们曾经谈到珠儿洋溢着光彩照人的美丽，是个浓墨重彩、生动活泼的小姑娘：她有晶莹的皮肤，一双大眼睛既专注深沉又炯炯有神，头发此时已是润泽的深棕色，再过几年就几乎是漆黑色的了。*她浑身上下有一团火，向四下发散着，像是在激情时刻不期而孕的一个子嗣*。她母亲在给孩子设计服装时呕心沥血，充分发挥了华丽的倾向，用鲜红的天鹅绒为她裁剪了一件式样独特的束腰裙衫，还用金丝线在上面绣满新奇多彩的花样。

译文 4： 我们曾说过，小珍珠的容貌美得光彩照人，她的肤色白皙亮洁，她的眼睛炯炯有神。她的头发光滑柔顺，现在是润泽的深棕色，再过几年就会变成亮丽的乌黑色。*她的着装更是特色鲜明，使她看上去像被一团美丽的火焰包围*。在为女儿设计这套装束时，海丝特将自己对华装丽服的偏好发挥得淋漓尽致。她为女儿裁剪了一件样式别致的猩红色天鹅绒束腰外衣，还用金线在上面绣制了许多精美的花边。

讲　评： 原文中的画线句子含有一个隐喻：Pearl is the unpremeditated offshoot. 意思是珍珠是意想不到的小分树枝。读过《红字》这部小说，我们知道，珍珠是海丝特·白兰的女儿，是作者始终不惜笔墨赞美的可爱精灵。虽然海丝特·白兰犯下通奸之罪，但孩子是无辜的。所以这里作者使用的 offshoot 就有隐喻不恰当之嫌，因为分叉树枝通常都是多余的，会被园丁修剪掉，因而它含有贬义。

为了突出重点部分，我们这里只解析译文中的隐喻翻译。

从译文 1"她从里到外都燃烧着烈火；她是激情勃发的瞬间意想不到的分蘖"

第八章 隐喻翻译

可以看到：隐喻在这里被直译了，不过由于分蘖（也就是接近地面的分杈树枝）具有一定的贬义，至少在多数中国读者心中具有贬义，而这种译法与作者全篇赞美珍珠的观点明显不符，所以直译隐喻的方式失败了。

从译文 2"她的周身上下犹如燃烧着一团火；像是激情迸发时不期而至的结晶"可以发现：隐喻在这里被替换了，句意是可以理解的，但结晶与"一团火"之间的关系可能会误导读者，好像是说这结晶是被火烧出来似的。其实，那团火是指小珍珠所穿的猩红色衣服。所以，这里的隐喻替换最多只能说是成功了一半。

从译文 3"她浑身上下有一团火，向四下发散着，像是在激情时刻不期而孕的一个子嗣"可以发现：隐喻在这里被意译，但却不够恰当，因为珍珠本来就是海丝特的子嗣，什么叫像是子嗣，所以这种意译隐喻的方式失败了。

从译文 4"她的着装更是特色鲜明，使她看上去像被一团美丽的火焰包围"看出：原来的隐喻被删除了，也突出了珍珠穿的这身红衣看起来非常漂亮，非常鲜艳。这样一来，原隐喻造成的矛盾得以解决，整个语境也和谐了。

下面通过图表小结一下：

原文：There was fire in her and throughout her: she seemed the unpremeditated offshoot of a passionate moment.		
她从里到外都燃烧着烈火；她是激情勃发的瞬间意想不到的分蘖。	直译隐喻	×
她的周身上下犹如燃烧着一团火；像是激情迸发时不期而至的结晶。	替换隐喻	√
她浑身上下有一团火，向四下发散着，像是在激情时刻不期而孕的一个子嗣。	意译隐喻	×
她的着装更是特色鲜明，使她看上去像被一团美丽的火焰包围。	删除隐喻	√

对于 offshoot 这个独特隐喻，译文 1 用直译隐喻的方式，结果失败了；译文 2 用了替换隐喻的方式，只能算成功一半；译文 3 用了意译隐喻的方式，也是失败；译文 4 采用删除隐喻的办法，结果是成功的。

由此得出的结论就是：对于表情型语篇，某些独特隐喻虽可理解，但若与整个语境的逻辑和情感不符，可以考虑删除。

通过这五个典型文本，表情型文本中的隐喻翻译策略可总结为：

1）通用隐喻或常见隐喻应予保留。

2）一般性独特隐喻只要读者接受，最好也要保留。

3）若是独特隐喻表达了作者特殊意图，而且能被译文读者理解和接受，那么应予保留；但若是很难理解，那么可以考虑用合适的隐喻替换或者只翻意思。

4）若是某些独特隐喻虽可理解，但若与整个语境的逻辑和情感不合，可以考虑删除。

其中，前三条是应该遵守的常规，而第四条删除隐喻则要非常慎重，毕竟作家不会经常犯错误，尤其是世界名著的作者。

不过，我们发现，这四条翻译策略与前面理论推导得出的四条原则有一定的不同。那么应该以哪个为准呢？当然是从实践中推导出的翻译策略。问题出在哪里呢？问题大概就出在赖斯与纽马克两位学者在对表情型文本做研究时只考虑了西方的语言。英法德俄等语言拥有类似的宗教和文化背景，而汉语和英语之间则差别巨大。因此，英汉文学隐喻翻译需要有更多的考虑。下面我们就隐喻的价值评估再深入探讨一下。

从前面的总结中，我们能明显感觉到，表情型文本中的独特隐喻是理解和翻译的难点，而文学又是独特隐喻时常光顾之地，那么我们在文学阅读和翻译时到底怎样才能做出正确的判断呢？不要担心，我们建议大家使用"前景化"，作为评估隐喻价值大小的有力工具。

首先，我们要说说"前景化"概念的缘起。"前景化（foregrounding）"是文体学中的常见术语，与背景（background）、自动化（automation）或常规（convention）相对应。该概念来自于绘画领域，指画家将其要表现的艺术形象在与其他人或物的对比中凸显出来，以吸引观者的注意，从而达到画家所期望的某种艺术效果，而其他的人或物则构成背景。请看一个前景与背景的例子：

在这个画面中，一对人的面孔构成了前景，而白色画面则成为背景。当然，我们也可以把白色背景看作一个沙漏，黑色部分当成沙漏的背景。不过通常说来，人们往往更容易看出的是一对人的面孔而非沙漏，而想画出这样的图景也是需要技巧的，并非人人都能，这体现了绘画的艺术性。与此类似，文学中的前景化也是一门艺术。下面我们就来谈谈文学中的前景化。

在文学研究领域，"前景化"作为一个完整概念，由俄国形式主义者穆卡罗夫斯基首先提出，经雅各布逊、利奇、韩礼德等学者的发展而最终形成。形式主义者认为，诗歌语言并不是标准语言，但与标准语言之间存在紧密联系。标准语言造就了诗歌语言的背景；对标准语言规则的违反使得语言诗意化成为可能；如果没有这种可能，也就没有了诗歌。文学语言与其他语言的差别就在于其特殊的表达方式。正因为如此，文学才有了独特的艺术效果，即具有了文学性（literariness）。换言之，文学中的独特表达往往构成前景，普通表达则成为背景。因此，独特文学隐喻成为前景是大概率事件，理应引起读者高度重视。

请看一组文学隐喻的例子。

第八章 隐喻翻译

【例 128】

原　文：Our love is *at a crossroads*.

译　文：我们的爱情已经*走到了十字路口*。

讲　评：at a crossroads 在这里是自动化隐喻，未能成为明显的前景，汉语中也很常见，无特别价值，可以释义，但保留更方便。

【例 129】

原　文：Soon we'll be *sliding down the razorblade of life*.

译　文：不用多久，我们就会*在生活的刀锋上径直滑落*。

讲　评：sliding down the razorblade of life 这个隐喻明显成为前景，非常震撼，很有价值，不宜释义。这个前景化隐喻明显非常独特，相信几乎没谁见过。它形象地说出了一个恐怖的事实，就是两人的爱情关系或婚姻关系已经处在非常危险的边缘。

那么，结合前景化这个工具，我们再来总结一下独特文学隐喻的翻译。首先，根据前面诸多论述和例证，我们可以对独特文学隐喻做出如下解读：

1）文学中独特隐喻往往不反映语言体系的特征。

2）文学中独特隐喻往往是有价值的表达。

那么如何界定有价值呢？

有价值可界定为"作者刻意安排的"，有价值的语言具有文学性。

那么又如何理解文学性呢？

文学性往往具有一定程度的前景化效果。文学性体现在文体方面、美学方面、艺术方面和主位意义方面。

那么又如何理解隐喻文学性的这四个方面呢？

文体方面（stylistic）指作家使用隐喻时显示出特定方法和技巧，使作品呈现出一种鲜明的风格。美学方面（aesthetic）指含有隐喻的语言能带给读者美的感受。艺术方面（artistic）指含有隐喻的语言表达或整体安排能引起人们的兴趣，而这些表达或安排本身需要技巧才能完成，并且充满了想象空间。主位意义方面（thematic）指在隐喻的写作中，通过信息顺序的精心安排，使得含有隐喻的重要信息或主旨得以凸显，进而给读者留下深刻印象。

简而言之，专业说法就是，隐喻文学性指能成为前景的表达，通俗说法就是，隐喻文学性指能吸引眼球的表达。

如此一来，独特文学隐喻翻译的整体策略便可概括如下：

1）独特文学隐喻若非作者故意写出，未必需要重视。

2）独特文学隐喻大多体现作者特定意图，价值较大。

3）独特文学隐喻具有较强文学性，译者要仔细揣摩。

4）独特文学隐喻通常不宜用解释意思的方式来翻译。

5）独特文学隐喻在译文中也须成为基本等重的前景。

本章小结

　　通常说来，隐喻翻译往往是翻译实践的重点之一。无论是信息型文本、表情型文本还是感染型文本，隐喻翻译都要小心应对。在进行文学翻译时，尤其要当心作者所使用的独特隐喻，也就是新鲜隐喻。在揣摩清楚作者意图之后，可以用合适的方式将其译出。正所谓"译无定法"，到底是直译，还是意译，或是其他方式，要取决于对隐喻价值、读者接受、意识形态等诸多因素的通盘考虑。这几章学过之后，可以说学习者基本学完了翻译实践的常规知识。但是，我们有必要了解同时可以作为翻译原则和翻译批评的另一项理论——合作原则。

第九章 合作原则
Cooperative Principle

本章的核心观点是：译者应具有识别和运用合作原则的能力。本章分为三个部分：一、合作原则；二、翻译实践中对合作原则的遵守；三、蕴含的翻译，也就是对上述准则违反后该如何翻译。第二部分又分为以下几小部分：（一）对数量准则的遵守；（二）对质量准则的遵守；（三）对关系准则的遵守；（四）对方式准则的遵守。

一、合作原则

20世纪50年代，英国牛津大学哲学家格莱斯（Grice）对日常语言运用规律展开研究，并于1967年在美国做讲座时将研究成果"会话含义理论"公布于世。1975年，格莱斯演讲稿的部分内容以《逻辑与会话》（*Logic and Conversation*）为题发表在柯尔和摩根等人编撰的论文集《句法学与语义学》（*Syntax and Semantics*）之中。本章的理论正是基于这篇论文。格莱斯注意到："人们的交流通常不是由一连串不相关联的话语组成，否则就会不合情理。这些对话至少在某种程度上很明显具有合作的倾向；每个对话参与者都在某种程度上承认交流过程中有一个或一组共同目标，或者至少有一个彼此都接受的谈话方向。"（1975：45）格莱斯的意思是说，我们在交流中似乎遵循着某种原则，这个原则就是："在会话发生的时候，使你所说的话，在其所发生的阶段，符合交谈目的或交谈方向。这可以被称之为合作原则。"（同上）人们在日常会话中一般都会自觉遵守所在语言社团的会话原则，即合作原则，而合作原则又被格莱斯细分成为四种"会话准则"，它们是数量准则、质量准则、关系准则和方式准则。这四种准则成为判断话语是否遵守交际原则的基础。遵守合作原则的话语，话语意在言内，语义比较容易理解；故意违反合作原则的话语，话语意在言外，被称为"蕴含"（implicature），需要推断才能得知真实意图。

下面先介绍一下合作原则的四条准则：
1）数量准则
a. 所说的话应包含当前交谈目的所需的信息。
b. 所说的话不应包含超出需要之外的信息。
2）质量准则
尽量让你说的话是真实的，尤其是
a. 不要说你认为是错误的话。

b. 不要说缺乏确切根据的话。
3）关系准则
话语要有关联。
4）方式准则
话语要语义清晰易于理解。
a. 表达要避免晦涩。
b. 表达要避免歧义。
c. 表达要简练。
d. 表达要有条理。

这里要简单说明一下为什么能将合作原则应用在翻译实践中。格莱斯的会话研究虽然不针对翻译，但对语篇的解读和翻译也同样具有重要意义。这是因为语篇翻译也是交际行为，而语篇翻译若想为读者所理解，也必然要遵守译语文化的合作原则。

二、翻译实践中对合作原则的遵守

合作原则要求话语发出者（译者）必须使自己的话语能被接受者（译文读者）听懂（读懂）。为实现这个目的，他必须要对他和接受者（译文读者）的共有知识做出预判，并在交际过程中适时调整说话策略（翻译策略），结果就是译文必然也要遵守合作原则。

根据语用学中的合作原则，可以推导出翻译中译者应遵守的合作原则：

在实践中，译者需要结合语境，使译文符合作者和译文读者的交际目的，并同时使译文受到译入语的语言和文化规范的制约。

四个翻译准则：
1）数量准则
a. 译文应包含符合当前交际目的所需的信息；
b. 译文不应包含原文信息之外的信息。
2）质量准则
译文的内容应是真实的，尤其要
a. 不译译者都认为是错误的信息；
b. 不译没有确切根据的信息。
3）关系准则
译文语篇信息应与语境关联。
4）方式准则
译文要语义清晰，易于理解。
a. 译文语言要避免晦涩；
b. 译文语言要避免歧义；
c. 译文语言要简练；

第九章 合作原则

d. 译文语言要有条理。

下面，我们结合实例看看这些准则都是如何被遵守的。

（一）对数量准则的遵守（Follow Quantity Maxim in Translating）

【例 130】

原　文：Mrs. Fairfax stayed behind a moment to fasten the trap-door; I, by drift of groping, found the outlet from the attic, and proceeded to descend the narrow garret staircase. I lingered in the long passage to which this led, separating the front and back rooms of the third storey: narrow, low, and dim, with only one little window at the far end, and looking, with its two rows of small black doors all shut, like a corridor in some *Bluebeard*'s castle. (Chapter 11, *Jane Eyre*)

译　文：为了关闭天窗，费尔法克斯太太耽搁了几分钟，落在了我后面。我摸索着找到了阁楼的出口，小心翼翼地走下那段狭窄的楼梯，然后在旁边的长走廊上逗留了一会儿。这条过道把三楼的前房和后房分隔开来，看上去狭窄、低矮而阴暗，只是在远远的尽头开了个小窗，而两边的黑色小门全都紧紧地关着，看起来活像*蓝胡子*[1] 城堡里的长廊。

讲　评：这里的语境是简·爱初次来到桑菲尔德府，并在管家费尔法克斯太太的引领下参观府宅，本段讲的是两人在三楼楼顶驻足后返回阁楼时的情景。虽然最后一句有"狭窄、低矮而阴暗""开了个小窗"和"两边的黑色小门全都紧紧关着"等暗示性言语，但是我们依旧猜不出蓝胡子城堡到底是什么东西，这里又暗示了什么信息。为解决这个问题，除了参考译文之外，请见脚注内容。这里译为"蓝胡子"城堡并且加脚注是在遵守量准则第 1 条：译文应包含符合当前交际目的所需的信息，同时也隐含了第 2 条——译文不应包含原文信息息之外的信息。若仅仅直译而不加脚注，或脚注未能提供明确解释，读者便无法深切感受到这个比喻所映射的危险。

【例 131】

原　文：Blanche and Mary were of equal stature,—straight and tall as poplars. Mary was too slim for her height, but Blanche was moulded like a *Dian*. I regarded her, of course, with special interest. First, I wished to see whether her appearance accorded with Mrs. Fairfax's description; secondly, whether it at all resembled the fancy

---

[1] 蓝胡子（Bluebeard）：法国诗人夏尔·佩罗（Charles Perrault，1628—1703）所创作的童话故事，出版于 1697 年，也是主角的名字。故事中，蓝胡子迎娶过很多女孩，但都被他杀害了。他家地下室走廊尽头的小屋子里便藏着被他接连杀害的一个又一个妻子。后来，"蓝胡子"就被用来指代连续杀妻者。

miniature I had painted of her; and thirdly—it will out!—whether it were such as I should fancy likely to suit Mr. Rochester's taste. (Chapter 17, *Jane Eyre*)

译　文：布兰奇和玛丽的身材别无二致，她们都像白杨树般高大挺拔。不过，就她们的身高来看，玛丽显得有些单薄，而布兰奇则像极了**月亮女神狄安娜**[1]。我当然会怀着强烈的好奇心打量布兰奇。首先，我想看看她的长相是不是和费尔法克斯太太说的一样；其次，我想知道她是不是和我凭想象画出来的那幅肖像画相似；再有一点，坦白直说了吧，是不是同我设想的一样，很符合罗切斯特先生的品味。

讲　评：这里的语境是罗切斯特先生从外地归来，同时还邀请了一群贵族朋友来家里做客，其中包括布兰奇·英格拉姆和玛丽·英格拉姆姐妹。在此之前，简·爱从费尔法克斯太太那里得知，布兰奇小姐非常漂亮。可是她到底有多漂亮，与月亮女神到底有什么关系，读者就很难猜出来了。为解决这个问题，除了参考译文之外，请见脚注内容。

这里译为"月亮女神狄安娜"并加脚注是在遵守数量准则第 1 条：译文应包含符合当前交际目的所需的信息，同时也隐含了第 2 条——译文不应包含原文信息之外的信息。若仅仅直译为"狄安娜"而不加脚注，或脚注未能提供明确解释，读者便无法感受到布兰奇到底美到什么程度，也无法体会简·爱当时的好奇、羡慕和嫉妒之情。

（二）对质量准则的遵守（Follow Quality Maxim in Translating）

【例 132】

原　文：In the clear embers I was tracing a view, not unlike a picture I remembered to have seen of *the castle of Heidelberg, on the Rhine*, when Mrs. Fairfax came in, breaking up by her entrance the fiery mosaic I had been piercing together, and scattering too some heavy unwelcome thoughts that were beginning to throng on my solitude. (Chapter 13, *Jane Eyre*)

译　文：我放下帷幔，回到壁炉边。对着炉火的余烬，渐渐地我陷入了沉思，眼前仿佛出现了一幅画面，一幅曾经见过的风景画，描绘的是**内卡河畔的海德堡城堡**[2]。正在这时，费尔法克斯太太走进屋来，扰乱了我刚刚拼凑起来的火焰镶嵌画，但也同时驱散了我的孤寂与沉闷。

---

[1] 狄安娜（Diana）：罗马神话中的月亮和狩猎女神，管理着大自然，是太阳与音乐之神阿波罗的孪生妹妹。她与阿波罗一样，喜欢森林、草原。按照神话的说法，狄安娜身材修长匀称，相貌美丽动人。

[2] 内卡河畔的海德堡城堡（原文为 the castle of Heidelberg, on the Rhine）：海德堡城堡是建于 13 世纪的古城，位于德国西南部，内卡河畔。内卡河（德语：Neckar）是莱茵河的第四大支流（次于阿勒河、摩泽尔河和美因河），流经海德堡，于曼海姆注入莱茵河，长 367 公里。故此处为作者的失误。

讲　评：这里的语境是简·爱来到桑菲尔德府做家庭教师已经三个月了，每天除了教阿黛勒学习各种课程，便再无其他事情可做。整日里面对的人只有阿黛勒和费尔法克斯太太，于是她会时不时地浮想联翩，其中有一次就依稀看到了某个城堡。这样理解似乎没什么问题，但其实存在一个陷阱，具体解释请看脚注。这里译为"内卡河畔的海德堡城堡"是在遵守质量准则第 1 条：译文的内容应是真实的，尤其要不译译者都认为是错误的信息。由于注释是经过认真考证之后做出的，所以这里也间接地遵守了第 2 条——不译没有确切根据的信息。若译为"莱茵河畔的海德堡城堡"，则在传递错误的地理知识，会有害读者的认知。

【例 133】

原　文：One morning, about a week after Bingley's engagement with Jane had been formed, as he and the females of the family were sitting together in *the dining room*, their attention was suddenly drawn to the window, by the sound of a carriage; and they perceived a chaise and four driving up the lawn. It was too early in the morning for visitors, and besides, the equipage did not answer to that of any of their neighbours. The horses were post; and neither the carriage, nor the livery of the servant who preceded it, were familiar to them. As it was certain, however, that somebody was coming, Bingley instantly prevailed on Miss Bennet to avoid the confinement of such an intrusion, and walk away with him into the shrubbery. They both set off, and the conjectures of the remaining three continued, though with little satisfaction, till the door was thrown open, and their visitor entered. It was Lady Catherine de Bourgh. (Chapter 56, *Pride and Prejudice*)

译　文：宾利和简订婚已有一个星期，这一天早上，宾利和太太小姐们正坐在贝内特家的**客厅**[1]里，忽然听到外面传来一阵马车驶近的声音，众人立刻循声来到窗前，只见一辆驷马马车驶进了贝内特家的草地。此时天色尚早，按理说不会有客人来访，而且从马车外观来看，也不像是邻居家的。马匹是驿站上的，马车和仆人的制服，大家也都没见过，但有人到访是确定无疑的。宾利立即提出和简去灌木林那边走走，以免被这位不速之客打扰。他们俩走后，贝内特母女三人仍在不断猜测，没有半点头绪。就在这时，门突然被推开了，访客走了进来，竟然是凯瑟琳·德波夫人。

讲　评：这里把"the dining room"译为"客厅"是在遵守质准则第 1 条：译文的内容应是真实的，尤其要不译译者都认为是错误的信息。同时也间接地遵守了第 2 条——不译没有确切根据的信息。若译为餐厅，会跟后面的语境产生冲突。所以，参考译文同时附上了脚注，以便做出必要的解释。

---

[1] 原文写的是餐厅（the dining-room），但是从后文凯瑟琳夫人的谈话可以看出，这里应该是客厅（the sitting-room），此处应该为作者的疏忽。

（三）对关系准则的遵守（Follow Relation Maxim in Translating）

【例 134】

原　文：　"Who recommended you to come here?"

"I advertised, and Mrs. Fairfax answered my advertisement."

"Yes," said the good lady, who now knew what ground we were upon, "and I am daily thankful for the choice Providence led me to make. Miss Eyre has been an invaluable companion to me, and a kind and careful teacher to Adèle."

"Don't trouble yourself to give her a character," returned Mr. Rochester: "eulogiums will not bias me; I shall judge for myself. She began by felling my horse."

"*Sir?*" said Mrs. Fairfax.

"I have to thank her for this sprain." (Chapter 13, *Jane Eyre*)

译　文：　"谁介绍你来这儿的？"

"我自己登的广告，然后费尔法克斯太太回复了我。"

"是这样的。"费尔法克斯太太说道，她现在终于知道我们在谈些什么了，"我每天都在感谢上帝，感谢他引导我做出了这个决定。爱小姐是我难得的伙伴，也是阿德拉友善细心的老师。"

"你不用费心帮她塑造良好形象。"罗切斯特先生这样答道，"任何溢美之词都不能左右我的看法，我会自己来做出判断。刚一见面，她就让我的马摔了一跤。"

"**什么，先生？**"费尔法克斯太太说道。

"我这次扭伤了脚，还要感谢她呢。"

讲　评：　这里的语境是简·爱来到桑菲尔德府三个月后，一次替费尔法克斯太太送信到海伊村途中，巧遇罗切斯特先生骑马归来，不过她当时并不知道骑马人是谁。由于路上结了薄薄一层冰，罗切斯特先生不小心摔下马来，结果扭伤了脚。后来在简·爱的帮助下，罗切斯特先生重新上马，飞快地离去。简·爱送信归来后，在府宅中见到了自己的主人——罗切斯特先生。至于两人在路上相遇一事，费尔法克斯太太并不知道，于是才有了上面那段对话。

这里"Sir?"译为"什么，先生？"是在遵守关系准则：译文语篇信息应与语境关联。若译为"先生？"，就难以与语境产生关联，阅读时容易产生语义断裂感。

【例 135】

原　文：　Old Roger Chillingworth, throughout life, had been calm in temperament, kindly, though not of warm affections, but ever, and in all his relations with the world, a pure and upright man. He had begun an investigation, as he imagined, with the severe and equal integrity of a judge, desirous only of truth, even as if the question involved no more than the air-drawn lines and figures of a geometrical problem, instead of human passions, and wrongs inflicted on himself. But, as he proceeded, a terrible fascination, a kind of fierce, though still calm, necessity, seized the old man within its gripe, and never set him free again until he had done all its bidding. He now dug into the poor clergyman's heart, like a miner searching for gold; or, rather, like a *sexton* delving into a grave, possibly in quest of a jewel that had been buried on the dead man's bosom, but likely to find nothing save mortality and corruption. Alas, for his own soul, if these were what he sought! (Chapter 10, *The Scarlet Letter*)

译　文：老罗杰·齐灵渥斯生性平和，虽说不上满怀慈爱，但也算为人厚道，而且在待人接物方面，始终纯洁而耿直。调查伊始，他便把自己想象成法官，办事态度严肃真诚，一心只为探求真相，似乎手中的案件不牵涉个人感情，也无关他所承受的委屈，不过是几何中的直线和图形而已。然而，在调查过程中，一种可怕的魔力，一种表面平静实则强烈的感觉，牢牢地控制了老罗杰，并且在其完成所有旨意前毫不放松。如今，这种感觉正向牧师的内心掘进，就像是一个矿工正在搜索黄金，或者确切地说，更像是一个*掘墓者*正努力寻找陪葬在死者胸前的珠宝，可是除了腐肉蚀骨外，最终一无所获。假如真是那样，那就让我们为这位*掘墓者*的灵魂哀叹吧！

讲　评：这里的语境是老罗杰·齐灵渥斯医生从欧洲来到北美殖民地马萨诸塞后，发现自己的妻子海丝特·白兰竟然有了私生女。在愤怒的驱使下，老罗杰开始秘密地调查与自己妻子通奸的男人到底是谁。在海丝特·白兰登台示众的过程中，老罗杰敏锐地感觉到丁梅斯代尔牧师有重大嫌疑。于是，老罗杰以看病为由，想方设法接近牧师，甚至与对方住在同一栋房子里，以便通过各种方式进行侦察。

这里把"Sexton"译为"掘墓者"是在遵守关系准则：译文语篇信息应与语境关联。若译为"教堂司事"，就难以与语境产生关联，译文读者反而会生出许多疑惑。毕竟教堂司事怎么会去偷东西呢，虽然他们负责管理教堂的地下墓穴，有监守自盗的条件，而译为掘墓者就很好地符合了读者的认知和预期。

（四）对方式准则的遵守（Follow Manner Maxim in Translating）

【例136】

原　文："And, besides, I once had a kind of rude tenderness of heart. When I was as old as you, I was a feeling fellow enough, partial to the unfledged, unfostered, and unlucky; but Fortune has knocked me about since: she has even kneaded me with her knuckles, and now I flatter myself I am hard and tough as an *India-rubber ball*; pervious, though, through a chink or two still, and with one sentient point in the middle of the lump. Yes. Does that leave hope for me?"

"Hope of what, sir?"

"Of my final re-transformation from *India-rubber* back to flesh?"

"Decidedly he has had too much wine," I thought; and I did not know what answer to make to his queer question: how could I tell whether he was capable of being re-transformed? (Chapter 14, *Jane Eyre*)

译　　文：　"不仅如此，我的心也曾一度怀有质朴的柔情。像你这么大时，我也是个有情有义的小伙子。对于生活中遭遇不幸的人，不管是羽翼未丰的、无人养育的，还是霉运缠身的，我总是深表同情。可是，从那时开始，命运之神一直在打击我，甚至将我的整个身心当成面团肆意踩躏。我现在非常自豪，尽管我的表面还有一两处孔隙，中心还有一个敏感点，但我感觉自己已经如*橡胶球*一样坚韧了。情况就是这样了，你看我还有希望吗？"

"什么希望呢，先生？"

"由*橡胶球*再次变回血肉之躯，你觉得有希望吗？"

"他显然是喝多了。"我心想。但我不知道该如何回答他这个奇怪的问题。他能不能变回去，我怎么知道呢？

讲　　评：　这里的语境是简·爱成为桑菲尔德府的家庭教师后，与罗切斯特先生第二次交谈。从后文可知，罗切斯特先生在第一次交谈后，对简·爱产生了强烈感情，于是邀请对方进行第二次长谈。

这里把"India-rubber ball"译为"橡胶球"是在遵守方式准则第 1 条：译文要语义清晰，易于理解。译文语言要避免晦涩。若译为"印度橡胶球"，读者很可能难以理解，还可能会产生不必要的联想。为什么是印度橡胶球而不是印度尼西亚橡胶球？都是盛产橡胶的地方嘛。这样的问题很可能会在善于思考的读者心中产生。其实，India-rubber 这个词跟印度在 19 世纪成为英国的殖民地有直接的关系。正是因为印度是英国海外最大的殖民地，而且又盛产橡胶，所以才会出现 India-rubber 这个派生词，可问题不在于橡胶球的产地，而在于橡胶球本身。众所周知，橡胶球非常结实，不怕摔，不怕踢，不怕挤压。罗切斯特先生把自身比喻成橡胶球，有破罐破摔的意思，毕竟他曾经历过很多伤心事，被骗婚就是其中最严重的一件。在碰到简·爱之前，他已经对爱情毫无感觉，所以才自比为橡胶球，意思是自己不惧怕任何伤害，对任何女性都毫无感觉。不过，他现在又说自己想从橡胶球变回血肉之躯，是表明想重新体验人间温情，尤其是自己最为缺欠的爱情。所以，参考译文由原文的"印度橡胶球"变为"橡胶球"是很明智的选择。从后文可知，这也是罗切斯特先生在向简·爱暗示好感，只是简·爱当时并不知道而已。

【例 137】

原　　文：　But the morning passed just as usual: nothing happened to interrupt the quiet course of Adèle's studies; only soon after breakfast, I heard some bustle in the

第九章 合作原则

neighbourhood of Mr. Rochester's chamber, Mrs. Fairfax's voice, and Leah's, and the cook's —that is, John's wife —and even John's own gruff tones. *There were exclamations of "What a mercy master was not burnt in his bed!" "It is always dangerous to keep a candle lit at night." "How providential that he had presence of mind to think of the water-jug!" "I wonder he waked nobody!" "It is to be hoped he will not take cold with sleeping on the library sofa,"* & c.

To much confabulation succeeded a sound of scrubbing and setting to rights; and when I passed the room, in going downstairs to dinner, I saw through the open door... (Chapter 16, *Jane Eyre*)

译　文：但是，整个上午很平静，阿黛勒的学习没有受到任何打扰。只是早餐过后没多久，我听到隔壁罗切斯特先生的房间有嘈杂声传来。从声音里可以听出，说话的人有费尔法克斯太太、莉娅和厨娘——约翰的妻子，我甚至还听到了约翰那粗哑的嗓音。

"主人在床上竟没被烧死，这可真是万幸！"
"不管怎么说，晚上点着蜡烛睡觉就是危险。"
"他那时竟然那么镇定，还能想到用水罐，多亏上帝保佑！"
"他居然谁都没吵醒，太奇怪了！"
"但愿他睡在书房的沙发上没有着凉。"
隔壁屋里的人七嘴八舌地议论着，说的都是诸如此类的话。

众人闲聊过后，隔壁又传出擦洗东西和摆放物件的声音。过了一会儿，我下楼去吃饭。经过罗切斯特先生的房间时，我发现他的房门开着，便朝里面望去。

讲　评：这里的语境是简·爱与罗切斯特先生有了几次交流，之后的一天夜里，罗切斯特先生的卧室突然着火了，简·爱发现后奋力将火扑灭，救了罗切斯特先生。劫后余生后，罗切斯特先生情不自禁地握住了简·爱的手，并且通过话语与眼神委婉地表达了爱意。简·爱回到房间后，竟再也无法入睡。第二天清晨，简·爱便听到了人们在隔壁对昨夜失火的一些议论。

原文那些直接引语在译文中被重新分段，并加上总结性话语，这其实遵守了方式准则第4条：译文要语义清晰，易于理解。译文语言要有条理。若是照原样直译，显然就会破坏译语的叙事规范，还会破坏阅读的流畅感受。

不过，在日常交流中，人们有时会故意违反合作原则中的某项准则，以凸显某些特定意图，这种情况被称为蕴含。下面我们再来谈谈蕴含的翻译。

三、蕴含的翻译

格莱斯注意到人们在日常交际中为了达到某种交际目的，实现某种交际效果，经常故意违反某一会话准则，在这种情况下，只要接受者坚信对方仍在遵守总的合作原则，只是在某个层次上违反了某个准则,那么他就会推导出这样一个结论:那个准则或者至少是总的合作原则一定是在隐含的层次上得到了遵守。换言之,一旦某个会话准则被违反了,话语的真实含义与话语的字面意义就不一样了。当接受者根据语境推导出真实意义时,该意义被称为蕴含,也被称为会话含义。

不过,就翻译而言,译者所面临的问题与语用学中的日常会话有很大不同。原文作者通常无法与译文读者使用同一种语言进行面对面交流,甚至更有时间和空间的距离。那么,当发现作者故意违反某一会话准则,从而造成蕴含的产生,译者这时该如何处理呢?

一般说来,作者都是为读者而创作的,因此语篇中的蕴含可以推导。蕴含在不同文体中都存在,文学语篇中尤为密集。语用学家称之为"蕴含"的语言现象在文学理论家那里被称为"陌生化"或"文学性",因此蕴含是一个本质上关乎作者意图的重点内容。而读者则乐于解读蕴含,进而获得美学享受。下面,我们将从代表性实例中归纳出蕴含的翻译策略。

【例138】

原　文：He looked at me for a minute.

"And a little depressed," he said. "What about? Tell me."

"Nothing—nothing, sir. I am not depressed."

"But I affirm that you are: so much depressed that a few more words would bring tears to your eyes—indeed, they are there now, shining and swimming; and a bead has slipped from the lash and fallen on to the flag. If I had time, and was not in mortal dread of some prating prig of a servant passing, I would know what all this means. Well, to-night I excuse you; but understand that so long as my visitors stay, I expect you to appear in the drawing-room every evening; it is my wish; don't neglect it. Now go, and send Sophie for Adèle. *Good-night, my—*" He stopped, bit his lip, and abruptly left me. (Chapter 17, *Jane Eyre*)

译　文：他看了我足足一分钟,然后才说道:"你好像心情不大好。怎么了?跟我说说吧。"

"没什么,真的没什么,先生。我没有心情不好。"

"我敢肯定你绝对心情不好,而且非常不好,感觉你再说几句眼泪就要落下了似的。其实,你眼睛里现在就闪现泪花了,有一滴已经从睫毛上滚下来,落在石板地上了。要不是因为现在没有时间,要不是因为担心过往的仆人说三道四,我准要问问这到底是怎么回事。好吧,今天晚上我先让你回去。但你要记住,在我的客人离开之前,我希望每天都能在客厅见到你。这是我的愿望,你一定要记在心里。去吧,顺便让索菲娅过来把阿黛勒接走。**晚安,我的……**"他突然打住,紧咬了一下嘴唇,蓦地转身离去。

讲　评：这里的语境是罗切斯特先生邀请一群贵族朋友来家里做客,同时要求简·爱在客厅里作陪。可是，到访客人中有不少都瞧不起简·爱的家庭教师身份，他们对简·爱要么盛气凌人，要么冷嘲热讽。简·爱不堪忍受，在听完罗切斯特先生唱歌之后便迅速离开，而罗切斯特先生很快就发现了这个情况，于是立刻追了出来。罗切斯特先生让简·爱作陪，这正是对简·爱珍视的表现，但是限于环境，他只能忍住心中的爱意。其实，他想对简·爱说："Good-night, my love"，但是时机还不成熟，于是只能说"Good-night, my—"。不过，这种蕴含是可以被领悟到的，因此可以用对等式蕴含的方式来翻译原文的蕴含，以达到言有尽而意无穷的效果。由此得出的翻译策略是：以对等式蕴含对蕴含。

【例 139】

原　文："Barbara," said she, "can you not bring a little more bread and butter? There is not enough for three."

Barbara went out: she returned soon—

"Madam, Mrs. Harden says she has sent up the usual quantity."

Mrs. Harden, be it observed, was the housekeeper: a woman after Mr. Brocklehurst's own heart, made up of equal parts of *whalebone and iron*. (Chapter 8, *Jane Eyre*)

译　文："芭芭拉，"坦普尔小姐说道，"你就不能多拿点面包和黄油来吗？这些东西不够三个人分的。"

芭芭拉走了出去，但很快又回来了。

"小姐，哈登太太说，她已按照平时的分量给了。"

需要说明一下，哈登太太是这里的管家，向来会让布罗克赫斯特先生满意。他们两个都是一样的**铁石心肠**。

讲　评：这里的语境是里德舅妈在把简·爱送到罗沃德学校之前，当着布罗克赫斯特先生的面，造谣中伤简·爱的人品。在简·爱到达学校之后，布罗克赫斯特先生当着全校师生惩罚简·爱，让她站在高高的凳子上示众。下课之后，海伦来安慰简·爱。后来，坦普尔小姐也来了，并请两个孩子到自己的房间做客，还招待她们吃东西。由于哈登太太和布罗克赫斯特先生是一个阵营的，因此他们在简·爱眼中都是坏人，于是简·爱使用 whalebone and iron（鲸鱼骨和生铁）这个隐喻来描述他们对自己的冷漠。我们知道，英国人是海洋性民族，出海捕鱼是他们的重要生活方式，所以他们对于鲸鱼是很熟悉的，再加上历经工业革命，英国人对冶铁也是非常熟悉的，所以文中才会出现 whalebone and iron 这种用法。不过，中国人只熟悉冶铁，对鲸鱼并不熟悉。考虑到作者的意图并不在这个隐喻本身，这里可以用我们熟悉的成语"铁石心肠"来表达同样的意思。由此得出的翻译策略是：以归化式蕴含对蕴含。

【例140】

原　文： "No, not to thee! not to an earthly physician!" cried Mr. Dimmesdale, passionately, and turning his eyes, full and bright, and with a kind of fierceness, on old Roger Chillingworth. "Not to thee! But, if it be the soul's disease, then do I commit myself to the one *Physician of the soul*! *He*, if it stand with *His* good pleasure, can cure, or he can kill. Let *Him* do with me as, in *His* justice and wisdom, *He* shall see good. But who art thou, that meddlest in this matter? that dares thrust himself between the sufferer and *his God*?" (Chapter 10, *The Scarlet Letter*)

译　文： "不！！！我绝不会告诉你！！！我绝不会告诉一个世俗的医生！！！"丁梅斯代尔牧师双眼圆睁，瞪着老罗杰·齐灵渥斯，情绪激动地咆哮起来，"要是我的灵魂真得了病，我只会向<u>上帝</u>坦白。<u>上帝</u>只要乐意，便可以治愈我，也可以杀死我。<u>上帝</u>会运用公正和智慧，爱怎么处理我就怎么处理我。可是，你又算什么？？？竟敢来插手这件事？？？竟敢把自己摆在受难者和<u>上帝</u>之间？？？"说罢，牧师发疯似的冲出了屋子。

讲　评： 这里的语境是老罗杰医生以看病为由，与丁梅斯代尔牧师住在一栋房子里，并且在言语上向对方步步紧逼，以期找到对方的蛛丝马迹。原文中的 Physician of the soul 是隐喻用法，指代上帝，类似于我们称教师为灵魂工程师，首字母大写的 He 和 Him 以及 his God 也都是指上帝。这些都是 God 的指称变化手段，没有其他意义。另外，对于中国人而言，上帝就是上帝，通常不会有其他称呼。由此得出的翻译策略是：以直白式表达对蕴含。

【例141】

原　文： "Where are you going?"
"To put Adèle to bed: it is past her bedtime."
"You are afraid of me, because I talk like a *Sphynx*."
"Your language is enigmatical, sir: but though I am bewildered, I am certainly not afraid." (Chapter 14, *Jane Eyre*)

译　文： "你要去哪儿？"
"带阿黛勒上床睡觉，她就寝的时间都过了。"
"你在怕我，就因为我说话像*斯芬克斯*[1]？"
"你的语言像谜一样，先生。不过，就算我很困惑，也不代表我怕你。"

讲　评： 这里的语境是罗切斯特先生与简·爱第二次长时间交谈。从后文可知，罗切

---

[1] 斯芬克斯（sphinx）：古代希腊神话中带翼的狮身女面怪物，它用缪斯所传授的谜语来为难人，回答不出谜语的要被它杀死。传说天后赫拉派斯芬克斯坐在忒拜城附近的悬崖道路上，向过路的行人问一个谜语。谜语的内容为：是什么动物，早上四条腿走路，中午两条腿走路而晚上三条腿走路？谜语的答案是"人"。早上、中午和晚上分别比喻人的幼年、中年和老年。传说，这个谜题后来被年轻的希腊人俄狄浦斯答对，斯芬克斯因而跳崖自杀。

第九章 合作原则

斯特先生在第一次交谈后，便对简·爱产生了强烈的感情，可是囿于身份，他不能直接表达爱意，只能是顾左右而言他，说一些奇奇怪怪的话。罗切斯特先生所说的斯芬克斯的故事是西方人都比较熟悉的，但对于中国人还相当陌生，因此有必要注释说明该故事的来龙去脉。读者从这个故事可以推断出，罗切斯特先生说话时在故意兜圈子，他一定是有难言之隐。鉴于读者能够轻松地推断出这一点，由此得出的翻译策略是：以注释式蕴含对蕴含。

通过上面有代表性的四个例子，蕴含的翻译策略可以总结为：

1）以对等式蕴含对蕴含；
2）以归化式蕴含对蕴含；
3）以直白式表达对蕴含；
4）以注释式蕴含对蕴含。

本章小结

译者翻译前必须牢记一点，就是承认作者是在遵循总的合作原则，无论是对会话准则的遵守还是违反，都要符合这个总原则。这就意味着译者要努力从作者的视角来看待语言的千变万化，并尽可能加以再现，而不该用一成不变的语言风格应对。另一方面，译者必须考虑译文读者的感受，要用译入语读者能接受的方式来翻译，这样译文才具有交际功能。因此，译者的合作原则是有底线的，这个底线应该是以译文读者的需求为倾向。

翻译理论：下编

系统功能语言学由韩礼德创立，并被国内外学者广泛应用于翻译研究。系统功能语言学将语言本质概括为三大元功能：语篇功能、人际功能和概念功能。通过对语言做系统功能分析，语言的意义就可以被充分解读，还可以为原文理解和译文质量评价提供一个虽然比较复杂但却相对客观的方法。本编将对三大元功能展开较为详细的论述。

第十章 语篇功能
Textual Metafunction

本章的核心观点是译者必须具备语篇功能解读及再现或再造的能力。本章分为两大部分：小句翻译和衔接手段。第一大部分的核心观点是译者应具有再现小句真实语义的能力分为以下几部分：一、小句的解读；二、小句的翻译策略；三、小句主位结构之案例分析。其中小句的解读又分为以下几个小部分：（一）小句定义；（二）主位结构；（三）信息结构；（四）主位推进。第二大部分的核心观点是译者须熟知英文的衔接手段及其翻译策略。这一部分一共有三个内容：一、衔接的定义；二、衔接的分类；三、衔接手段的翻译策略。其中衔接包括语法衔接和词汇衔接。语法衔接共有四类——照应、替代、省略和连接；词汇衔接共有六类——同词重复关系、近义关系、反义关系、上下义关系、整体局部关系和语境同现关系。

第一部分 小句翻译（Clause Translation）

一、小句的解读

（一）小句定义（Clause Definition）

如果把语篇比喻成一个社会，其中的每一个词语比喻成社会中的每一个人，那么位于这二者之中的小句（包括复合小句）就是一个个家庭。家庭是社会的基本单位，家庭的稳定和谐是社会健康发展的基石，家庭对于社会的重要意义不言而喻。同理，小句翻译对于做好语篇翻译有着极为重大的意义。小句翻译若有问题，语篇翻译必有问题。正所谓"小句不译，何以译语篇"说的就是这个道理。

在给出小句的定义之前，必须先说说语法级阶的概念。根据系统功能语法（Thompson, 2004/2008: 21-23），语法分析自小到大的顺序是：词素、单词、词组或短语、小句、复合小句。韩礼德所开创的系统功能语法把"小句"当作语法分析的基本单位，这是因为小句由一个主语加一个谓语构成，能够表达出相对完整的语义。我们一直提倡的语篇翻译则是语义单位，而不是语法单位。要想做好翻译，首先要对语法的基本单位"小句"做到透彻的了解。另外，我们还要谈谈复合小句（也被称为小句复合体）是如

第十章 语篇功能

何翻译的。系统功能语言学不使用 sentence 这个概念，因为 sentence 只是用来标识以句号、问号、叹号或省略号来界定的一个语言片段，属于传统语法的范畴，而 clause complexes（复合小句）则是系统功能语言学使用的概念，更有利于彰显小句间的语义关系。

下面再说说小句分类。从不同角度看，小句有不同的划分。我们要知道这里谈论的是什么样的小句，才能给出准确的定义。如果从是否含有谓语（predicator）来看，小句可分为基本小句（major clause）和非基本小句（minor clause），前者有一个动词，后者没有动词。本章要谈的小句指基本小句，这也是人们在进行小句研究时已经一致认可的对象。要是按照语气来划分，基本小句可分为三种：陈述句（declarative clause）、疑问句（interrogative clause）和祈使句（imperative clause），这种划分是从系统功能语法的角度进行的，不是传统语法的视角，传统语法中的感叹句在这里被归入陈述句之中。要是从数量来划分，小句可分为简单小句（simple clause）和复合小句（clause complex），前者是指一个小句便构成了一个句子（sentence），后者指两个以上小句所构成的句子。

下面请看两个专业的小句定义：

1) A group of words which form a grammatical unit and which contain a subject and a FINITE VERB. A clause forms a sentence or part of a sentence and often functions as noun, adjective, or adverb.

For example:

I hurried home.

Because I was late, they went without me.

Clauses are classified as dependent or independent, e.g.

I hurried   because I was late.
(independent clause)   (dependent clause)

(*Longman Dictionary of Language Teaching & Applied Linguistics*)

含有主语和限定动词的一组词所构成的语法单位。小句可以构成句子，或句子的一部分，其功能相当于名词、形容词或副词。

例如：

I hurried home.（我急忙赶回家里。）

Because I was late, they went without me.

（因为我迟到了，所以他们没等到我就走了。）

小句分为从属句（dependent）和独立句（independent），例如：

I hurried   because I was late.
（独立句）   （从属句）

(《朗文语言教学及应用语言学辞典》)

2) A set of words consisting of a SUBJECT and a PREDICATE, and expressing a proposition. Halliday's SYSTEMIC FUNCTIONAL GRAMMAR considers the clause rather than the sentence, as the basic unit of grammatical analysis. A clause can exist on its own as a sentence, for example, "*The man replied*" (NBC, A0R), but more complex sentences can

contain multiple clauses or clauses embedded within clauses. Clauses which cannot exist on their own as a sentence are referred to as dependent clauses. Clauses can be classified further; for example, adverbial clauses function as adverbs: "I left *when I was about eight*" (BNC, CH8). Relative clauses modify nouns: "We can return for a moment to talk to the girl *who went to Italy*", while complement clauses are arguments of predicates: "I am sure *that it would be welcomed by them*". (*Key Terms in Discourse Analysis*)

小句是由一个主语和一个谓语组成的一组词语，用来表达一个命题。韩礼德的系统功能语法认为：小句而非句子才是语法分析的基本单位。小句，若是作为一个句子，能够单独存在，例如，"*The man replied*"（源自英国国家语料库，编号 A0R），但是更复杂的句子包含多个小句，或者小句之中内嵌小句。不能独立用作句子的小句被称为从属小句。小句还可以进一步划分：状语小句担任状语的功能，例如"I left *when I was about eight*"（源自英国国家语料库，编号 CH18）；关系小句用来修饰名词，例如"We can return for a moment to talk to the girl *who went to Italy*"（源自英国国家语料库，编号 A04）；补语小句是对谓语的表述，例如"I am sure *that it would be welcomed by them*"。（《话语分析核心术语》）

综上所述，小句的基本特征可归纳为：
1）小句是系统功能语法分析的基本单位。
2）小句由主语（或主词）和谓语（或限定动词）构成。
3）小句用来表达一个命题，也就是用来表达某个观点或主张。
4）小句能成为独立句子（即简单小句），也能成为复合小句中的某个成分（即充当定语、状语、补语等）。
5）从不同角度划分，小句有不同的种类，但基本小句是研究的重点。

（二）主位结构（Thematic Structure）

当我们从语篇功能角度来看待语言的时候，我们就是在谈论说话者如何组织信息，如何把这些信息流畅地组织成更多的信息。系统功能语法认为，语篇功能在小句上的体现就是主位结构，而理解主位结构的重点是确定主位是什么（Halliday, 1985, 1994, 2004, 2014; Thompson, 1996, 2004）。根据系统功能语法的解释，主位结构（Thematic Structure）由主位（Theme）和述位（Rheme）两部分构成。谈到系统功能语法，人们言必称韩礼德，但是主位和述位这对概念却早在20世纪40年代就有人提出了，请看《话语分析》（*Discourse Analysis*）这部专著中布朗和尤尔两位学者的论述：

Each simple sentence has a theme "the starting point of the utterance" and a rheme, everything else that follows in the sentence which consists of "what the speaker states about, or in regard to, the starting point of the utterance" (Mathesius, 1942). The theme, then, is what speakers/writers use as what Halliday calls a "point of departure" (1967: 212). (Brown & Yule, 1983/2000: 126)

每个简单句都由一个主位（theme）和一个述位（rheme）构成，主位是"话语的出发点",述位是主位后表述的部分,由"说话者所讲的内容或者与话语出发点相关的内容"构成。(Mathesius, 1942)因此,主位就是说话者或作者所使用的,被韩礼德称之为"出发点"的东西。(1967: 212)

下面我们再看看系统功能语言学的开创者韩礼德是怎么说的。

The Theme is the element which serves as the point of departure of the message; it is that which locates and orients the clause within its context. The remainder of the message, the part in which the Theme is developed, is called in Prague school terminology the Rheme. As a message structure, therefore, a clause consists of a Theme accompanied by a Rheme; and the structure is expressed by the order—whatever is chosen as the Theme is put first. (Halliday & Matthiessen, 2004/2008: 64-65)

主位是这样一个小句成分,它担任信息出发点的功能;主位是在小句的语境之内进行定位并确定发展方向的部分。小句信息的剩余部分,即主位所发展出的部分,被布拉格学派称为述位。因此,作为一个信息结构,小句由一个主位后接一个述位构成;这种结构由语序来体现,即被选作主位的内容要放在小句的开头。

最后,我们再看看《符号学核心术语》对这组概念的描述。

Theme is a formal grammatical category which refers to the initial element in a clause serving as the point of departure for the message. It is the element around which the sentence is organized and to which the writer/speaker wishes to give prominence. Everything that follows the theme, i.e. the remainder of the message or part in which the theme is developed, is known as the *rheme*. A message, therefore, consists of a theme combined with a rheme. (*Key Terms in Semiotics*)

主位是一个形式化的语法范畴,指小句中的起始部分,并作为信息的出发点而存在。围绕主位,句子得以组织起来,作者或说话人借以将其突出。主位后面跟着的所有东西,也就是小句信息的其他部分,或者说主位发展起来的部分,被称为述位。因此,小句信息由一个主位加一个述位构成。(《符号学核心术语》)

因此,同一个句子,由于语序不同,它的主位和述位也变得不同,例如:

Theme	Rheme
1) The reporter	repeatedly interrupted her replies.
2) Her replies	were repeatedly interrupted by the reporter.
3) Repeatedly,	the reporter interrupted her replies.

根据上述三个定义,我们可以大致勾勒出主位、述位的轮廓:

1)小句都是由一个主位加一个述位构成,这种结构由主位在前、述位在后的语序来体现。

2)在小句的语境之内,主位确定信息的起始点和发展方向,述位则是信息发展的具体表现,即述位围绕主位展开。

3）主位是语法范畴，可能很短，也可能很长；可能结构简单，也可能结构复杂；并不特指某一类词或某一类语法成分。

不过，还有些问题需要明确，就是作为信息起始点的主位到哪里终止，上述定义并没有提及。而主位与述位哪个承载更重要的信息，也并没有讲到。显然，这些都是极为重要的问题，因为只有主位确定了，述位才能确定，只有清楚了信息焦点是在主位还是述位，才能对小句意义有正确的理解，才能做好小句的翻译。对于主位的判定问题，吉奥夫·汤普森（Geoff Thompson）做过非常详尽的研究（2004/2008: 141-164）。我们将在稍后进行详细介绍。对于主位、述位的价值判定，我们现在就要引入一组概念：有标记（marked）、半有标记（less marked）和无标记（unmarked）。这组概念同时也与主位的判定有密切关系。

Markedness / Marked:

The theory that in the languages of the world certain linguistic elements are more basic, natural, and frequent (unmarked) than others which are referred to as "marked". For example, in English, sentences which have the order

Subject – Verb – Object: *I dislike such people.*

are considered to be unmarked, whereas sentences which have the order

Object – Subject – Verb: *Such people I dislike.*

are considered to be marked.

(*Longman Dictionary of Language Teaching & Applied Linguistics*)

标记性 / 有标记的：

一种理论认为世界上的各种语言中，某些语言成分比其他的更基本、更自然、更常见（即无标记的），这些其他的语言成分被称为"有标记的"。例如，英语句子顺序如下：

主语 – 动词 – 宾语：我不喜欢这样的人。

被认为是无标记的，而如果句子顺序为这样：

宾语 – 主语 – 动词：这样的人我不喜欢。

则被认为是有标记的。

（《朗文语言教学及应用语言学辞典》）

不过，语言成分的划分并非总是泾渭分明，有些成分可能处于有标记和无标记之间，这种情况可以被称为"半有标记"（less marked）。

按照无标记、半有标记和有标记的划分标准，我们结合吉奥夫·汤普森（2004/2008: 141-164）的研究，将英语小句中的主位分类总结为如下图表：

主位结构
- 常规主位结构（共四类）
- 特殊主位结构（共九类）
- 多项主位结构（共六类）
- 复合小句中的主位结构（共两类）

在我们具体分析小句的主位和述位之前，有三点需要牢记：首先，主位永远都位于句首；其次，多数情况下，主位都是无标记的，只是信息的起始点，价值相对而言不如述位重要；再次，我们对某个小句的主位到底是无标记还是有标记的讨论，暂时是脱离语境的，也就是只局限在本小句之内。下面，我们来详尽了解一下小句的主位结构。

1. 常规主位结构（Common Thematic Structure）

1) 陈述句中的主位（Theme in declarative clauses）

（1）主语作为主位（Subject as Theme）

Theme	Rheme
a. You	probably haven't heard of the story before.
b. We	love our country.

第一个小句的主位是"you"，这是信息的起始点。这个"you"如何了呢，"probably haven't heard of the story before"就是"you"的发展情况，通常就是说话人想强调的，以及听话人应该知道的焦点信息。在这类小句中，主位是无标记的，述位提供焦点信息。限于篇幅，我们只能"举一"例说明，而"反三"理解的任务就交给读者了。

（2）长主语作为主位（"Heavy" subject as Theme）

Theme	Rheme
a. Sending the final result through to Faculty before all the required documents have arrived	will probably just confuse matters.
b. The man who was here yesterday	was John's brother.

第一个小句的主位"Sending the final result through to Faculty before all the required documents have arrived"尽管很长，但是它仍然是无标记主位，小句的焦点信息是后面的述位"will probably just confuse matters"。

（3）状语作为主位（Adjunct as Theme）

Theme (less marked)	Rheme
a. Last night	a man was helping police enquiries.
b. As a tax-payer,	I object to paying for the restoration of Windsor Castle.

第一个小句的主位"Last night"是半有标记主位，也就是说，这个短语放在句子结尾更常见，但是出现在句首的时候也不算很少。对于这种情况，我们一般认为小句焦点还是后面的述位"a man was helping police enquiries"。

（4）补语作为主位（Complement as Theme）

Theme (marked)	Rheme
a. All the rest	we'll do for you.
b. Friends like that	I can do without.
c. Particularly significant	was the way the subjects reacted to the third task.

　　第一个小句的主位"All the rest"是有标记主位，对于这种情况，我们通常认为小句焦点就是主位，后面的述位"we'll do for you"变得相对次要。
　　（5）完整感叹句中的主位（Theme in exclamative clauses）

Theme (marked)	Rheme
a. What a nice plant	you've got!
b. How absolutely lovely	she looks tonight!

　　第一个小句的主位"What a nice plant"是有标记主位，对于这种情况，我们通常认为小句焦点就是主位，后面的述位"you've got"不太重要。
　　2) 疑问句中的主位（Theme in interrogative clauses）
　　（1）特殊疑问句中的主位（Theme in WH-questions）

Theme (marked)	Rheme
a. What	happened to her?
b. How often	are you supposed to take them?

　　第一个小句的主位"What"是有标记主位，对于这种情况，我们通常认为小句焦点就是主位，后面的述位"happened to her"变得相对次要。也就是说，特殊疑问词都是焦点信息，都是有标记主位。
　　（2）特殊疑问句中的有标记主位（Marked Theme in WH-questions）

Theme (marked)	Rheme
a. After the party,	where did you go?
b. An hour before supper,	what did you eat?

　　还有一种情况，当特殊疑问词前面出现状语时，该成分就是有标记主位。例如第一个小句，述位"where did you go"变得相对次要，而主位"After the party"就有被强调的意味，特指聚会之后你去了哪里，而不关注其他时间段。
　　（3）一般疑问句中的主位（Theme in yes/no questions）

Theme (less marked)	Rheme
a. Did he	tell you where I was?
b. Hasn't he	changed his name?

第一个小句的主位"Did he"是半有标记主位。对于这种情况，我们一般认为小句焦点还是后面的述位"tell you where I was"。主位中的限定词"Did"主要作用是形成选择性疑问语气，并请求对方给予信息，即到底是"yes"还是"no"。

3) 祈使句中的主位（Theme in imperative clauses）

（1）祈使句中的常规主位（Theme in imperative clauses）

Theme	Rheme
a. Leave	the lamp here.
b. Don't cry	about it.
c. Do have	some cheese.
d. Let's	go for a walk, shall we?

第一个小句的主位是"Leave"，这是信息的起始点，"the lamp here"是"leave"的发展情况。在这类小句中，句首动词是无标记主位，信息焦点在述位上。

（2）祈使句中的有标记主位（Marked Theme in imperative clauses）

Theme (marked)	Rheme
a. You	just shut up, will you?
b. On arrival in Liverpool	take a taxi to the University.
c. For a sharper taste	squeeze some lime over it.

祈使句还有一种情况，就是当动词前出现其他成分时，该成分就成为主位，而且是有标记主位，例如第一个小句的主位"You"通常不出现，现在出现了，强调的意味非常明显。对于祈使句的这种情况，我们通常认为主位是小句焦点，后面的述位变得相对次要。

4) 省略式小句中的主位（Theme in elliptical clauses）

Theme (It depends)	Rheme
a. Who	(would you most like to meet)?
(I	'd most like to meet) Your real father.
b. (That	's an) Amazing discovery!
c. (Are you)	Not sure what a special delivery is?

省略式小句如果只有主位，像第一个小句中的"Who"，那么该主位就是有标记主位，是说话人强调的对象，如果主位被省略了，像第二个小句的"Amazing discovery"，这时被省略的主位就是无标记主位，述位是小句的焦点。所以，省略式小句中的主位到底是不是有标记的，要视情况而定。通常说来，被省略的都不重要，剩下的小句成分是焦点信息。如果小句只存在主位，则该主位是有标记主位。

2. 特殊主位结构（Uncommon Thematic Structure）

1) 等价类主位（Thematic equatives）

（1）无标记等价类主位（Thematic equatives）

Theme	Rheme
a. What I really want to know	is the way you solve the problem.
b. What happened	was that they did not get married.
c. What one will not learn here	is anything about the Enlightenment.

无标记等价类主位其实就是"what"引导的主语从句做主位，这个主位是无标记的，后面的述位是小句的焦点。例如第一个小句，"What I really want to know"是无标记主位，"is the way you solve the problem"是小句的述位，关注的焦点。

（2）有标记等价类主位（Marked thematic equatives）

Theme (marked)	Rheme
a. That	's not what I meant.
b. And nothing	is precisely what we got.
c. Making the Party feel good about itself	is, after all, what he does best.

在这类小句中，"what"引导的从句依然存在，只不过出现在小句的后面，做了补语。主位还是在前面，而且是有标记的，明显是在强调。例如第一个小句，"That"作为主位是在表明说话人指的是"那件事情"，而不是"这件事情"或"其他事情"，"'s not what I meant"是小句的述位，并非句子焦点。

2) 谓化类主位（Predicated Theme）

Theme (marked)	Rheme
a. It was Helen	that Henry kissed in the park last night.
b. It was in the park	where Henry kissed Helen last night.
c. It was last night	when Henry kissed Helen in the park.

这类主位是有标记的，里面包含谓语动词，整个小句使用的是传统语法中所说的"强调句式"。例如第一个小句，主位是"It was Helen"，强调的是"Helen"而不是"Mary"等其他女子。"that Henry kissed in the park last night"则是小句的述位，是次要信息。

3) 评价类主位（Thematized comment）

Theme (less marked)	Rheme
a. It is true	that it took five days to do so.
b. It's interesting	that you should say that.
c. It is regretted	that the University is unable to provide continuous nursing or domestic care.

这类小句比较特殊，焦点信息相对集中在"that"引导的主语从句上，也就是述位上，而主位中含有说话人的评价，属于半有标记性质。对于这类小句，请牢记小句主要信息在述位部分。

4) 前置类主位（Preposed Theme）

Theme (marked)	Rheme
a. Happiness	that's what life is about.
b. Your Mum,	does she know you're here?
c. That picture of a frog,	where is it?

在这类特殊主位中，说话人把主语提到句首，然后在小句后面用代词指代，结果就形成了有标记主位，例如第一个小句，"Happiness"是有标记主位，是说话人强调的对象，后面的"that's what life is about"是述位，是次要信息。

5) 同位类主位（Apposition Theme）

Theme (less marked)	Rheme
a. They *both*	arrived last night.
b. Nina, *my best friend,*	has written another book.
c. The news *that Paris had fallen*	was a terrible blow to French pride.

这类主位由常规主位和它的同位语共同构成，是半有标记主位，例如第一个小句，"They both"是半有标记主位，"arrived last night"是述位，是小句的信息焦点。对于这类常规主位加同位语而形成的新主位，我们认为最多只是形成半有标记主位，如果同位语出现在小句中间或句尾，那又另当别论，具体请参看"文体变异"那一章。

6) 被动句中的主位（Theme in passive clauses）

a. *They* arrived at the airport at 7.00 last night *and they* were met by the Mayor of Beijing.	√
b. *They* arrived at the airport at 7.00 last night *and the Mayor of Beijing* met them.	×

这两个小句（也可称小句复合体）的语义基本一致。第一个小句复合体中的两个小句都是用"They"做主位，这样便形成了比较连贯的语义陈述，而第二个小句复合体中的两个小句分别使用了"They"和"the Mayor of Beijing"做主位，语义叙述连贯性因而降低。若无特殊原因，第一个小句复合体中的主位选择更值得提倡。

7) 存现句中的主位（Existential "there" in Theme）

Theme	Rheme
a. There was	no question of Kate's marrying Ted.
b. There is	something special about this situation.
c. There are	an infinite number of other special ones that follow.

对于存现句，就是所谓的"There be"句型，小句的主位就是"There be"本身，后面的内容是小句焦点。例如，第一个小句的主位是"There was"，"no question of Kate's marrying Ted"是述位，人们关注的焦点。

8) 引语句和投射句中的主位（Theme in reported and projected clauses）

Theme 1	Rheme 1	Theme 2	Rheme 2
a. He	said:	"Some people	won't like it."
b. "What deters them	is the likelihood of being caught,"	he	said.
c. Baker (1999)	suggests	that certain features	might be observed more systematically using corpora.

无论是引语句还是投射句，都由两个小句构成。两个小句的主位都是无标记主位，例如第一个小句，"He"是主位，"said"是述位，在后面的宾语从句中，"some people"是主位，"won't like it"是述位，不过为方便分析，可以整体上将第一个小句"He said:"看作主位，将第二个小句"Some people won't like it."看作述位。另外，如果从整体上进行分析，第二个小句的"What deters them is the likelihood of being caught"就变成了有标记主位，而"he said."则是不重要的述位。

9) 主位中的前置定语（Preposed attributives in Theme）

Theme (marked)	Rheme
a. *Standing in extensive gardens,* the house	has been carefully maintained to a high standard.
b. *Always ready the instant you need it,* the torch	needs no battery or mains recharging.
c. *Priced from under $200 to around $20,000,* our choice of rings	is seemingly endless.

英语中的短语类定语通常要放在所修饰名词的后面，前置之后被强调的意味非常明显，于是前置定语与核心名词一起构成了有标记主位。例如第一个小句，主位是"Standing in extensive gardens, the house"，述位是"has been carefully maintained to a high standard"。在翻译时，有标记主位中的前置定语常常被处理为谓语，形成最为常见的主谓结构，以此凸显前置定语的价值。

3. 多项主位结构（Multi-thematic Structure）

1) 连接词 + 主位（Conjunctions as part of Theme）

Theme	Rheme
a. But all rooms	look out onto the secluded garden.
b. But by the morning	the snow had all melted.
c. But if she missed those in Hyde Park in 1838,	she made up for it in the following year.

在现实语篇中，小句与小句总要衔接，主位之前经常会出现连接词，这时会形成复合主位，即连接词加上常规主位。例如第一个小句，主位是"But all rooms"，也就是连接词"But"加上常规主位"all rooms"，述位是后面的"look out onto the secluded garden"。这种主位是无标记的，翻译时往往只需要按照小句顺序直译即可。

2) 连接副词/情态副词 + 主位（Conjunctive and modal adjuncts in Theme）

Theme	Rheme
a. Thus disorder	will tend to increase with time.
b. Nevertheless, we	can reflect on our own activities.
c. Admittedly, he	took the trouble to destroy all the papers in the cottage.
d. Please may I	leave the table?

小句与小句在衔接时，除了使用连接词以外，还常使用连接副词或情态副词，以构成复合主位。例如第一个小句，主位是"Thus disorder"，述位是后面的"will tend to increase with time"。这种主位依然是无标记主位，翻译时往往只需要按照小句顺序直译即可。

3) 语篇主位 + 人际主位 + 经验主位（Textual^ interpersonal^ experiential Theme）

Theme			Rheme
textual	interpersonal	experiential	
a. But	surely	the course	doesn't start till next week.
b. Well,	certainly,	sanity	is a precarious state.
c. And,	oddly,	he	was right.

小句与小句在衔接时，还有一种常见情况，就是具有衔接功能的语篇主位，情态功能的人际主位，以及具有经验功能的常规主位，三者依次出现。汤普森用"^"符号表示三者之间的关系。例如第一个小句，主位是"But surely the discourse"，述位是后面的"doesn't start till next week"。这种主位还是无标记主位，翻译时往往只需要按照小句顺序直译即可，有时可能需要调整一下个别词语的顺序，以便符合译入语的搭配需要。

4) 人际主位 + 语篇主位 + 经验主位（Interpersonal^ textual^ experiential Theme）

Theme (less marked)			Rheme
interpersonal	textual	experiential	
a. Unfortunately,	however,	he	was late.
b. Not surprisingly,	then,	its operations	were viewed with admiration.

小句与小句在衔接时，第三种情况还有一种变体，就是具有情态功能的人际主位，衔接功能的语篇主位，以及具有经验功能的常规主位，三者依次出现。例如第一个小句，主位是"Unfortunately, however, he"，述位是后面的"was late"。这种主位是半有标记主位，在一定程度上通过情态主位来凸显作者的情感或观点，不过翻译时基本只需按照小句顺序直译，有时可能需要调整个别词语顺序，以便符合译入语的搭配需要。

5) 一般疑问句中的多项主位（Yes/no interrogatives as multiple Theme）

Theme			Rheme
textual	interpersonal	experiential	
Well,	had,	she	missed her Mum?
	Mrs. Lovatt, would	you	say it is untrue?

一般疑问句也会形成多项主位，也是无标记主位，与第三种多项主位的情况一样，这里不再赘述。

6) 祈使句中的多项主位（Imperatives as multiple Theme）

第十章 语篇功能

	Theme		Rheme
textual	interpersonal	experiential	
Well,	do	have	one of these eclairs.
	please don't	make	me out as some kind of hysterical idiot.

祈使句也会形成多项主位，也是无标记主位，与第三种多项主位情况一样，这里也不再赘述。

4. 复合小句中的主位结构（Thematic Structure in Clause Complexes）

1) 对复合小句主位的局部和整体分析（The local and global analysis of Theme in clause complexes）

Theme		Rheme	
Theme 1	Rheme 1	Theme 2	Rheme 2
a. As the universe	expanded,	the temperature of the radiation	decreased.
b. After the police	arrived,	I	brought them to this cottage.

对复合小句（也称小句复合体）进行主位分析时，有两种方式。第一种就是把出现在前面的从属小句视为无标记主位，把在后面出现的独立小句视为述位。第二种就是对从属小句和独立小句分别做主位结构分析，这两种主位结构中的主位通常都是无标记主位。具体如上图所示。从翻译实践来看，整体分析的价值更大一些，因为可以把握住整个句子的语义和逻辑。不过局部分析法也有价值，毕竟小句内部也要考虑语序。

下面是对复合小句主位整体分析的更多例子：

Theme	Rheme
a. Since he's already paid the bill	there's not much point in arguing.
b. If he was in the house,	would he keep out of sight?
c. Without replying	he put his head under the blankets.

下面是对复合小句主位局部分析的更多例子：

Theme 1	Rheme 1	Theme 2	Rheme 2
a. When we talked	I was thinking of myself,	and you	may have thought me very selfish.
b. Then, as the universe expanded and cooled,	the antiquarks would annihilate with the quarks,	but since there would be more quarks than antiquarks,	a small excess of quarks would remain.

2) 从属小句成为述位一部分（Dependent clause in Rheme）

Theme	Rheme
a. My dad	died when I was five.
b. I	do it because it's an addiction.
c. Down	she ran to the kitchen, where there were voices.
d. He	was sad although he was rich.

对复合小句分析还有另外一种常见情况，就是独立小句在前，从属小句在后。这时会把独立小句中的主位视为整个句子的主位，独立小句中的述位和从属小句被统一视为述位。这种分析模式下的主位是无标记主位。例如第一个复合小句，主位是"My dad"，述位是"died when I was five"。不过，翻译时并不一定要按照这个顺序来进行，有可能在考虑前后语境之后，重新确定译文语序。汉语译文一般会把被强调的独立小句放在后面，这种情况较多。

虽然汤普森对小句的主位述位划分做了非常详尽的描述，但是现实中经常会出现一些特殊情况的小句或小句复合体，这时需要我们运用相关理论知识做充分的分析，主位结构分析的问题最终是可以解决的。

（三）信息结构（Information Structure）

主位结构是从说话人或作者的视角对小句信息进行编排，而信息结构是从听话人或读者的视角，来对小句的意义进行理解的相反路径，对语篇意义的理解也很重要。下面请看信息结构的定义：

The use of WORD ORDER, INTONATION, STRESS and other devices to indicate how the message expressed by a sentence is to be understood. Information structure is communicated by devices which indicate such things as which parts of the message the speaker assumes the hearer already knows and which parts of the message are new information contrast, which may be indicated by stressing one word and not another (e.g. *I broke MY pen; I broke my PEN; I BROKE my pen*).

(*Longman Dictionary of Language Teaching & Applied Linguistics*)

信息结构：

运用词序、语调、重音及其他方式表明句子所表达的信息该如何理解。信息结构实现的方式是通过表明以下内容：哪部分信息说话者认为听话者已经知道，哪部分属于新信息。对此，可以通过一个词重读而另一个词不重读的方法来体现（例如，*I broke MY pen; I broke my PEN; I BROKE my pen*）。

(《朗文语言教学及应用语言学辞典》)

根据韩礼德和迈西森（2004/2008: 93），信息结构与主位结构之间存在着密切的语

第十章 语篇功能

义联系。在主位是无标记的状态下，信息结构与主位结构是对等的，也就是"旧信息"（Given information）等同于"主位"，而"新信息"（New information）等同于"述位"。尽管如此，我们还是不能把两个概念完全视为是相等的，因为主位是言语发出者所选择的话语表达的起始点，而旧信息是听话人所选择的信息接收的起始点。因此，主位述位是以说话者为倾向的理论，而旧信息新信息是以听话人为倾向的理论。

对信息结构这一概念研究最早的是布拉格学派，马泰修斯等人在二战前就对句子功能做了初步而有益的探讨，但当时影响并不太大。直到 1967 年，韩礼德发表了一篇极有影响的论文——《关于英语及物性和主位的研究》（*Notes on Transitivity and Theme in English*），信息结构在语言学研究中的受重视程度才达到一个新高度。在这篇文章中，韩礼德对信息结构的研究是跟英语口语的调群（tone group）结合在一起的。从语法方面分析，一个调群就是一个信息单位（information unit）。一个信息单位必须有新信息存在，也可以带上已知信息。因此，刚才的定义中提到了句子中某些单词重读的问题，就不难理解了。

根据系统功能语言学（胡壮麟等，2017），信息交流要靠信息单位的运用来完成。所谓信息交流，就是言语活动过程中已知信息和新信息的互相作用。已知信息，也被称为旧信息，指前文中已经出现过的或者借助语境可以轻松推导出的信息，而新信息指语篇中尚未出现的或者根据语境难以断定的内容。例如：

——What has John written?
——He has written a letter.

在前面问句的背景下，对于读者而言，"He has written"就成了已知信息，而"a letter"则是新信息。但有时候，在语境关照下，已知信息可能会被省略。例如：

——Who saw the play yesterday?
——(A)John.
——(B)John saw the play yesterday.

在回答上面的问题时，一般都使用 (A) 的回答方式，因为 John 是新信息，是读者关心的内容，而 (B) 的回答方式往往较为罕见，因为"saw the play yesterday"属于已知信息，完全重复这些内容没有意义，除非有特殊理由。

从主位情况的分析可知，主位大多数情况下都是旧信息，而述位是新信息，但不能绝对化地认为主位就是旧信息，述位就是新信息。有时候新信息会出现在主位的位置，这样的主位就被称为有标记主位，例如：

What（新信息，有标记主位）do you mean?（旧信息，述位）
Me（新信息，有标记主位）they blame for it.（旧信息，述位）

另外，还有两种情况比较复杂，即新信息与旧信息交织在一个小句中。它们是"新信息 + 旧信息 + 新信息"和"旧信息 + 新信息 + 旧信息"。例如：

——John loved Ann and Mary.
——But Helen（新信息）he（旧信息）hated（新信息）.
——John loved Ann and Mary.

—Yes, but he（旧信息）hated Helen（新信息），as you know（旧信息）.

（四）主位推进（Thematic Progression）

无论是主位述位理论，还是旧信息新信息理论，揭示的都是小句内部的语义结构。但是，语义在现实中往往都是生成于语篇层面的，也就是由多个连续相关的小句来共同展示说话人的意图。所以，当我们研究小句语义结构中的主位信息是如何一步一步向前推进的时候，就是在谈论主位推进这个概念。

根据胡壮麟等学者编写的《系统功能语言学概论》（2017：170-172），常见的主位推进模式有四种：放射型；聚合型；阶梯型；交叉型。

1）放射型（Radiation Pattern）

放射型主位推进就是几个小句的主位相同，而述位各不相同。结构如下图所示：

例如：

① Mary is from London. She is 20 years old. She is now studying Chinese at Peking University.

② Tokyo is a city. It is a big city. It is the capital of Japan.

在第一个语篇中，一共有三个小句。第一个小句的主位是"Mary"，第二个和第三个小句的主位是"She"，是"Mary"的人称照应。三者都是相同的主位，于是就构成了放射型主位推进模式。这种主位推进模式比较常见，对于汉语流畅的表达尤其重要。

2）聚合型（Focus Pattern）

聚合型主位推进就是几个小句的主位各不相同，但述位一致。结构如下图所示：

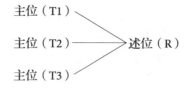

例如：

① China is in Asia. Japan is in Asia. And India is in Asia, too.

② John likes football. Jimmy likes football. Every man likes football.

在第一个语篇中，一共有三个小句。第一个小句的主位是"China"，第二个小句的主位是"Japan"，第三个小句的主位是"And India"。三者都拥有相同的述位"is in Asia"，第三个小句的述位多了一个"too"，不过这是语义表达连贯的需要。于是，这三个小句就构成了聚合型主位推进模式。

第十章 语篇功能

3）阶梯型（Stair Pattern）

阶梯型主位推进就是在由一连串相关小句组成的语篇中，前一个小句的述位或述位的部分是后一个小句的主位。结构如下图所示：

主位（T1）──── 述位（R1）
　　　　　　　　　│
　　　　　　（R1=T2）主位（T2）──── 述位（R2）

例如：

① Mary bought a carpet. It was made in Turkey. Turkey is a country in Asia.

② We visited the Great Wall. The Great Wall is in the northern part of China. China has witnessed many changes since the Great Wall was built.

在第一个语篇中，一共有三个小句。第一个小句的主位是"Mary"，第二个小句的主位是"It"，这个主位是第一个小句述位的成分。第三个小句的主位是"Turkey"，这个主位是第二个小句述位的成分。三个小句的语义表述犹如下台阶一样向前自然推进。于是，这三个小句就构成了阶梯型主位推进模式。

4）交叉型（Intersection Pattern）

交叉型主位推进就是在由一连串相关小句组成的语篇中，后一个小句的主位和述位与前一个小句的主位和述位（或部分主位和/或部分述位）相互交叉或部分交叉。结构如下图所示：

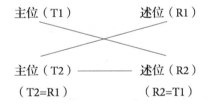

例如：

① The play was interesting, but I didn't enjoy it. A young man and young woman troubled me. I turned round and looked at them, but they didn't pay any attention to me.

② Norman Logan paid for his apple pie and coffee, then carried his tray toward the front of the cafeteria. From a distance, he recognized the back of William Tritt's large head. The tables near Tritt were empty, and Logan had no desire to eat with him, but they had some unfinished business that Logan wanted to clear up.

在第一个语篇中，一共有五个小句。第二个小句的述位成分中包括"it"，这恰好是第一个小句的主位。第三个小句的述位成分有"me"，这又恰好与第二个小句的主位"I"语义相等。第四个小句的主位是"I"，这正好与第三个小句的述位成分"me"语义相等。第四个小句的述位成分"them"等同于第三个小句的主位"A young man and young woman"。第五个小句的主位"but they"又呼应了第四个小句的述位成分"them"，第五个小句的述位成分"me"又与第四个小句的主位"I"呼应。于是，五个小句的主位和述位完全或部分呼应，语义表述被编织成了网络，自然向前推进。因此，该语篇小句使用的是交叉型主位推进模式。交叉型主位推进模式较为复杂，在成人阅读的各类文章中出现频率较高。

二、小句的翻译策略

基于前面详尽的论述，小句的翻译策略可以总结如下：依据语境，判断清楚英语原文小句的主位是无标记的还是有标记的。如果是无标记的或半有标记的，那么通常可以直译，即汉语译文小句主位述位顺序与原小句相同。如果原文小句主位是有标记的，那么汉语译文小句经常会把重要信息放在句尾，或采用其他合适的表达，以形成强调的效果。在确定小句主位是否为有标记时，可以使用信息结构理论辅助判断。另外，在凸显小句焦点信息时，要注意使用合适的主位推进模式，以保证小句间的语义连贯。通常说来，小句主位大多数时候是无标记的，有标记的情况并不常见。

三、小句主位结构之案例分析
—— 以"After Twenty Years"第 1~2 段为例

After Twenty Years

O. Henry

The policeman on the beat moved up the avenue impressively. The impressiveness was habitual and not for show, for spectators were few. The time was barely 10 o'clock at night, but chilly gusts of wind with a taste of rain in them had well nigh depeopled the streets.

一个警察正威风凛凛地在大街上巡逻。这种威风是习惯使然，并不是在显摆什么。虽然时间还不到晚上十点，但是一阵阵裹挟丝丝雨意的寒风呼啸而过，几乎把街上的行人赶得一干二净。

经过分析，原文五个小句的主位结构可以做如下划分：

Theme	Rheme
1) The policeman on the beat	moved up the avenue impressively.
2) The impressiveness	was habitual and not for show, for spectators were few.
3) The time	was barely 10 o'clock at night,
4) but chilly gusts of wind with a taste of rain in them	had well nigh depeopled the streets.

第十章 语篇功能

从上述表格可以看出，这四个小句的主位都是无标记的。

鉴于系统功能语言学也同样适用于汉语小句分析，我们再看对应译文小句的主位结构的情况。

Theme	Rheme
1) 一个警察	正威风凛凛地在大街上巡逻。
2) 这种威风	是习惯使然，并不是在显摆什么。
3) 虽然时间	还不到晚上十点，
4) 但是一阵阵裹挟丝丝雨意的寒风	呼啸而过，几乎把街上的行人赶得一干二净。

经过比较，我们发现，该语篇汉语小句的主位述位与英语的主位述位除了在细节处稍有区别，整体上完全一样。细节的差别跟汉语表达特征、小句间衔接、逻辑是否凸显等有关，而跟小句主位结构无关，因此这里暂时不做讨论。

鉴于本段一共有五个小句，自然要关系到小句的主位推进模式，让我们看看它们是如何推进的，具体内容请见下列图表。英语的第一个小句与第二个小句使用了阶梯式主位推进模式；第三个小句述位中的从属小句与第四个小句使用了交叉式主位推进模式，这里名词 spectators 与动词 depeopled 存在语义上的关联。另外，第一个小句与第四个小句具有词汇上的衔接关系，具体说来，就是 avenue 与 street 之间存在词汇衔接中的近义关系。

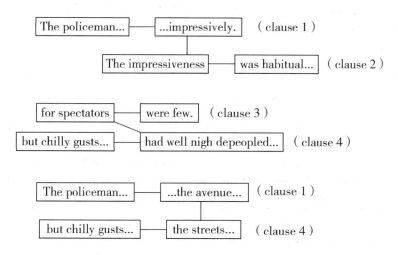

下面看看汉语译文中小句的推进模式是什么情况。具体分析也请见下列图表。可以看到，第一个小句与第二个小句之间是阶梯式主位推进模式；英文中第三个小句述位中的从属小句在汉语译文中消失了，但其实并没有真的消失，因为它的语义已经隐含在语篇中了，这可以通过第四个小句的述位看出来。之所以会有小句消失或隐含的现象，是因为译文毕竟在用汉语表达，要遵循汉语的写作规范，不可能跟英文完全对应。另外，像英文小句一样，汉语译文第一个小句与第四个小句也有关联，也是词汇上的近义关系，体现在"大街"与"街上"这对近义词的使用上。

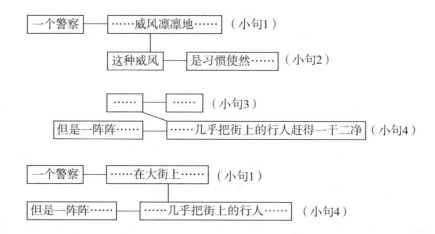

从上述分析可以看出，如果英语小句的主位是无标记的，那么汉语小句的主位结构很容易与英语小句的一致。在主位结构一致的前提下，很可能汉语译文会根据自身规范，在表达上进行局部调整。总而言之，无标记主位结构对翻译造成的困难并不算大。

下面再看 "After Twenty Years" 的第二段的第一句话，这是一个长句，也是一个小句。

Trying doors as he went, twirling his club with many intricate and artful movements, turning now and then to cast his watchful eye adown the pacific thoroughfare, the officer, with his stalwart form and slight swagger, made a fine picture of a guardian of the peace.

这个警察身材魁梧，步伐威严，边走边查看每家商户的门窗，警棍在他手里不停地翻转，灵巧地挥舞出各种复杂动作，目光还时不时警觉地扫过宁静的街道，那样子完全就是一个和平守卫者。

经过分析，可以看到，这是一个有标记主位结构，具体说来，主位中的核心词 the officer 有前置定语，从而导致该主位变成有标记主位。具体请见下表。

Theme (marked)	Rheme
Trying doors as he went, twirling his club with many intricate and artful movements, turning now and then to cast his watchful eye adown the pacific thoroughfare, the officer,	with his stalwart form and slight swagger, made a fine picture of a guardian of the peace.

再看看汉语译文小句的主位结构是什么情况。具体请见下表。

Theme	Rheme
a. 这个警察	身材魁梧，步伐威严，边走边查看每家商户的门窗，
b. 警棍	在他手里不停地翻转，灵巧地挥舞出各种复杂动作，
c. 目光	还时不时警觉地扫过宁静的街道，
d. 那样子	完全就是一个和平守卫者。

第十章 语篇功能

通过表格，我们可以看到，原文小句经过翻译之后，变成了四个汉语小句，也是中规中矩的无标记主位结构。不过，这个表格不容易显示出这些小句的主位推进模式，也不容易看出小句之间的内在逻辑联系。请看下面的结构图：

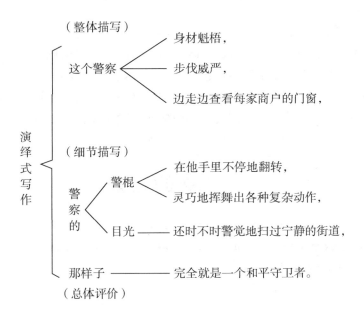

可以看出，第一个小句采用的是放射型主位推进模式；第二个小句采用的也是放射型主位推进模式。而四个小句之间是演绎式写作的关系：第一个小句对警察巡逻做了整体描写；第二个小句和第三个小句对警察做了细节描写——警棍和目光；第四个小句对警察的形象做了一个积极评价——完全就是一个和平守卫者。

根据本章所讲的理论，整个小句主位中的 the officer 其实是无标记的，因为第一段中已经提到，而"真正的"述位内容（焦点信息）则有很多——（警察的）身材如何如何，步伐如何如何，行为如何如何，警棍如何如何，目光如何如何，样子如何如何。这些述位内容多数放在了句子主语 the officer 前面，从而使得主位变得重要起来（即有标记），当然，主语后面的述位内容在意义上也同样重要。毕竟从信息结构理论的角度看，对警察的各种描写和评价都是新信息，都值得读者关注。所以，这个小句因为结构复杂而变得稍微有些特殊——主语前后都有语义焦点存在，主位是有标记的，述位同样重要。不过，这并不影响我们准确理解和巧妙翻译。

从上述分析可以看出，如果英语小句的主位是有标记的，那么汉语小句主位结构与英语小句相比可能会发生很大变化。容易出现一个长长的英语小句变成多个汉语小句的现象。这时，汉语译文很可能要根据自身写作规范，考虑汉语多用主谓结构的特点，将英语有标记主位或其中的新信息放在谓语的位置，以此强调。总之，有标记主位结构对翻译造成的困难较大，但只要把握规律，是可以很好解决的。

第二部分 衔接手段（Cohesive Devices）

衔接手段是语篇翻译研究与实践的重要内容。韩礼德和哈桑（1985）认为，语篇通常都具有语篇属性（texture）。语篇属性体现为两方面：主位信息结构和衔接。前者侧重的是小句内不同成分之间（主位与述位，旧信息与新信息）的语义联系，后者侧重的是小句间不同成分（语法衔接、词汇衔接）的语义联系。因此，衔接对于语篇的形成同样具有不可或缺的作用。所以，我们要对英语衔接手段予以充分了解。

一、衔接的定义

Cohesion refers to the grammatical and lexical relationships between the different elements of a text. This may be the relationship between different sentences or between different parts of a sentence. For example,

A: *Is Jenny coming to the party?*

B: *Yes, she is.*

There is a link between Jenny and she and also between is ... coming and is.

In the sentence "*If you are going to London, I can give you the address of a good hotel there.*", *t*he link is between London and there.

(*Longman Dictionary of Language Teaching & Applied Linguistics*)

衔接指语篇不同成分之间所存在的语法和/或词汇关系，这种联系可能存在于句子之间，也可能存在于一个句子的不同成分之间（即小句之间）。例如：

<u>A：珍妮来参加聚会吗？</u>

<u>B：是的，她要来。</u>

在这个对话中，Jenny 和 she 以及 is... coming 和 is 之间就存在着联系。

再比如，在下面这个句子中，

<u>你如果去伦敦，我可以给你一个上好旅馆的地址。</u>

上述句子中的 London 和 there 就存在着联系（具体说来，就是前指照应的关系）。

（《朗文语言教学及应用语言学辞典》）

上述定义说得比较清楚，但是不够详尽，需要展开论述。因此，接下来我们有必要了解衔接的分类。

二、衔接的分类

根据韩礼德和哈桑（1976，1985）的划分，衔接手段可以分为语法衔接和词汇衔接。其中语法衔接包括照应、替代、省略和连接，而词汇衔接则包括同词重复关系、近义关系、反义关系、上下义关系、整体局部关系和语境同现关系。上述十种衔接手段的共性就是，它们都反映出语篇内部两个小句在意义上的相互关联，也就是一个成分的理解需要参照另一个成分。

（一）语法衔接（Grammatical Cohesion）

1. 照应（Reference）

照应是指能使小句与小句通过指称词语而建立起来的衔接关系。照应分为外指和内指两类。外指是指语篇中某个词语的理解不能在语篇内部找到答案，而需要去情景语境中寻求，例如交传会议上译者对现场某事物的翻译。内指是指语篇中某个词语的理解可以在本语篇的上下文中求得答案。内指又可进一步分为前指（anaphora）与后指（cataphora）两种；如果所指词语或语篇在该词前面，就叫前指，如果在后面，就叫后指。

英语照应系统有三种类型：人称照应、指示照应和比较照应。

1) Personal Reference（人称照应）

Semantic category（语义范畴）	Existential（存在性的）	Possessive（归属性的）	
Grammatical function（语法功能）	Head（中心词）		Modifier（修饰词）
Class（词类）	Noun (Pronoun)（名词性代词）	Determiner（限定词）	
Person（人称）	英语　汉语翻译	英语　汉语翻译	英语　汉语翻译
Speaker (only)（发话者自己） Addressee(s), with/without other person(s)（受话者，包括或不包括他人）	I me　我 you　你（们） we us　我们	mine　我的 yours　你（们）的 ours　我们的	my　我的 your　你（们）的 our　我们的
Other person, male（他人，男性）	he him　他	his　他的	his　他的
Other person, female（他人，女性）	she her　她	hers　她的	her　她的
Other persons; objects（他人或物体，复数）	they them 他（她、它）们	theirs 他她、它们的	their 他（她、它）们的
Object; passage of text（物体或语篇段落）	it　它	[its]　[它的]	its　它的
Generalized person（一般人称）	one（无固定对应词汇）		one's（无固定对应词汇）

（Halliday & Hasan，1976：38）

上面表格中的英文一眼看去，感觉非常简单，初学英语时便接触过。但若是涉及翻译，麻烦就来了。为什么呢？因为英文和中文两种语言的代词系统及其应用有很大不同。上面表格中的汉语只是英文表达的对应翻译，但不代表实际的语篇翻译时必须要这样说。一般说来，除非有意强调或是出于修辞的需要，英语表达总的原则是避免重复。英语使用者对于名词重复的解决方法之一就是使用代词。相比英语，汉语代词数量比较有限，常用的有"其、之、自己、对方、彼此、大家、人们、有人"等，所以结果就是，一方面汉语习惯于重复名词，另一方面那些有限的汉语代词会反复出现。至于代词的翻译方法，应该以体现原语言功能和译入语表达自然为最终标准。

2) Demonstrative Reference（指示照应）

Semantic category （语义范畴）	Selective （选择性的）		Non-selective （非选择性的）
Grammatical function （语法功能）	Modifier/Head （修饰语/中心词）	Adjunct（附加语）	Modifier（修饰语）
Class（词类）	Determiner（限定词）	Adverb（副词）	Determiner（限定词）
Proximity（远近程度） near 近 far 远 neutral 一般	英语　　　汉语翻译 this these　这 这些 that those　那 那些	英语　汉语翻译 here　这里/儿 [now]　[现在] there　那里/儿 then　那时	英语　汉语翻译 the（无固定对应项）

（Halliday & Hasan，1976：38）

相比较英语的人称照应，英语的指示照应数量更少，似乎也更简单。没错，从翻译的角度而论，指示照应确实很简单，基本只要对应翻译即可，但有时也需要考虑原文的意义和功能，以便做出相应调整。指示照应翻译的最终标准就是要使译入语的表达意义清晰，流畅自然。

3) Comparative Reference（比较照应）

Grammatical function （语法功能）	Modifier：Deictic/Epithet （修饰语：指示词/修饰词）	Submodifier/Adjunct （副修饰语/附加语）
Class（词类）	Adjective（形容词）	Adverb（副词）
General comparison：总体比较： identity 相同 similarity 相似 difference (ie. Non-identity or similarity) 不同（也就是不相同或不相似）	英语　　　汉语翻译 same　　　相同的 identical　同样的 equal　　　相等的 similar　　相似的 additional　另外的 other　　　其他的 different　　不同的 else　　　别的	英语　　　汉语翻译 identically　完全一样地 similarly　　相似地 likewise　　同样地 so much　　如此多/这么多 differently　不同地 otherwise　另外/除此以外

第十章 语篇功能

续表

Particular comparison（具体比较）	better more etc. [comparative adjectives and quantifiers] 更好的，更多的，等等 [表示比较的形容词和量化词]	so more less equally	如此 更（多、大、高等） 更（少、小、低等） 相等地

（Halliday & Hasan，1976：39）

相较于英语的人称照应和指示照应，英语的比较照应数量虽然不少，但其实翻译难度很小，也就是只需要对应翻译即可。唯一需要考虑的，也许就是如何使比较照应的翻译与句子整体表达和谐一致，也就是使译文句子表达清晰自然。

简而言之，照应的翻译就是要求译者用具有同等功能和效果的方式重构衔接关系。虽然照应这种衔接手段通常没有审美价值，但是对于翻译初学者或翻译水平不高的人却是个不小的陷阱。

【例142】

原　文：Though *he* had detected with a critical eye more than one failure of perfect symmetry in *her* form, *he* was forced to acknowledge *her* figure to be light and pleasing; and in spite of *his* asserting that *her* manners were not those of the fashionable world, *he* was caught by their easy playfulness. (Chapter 6, *Pride and Prejudice*)

译文1：虽说<u>他</u>带着挑剔的目光，发觉<u>她</u>身条这儿不匀称那儿不完美，但<u>他</u>不得不承认<u>她</u>体态轻盈，招人喜爱。尽管<u>他</u>一口咬定<u>她</u>缺乏上流社会的风度，可<u>他</u>又被<u>她</u>那大大落落的调皮劲儿所吸引。

译文2：<u>达西</u>起初认为<u>伊丽莎白</u>身材不够匀称，现在却不得不承认<u>她</u>体态轻盈，讨人喜欢。<u>达西</u>还曾认为<u>伊丽莎白</u>举止不够端庄，与上流社会格格不入，现在却觉得<u>她</u>活泼俏皮、大方可爱。

讲　评：经过比较，我们发现，译文1采用的都是人称照应，不是"他"就是"她"，可是这两个代词在中文里发音相同，我们的耳朵无法识别，于是就很容易产生逻辑混乱的感觉。可能有人会反驳说，译文是用眼睛看的，是可以识别"他"和"她"的。可即便如此，我们在阅读时依然要一定程度上依赖心中的"默读之声"，这是人类语言的基本特性之一，也就是说，无论是否出声阅读，声音的特性都存在，都会影响到读者。而译文2使用了"照应+词汇衔接+省略"的方式，这样就解决了汉语译文的衔接问题。无论用眼睛看还是用耳朵听，读者都会觉得很舒服。

【例 143】

原　文：Yet Mr. Dimmesdale would perhaps have seen this individual's character more perfectly, if a certain morbidness, to which sick hearts are liable, had not rendered him suspicious of all mankind. Trusting no man as his friend, he could not recognize his enemy when the latter actually appeared. *He* therefore still kept up a familiar intercourse with *him*, daily receiving *the old physician* in *his* study, or visiting the laboratory, and, for recreation's sake, watching the processes by which weeds were converted into drugs of potency.

One day, leaning *his* forehead on *his* hand, and *his* elbow on the sill of the open window, that looked towards the grave-yard, *he* talked with *Roger Chillingworth*, while *the old man* was examining a bundle of unsightly plants. (Chapter 10, *The Scarlet Letter*)

译文1：而丁梅斯代尔先生如果没有病人常有的某种病态，以致对整个人类抱着猜疑的态度的话，他或许会对此人的品性看得更充分些。由于他不把任何人视为可信赖的朋友，故此当敌人实际上已出现时，仍然辨认不出。所以，*他*依旧同*老医生*随意倾谈，每天都在书斋中接待*他*；或者到*他*的实验室去拜访*他*，并且出于消遣的目的，在一旁观看*他*如何把药草制成有效的药剂。

一天，*他*用一只手支着前额，肘部垫在朝坟墓开着的窗子的窗台上，同*罗杰·齐灵渥斯*谈话，*那老人*正在检看一簇难看的植物。

译文2：要是丁梅斯代尔牧师不抱有怀疑心态，不像其他病人那样对人都疑心重重，那么他或许会对老罗杰医生的品行看得更加清楚。由于他不相信任何人会成为自己的朋友，故而敌人出现在面前时他也无法觉察。因此，*他*跟*医生*仍像平常一样密切来往，每天在书房中*予以接待*，或者去*对方*的实验室闲聊，看看*人家*如何把草根树叶变成灵丹妙药。

一天，*他*同*医生*闲谈起来。当时，*他*一手支着前额，肘部撑在窗台上，眼睛看着窗外的墓地，而*医生*正在察看一簇难看的植物。

讲　评：在译文1中，一个非常明显的问题就是照应混乱，也就是说，"他"与"他"在同一个句子中出现，我们也就难以容易辨认"谁"是"谁"了。另外，原文使用的词汇衔接 the old physician、Roger Chillingworth、the old man，明明是指一个人，结果译文完全复制了原文的词汇衔接表达，即翻译成"老医生""罗杰·齐灵渥斯"和"那老人"，读过之后恐怕会有崩溃的感觉。那么，应该如何翻译呢？

我们可以看到，译文2所有的"他"都有固定所指，就是指丁梅斯代尔牧师，而那个医生的照应方式则为"医生、对方、人家、医生、医生"，其中还有一个"予以接待"，这是省略衔接。读过之后，我们感觉译文语义清晰，毫不混乱。换言之，原文使用的是"照应+词汇衔接"，而译文2采用的是"照应+词汇衔接+省略"的办法。

第十章 语篇功能

通过上述两个例子，可以看出，照应衔接的翻译真有可能引发大问题。解决方法就是以功能对等为主，不一定要形式对应。

2. 替代（Substitution）

替代是指用具有替代功能的词语来取代前文中的某个词语或某个部分，这是为避免重复而采用的句际衔接手段。

根据韩礼德和哈桑（1976）的划分，英语中的替代可以分为三种：

1）名词性替代（Nominal Substitution）：one、ones、the same；
2）动词性替代（Verbal Substitution）：do、does、did；
3）小句性替代（Clausal Substitution）：so、not。

英语中常见的名词性替代只有 one、ones 和 the same 三个。One 用于替代上文中已经出现的可数名词单数，复数名词用 ones 替代，要是替代名词词组，就使用 the same。英语中可用的动词性替代其实只有 do 这一个，即指代前文中出现的动词或动词词组，does 是第三人称单数情况下的替代，did 是在一般过去时中的替代。小句性替代是指用替代词来取代前文中的小句，肯定情况就使用 so，否定情况就使用 not。

【例 144】

原　文：① The days of his youth appeared like dreams before him, and he recalled the serious moment when his father placed him at the entrance of *the two roads*—*one* leading to a peaceful, sunny place, covered with flowers, fruits and resounding with soft, sweet songs; the other leading to a deep, dark cave, which was endless, where poison flowed instead of water and where devils and poisonous snakes hissed and crawled.

② Whatever our souls are made of, yours and mine are *the same*.

③ But we accept—at least we say we *do*. All of parenting is a series of letting go by degrees.

④ ...Surely something marvelous was going to happen.
　　And then it *did*.

⑤ — "Is Matthew still there?"
　　— "Oh yes, I think *so*—I've just seen him."

⑥ ...She was willing to accept the relationship on these terms. I was *not*.

译　文：① 过往的青春岁月梦幻般地浮现在他的眼前，他回想起那庄严的时刻，父亲把他领到了人生的*岔路口*前——*一条路*通向和平安宁、阳光明媚的世界，那里有遍地鲜花，满园果实，处处回荡着洪亮悦耳、柔和甜美的歌声；另一条路则通向黑暗无底的深渊，流淌的毒浆替代了清泉，恶魔张牙舞爪在此横行、毒蛇遍地游走嘶嘶蹿动。

② 无论我们的灵魂是由什么做成的，你的跟我的*都是一样的*。

③ 不过，我们还是接受了杰夫离开的事实，至少表面上是*接受了*。养儿育女实际上就是一个逐步放手的过程。

④ ……由此看来，某种绝妙的场景就要出现。

它*真的来了*。

⑤ ——"马修还在那里吗？"

——"是的，我想他*还在*，因为我刚刚见过他。"

⑥ ……母亲愿意我们之间保持这样的关系，可是我*不愿意*。

讲　评：通过对比原文与译文，我们可以看到，英文的替代手段与中文的替代手段都起到了避免重复，同时使句子紧凑的效果。在语篇层面上，替代起到了建构句际衔接的作用。一般说来，替代造成的翻译困难较小，只要能考虑到语言的功能和意义，"直译"就可以解决问题。

3. 省略（Ellipsis）

省略是指把语言结构中的某个成分省去不提。人们使用省略是为了消除语言的重复感，同时使语言变得精炼，使语义变得清晰，使交际效率变得更高。省略现象的出现符合了语言使用中的经济原则，即人们在使用语言时倾向于用较少的精力去表达尽可能多的信息，同时还能保证交际获得成功。

省略现象在语言的许多维度都存在，例如口语中的省音，词汇中的缩略词，但是作为衔接手段的省略就是指句法层面某些成分的省略。单纯看省略现象所在的句式，结构虽然不完整，但并不意味着不能理解，因为缺失的部分可以从上下文中找到。

韩礼德和哈桑（1976）把省略分成名词性省略（nominal ellipsis）、动词性省略（verbal ellipsis）和小句性省略（clausal ellipsis）。

【例145】

原　文：① 名词性省略

"I think I have heard you say, that their uncle is an attorney in Meryton."

"Yes; and they have another, who lives somewhere near Cheapside."

(Chapter 8, *Pride and Prejudice*)

② 动词性省略

——Is John going to come?

——He might. He was to, but he may not.

③ 小句性省略

——What did you draw it with?

——A pencil.

译　文：① 名词性省略

"我记得听你说过，她们的姨夫在梅里顿当律师。"

"没错，她们还有一个舅舅，住在奇普赛德。"

（《傲慢与偏见》第八章）

② 动词性省略

——约翰打算来吗？

——他也许吧。他那时候想，不过现在也许不了吧。

③ 小句性省略

——你拿什么画的？

——铅笔。

讲　评：第一个例子中的 another 相当于 another uncle，这里的名词 uncle 被省略，修饰成分 another 成为中心词。不过，汉语译文却不能省略"uncle"，因为这个词在汉语文化中没有固定对应词，不同场合需要表达为"伯父、叔父、姑父、姨夫、舅舅"等，所以在这里必须区分清楚，否则中国读者一定会困惑。根据小说的人物关系，一个要译为"姨夫"，另一个要译成"舅舅"。在第二个例子中，动词 come 被省略，只留下表达情态意义的词语 might、was to 和 may not。在第三个例子中，A pencil 前面省略了小句 I drew it with。之所以能被省略，是因为那些表达在问句中就已经预设了。第 2 句和第 3 句译文的省略情况与原文一致，体现了对语言经济性原则的遵守。

通过上述三个例子，可以看出，省略现象在英语和汉语中都很普遍，也比较容易识别，因此只要能够保证语义连贯，处理省略翻译的原则就是"能省就省，实在不能省的地方，以某种方式把语义说明即可"。

4. 连接（Conjunction）

连接本身就是"在前言与后语之间建立系统联系的专门用语"。通过这类连接词语，"人们可以了解句子之间的语义联系，甚至可以经前句从逻辑上预见后续句的语义"。（胡壮麟，1994：92）在《英语中的衔接》（*Cohesion in English*）一书中，韩礼德和哈桑（1976）将连接划分为四种类型：附加关系（additive）；转折关系（adversative）；因果关系（causal）；时间关系（temporal）。

附加关系就是在当前句子之后还有扩展的空间，可以再增加新的信息，也可视为补充关系或递进关系。转折关系就是前一句与后一句的意义完全相反。因果关系就是前一句与后一句之间体现出原因和结果，或者是结果与原因。时间关系体现出事件发生时的先后顺序，有的是有先有后，有的是同时出现。

后来，韩礼德在《功能语法导论》（*An Introduction to Functional Grammar*）一书中又提出了新的划分，即把连接分为扩展关系和投射关系，并把前者分为"详述""延伸"和"增强"三种类型，后者分为"话语"和"主意"两种类型。它们与"并列"和"主从"又存在交叉关系。（详见本编最后一章逻辑功能部分）对于英语语法研究而言，这种划分更加严谨和全面，但却使应用于翻译实践难度陡增，而且可操作性不强，因此本章还是采用韩礼德和哈桑在《英语中的衔接》一书中的划分，即把连接分为"附加、转折、因果和时间"四种。下面请看韩礼德和哈桑（1976：238-239）给出的一个经典例子。

【例 146】

原　文：For the whole day he climbed up the steep mountainside, almost without stopping.

　　　　a. *And* in all this time he met no one. (additive)

b. *Yet* he was hardly aware of being tired. (adversative)

c. *So* by night time the valley was far below. (causal)

d. *Then*, as dusk fell, he sat down to rest. (temporal)

译　　文：整整一天，他都在陡峭的山坡上攀爬，几乎没有停过。

a. *而*在这段时间里，他没有碰到过任何人。（附加）

b. *然而*，他好像一点也没觉得累。（转折）

c. *因此*，到了晚上，山谷被远远甩到了下面。（因果）

d. *后来*，黄昏降临了，他才坐下来休息。（时间）

讲　　评：可以看到，同样一个小句，由于后面的连接词语不同，小句语义也变得不同，也可以这样说，由于后面小句所暗含的逻辑关系不同，所以要求前面使用的连接词语也变得不同。

【例 147】

原文 1： "She is in the window-seat, to be sure, Jack."

And I came out immediately, for I trembled at the idea of being dragged forth by the said Jack. (Chapter 1, *Jane Eyre*)

译文 1： "她在窗台上，杰克，我敢肯定。"

一想到要被约翰揪出来，我就禁不住全身颤抖，*于是*只好主动站了出来。

原文 2： Bessie answered not; but ere long, addressing me, she said—"You ought to be aware, Miss, that you are under obligations to Mrs. Reed: she keeps you: if she were to turn you off, you would have to go to the poorhouse."

I had nothing to say to these words: they were not new to me: my very first recollections of existence included hints of the same kind. This reproach of my dependence had become a vague singsong in my ear: very painful and crushing, but only half intelligible. Miss Abbot joined in—

"*And* you ought not to think yourself on an equality with the Misses Reed and Master Reed, because Missis kindly allows you to be brought up with them. They will have a great deal of money, and you will have none: it is your place to be humble, and to try to make yourself agreeable to them." (Chapter 2, *Jane Eyre*)

译文 2： 贝茜没有回答，但没过多久她就冲我说道："小姐，你应该知道，你是在受里德太太的恩惠。她要是把你赶出去，你就只能进济贫院了。"

这番话令我无话可说，对此我也并不陌生，在我小时候就有过类似的记忆。这种指责如今还会时常在我耳边响起，我虽懵懵懂懂，却也痛苦万分，难过至极。艾博特也在一旁附和道："太太好心把你和少爷小姐放在一起抚养，你可别自以为能跟他们平起平坐。他们将来都会有很多钱，而你却一分钱也不会有。你必须低声下气，顺着他们，这才是你的本分。"

讲　　评：and 在原文 1 中起顺承作用，强调前后小句存在因果关系，在原文 2 中起附

第十章 语篇功能

加作用，与前段的前段存在呼应关系。不过，看过参考译文，我们可知，第一个 and 要翻译成"于是"；第二个 and 却隐身于句子之中了，并没有翻译成某个直接对应的词语。因此，连接词语到底要如何翻译，要视语境和搭配而定。

总的说来，从词性上来讲，连接成分不外乎是连词和副词；从功能上来讲，有连接作用的连词和副词往往出现在句首，或者接近句首的位置，作用就是使前后句之间的逻辑关系得以畅通。鉴于逻辑体现的是前后小句间的基本关系，因此译者一般可采用形式对应的直译方式，但有时候也未必一定要翻译出来，因为逻辑关系可以隐藏在字里行间。

（二）词汇衔接（Lexical Cohesion）

英语小句间的语义关系也需要词汇衔接来保证。韩礼德和哈桑（1976）将词汇衔接分为复现（reiteration）和同现（collocation）两种。为了使语义阐释更为清晰，同时使对翻译实践的指导更具操作性，这里将两种展开，变成独立的六类：同词重复关系（repetition）、近义关系（synonymy）、反义关系（antonymy）、上下义关系（hyponymy）、整体局部关系（meronymy）和语境共现关系（collocation）。

1. 同词重复关系（Repetition）

同词重复关系就是单个词语、短语或小句的重复出现，以此形成语义衔接和逻辑推进。从词语相隔距离角度来看，同词重复关系可分为连续重复和间隔重复。同词重复不仅可以使语义信息向前传递，有时还可以起到加强语气的作用。例如：

Algy met a bear. The bear was bulgy.

在这个句子中，the bear 指代了前面的 a bear，这样便使得叙述得以继续。

再比如，马丁·路德·金那篇著名的演讲"I have a dream"：

I have a dream that ...

...

I have a dream that ...

...

I have a dream that ...

...[1]

"I have a dream that"这个表达反复出现，对意义和气势起到了明显的加强作用。通常情况下，英汉翻译时对同词重复关系最为有效的翻译方法是重复直译，也就是说不要更换表达。所以，"I have a dream"在本文中永远要译为"我有一个梦想"。再比如 *The Two Roads* 这篇散文中"youth"这个词语：

【例 148】

原　文：The days of his *youth* appeared like dreams before him, ...

---

[1] 演讲的具体内容请见上编第四章。

He looked towards the sky and cried painfully, "O *youth*, return! ... But both his father and the days of his *youth* had passed away.

His darkened eyes were full of tears, and with a despairing effort, he burst out a cry: "Come back, my early days! Come back, my lost *youth*!"

And his *youth* did return, for all this was only a dream, which he had on New Year's Night.

...you will cry bitterly, but in vain: "O *youth*, return! Oh give me back my early days!"

译　　文：**青春**梦幻般地浮现在他眼前。

老人又抬起头，仰天悲叹："**青春**啊，归来吧！……然而他的父亲和他的**青春**却都早已逝去。

他黯淡的双眼充满了泪水，绝望中他鼓足余力高声呼唤："归来吧，我虚度的年华！归来吧，我逝去的**青春**！"

他的**青春**真的归来了，刚才的一切不过是他新年之夜的一场梦。

……你们也会痛苦而徒然地呼唤："归来吧，我虚度的年华！归来吧，我逝去的**青春**！"

讲　　评：可以看到，youth 从头至尾都译成了"青春"，而不是"韶华"或"韶光"等近义词。因为只有这样，才能突出作者呼吁大家珍惜美好青春的强烈心声。也只有这样翻译，才能保证 youth，即原文中的核心词语不会被更换，才能保证语篇核心思想的流畅，也就是体现出韩礼德所说的"经验功能"（experiential function）的一致，因而要重复表达，以达到实现同等功能的效果。

2. 近义关系（Synonymy）

虽然有很多人把 synonymy 称为同义关系，但是这里还是称之为"近义关系"，因为绝对的同义词是不存在的。从修辞角度来看，近义关系主要有防止单调，使表达富于变化的作用。从衔接角度来看，近义关系还体现出解释的作用，这样就使得同一个段落之内甚至不同段落之间的句子有了逻辑关系，衔接关系因而得以建立。

【例 149】

原　　文：I'm sitting at my mother's *desk*, a mahogany *secretary* with a writing leaf that folds down to reveal rows of cubbyholes and tiny drawers—even a sliding secret compartment. (*My Mother's Desk*)

译　　文：我坐在母亲的**书桌**旁，这是一个红木做的**带书架的写字桌**，上面有个可以折叠的活动桌面，桌面翻下来就可以看见几排小格子和一些小抽屉，甚至还有一个可以拉动的暗格。

讲　　评：这里 secretary（带书架的写字桌）与前面的 desk（书桌）构成了近义关系。

【例 150】

原　　文：... Some of my happiest moments were spent *daydreaming* about someone wonderful and exciting but too shy or eccentric to make known his or her identity.

My mother contributed to these *imaginings*. She'd ask me if there was someone for whom I had done a special kindness who might be showing appreciation... (*Mystery of the White Gardenia*)

译　　文：……我最快乐的时刻便是去**浮想联翩**，揣测大概有那么一个人，令人赞叹，使人激动，可却腼腆或者古怪，以至于隐姓埋名。

冒出这许多**遐想**，自然要归功于我的母亲。她会问我，是否替谁做了件特殊的好事，因此人家想表示谢意。

讲　　评：在这个例子中，imaginings（遐想）与前面的 daydreaming（浮想联翩）构成了近义关系。

3. 反义关系（Antonymy）

韩礼德和哈桑虽然在《英语中的衔接》一书里列出了反义关系，但并未展开论述，这里有必要引入其他学者的观点。根据利奇（1983：92-109）的研究，反义关系主要有四种：（1）二项分类，即非此即彼，如 alive/dead（生/死）；（2）多项分类，即共同下义关系，如 gold/silver/copper/iron（金/银/铜/铁）；（3）两极关系，即中间区域可以分级，如 large/small（大/小），中间可以有 middle-sized（中等尺寸的）；（4）方向关系，即表示相对，如 before/after（前/后），parent/child（父母/孩子）。简而言之，只要两个表达能在意义上形成对照，就构成反义关系。由于语义上的对立或反衬，反义词可以帮助读者意识到，同一个事物中有两个相反的特性共存，或者是认识到两个事物因为某些特征相反而显得完全不同。

【例151】

原　　文：Then he is driving a car, and we are *falling asleep* before he gets home, *alert*, even in our dreams, to the sound of his motor gearing down. (*A Room of His Own*)

译　　文：现在他又学会了开车，每晚在他回家前，我们都难以**入眠**，**屏息倾听**着他把车子的引擎慢慢熄火，甚至有时在梦中都是如此。

讲　　评：falling asleep（入眠）与 alert（屏息倾听）就构成了反义关系，作者以此说明，父母亲无论是清醒还是梦中，都始终惦记着晚归的儿子。

【例152】

原　　文：Finally, my teacher took me aside. She explained that she had written a narrator's part to the play, and asked me to switch roles. Her words, *kindly* delivered, still *stung*, especially when I saw my part to go to another girl. (*My Mother's Gift*)

译　　文：终于，老师把我带到一边，然后解释说，她还写了一个旁白的角色，现在想把我换成旁白。尽管老师说话时很**温柔**，可还是**刺痛**了我，尤其是当我看到自己的公主角色为另一个女孩顶替时，更是万分难过。

讲　　评：在这个例子中，我们发现，kindly（温柔）虽然与 stung（刺痛）的词性不同，前者是副词，后者是过去分词，但是语义却是相对立的，因此也构成了反义关系。这对反义词语表明了女孩在看到自己的公主角色被人顶替时，是多么心痛，哪怕老师的话语非常温柔。这里需要注意的是，处于反义关系的一组词语未必要词性相同，只要语义相反，就可构成反义关系。前面刚刚提到的近义关系也是如此，我们要多加留意。

4. 上下义关系（Hyponymy）

所谓上下义关系，就是指某个表达的意义在另一个表达的意义范围之内，或者是其中的一种类型，也就是说，下义词是上义词中的一种情况。上下义关系可以分为三类：（1）上义词先出现，下义词后出现；（2）下义词先出现，上义词后出现；（3）下义词出现，上义词不出现，但是又人人皆知上义词是什么。

【例 153】

原　　文：Unmistakable *noises* are coming through my bedroom wall. Now a *scuffling*, now a *bumping*, a long, drawn-out *scraping*. (*A Room of His Own*)

译　　文：隆隆的**噪音**穿透了我卧室的墙壁，时而是**拖拽东西的咔咔声**，时而是**物体撞击的砰砰声**，时而是又长又尖的**吱吱声**。

讲　　评：在这个例子中，noises（噪音）是上义词，scuffling（拖拽东西的咔咔声）、bumping（物体撞击的砰砰声）和 scraping（吱吱声）都是它的下义词，表示各种各样的噪声，以此说明文章中的"我"已经非常不耐烦了，所以才会把噪声一一罗列出来。

【例 154】

原　　文：The day before my father died, my mother and I had gone shopping for a prom dress. We'd found a spectacular one, with yards and yards of dotted swiss in *red*, *white* and *blue*, it made me feel like Scarlett O'Hara, but it was the wrong size. (*Mystery of the White Gardenia*)

译　　文：父亲去世的前一天，母亲和我一起去商店买参加舞会所穿的裙子。我们选中的那件特别亮丽，是用薄纱缝制的，上面印有许多**红**、**白**、**蓝**三色圆点。穿上它的感觉非常棒，我就像斯佳丽·奥哈拉一样美丽，但是大小不合适。

讲　　评：这个例子比较有特点，因为它只有下义词，即 red、white、blue（红、白、蓝三色），可是找不到上义词，然而我们又知道那是什么。答案很简单，colour——颜色。

5. 整体局部关系（Meronymy）

所谓整体局部关系，就是指某个表达的意义与另一个表达的意义之间有整体和局部的联系，也就是说，二者之间是包含和被包含的状态。有时，整体与局部之间的关系并非一目了然，需要去上下文寻找，甚至要根据经验去体会。有时，原文中有明确的整体局部关系，但是译文中却未必在词语上直接体现。

【例155】

原　文：Then he is driving a *car*, and we are falling asleep before he gets home, alert, even in our dreams, to the sound of his *motor* gearing down. (*A Room of His Own*)

译　文：现在他又学会了开<u>车</u>，每晚在他回家前，我们都难以入眠，屏息倾听着他把车子的<u>引擎</u>慢慢熄火，甚至有时在梦中都是如此。

讲　评：在这个例子中，car 和 motor，即汽车和引擎，或者说汽车和马达，就是典型的整体与局部的关系，这样前后句的语义联系因为这两个词语而显得紧密了。

【例156】

原　文：As conscientious parents, we strive to foster independence. But when it happens, when you pause outside that *door* and look at *the blank panels* it is always a little unsettling. (*A Room of His Own*)

译　文：作为有强烈责任心的父母，我们会努力培养孩子独立。可是，一旦他们独立了，而你却只能在紧闭的<u>门扉</u>外徘徊，这种情况总会让人有些担忧和不安。

讲　评：在这个例子中，door 与 the blank panels，即"门"与"门板"，也是整体与局部的关系，可是译者却不一定要将其全部翻译出来。在译文中，我们只见"门扉"，即"门板"，却不见了包括门框和门板在内的作为整体的"门"，但我们知道，"门"当然是存在的，是不言自明的。从这个例子，我们也体会到这样一个道理，译者并不需要把原文的每一个词都一一对应式地转换过来，而只需要翻译那些有必要、有价值的词语。关于本句翻译更详尽的解释，请见本书【例13】。

6. 语境同现关系（Collocation）

语境同现关系不是简单的词语搭配关系，而是一种依赖有关词汇的特定联想而形成的词汇语义衔接，即一些词项倾向于在同一语境中出现，因此具有了衔接功能。语境同现词语不仅存在于搭配中，例如"虎虎有生气"，说到"生气"，我们想到的就是"虎虎"，而非其他动物词语的叠用，并且也体现在同一语境中词语的习惯性共现方面，例如"寒冷"往往就会跟"冰雪""棉衣"等词语同现，而通常不会跟"电视""书包"等词语同现，除非是有特定的语境支持。

【例157】

原　文：It was New Year's *Night*. An aged man was standing at a window. He raised his mournful eyes towards *the deep blue sky*, where *the stars* were floating like white lilies on the surface of a clear calm lake. (*The Two Roads*)

译　文：那是个新年之<u>夜</u>，一位老人伫立在窗前。他忧伤地抬起头，仰望<u>深蓝的夜空</u>，那满天<u>繁星</u>就像朵朵白色睡莲，漂浮在清澈静谧的湖面上。

讲　评：在这个例子中，night、the deep blue sky 和 the stars，即"夜晚""深蓝的天空"和"繁星"，就构成了语境同现关系，这是基本常识，人们读到这里，会觉得自然而和谐。

【例 158】

原　文：Every year on my birthday, from the time I turned 12, *a white gardenia* was *delivered* to my house in Bethesda, Md. No *card* or *note* came with it. Calls to *the florist* were always in vain—it was *a cash purchase*. (Mystery of the White Gardenia)

译　文：自打十二岁起，每年生日那天，**一枝洁白的栀子花**便会**送**到我在马里兰州贝塞斯达小镇的家中。花枝上不附**名片**，也无**便条**。多次打电话询问**鲜花店**，均无所获，大概是**现金支付**的缘故。

讲　评：在这个例子中，a white gardenia、delivered、card、note、the florist，以及 a cash purchase 也构成了语境同现关系。这是因为"一枝洁白的栀子花"被"送"到某人的家中，这是现代社会最常见的一种服务，送花人往往在送鲜花的同时，附上自己的"名片"，或者是祝福的"卡片"或"便条"。而鲜花呢，往往都是从"鲜花店"购买的。另外，在过去的那个年代，买花支付的方式主要是"现金"。所以，上述词语共同构成了一个和谐的语境。

这里，我们要特别指出，语境同现衔接关系的识别对于翻译意义重大。因为英文词语通常是一词多义，所以对词义进行准确定位就是译者必须要完成的任务。我们所依靠的语境本质上是语境同现关系，因此译者就可以根据同现语境来定位词义，同时根据语境同现这个定律，来选择合适的译文词语。

最后，让我们再回顾一下英语的衔接手段：英语的衔接手段反映出语篇内部两个小句在意义上的相互关联，可分成语法衔接与词汇衔接两大类。语法衔接包括照应、替代、省略和连接；词汇衔接包括同词重复关系、近义关系、反义关系、上下义关系、整体局部关系和语境同现关系。这些衔接手段如下图所示：

三、衔接的翻译策略

语法衔接中的替代、省略和连接引发的翻译困难较小,通常的做法是替代对替代,省略对省略,连接对连接。唯有照应中的人称照应需要格外当心,需要以功能对等的方式处理。词汇衔接虽然类型多一点,但基本上可考虑以直译为主,意译作为补充。但是无论怎样,都要保证功能对等。

本章小结

作为三大元功能之一,语篇功能与翻译和写作的关系最为密切。虽然我们在前面讲了很多内容,但语篇功能的翻译其实可以简单概括为做好小句主位述位的表达,同时兼顾小句间衔接手段的复现或再造。对于原文理解,除了具有主位和信息结构的意识之外,还要具备标记的识别意识,这样在翻译时才有可能写出既符合译语语言规范,又能凸显作者意图的正确句子。同时,译者还要注意原文的衔接特征,做到尽力正确再现。原则上说,原文凸显衔接手段的特点比较突出,也就是凸显逻辑关系,译文也理应如此,反之亦然。语篇功能犹如一个人的外在着装,是可以看到并把握的,只是需要我们花费些时间去揣摩和再现。接下来要学习的人际功能犹如一个人的态度与情感,需要我们更加仔细地观察和体会。

第十一章 人际功能
Interpersonal Metafunction

> 本章的核心观点是：译者应该始终具有人际功能转换的意识。本章分为四个部分：一、人际功能的定义；二、人际功能的体现；三、人际功能的翻译策略；四、小句人际功能之案例分析。第二部分又分为以下几个小部分：（一）语气系统；（二）代称系统；（三）情态系统；（四）评价系统。

一、人际功能的定义

韩礼德（1967/1968）把语言元功能划分为三种：概念功能、人际功能和语篇功能。概念功能还可分为经验功能和逻辑功能。根据《系统功能语言学核心术语》给出的定义，人际功能指语言作为一种资源，可以在说话人和受话人之间扮演角色，展示关系，以表达意义。

汤普森（2004/2008：30）指出，我们用语言来与他人沟通，建立并维系关系，影响他们的行为，表达我们对世界的看法，以及探出或改变对方的观点。

胡壮麟等（2017：110）认为，语言除具有表达讲话者的亲身经历和内心活动功能外，还具有表达讲话者的身份、地位、态度、动机和他对事物的推断、判断和评价等功能。语言的这一功能称作"人际功能"。语言的人际功能是讲话者作为参与者的"意义潜势"，是语言的参与功能。通过这一功能，讲话者使自己参与到某一情景语境之中，来表达他的态度和推断，并试图影响别人的态度和行为。此功能还表示与情景有关的角色关系，包括交际角色关系，即讲话者或听话者在交际过程中扮演的角色之间的关系，如提问者与回答者、告知者与怀疑者等之间的关系。

根据上述观点，人际功能可以重新定义如下：

1) 作为语言三大元功能之一，人际功能指语言作为一种资源，可以在说话人和受话人之间扮演角色，展示关系。

2) 人际功能体现出语言的参与功能，对人际关系有沟通、建立、维系、影响和改变的作用。

3) 人际功能具有表达讲话者身份、地位、情感、态度、动机和表达讲话者对事物或他人的推测、判断和评价等功能。

第十一章 人际功能

二、人际功能的体现

（一）语气系统（Mood）

1. 语气系统的语法范畴（Grammatical Category）

语气系统是小句语义系统的语法化体现，是人际功能的基本系统之一，包括信息求取者和信息提供者两种言语交流角色。语气系统的选择项有直陈（indicative）和祈使（imperative）两个基本语法范畴，前者用于交换信息，可以进一步区分为陈述（declarative）和疑问（interrogative）两种语气，而后者用于交换商品和服务（goods-&-services），只有祈使（imperative）一种语气。语气系统可用下表来体现其内部关系：

```
                    ┌─ 直陈（Indicative）─┬─ 陈述（Declarative）
语气（Mood）────────┤                     └─ 疑问（Interrogative）
                    └─ 祈使（Imperative）
```

2. 语气系统的言语功能（Speech Function）

在言语交流过程中，说话人表达的语言千变万化，但本质上只扮演两个角色：给予（giving）或求取（demanding）。也就是说，讲话人或者给予听话人某种东西，或者向对方求取某种东西。这意味着，讲话者不但自己做事，同时要求听话人为自己做事。因此，言语交流过程实际上就是双方交流内容的过程。双方能够交流的内容不仅是信息（information），也可以包括物品和服务（goods&services）。

交流角色和交换物品相互组合，就构成了语气系统的四种言语功能：提供（offer）、命令（command）、陈述（statement）和提问（question）。具体如下表所示：

Role in exchange（交流角色）	Commodity exchanged（交换物品）	
	goods-&-services（物品与服务）	Information（信息）
(i) Giving（给予）	"offer"（提供） e.g. Would you like this teapot?	"statement"（陈述） e.g. He's giving her the teapot.
(ii) Demanding（求取）	"command"（命令） e.g. Give me that teapot!	"question"（提问） e.g. What is he giving her?

（Halliday & Matthiessen, 2004: 108）

要是有人说出"He's giving her the teapot."这种类型的句子，那就意味着说话人是在给予信息，这被称之为 Statement（陈述）。要是有人说出"What is he giving her?"这种类型的句子，那就意味着说话人是在求取信息，这被称之为 Question（提问）。要是有人说出"Would you like this teapot?"这种类型的句子，那就意味着说话人是在给予物品与服务，这被称之为 Offer（提供）。要是有人说出"Give me that teapot!"这种类型的句子，那就意味着说话人是在求取物品与服务，这被称之为 Command（命令）。

那么，问题来了，这个表格对于翻译实践的意义在哪里呢？回答：意义重大。也就是说，如果原文表达的是给予信息，那么译文必然是给予信息；如果原文表达的是求取信息，那么译文必然是求取信息；如果原文表达的是给予物品与服务，那么译文必然是给予物品与服务；如果原文表达的是求取物品与服务，那么译文必然是求取物品与服务。翻译实践中，有一部分错误确实是由于言语功能的错位，这是我们必须要注意的。

3. 语气系统的句法结构（Syntactic Structure）

在系统功能语言学中，语气系统的句法结构是体现人际功能的核心，是在小句中实现语气的部分。它由主语（Subject）和限定成分（Finite）组成。其中主语由具有名词特性的词、词组或小句来充当，而限定成分是小句中动词词组的第一个功能成分。语气之外的部分被称为剩余成分（Residue）。例如，在"Would you like this teapot?"这个小句中，Would 是限定成分，you 是主语，like this teapot 是剩余成分。整个小句表达的是疑问语气。

小句的语气系统句法结构有三种类型：陈述句中的语气结构、疑问句中的语气结构、祈使句中的语气结构。汤普森（2004/2008：49-57）对此做过较为详尽的研究，具体分类及举例如下：

1）陈述句中的语气结构（Mood in declarative clauses）

a）Assessment	will	be by coursework.
b）We	[present]	take conversation for granted most of the time.
Subject	Finite	Residue
Mood		

在例句 a）中，Assessment 是小句的主语，will 是小句的限定成分，be by coursework 是小句的剩余成分。而在例句 b）中，We 是主语，一般现在时，也就是斜中括号内的 present 是限定成分，take conversation for granted most of the time 是剩余成分。无论小句内容是什么，只要语气结构是陈述句，那么就表示对一个事情的表达或宣布，就是在给予听话人一些信息。

不过，下面这种情况会稍有一点特殊，请看：

感叹句中的语气结构（Mood in exclamative clauses）

a）What an epitaph	that	would	make!
b）How simple	it all	[past]	seemed at the time.
Residue	Subject	Finite	Residue
	Mood		

第十一章 人际功能

在例句 a）中，that 是小句的主语，would 是小句的限定成分，开头的 What an epitaph 和后面的 make 是小句的剩余成分。在例句 b）中，it all 是小句主语，一般过去时，也就是斜中括号内的 past 是小句的限定成分，How simple 和 seemed at the time 是小句的剩余成分。无论是 What 引导的感叹句，还是 How 引导的感叹句，在系统功能语言学中都被认为是表达陈述语气，虽然这种陈述语气比较强烈，可依旧是在给予听话人某种信息。

2）疑问句中的语气结构（Mood in interrogative clauses）

（1）一般疑问句中的语气结构（Mood in yes/no interrogative clauses）

a）Can	he	paint well enough?
b）Do	we	have anything in common?
Finite	Subject	Residue
Mood		

一般疑问句的语气结构特征是：助动词作为小句的限定成分，会出现在句首，接着出现的是小句的主语，后面是小句的剩余成分。这种语气结构表达的是说话人想要向对方或自身索取肯定或否定的信息，或者索取肯定或否定的物品或服务。例句 a）"Can he paint well enough?"就是说话人在向对方索取信息——"他"的绘画能力是否足够优秀？而例句 b）"Do we have anything in common?"就是在向自身，即"我们"，索取信息——"我们"是否有任何共同之处？

（2）特殊疑问句中的语气结构 [1]（Mood in WH-interrogative with known subject）

	a）Why	did	the affair	end?
	b）What	do	you	expect me to do?
	c）How many	are	there?	
Residue		Finite	Subject	Residue
		Mood		

特殊疑问句语气结构 [1] 的特征是：除了提问"人"以外的其他特殊疑问词作为剩余成分的一部分会出现在句首，助动词作为小句的限定成分，会紧跟其后，接着出现的是小句的主语，这是明确的主语，后面是小句的其他剩余成分，也可能其他剩余成分不出现。这种语气结构表达的是说话人想要向对方或自身索取某些特定信息，或者索取某些特定物品或服务。例句 a）"Why did the affair end?"是对事情结束的原因提出疑问；例句 b）"What do you expect me to do?" 是在就对方的期待提出疑问；例句 c）"How many are there?"是对数量提出疑问。

（3）特殊疑问句中的语气结构 [2]（Mood in WH-interrogative with Wh-element as subject）

a）Who	's	been sleeping in my bed?
b）What kind of idiot	would	do something like that?
c）Who	[past]	typed out that note?
Subject/WH-	Finite	Residue
Mood		

特殊疑问句语气结构 [2] 的特征是：用来提问"人"的特殊疑问词，或含有这种特殊疑问词的短语，会出现在句首，动词词组的第一个成分作为小句的限定成分，会紧跟其后，接着出现的是小句的其他剩余成分。这种语气结构表达的是说话人想要向对方或自身就谁发出的动作或状态而索取信息。例句 a）"Who's been sleeping in my bed? "是在询问一直睡在我床上的人是谁？例句 b）"What kind of idiot would do something like that? "是在询问能做出那样事情的白痴到底是什么样的？例句 c）"Who typed out that note?"是在询问打印出来那个材料的人是谁？

3）祈使句中的语气结构（Mood in imperative clauses）

（1）无标记祈使句中的语气结构（Mood in unmarked imperative clauses）

		a）Go away.
		b）Answer no more than three of the following questions.
c）Don't		look at me like that.
Finite	[Subject]	Residue
Mood		

无标记祈使句语气结构的特征是：小句的限定成分以隐形方式出现在句首，但限定成分若是 Don't 之类的否词表达，则会出现在句首，小句的主语也以隐形方式紧随限定成分出现，之后就是小句的剩余成分。这种语气结构表达的是说话人想要向对方索取物品或服务。例句 a）"Go away."就是在命令对方离开；例句 b）"Answer no more than three of the following questions."是在要求对方回答下面的问题时不要超过三个；例句 c）"Don't look at me like that."是在要求对方不要以那种方式看着自己。

（2）有标记祈使句中的语气结构（Mood in marked imperative clauses）

第十一章 人际功能

	a）You	listen to me, young man.
b）Do		hurry up, for goodness' sake.
c）Don't	you	take that tone of voice to me.
Finite	Subject	Residue
Mood（marked）		

有标记祈使句语气结构的特征是：小句的限定成分可能会以显形方式出现在句首，小句的主语可能也会以显形方式紧随限定成分出现，之后就是小句的剩余成分。这种语气结构表达的是一种比较强烈的祈使语气，即说话人非常强烈地想要向对方索取物品或服务。例句 a）"You listen to me, young man."就是语气强硬地要求年轻人照自己说的去做；例句 b）"Do hurry up, for goodness'sake."就是在表达强烈的情绪，请求对方无论如何一定要快一点；例句 c）"Don't you take that tone of voice to me."就是以特别强调的口吻，要求对方不要用那种口气跟"我"说话。

（3）"Let's"祈使句中的语气结构（Mood in "Let's" imperative clauses）

	a）Let's	call it a day.
b）Don't	let's	argue about it.
c）Do (marked)	let's	try and get it right this time.
Finite	Subject	Residue
Mood		

"Let's"祈使句语气结构的特征是：小句的主语是"Let's"，前面的限定成分如果表示肯定意义，那么该限定成分不出现，但是如果表达否定意义，则小句的限定成分 Don't 会出现在主语之前。而无论限定成分表达肯定还是否定，主语之后都会跟随剩余成分。这种语气结构表达的是普通的祈使语气，即说话人希望对方跟自己都可以接受某种物品或服务。例句 a）"Let's call it a day."表示说话人要求对方接受今天到此为止的现状；例句 b）"Don't let's argue about it."在表达否定，说话人不希望对方因为这个而与自己争辩。然而，例句 c）"Do let's try and get it right this time."虽然在表达肯定语气，但是语气明显加强了，因为 Let's 前面出现了"Do"，所以限定成分是有标记的。

（二）代称系统（Pronouns and Address Terms）

代称系统指能够体现人际功能的人称代词的选择性运用和称谓语的选择性运用。在这里，人称代词不仅体现语篇功能，更体现出人际功能。语言使用者在使用第一人称时，到底使用表示单数的"I/me"，还是表示复数的"We/us"，在使用第二人称时，到底使用表示单数的"you/thou/thee"，还是表示复数的"you/ye"，在使用第三人称时，到底使用表示单数的 he/him/she/her/it，还是使用表示复数的 they/them，这些都能体现出不同的人际功能和人际意义。同样，对同一个说话对象，不同的称谓语也会体现出不同的人际功能和人际意义。译者必须对此积极应对，以求人际功能和交际意义的对等转换。代称系统可以用下图表示：

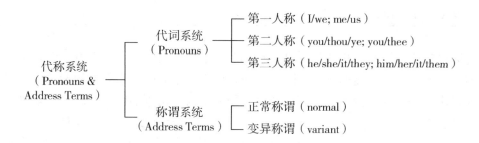

代词系统人际功能实例分析 1

President Barack Obama's Inaugural Address (2009)

My fellow citizens:

  I stand here today humbled by the task before us, grateful for the trust you have bestowed, mindful of the sacrifices borne by our ancestors. *I* thank President Bush for his service to our nation, as well as the generosity and cooperation he has shown throughout this transition.

  ...

  Today *I* say to you that the challenges we face are real. They are serious and they are many. They will not be met easily or in a short span of time. But know this, America—they will be met.

  ...

  As for our common defense, <u>we</u> reject as false the choice between our safety and our ideals. Our Founding Fathers, faced with perils <u>we</u> can scarcely imagine, drafted a charter to assure the rule of law and the rights of man, a charter expanded by the blood of generations. Those ideals still light the world, and <u>we</u> will not give them up for expedience's sake. And so to all other peoples and governments who are watching today, from the grandest capitals to the small village where my father was born: know that America is a friend of each nation and every man, woman, and child who seeks a future of peace and dignity, and that <u>we</u> are ready to lead once more.

在整篇演讲当中，奥巴马只使用了三次"I"，上面的段落中都列出来了。与之形成强烈对比的是，奥巴马在演讲中使用了 62 次"We"。造成这种差别的原因究竟在哪里呢？演讲一开头，奥巴马首先以个人的身份，表明了自己肩负责任之重大，然后还是以个人的身份感谢了美国前总统小布什对自己工作的配合，此后第一人称单数"I"几乎就再未出现，代替出场的是第一人称复数"we"，这是因为他这时已然是美国总统，演讲时代表的是美国政府，需要弥合民主党与共和党之间的裂痕，同时也需要团结美国

第十一章 人际功能

民众。所以后面他一直以第一人称复数"we"出现，这是合情合理的。另外，"we"的频繁使用也在表达奥巴马背后有强大的支持力量，这会给美国民众以及盟国政府和它们的人民以巨大的信心。

可要是你以为奥巴马演讲时总会使用"we"，很少使用"I"，那可就大错特错了。请看奥巴马 2009 年 9 月 8 日访问弗吉尼亚州阿灵顿市韦克菲尔德高中时发表的演讲，这篇演讲相当于在开学第一课发表讲话。

代词系统人际功能实例分析 2

Remarks by the President in a National Address to America's School Children (2009)

THE PRESIDENT: Hello, everybody! Thank you. Thank you. Thank you, everybody. All right, everybody go ahead and have a seat. How is everybody doing today? (Applause.) How about Tim Spicer? (Applause.) *I* am here with students at Wakefield High School in Arlington, Virginia. And we've got students tuning in from all across America, from kindergarten through 12th grade. And *I* am just so glad that all could join us today. And *I* want to thank Wakefield for being such an outstanding host. Give yourselves a big round of applause. (Applause.)

...

Now, your families, your teachers, and *I* are doing everything *we* can to make sure you have the education you need to answer these questions. *I*'m working hard to fix up your classrooms and get you the books and the equipment and the computers you need to learn. But you've got to do your part, too. So *I* expect all of you to get serious this year. *I* expect you to put your best effort into everything you do. *I* expect great things from each of you. So don't let us down. Don't let your family down or your country down. Most of all, don't let yourself down. Make us all proud.

经过统计，在这个演讲中，奥巴马一共使用了 48 次"I"，上面的段落只是其中的一小部分。而使用"we"的次数是多少呢？答案是一共 6 次。这个情况与就职演讲简直完全颠倒过来。原因是什么呢？因为这个演讲是对全美学生直播的，观看的对象基本是中小学生和幼儿园的孩子。为了能够让自己的演讲更容易被孩子们接受，奥巴马当然要放下总统的身段，更多地使用"I"，并把自己当年求学时的感受与大家分享，以凸显个人的经历和体会，这样才更有可能达到教育学生的初衷。要是过多地使用"we"，就容易产生一种高高在上的感觉，容易拉开与学生的距离。因此，我们在写作和翻译时都要注意这一点。

代词系统人际功能统实例分析 3

HAMLET	Now, mother, what's the matter?
QUEEN GERTRUDE	Hamlet, *thou* hast thy father much offended.
HAMLET	Mother, *you* have my father much offended.
QUEEN GERTRUDE	Come, come, *you* answer with an idle tongue.
HAMLET	Go, go, *you* question with a wicked tongue.

183

QUEEN GERTRUDE	Why, how now, Hamlet!
HAMLET	What's the matter now?
QUEEN GERTRUDE	Have *you* forgot me?
HAMLET	No, by the rood, not so:
	You are the queen, your husband's brother's wife;
	And—would it were not so!—*you* are my mother.
QUEEN GERTRUDE	Nay, then, I'll set those to *you* that can speak.
HAMLET	Come, come, and sit *you* down; *you* shall not budge;
	You go not till I set *you* up a glass
	Where *you* may see the inmost part of *you*.
QUEEN GERTRUDE	What wilt *thou* do? *thou* wilt not murder me?
	Help, help, ho!

(Scene iv, Act III, *Hamlet*)

哈　母亲，您叫我有什么事？

后　哈姆雷特，你已经大大得罪了你的父亲啦！

哈　母亲，您已经大大得罪了我的父亲啦！

后　来，来，不要用这种胡说八道的话回答我。

哈　去，去，不要用这种胡说八道的话问我。

后　啊，怎么，哈姆雷特！

哈　现在又是什么事？

后　你忘记了我吗？

哈　不，凭着十字架起誓，我没有忘记你；你是王后，你的丈夫的兄弟的妻子；你又是我的母亲，——但愿你不是！

后　哎哟！那么我要去叫那些会说话的人来跟你谈谈了。

哈　来，来，坐下来，不要动；我要把一面镜子放在你的面前，让你看一看自己的灵魂。

后　你要干什么呀？你不是要杀我吗？救命呀，救命呀！

（朱生豪译）

上例是哈姆雷特用一出名为"捕鼠器"的戏剧弄清了国王克劳迪厄斯是谋害父亲的凶手，其母葛楚德王后认为哈姆雷特的做法冒犯了新王，于是召见哈姆雷特问话，哈姆雷特借机质问母亲。上例中"you/thou"交替使用，"you"共出现13次，"thou"共出现3次：王后开始以"thou"称呼儿子，表示母子关系亲密；听到儿子语气生硬后改用"you"表示对儿子的不满；感觉生命受到威胁时又改用"thou"借以拉近距离，唤起怜悯。哈姆雷特始终以尊称"you"来称呼母亲，但语气生硬，饱含讽刺。王后交替使用"you"和"thou"，表现其态度和情感的变化，哈姆雷特使用礼貌性代词的背后暗含着对母亲的不满，此处"you"和"thou"体现的社会语用意义需要在译文中有所体现。

第十一章 人际功能

称谓系统人际功能实例分析 1：简·爱与约翰的关系

With Bewick on my knee, I was then happy: happy at least in my way. I feared nothing but interruption, and that came too soon. The breakfast-room door opened.

"Boh! *Madam Mope!*" cried the voice of John Reed; then he paused: he found the room apparently empty.

"*Where the dickens is she!*" he continued. "*Lizzy! Georgy!* (calling to his sisters) Joan is not here: tell mama she is run out into the rain—*bad animal!*" (Chapter 1, *Jane Eyre*)

此处的语境是在一个深秋的下午，外面下着冷雨，小简·爱独自一人在早餐室看书。为了躲避表哥约翰的欺辱，她躲在窗帘后面，坐在窗台上，专心致志地翻看《英国鸟类史》。这时，约翰走进早餐室来寻找简·爱，他平日里欺负表妹都已成为习惯，于是使用的称谓语是"Madam Mope"。Madam 意思是指任性妄为的年轻女子，该词不同于 Madame，那个词才是对女士的尊称，而 Mope 是闷闷不乐的意思，约翰这么称呼简·爱，明显是在嘲讽对方，也间接地反映了简·爱平时极不开心的生活状态。约翰还使用了表达强烈情绪并带有粗俗特征的短语"the dickens"，最后又称呼简·爱为"bad animal"然而，约翰对自己的两个亲妹妹使用的却是正常的昵称"Lizzy"和"Georgy"。这些称谓语真实体现了约翰与小简·爱之间恶劣的人际关系。

"It is well I drew the curtain," thought I; and I wished fervently he might not discover my hiding-place: nor would *John Reed* have found it out himself; he was not quick either of vision or conception; but *Eliza* just put her head in at the door, and said at once—

"She is in the window-seat, to be sure, *Jack*."

And I came out immediately, for I trembled at the idea of being dragged forth by the said Jack. "*What do you want?*" I asked, with awkward diffidence.

"*Say, 'What do you want, Master Reed?*'" was the answer. "I want you to come here;" and seating himself in an arm-chair, he intimated by a gesture that I was to approach and stand before him. (Chapter 1, *Jane Eyre*)

此处语境承接上一个例子，小简·爱对表哥约翰的称谓语为"John Reed"，这种称呼全名而非称呼名字的做法体现了二人之间冷漠的人际关系。小简·爱接下来称呼自己的表姐为"Eliza"，就是 Elizabeth 的简称，不是昵称"Lizzy"，也不是全称"Elizabeth Reed"，这体现了她与表姐之间不冷不热的状态。而 Eliza Reed 称呼约翰为"Jack"，这明显体现出良好的姐弟关系。在被约翰发现藏身之处后，小简·爱对表哥脱口而出的竟是"What do you want?"，这里面没有任何称谓语，除了体现出两人的冷漠关系之外，还体现了小简·爱当时非常害怕的心情。约翰则使用了祈使句的语气结构，并强迫表妹称呼自己为"Master Reed"，这明显说明约翰是把简·爱当作仆人来看待，而非自己的表妹。通过称谓的选择，这个例子进一步显示了小简·爱与表哥约翰之间的关系有多么糟糕。

称谓系统人际功能实例分析 2：简·爱与里德舅妈的关系

"I don't know. I asked *Aunt Reed* once, and she said possibly I might have some poor, low relations called Eyre, but she knew nothing about them."

...

"I cannot tell; *Aunt Reed* says if I have any, they must be a beggarly set: I should not like to go a begging." (Chapter 3, *Jane Eyre*)

这里的语境是，小简·爱在与表哥约翰发生严重冲突之后便生病了，而且还病得比较严重。劳埃德医生当晚便被请来给小简·爱看病，第三天中午又来看望小简·爱。这两段是小简·爱与劳埃德医生的对话。由于里德舅妈一家人不在场，再加上小简·爱的身体变好了一些，于是小简·爱的情绪较为平静。面对劳埃德医生，小简·爱提起里德舅妈时，用的是"Aunt Reed"这种比较正常的称谓语。

"Who could want me?" I asked inwardly, as with both hands I turned the stiff doorhandle, which, for a second or two, resisted my efforts. "What should I see besides *Aunt Reed* in the apartment?—a man or a woman?" The handle turned, the door unclosed, and passing through and curtseying low, I looked up at—a black pillar!—such, at least, appeared to me, at first sight, the straight, narrow, sable-clad shape standing erect on the rug: the grim face at the top was like a carved mask, placed above the shaft by way of capital. (Chapter 4, *Jane Eyre*)

这里的语境是，在与约翰那次冲突之后，又过了两个多月，小简·爱虽然与里德舅妈一家人的关系依旧冷淡，可是这时的心情已经比较平静了。有一天，里德舅妈派保姆贝茜去找小简·爱，并告诉她去早餐室见一位客人。在推门去见客人之前，小简·爱的心里有了这段独白，此时她有些忐忑，但情绪还算平静，因此指代舅妈时用的是正常的称谓语"Aunt Reed"。

"How dare I, Mrs. Reed? How dare I? Because it is the truth. You think I have no feelings, and that I can do without one bit of love or kindness; but I cannot live so: and you have no pity. I shall remember how you thrust me back—roughly and violently thrust me back—into the red-room, and locked me up there, to my dying day; though I was in agony; though I cried out, while suffocating with distress, 'Have mercy! Have mercy, *Aunt Reed!*' And that punishment you made me suffer because your wicked boy struck me—knocked me down for nothing. I will tell anybody who asks me questions, this exact tale. People think you a good woman, but you are bad, hard-hearted. You are deceitful!" (Chapter 4, *Jane Eyre*)

这里的语境是，小简·爱在进入早餐室后，知道了要见自己的人是布罗克赫斯特先生。不过，小简·爱与这位先生的会面并不愉快，而里德舅妈还当着客人的面污蔑简·爱喜欢撒谎。在客人离开后，小简·爱与舅妈发生了激烈的争吵，争吵期间她回忆起两个多月前与约翰的那次冲突，当时里德舅妈非常粗暴地把她关进了红屋子。小简·爱毕竟只是个十岁的孩子，心里还是很害怕里德舅妈的，于是请求舅妈不要粗暴对待自己，并且使用了"Aunt Reed"的称谓。对于一个孩子来说，这也是无奈却合乎情理的选择。

"Is this Jane Eyre?" she said.

第十一章 人际功能

"Yes, <u>Aunt Reed</u>. How are you, <u>dear aunt</u>?"
...
"It is I, <u>Aunt Reed</u>."
"Who—I?" was her answer. "Who are you?" looking at me with surprise and a sort of alarm, but still not wildly. "You are quite a stranger to me—where is Bessie?"
"She is at the lodge, <u>aunt</u>."
"<u>Aunt</u>," she repeated. "<u>Who calls me aunt?</u> You are not one of the Gibsons; and yet I know you—that face, and the eyes and forehead, are quiet familiar to me: you are like—why, you are like Jane Eyre!" (Chapter 21, *Jane Eyre*)

这里的语境是，随着故事的发展，小简·爱长成了十八九岁的大姑娘，不仅在罗沃德学校顺利完成了学业，还留在那里工作了两年，最后通过应聘的方式，去罗切斯特先生家里当了家庭教师。有一天，简·爱收到一封信，得知里德舅妈生了重病，将不久于人世。知道这个消息后，简·爱跟罗切斯特先生请了个假，然后便即刻前往盖茨黑德府探望舅妈。此时的简·爱已经是大人了，而且成熟了很多，她知道这时自己应该做的就是对临终前的舅妈给予原谅和温暖。所以，简·爱对舅妈使用的称谓语是"Aunt Reed""dear aunt"和"aunt"。而里德舅妈听到有人叫自己"aunt"之后，显得很困惑，因为这种称谓语在她的记忆中非常模糊，毕竟简·爱全书中称呼她为"Aunt Reed"一共才六次，这足以显示出两人的关系多么冰冷。

I was a discord in Gateshead Hall: I was like nobody there; I had nothing in harmony with <u>Mrs. Reed</u> or <u>her children</u>, or her chosen vassalage. If they did not love me, in fact, as little did I love them. They were not bound to regard with affection a thing that could not sympathise with one amongst them; a heterogeneous thing, opposed to them in temperament, in capacity, in propensities; a useless thing, incapable of serving their interest, or adding to their pleasure; a noxious thing, cherishing the germs of indignation at their treatment, of contempt of their judgment. I know that had I been a sanguine, brilliant, careless, exacting, handsome, romping child—though equally dependent and friendless—<u>Mrs. Reed</u> would have endured my presence more complacently; <u>her children</u> would have entertained for me more of the cordiality of fellow-feeling; the servants would have been less prone to make me the scapegoat of the nursery. (Chapter 2, *Jane Eyre*)

简而言之，简·爱在绝大部分时间里对里德舅妈以"Mrs. Reed"进行称谓，用以称呼对方或叙述事件，正如上面这一段落所显示的那样。根据对全书的统计，简·爱使用"Mrs. Reed"来称呼里德舅妈的次数高达71次，这充分反映出简·爱与舅妈非常冷漠的人际关系。而在上面一段指称表哥和表姐时，简·爱使用的是"her children"，而不是"my cousins"，这些证据足以说明了简·爱与里德舅妈一家人关系冷漠，毫无感情。

总之，上述称谓语的使用变化清晰地勾勒出简·爱与盖茨黑德府一家人偶有温情，但人际关系总体上冷漠乃至仇恨的状态。

(三) 情态系统 (Modality System)

情态系统是人际意义的重要组成部分，是讲话者对自己所讲观点的成功性和提议的有效性所做的判断，体现为归一性和情态性两种情况。归一性体现为肯定与否定二者的对立，是语法化的范畴。情态性要么体现为在陈述或提问中对概率或频率的判断，要么体现为在命令或提供中要求对方承担义务或自我表达意愿的程度。下面请看归一性和情态性的定义：

1. 归一性 (Polarity)

POLARITY is the resource for assessing the arguability value of a clause: yes or no—the validity of a proposition ("it is/it isn't") or the actualization of a proposal ("do/don't!"). In the system of POLARITY, the option "positive" is unmarked, whereas "negative" is marked. (*Key Terms in Systemic Functional Linguistics*)

归一性是一种评价小句争议性的量值："是"还是"否"——观点的正确性（即"it is"还是"it isn't"）或者是提议的可行性（即"do"还是"don't!"）。在归一性这个系统中，"肯定"选项是无标记的，而"否定"选项是有标记的。

(《系统功能语言学核心术语》)

归一性的理论价值在于，一个小句的意义若是涉及到了归一性，即观点要么正确，要么错误，或者是提议要么可行，要么不可行，这时译者要对归一性进行准确地再现。换言之，在原小句中，正确就是正确，错误就是错误，可行就是可行，不可行就是不可行，译者绝对不可以弄错。

简而言之，归一性谈论的是情态系统中肯定与否定两极表达的问题，但我们深知，这个世界的许多事情并不是非黑即白那么简单，而肯定与否定中间还有大片过渡地带，这就是情态性要探讨的问题了。

2. 情态性 (Modality)

Expressions of indeterminacy between the positive and negative poles, which interpersonally construct the semantic region of uncertainty that lies between "yes" and "no". Interpersonal meanings that grade **propositions** (statements, questions) and **proposals** (commands, offers) in terms of these poles include "probability", for example, *of course she **might** have changed recently*, "usuality", for example, *it is **usually** military, economical and political terror*, "obligation", for example, *you **should** not tantalize your commanding officer*, and "inclination", for example, *I **would** rather get married to my husband*. Both probability and usuality modalize propositions whereas obligation and inclination modalize proposals. In order to keep them distinct, the former is referred to **modalization** and the latter **modulation**. (*Key Terms in Systemic Functional Linguistics*)

在肯定与否定两极间的不确定表达，即在人际功能上构建出居于"是"和"否"之间的不确定语义表达区。在肯定和否定间为**"观点"**（陈述，提问）和**"提议"**（命令、提供）分级的人际意义包括"概率"，例如，当然，她近来**也许**（*might*）做出了改变，"频率"，例如，这**通常**（*usually*）是出于军事目的、经济目的和政治目的的恐怖行动，"义务"，

第十一章 人际功能

例如，你**不应该**（*should*）挑逗你的指挥官，"意愿"，例如，我**宁愿**（*would rather*）跟我丈夫结婚。概率和频率使得观点具有情态性，而义务和意愿使得提议具有情态性。为了使二者有区分，前者被称为**情态化**（modalization），后者被称为**意态化**（modulation）。

（《系统功能语言学核心术语》）

韩礼德等（2017: 148）对情态性的两种类型情态化与意态化归纳为如下表格。为方便读者准确理解，表格中的英文词语和例句特别添加了汉语翻译。

交换物	言语功能		中介类型		典型体现	例子
信息	观点	陈述	情态化	概率 possible（有可能的） /probable（比较有可能的） /certain（确定无疑的）	情态动词 情态副词 以上二者	① They must have known. 他们一定已经知道。 ② They certainly know. 他们当然知道（这一点）。 ③ They certainly must have known. 他们毫无疑问肯定都知道了。
		提问		频率 sometimes（有时） /usually（通常） /always（每次都是）	情态动词 情态副词 以上二者	① It will happen. 这经常会发生。 ② It always happens. 这总是会发生。 ③ It must always happen. 确定无疑，这总会发生。
物品与服务	提议	命令	意态化	义务 allowed（可以） /supposed（应该） /required（按照规定，应该去作）	情态动词 被动谓语动词	① You must be patient. 你必须要耐心。 ② You're required to be patient. 按照规定，你必须耐心。
		提供		意愿 willing（愿意做某事） /anxious（渴望做某事） /determined（决意做某事）	情态动词 谓语化形容词	① I must win. （因为某些规定，或因为形势需要）我必须要获胜。 ② I'm determined to win. 我决意去获取胜利。

（胡壮麟等，2017: 148）

我们之前在学习语气系统时了解到，人们的言语沟通中有两种交换物，一是信息，二是物品与服务。信息包括陈述与提问两种言语功能，物品与服务包括命令与提供两种言语功能。在这个表格里，我们可以看到，陈述与提问这两种言语功能被称为观点，而命令与提供这两种言语功能被称为提议。观点的中介是情态化表达，有概率和频率两种类型；其中概率的典型体现方式有情态动词、情态副词，或者是二者的结合；频率的典型体现方式也是情态动词、情态副词，或者是二者的结合。而提议的中介是意态化表达，有义务和意愿两种类型。其中命令的典型体现方式有情态动词和被动谓语动词；提供的典型体现方式有情态动词和谓语化形容词。不难看出，情态动词对于情态性的表达至关重要，这也是我们在学习英语时碰到的难点之一。需要特别说明的是，表达概率、频率、义务和意愿的情态性词汇是按照程度由低到高的顺序排列，但并不表示情态性词汇只有表格中的这些，它们只是代表和典型而已。

根据韩礼德和迈西森（2004/2008：620）的研究，情态性具有四种取向，即在表达时可能会体现为主观显性、主观隐性、客观显性或客观隐性。也就是说，因为措辞不同，头脑中的某些想法表达出来后，给人的感觉很不一样。具体请看下面的表格。为方便读者准确理解，表格中的英文词语和例句特别添加了汉语翻译。

情态性	主观显性	主观隐性	客观显性	客观隐性
情态化：概率	I think (in my opinion) Mary knows. 我认为（在我看来）玛丽是知道的。	Mary'll know. ('ll：可能) 玛丽可能知道（这个事情）。	It's likely that Mary knows. 玛丽知道（这个事情），这看起来是很有可能的。	Mary probably knows. 玛丽比较有可能知道（这个事情）。
情态化：频率	无	Fred'll sit quite quiet. ('ll：总是) 弗雷德总是安静地坐着。	It's usual for Fred to sit quite quiet. 多数时候，弗雷德会安静地坐着。	Fred usually sits quite quiet. 弗雷德多数时候会安静地坐着。
意态化：义务	I want John to go. 我想让约翰去。	John should go. 约翰应当去。	It's expected that John goes. 约翰去，这是人们的期望。	John's supposed to go. 约翰按理说会去。
意态化：意愿	无	Jane'll help. ('ll：愿意) 简愿意帮忙 / 简准备帮忙。	无	Jane's keen to help. 简渴望帮忙 / 简很想帮忙。

（Halliday & Matthiessen, 2004/2008: 620）

鉴于表格的理解有些难度，这里做一些较为详尽的解释。请看第二行。同样是在体现情态化，表达你对事情发生可能性的判断，也就是表达概率，要是你说"I think Mary knows.（In my opinion Mary knows.）"你的意思就是"我认为玛丽是知道的（在我看来，玛丽是知道的。）"这种表达是在突出你的主观看法，而且 I think 或者 In my opinion 显而易见具有主观色彩，这叫做主观显性表达。要是你说"Mary'll know."你就是在说，玛丽可能知道（这个事情）。这种句子因为使用了情态动词 will，所以也是

第十一章 人际功能

在表达你的主观看法，不过比较隐晦，这叫做主观隐性表达。要是你说"It's likely that Mary knows."你的意思是说，玛丽知道（这个事情），这看起来是很有可能的。这种 It 做形式主语，后接 that 主语从句的句式很巧妙，它比较容易呈现出客观的感觉，而且这种客观感觉显而易见，好像玛丽知道这个事情是人人都知道的，不单单是你自己的看法，这叫做客观显性表达。要是你说"Mary probably knows."你的意思就是，玛丽比较有可能知道（这个事情）。这种说法看起来也比较客观，因为没有情态动词出现，使用的只是情态副词 probably，所以这叫做客观隐性表达。

再看一下表格里意态化中表达义务的例子。要是你说"I want John to go."意思就是，我想让约翰去。这样的表达是在突显你的主观想法，你在表达你的意愿，而这个意愿会变成约翰的义务，他得前去。这叫做主观显性表达。要是你说"John should go."你的意思就是，约翰应当去。这种句子因为使用了情态动词 should，所以也是在表达你的主观看法，不过比较隐晦，这叫做主观隐性表达。要是你说"It's expected that John goes."你的意思就是，约翰去，这是人们的期望。这种 It 做形式主语，后面接 that 主语从句的句式很巧妙，它比较容易呈现出客观的感觉，而且这种客观感觉显而易见，结果就是约翰去不是你的期望，而是大家期盼他去，你则躲在了幕后，这叫做客观显性表达。要是你说"John's supposed to go."你的意思就是，约翰按理说会去。这种说法看起来也比较客观，因为没用情态动词，用的只是谓语化形容词 supposed，重点在于强调按照规定，或者说按照常理，约翰会去的，结果说话人自己的意愿被隐藏了起来，所以这叫做客观隐性表达。

剩下的两组例句，大家可以自行分析和感悟一下，这种主观和客观的划分，对于我们中国人尤其重要。因为我们使用汉语时，往往习惯于从主观视角出发，这样久而久之，会对英语的客观性说法反应迟钝，依然使用我们所熟悉的主观表达形式去翻译，这样容易造成意义的扭曲，也会对译文读者产生不好的影响。

简而言之，语言表达真的是一门艺术。你在写作时到底是想突出自己的主观想法，还是想把自己的表达伪装得客观一些，这都取决于你的措辞水平。所以，我们不能不慎重。同样，译者在翻译时也要注意这一点，要审视译文的情态性与原文的情态性是否已经一致，还是不经意间改变了原文作者的说话口吻。这些都特别值得我们关注。

韩礼德和迈西森（2004/2008: 620）对情态性的三种量值也用下面的表格做了归纳。为方便读者准确理解，表格中的英文词语和例句特别添加了汉语翻译。

情态性	概率	频率	义务	意愿
高值	certain 确定无疑的	always 每次都是	required 按照规定，应该去做	determined 决意做某事
中值	probable 比较有可能的	usually 通常	supposed 应该	keen 渴望做某事
低值	possible 有可能的	sometimes 有时	allowed 可以	willing 愿意做某事

（Halliday & Matthiessen, 2004/2008: 620）

这个简单的表格告诉我们，情态性可以较为简单地划分为低值、中值和高值。在表达概率的代表性词汇中，possible 表达的概率最低，大概只有一半的可能；probable 在说话人看来，可能性肯定要高于 50%，不过最高也就是 80%~90%；而 certain 的可能性就近乎于 100% 了。在表达频率的代表性词汇中，sometimes 意思是有时会出现，但次数不多；usually 表示次数很多，多数时候都会出现；而 always 则表示每次都会这样，从无例外，也就是"总会、总是"。在表达义务的代表性词汇中，allowed 表示的是经人允许后，可以去做，自身要做的义务性比较弱；supposed 表示了较强的义务性，往往符合了人们的期待；而 required 的义务性最强，这不仅是人们的期待了，而是规定、规则要求人们必须去做。在表达意愿的代表性词汇中，willing 只表示某人对做某事有一定的意愿，表达的是较为喜欢的意思；keen 也表达喜欢，只是这种想做的想法已经比较强烈了；而 determined 则不仅仅是非常喜欢的问题，该词还强调了内在的决心，强调哪怕碰到再多的困难，也要努力去做好的坚定意愿。总而言之，作为译者，我们要对情态性的量值比较敏感，人家本来表达高值，我们也要翻译成高值，不能翻成中值，更不能翻成低值。

基于上述研究，情态系统整体结构可以用下面的树形结构图显示：

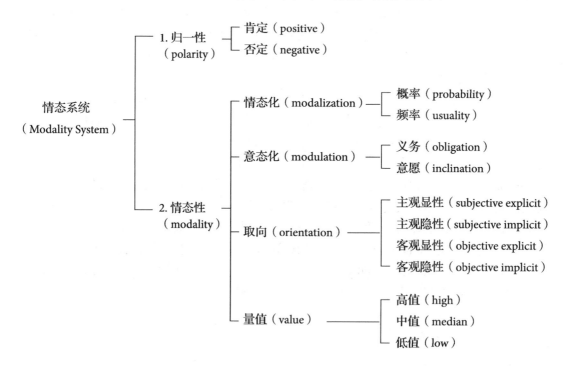

（四）评价系统（Appraisal）

评价系统（也称评价理论）是系统功能语言学在对人际意义研究中发展起来的新的语法框架，它主要关注协调社会关系的态度的表达。评价系统分为三个子系统：态度、介入和级差。态度系统是评价系统的核心理论，分为情感（对自身情感的评价）、判定

（对他人品行的评价）、鉴别（对事物价值的评价）三个次子系统。介入系统指态度的来源，分为单声，也称自言（态度源于自身）和多声，也称借言（态度源于他者）两个次子系统。级差系统指评价的强度，分为语势（评价力度是大还是小）和聚焦（评价表达清晰还是模糊）两个次子系统。整个评价系统结构如下图所示：

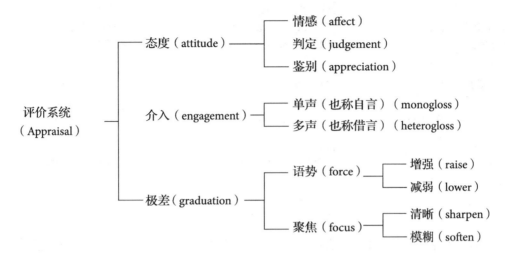

1. 态度系统（Attitude）

态度系统是评价系统的核心理论，包括情感、判定和鉴别三个子系统。说话人在用态度系统表达自身、评价人物或事件时，其实是在邀请听话人去理解及分享那种情绪反应，或者至少希望对方不对这种反应产生负面情绪。而一旦人们接受了这种情绪表达，交际双方的情感便有可能产生共鸣，进而产生深入交流的可能，甚至会对彼此的意识形态持包容的态度。反过来说，态度系统的表达若未收到良好的反应，后续交流便可能难以为继。下面我们将对情感系统、判定系统和鉴别系统的定义和主要内容做系统而简明的介绍。

1) 情感系统（Affect）

Affect is one of the basic types of APPRAISAL in the description of English presented in Martin & White (2005/2007). It is a term in the system of attitude, contrasting with judgement and appreciation. In the typology of affect proposed by Martin & White (2007: 49-64), three are three types: un/happiness——affairs of heart, in/security——emotions concerned with ecosocial well-being and dis/satisfaction——emotions concerned with the pursuit of goals.

(*Key Terms in Systemic Functional Linguistics*)

情感是马丁和怀特（2005/2007）在描绘英语时提出的评价系统中的基本类型之一，是态度系统中的一个术语，与判定和鉴别相对。在两人提出的情感类型中，共有三种划分：不幸福/幸福——有关心的感觉，不安全/安全——有关生态社会的福祉，不满意/满意——关系到对目标追求的情感。

（《系统功能语言学核心术语》）

马丁和怀特（2005: 46-51）将情感系统的特征和分类总结为如下两个表格：

（1）情感系统的特征（The Characteristics of Affect）

情感系统	举例	语法分析
情感成为"特征" - 描写参与者 - 成为参与者属性 - 过程的方式	A *sad* captain. The captain was *sad*. The captain left *sadly*.	成为修饰语 描写主语属性 描写环境角色
情感成为"过程" - 受情感影响的心理过程 - 受情感影响的行为过程	His departure *upset* him. He *missed* them. The captain *wept*.	担当心理过程 担当心理过程 担当行为过程
情感成为"评论" - 表达意愿	*Sadly*, he had to go.	由情态副词担任
情感成为"话题" - 表达潜在情绪	My *happiness* then was beyond words.	由抽象名词担任

上面这个表格给我们如下启示：第一，情感成为"特征"时，可以用于描写参与者，例如，"a sad captain"，sad 是参与者 captain 的修饰语，成为该词的特征；情感还能成为参与者属性，例如，"The captain was sad."，sad 就是参与者 captain 的属性，也可以说是主语 captain 的属性；情感也可以成为过程的方式，例如，"The captain left sadly." sadly 就是 left 这个动作过程的方式，也可以说是扮演了环境角色。

第二，情感可以成为"过程"，例如，这两个小句——"His departure upset him."和"He missed them." upset 和 missed 这两个动词都体现了心理过程，也就是跟我们的心理思维活动有关系；而在"The captain wept."这个例子中，wept 则表示行为过程，是受情感影响后而产生的行为——哭泣。

第三，情感也能成为"评论"，例如，"Sadly, he had to go." Sadly 作为表达情态的副词，在这里成为说话人的评论，表达了说话人的意愿，即不希望这样悲伤的事情发生。

第四，情感还能成为"话题"，例如，"My happiness then was beyond words."，抽象名词 happiness 在小句中表达了一种潜在的情绪——说话人很不开心。

综合上面的例子，我们发现情感可能无处不在。所以，我们做翻译时要留意潜藏于字里行间的情感，毕竟不仅形容词和副词能表达情感，就连名词和动词也可以表达情感。

（2）情感系统的分类（The Classification of Affect）

限于篇幅，这里只选取了原表格中的部分例子。

情感系统分类 （Affect）	积极情感倾向 （Positive）	消极情感倾向 （Negative）
a. 幸福 vs. 不幸福 (happiness vs. unhappiness)	cheerful, buoyant, jubilant; like, love, adore	sad, melancholy, despondent; broken-hearted, heavy-hearted, sick at heart

续表

情感系统分类 （Affect）	积极情感倾向 （Positive）	消极情感倾向 （Negative）
b. 安全 vs. 不安全 (security vs. insecurity)	together, confident, assured; comfortable, confident, trusting	uneasy, anxious, freaked out; startled, surprised, astonished
c. 满意 vs. 不满意 (satisfaction vs. dissatisfaction)	involved, absorbed, engrossed; satisfied, pleased, chuffed; impressed, charmed, thrilled	flat, stale, jaded; cross, angry, furious; bored with, sick of, fed up with

对于情感系统的分类，我们不必关注，要把握的是它的两种倾向：积极情感倾向和消极情感倾向。这种划分其实类似于我们所说的褒义和贬义。例如：cheerful（令人愉快的）、buoyant（愉快而充满信心的）、jubilant（喜气洋洋的），这一组词都表达幸福的情感，具有积极情感倾向，而sad（令人悲哀的）、melancholy（令人沮丧的）、despondent（垂头丧气的），这一组词都表达不幸福的情感，具有消极情感倾向。我们翻译的时候只需要把握词汇的准确含义和情感倾向即可。

2）判定系统（Judgement）

One of the basic types of APPRAISAL in the description of English presented in Martin & White (2005/2007). It is a term in the system of attitude, contrasting with affect and appreciation. Judgement is the resource for enacting judgements in terms of some parameter of people, typically of their behaviour. The parameters in terms of which judgements are made are social esteem and social sanction. Lexical realization of personal judgement depends on "normality" (how special? For example, lucky/unlucky), "capacity" (how capable? for example, powerful/weak) and "tenacity" (how dependable? for example, brave/cowardly), and moral judgement depends on "veracity" (how honest? for example, honest/dishonest) and "propriety" (how ethical? for example, good/bad). Grammatically, judgements are realizationally linked to modality.

(*Key Terms in Systemic Functional Linguistics*)

判定是马丁和怀特（2005/2007）在描绘英语时提出的评价系统中的基本类型之一，是态度系统中的一个术语，与情感和鉴别相对。判定作为一种资源，用于对人们的一些方面做出判定，尤其是行为。判定参数有社会尊严（即个人判定）和社会许可（即道德判定）两种类型。个人评判的词汇体现取决于"常态"（即有多特别？例如，幸运/不幸运），"能力"（即多有能力？例如，强大/虚弱），"韧性"（即可信任程度？例如，勇敢/怯懦）；道德评判取决于"真实性"（即有多诚实？例如，诚实/不诚实）和"适当性"（即有多符合道德规范？例如，正派/邪恶）。在语法方面，判定的实现与情态系统有关。

（《系统功能语言学核心术语》）

马丁和怀特（2005: 53）将判定系统分为社会尊严和社会许可两大类，并从积极倾向和消极倾向两个角度对这两类再进行细分，具体请见下面两个表格。限于篇幅，这里只选取了原表格中的部分例子。

社会尊严（指个人判定） （Social Esteem）	积极判定倾向 （Positive [admire]）	消极判定倾向 （Negative [criticise]）
① 常态 （normality "how special?"）	normal, natural, familiar...; in, fashionable, avant garde...; lucky, fortunate, charmed...	odd, peculiar, eccentric...; dated, daggy, retrograde...; unlucky, hapless, star-crossed...
② 能力 （capacity "how capable?"）	powerful, vigorous, robust...; sound, healthy, fit...; insightful, clever, gifted...	mild, weak, whimpy...; unsound, sick, crippled...; slow, stupid, thick...;
③ 韧性 （tenacity "how dependable?"）	plucky, brave, heroic...; cautious, wary, patient...; faithful, loyal, constant...	timid, cowardly, gutless...; rash, impatient, impetuous...; unfaithful, disloyal, inconstant...

社会许可（指道德判定） （Social Sanction）	积极判定倾向 （Positive [admire]）	消极判定倾向 （Negative [criticise]）
① 真实性 （veracity [truth] "how honest?"）	truthful, honest, credible...; frank, candid, direct...; discrete, tactful...	dishonest, deceitful, lying...; deceptive, manipulative, devious...; blunt, blabbermouth...
② 适当性 （propriety [ethics] "how far beyond reproach?"）	good, moral, ethical...; law abiding, fair, just...; sensitive, kind, caring...; polite, respectful, reverent...	bad, immoral, evil...; corrupt, unfair, unjust...; insensitive, mean, cruel...; rude, discourteous, irreverent...

简单地说，判定系统就是对人的道德方面和道德以外的其他方面所作的评价，这个分类对于社会学的研究有一定的价值，但是对翻译实践没有意义，不过积极判定倾向和消极判定倾向还是有意义的。例如，在对人们的社会许可（即道德）进行判定时，我们应该知道 truthful（诚实的）、honest（正直的）、credible（可以信任的）这一组词汇对个人道德给予了积极倾向的判定。而另一组词汇 dishonest（不正直的）、deceitful（欺骗人的）、lying（说谎的）则对个人道德给予了消极倾向的判定。作为译者，我们要把握住词语的准确含义，同时要把握住词语的情感倾向，即到底是积极判定倾向，还是消极判定倾向。

3）鉴别系统（Appreciation）

One of the basic types of APPRAISAL in the description of English presented in Martin & White (2005/2007). It is a term in the system of attitude, contrasting with judgement and affect. Appreciation is a resource for evaluating phenomena in "aesthetic" terms, either subjectively ("I like it") or objectively ("it is pleasing"). Martin & White classify appreciation into three subtypes—reaction (glossed as "did it grab me?" "did I like it?"), composition ("did it hang together?" "was it hard to follow?"), and valuation ("was it worthwhile?").

(*Key Terms in Systemic Functional Linguistics*)

第十一章 人际功能

鉴别是马丁和怀特（2005/2007）在描绘英语时提出的评价系统中的基本类型之一，是态度系统中的一个术语，与判定和情感相对。鉴别作为一种资源，用于从美学视角对现象做出评价，而评价方式或者突出主观（例如，"我喜欢这个"）或者突出客体（例如，这很令人喜欢）。马丁和怀特把鉴别分成三种次类型——反应（可解释为"它吸引我了吗？""我喜欢它吗？"），构成（可解释为"它组合在一起了吗？""它难以跟上吗？"），和估值（可解释为"它值得付出多少时间、金钱或努力？"）。

（《系统功能语言学核心术语》）

马丁和怀特（2005: 56）将鉴别系统分为反应、构成和估值三类，并依然从积极倾向和消极倾向两个角度对这三类再进行细分，具体请见下面表格。限于篇幅，这里只选取了原表格中的部分例子。

鉴别 （appreciation）	积极鉴别倾向 （positive [admire]）	消极鉴别倾向 （negative [criticise]）
1. 反应： ① 影响 （"did it grab me?"） ② 品质 （"did I like it?"）	fascinating, exciting, moving ...; lively, dramatic, intense ...; okay, fine, good ...; lovely, beautiful, splendid ...	dry, ascetic, uninviting ...; flat, predictable, monotonous ...; bad, yuk, nasty ...; plain, ugly, grotesque ...
2. 构成： ① 均衡性 （"did it hang together?"） ② 复杂度 （"was it hard to follow?"）	balanced, harmonious, unified, symmetrical, proportioned ...; consistent, logical ...; lucid, clear, precise ...; intricate, detailed, precise ...	unbalanced, discordant, irregular, uneven, flawed ...; contradictory, disorganised ...; arcane, unclear, woolly ...; plain, monolithic, simplistic ...
3. 估值： （"was it worthwhile?"）	authentic, real, genuine ...; valuable, priceless, worthwhile ...; appropriate, helpful, effective ...	fake, bogus, glitzy ...; worthless, shoddy, pricey ...; ineffective, useless, write-off ...

简而言之，鉴别是对事物或现象做出的评价。与前面的情感系统和判定系统一样，鉴别系统的分类对于翻译没什么意义，但是积极鉴别倾向和消极鉴别倾向的划分还是有意义的，我们在翻译实践时要注意这一点。

2. 介入系统（Engagement）

作为区分责任的语言资源，介入是评价系统中关于态度来源方式的子系统，它关注的是言语进行人际意义或概念意义协商的方式。介入可以分为两种来源：来源于说话者本人，来源于他者。也就是说，介入系统的主要选择是基于，在对话性的交流语境中，评价是否引入了其他声音或立场。如果没有引入，就是单声，也称自言；如果引入了其他声音或立场，就是多声，也称借言。马丁和怀特（2005: 100）对于单声和多声之间的区别，给出了一个经典实例，具体请看下表。为了让大家更好地理解这些例句的内涵，特别在每个句子的下面加上了翻译。

介入系统（engagement）	举例
单声（monogloss）	The banks have been greedy. 银行业一直都是贪婪的。
多声（heterogloss）	*There is the argument though that* the banks have been greedy. <u>不过，有观点认为，</u>银行业一直都是贪婪的。 *In my view* the banks have been greedy. <u>在我看来，</u>银行业一直很贪婪。 *Callers to talkback radio see* the banks as being greedy. <u>把电话打到对讲系统内部的人们看清了</u>银行业贪婪这个事实。 *The chairman of the consumers association has stated* that the banks are being greedy. <u>消费者协会主席宣称，</u>银行业是贪婪的。 *There can be no denying* the banks have been greedy. <u>没人能否认，</u>银行业一直是贪婪的。 *Everyone knows* the banks are greedy. <u>人人都知道，</u>银行业是贪婪的。 The banks have*n't* been greedy. 银行业<u>并不</u>贪婪。

看过上面的表格，"The banks have been greedy."给人的感觉是这个句子自己在陈述一个事实：银行业一直都是贪婪的。这就是单声句子带给人的感受——客观、理性，容易让人接受或相信。与之相对应的多声句子，我们能觉察到，除了陈述本身之外，至少还有一种声音存在，这样就使得陈述本身蒙上了一层主观色彩。从这些例句可以感受到，多声表达比较复杂，因此多声也是介入系统的研究重点之一。

马丁和怀特（2005: 97-135）将多声分为对话的扩展和压缩两种类型。扩展是指话语中的介入或多或少地引发了对话中的其他声音或立场，包括"引发"和"摘引"两种情况；而压缩则意味着话语中的介入在形式上挑战、反击或限制了其他声音和立场，包括"否定"和"声明"两种情况。具体情况请见下表。为方便理解，特别在英语例句下面附上了翻译。

多声（借言）		含义	举例
压缩（contract）	否定（disclaim）	意味着语篇中的声音和某种相反的声音相互对立。	It is a review which *doesn't* consider the feelings of the Chinese community. *What is surprising* is to find such offensive opinions in *The Guardian*. 这是一个<u>不</u>考虑华人社区感情的评论。 <u>令人惊讶的是，</u>在英国《卫报》上发现了这种冒犯性的观点。

第十一章　人际功能

续表

多声（借言）		含义	举例
压缩（contract）	声明（proclaim）	语篇中的声音将观点表现为不可推翻，从而排除了其他声音。	Naturally..., of course..., obviously..., admittedly..., I contend..., the truth of the matter is..., there can be no doubt that..., X has demonstrated that..., X has compellingly argued... 顺理成章地……，不言而喻地……，显而易见地……，无可否认地……，我坚决主张……，事实的真相是……，毫无疑问……，某事已经证明……，某事令人信服地证明了……
扩展（expand）	引发（entertain）	指语篇中的声音所表现的观点建立在和其他观点的联系之中，因而表现为许多声音中的一种，从而引发了对话。	It seems, the evidence suggests, apparently, I hear, perhaps, probably, maybe, it's possible, may/will/must 看起来，证据表明，显然地，我听说，也许，很可能，大概，那是有可能的，可能/将会/一定
	摘引（attribute）	指语篇中的声音所表现的观点来自语篇外部的声音，因而表现为许多声音中的一种，进而引发了对话。	X said..., in X's view, X believes..., according to X, X claims that, the myth that..., it's rumoured that... 某某曾说……，在某某看来，某某认为……，根据某某的报道，某某声称，某某荒诞的说法……，据传闻……

（胡壮麟等，2017:335-336）

请看压缩的第一种情况：否定。否定"意味着语篇中的声音和某种相反的声音相互对立。"例如，<u>What is surprising</u> is to find such offensive opinions in *The Guardian*.（<u>令人惊讶的是，</u>在英国《卫报》上发现了这种冒犯性的观点。）What is surprising（令人惊讶的是）的意思是人们没有想到，这与人们的心理预期正好相反。

压缩的第二种情况：声明。声明指的是"语篇中的声音将观点表现为不可推翻，从而排除了其他声音。"例如，Naturally...（顺理成章地……），of course...（不言而喻地……），这些表达都体现出很明确、很清楚、很坚决的意思，从而排除了其他人的声音，也就是拒绝了其他人的观点。

再看扩展的第一种情况：引发。引发"指语篇中的声音所表现的观点建立在和其他观点的联系之中，因而表现为许多声音中的一种，从而引发了对话。"例如，It seems（看起来），the evidence suggests（证据表明），这些表达都暗示着后面会有其他观点出现，从而引发对话。

扩展的第二种情况：摘引。摘引"指语篇中的声音所表现的观点来自语篇外部的声音，因而表现为许多声音中的一种，进而引发了对话。"例如，X said...（某某曾说……），in X's view（在某某看来），这些表达也暗示着后面有其他观点出现，从而引发对话。

介入理论的价值在于，我们翻译时首先要看清楚原文是单声还是多声。原则上应该是单声转换成单声，多声转换成多声。要是混为一谈，小句的意义必将发生改变。

3. 级差系统（Graduation）

级差系统分为语势和聚焦两个子系统。语势出现在情感系统和介入系统之中，是高值与低值之间的连续体，可以使程度增强或减弱。英语常用副词表达语势，例如，very、too、quite、really、sharply、extremely。聚焦是对人或物等不可分级范畴的"清晰"或"模糊"的描述，例如，purely/partly、exactly/approximately、real/sort of、precisely/vaguely、quite/slightly。级差系统贯穿了态度系统和介入系统，它们之间的关系如下面两个表格所示。为了便于大家理解，将表格中的英文单词和句子都附上了翻译。

1）态度系统中的级差（Graduation in Attitude）

态度系统(Attitude)	低值（low degree） ←		→ 高值（high degree）	
情感系统 （Affect）	contentedly 满足地	happily 幸福地	joyously 欢天喜地地	ecstatically 欣喜若狂地
	slightly upset 有点难过	somewhat upset 有些难过	very upset 非常难过	extremely upset 极其难过
判定系统 （Judgement）	competent player 具有资格的选手	good player 水平良好的选手		brilliant player 技艺高超的选手
	reasonably good player 说得过去的选手	quite good player 相当不错的选手	very good player 非常优秀的选手	extremely good player 极为出色的选手
鉴别系统 （Appreciation）	a bit untidy 有点凌乱	somewhat untidy 有些凌乱	very untidy 非常凌乱	completely untidy 极为凌乱
	attractive 引起兴趣的	beautiful 美丽的		exquisite 精美的

（Martin & White, 2005:136）

2）介入系统中的级差（Graduation in Engagement）

介入系统 （Engagement）	较低值（lower） ←	→ 较高值（higher）
否定 （Disclaim）	I didn't hurt him. 我没有伤害他。	I never hurt him. 我从没伤害过他。

第十一章 人际功能

续表

介入系统 (Engagement)	较低值 (lower) ←		→ 较高值 (higher)
声明 (Proclaim)	I'd say he's the man for the job. 我会说，他是适合这份工作的人。	I contend he's the man for the job. 我认为，他是适合这份工作的人。	I insist that he's the man for the job. 我坚持认为，他是适合这份工作的人。
	Admittedly he's technically proficient (but he doesn't play with feeling). 应当承认，他技术娴熟，（但是他并没有带着情感去做）		Certainly he's technically proficient (but ...). 确定无疑，他技术娴熟，（但是他……）
引发 (Entertain)	I suspect she betrayed us. 我猜测他背叛了我们。	I believe she betrayed us. 我认为他背叛了我们。	I am convinced she betrayed us. 我坚信他背叛了我们。
	Possibly she betrayed us. 她可能背叛了我们。	Probably she betrayed us. 她很可能背叛了我们。	Definitely she betrayed us. 她绝对背叛了我们。
	She just possibly betrayed us. 她仅仅是可能背叛了我们。	She possibly betrayed us. 她可能背叛了我们。	She very possibly betrayed us. 她非常有可能背叛了我们。
摘引 (Attribute)	She suggested that I had cheated. 她言下之意是，我作弊了。	She stated that I had cheated. 她说我作弊了。	She insisted that I had cheated. 她坚持认为我作弊了。

(Martin & White, 2005:136)

从上面两个表格可以看出，极差系统能够存在于态度系统和介入系统的每一个子系统中。例如，情感系统中的"有点难过、有些难过、非常难过、极其难过"。判定系统中的"说得过去的选手、相当不错的选手、非常优秀的选手、极为出色的选手"。鉴别系统中的"有点凌乱、有些凌乱、非常凌乱、极为凌乱"。否定系统中的"我没有伤害他。/ 我从没伤害过他。"声明系统中的"我会说，他是适合这份工作的人。/ 我认为，他是适合这份工作的人。/ 我坚持认为，他是适合这份工作的人。"引发系统中的"她可能背叛了我们。/ 她很可能背叛了我们。/ 她绝对背叛了我们。"摘引系统中的"她言下之意是，我作弊了。/ 她说我作弊了。/ 她坚持认为我作弊了。"

上面两个表格和诸多例子让我们深刻地意识到，语言的意义有"增强与减弱"之分，也有"清晰和模糊"之别。因此级差系统分为语势和聚焦两个子系统就是合情合理的界定了。作为译者，我们对于小句意义到底是增强还是减弱，到底是清晰还是模糊，要有准确的理解和再现。

三、人际功能的翻译策略

基于前面详尽的论述，人际功能的翻译策略可以归纳如下：

人际功能的翻译必须要实现功能和意义方面的对等。第一，原文的语气系统翻译时原则上应该实现形式对等，也就是直陈语气对直陈语气，疑问语气对疑问语气，祈使语气对祈使语气，同时做好有标记语气系统的翻译。但是也不排除某些语境下语气做出调整后，语言的功能和意义依然对等的可能。

第二，原文的代称系统的翻译必须优先传递出人际意义，体现人际关系，展示说话人的态度，原则上可考虑形式对应，但必须牢记，要兼顾人际功能对等，即对于变异的代称系统要充分理解，翻译时可根据需要做出调整。

第三，原文情态系统的翻译也要首先秉持着意义正确的原则，在此基础上再尽可能保证形式对应。对于归一性翻译，意义上肯定就是肯定，否定就是否定，而情态性中的概率、频率、义务和意愿的翻译要尽可能用词准确，以再现出作者真实的想法。对于情态的取向，无论是主观显性、主观隐性，还是客观显性、客观隐性，翻译时原则上要与原文意义保持一致，而对于情态量值的翻译，译文也要尽可能与原文力度相当。

第四，至于评价系统中态度系统的翻译，要尽可能接近原作者的真实态度，把握好积极倾向还是消极倾向；而处理介入系统时要很准确，把握好单声与多声的区别；级差系统则要选择合适的修饰语和词语，使意义与原文一致。说到具体操作，除了要特别关注作者所使用的形容词、副词和情态动词外，也要对动词、名词、短语和句子保持敏感，因为作者要表达的人际意义可能无处不在，正如语言学家帕默（1989）所言，人们说的话大多数时候都不是在陈述事实，而是在表达态度和情感。

四、小句人际功能之案例分析
——以 "After Twenty Years" 第 1~4 段为例

After Twenty Years

O. Henry

【例 159】

原　文：The policeman on the beat moved up the avenue *impressively*. The *impressiveness* was *habitual and not for show*, for spectators were *few*. The time was *barely* 10 o'clock at night, but *chilly* gusts of wind with a taste of rain in them had *well nigh* depeopled the streets.

译　文：一个警察正**威风凛凛地**在大街上巡逻。这种**威风**是*习惯使然*，*并不是在显摆什么*。虽然时间**还不到**晚上十点，但是一阵阵裹挟**丝丝**雨意的**寒**风呼啸而过，**几乎**把街上的行人赶得一干二净。

讲　评：

人际表达	类别	人际意义
impressively	副词	该词属于评价系统中的态度系统中的判定系统，是对警察行为的积极判定，奠定了本文中警察正面形象的总基调。
impressiveness	名词	该词属于评价系统中的态度系统中的判定系统，是对警察形象的积极判定。
habitual and not for show	形容词联合短语	该短语是对 impressiveness 的说明，是评价系统中的态度系统中的判定系统中的积极判定。
few	形容词	该词属于评价系统中的态度系统中的鉴别系统，略显为消极鉴别。
barely	副词	该词属于评价系统中的级差系统中的聚焦中的模糊表达，是对故事发生环境的描写。
chilly	形容词	该词属于评价系统中的态度系统中的鉴别系统，略显为消极鉴别，是对环境的细致描写，大概预示着不好的事情即将发生。
well nigh	副词短语	该短语属于评价系统中的级差系统中的聚焦中的模糊表达，是对环境的描写。

【例 160】

原　文：Trying doors as he went, twirling his club with *many intricate and artful* movements, turning *now and then* to cast his *watchful* eye adown the *pacific* thoroughfare, the officer, with his *stalwart form and slight swagger*, made *a fine* picture of *a guardian of the peace*. The vicinity was one that kept *early* hours. *Now and then* you *might* see the lights of a cigar store or of an *all-night* lunch counter; but the majority of the doors belonged to business places that had *long since* been closed.

译　文：这个警察*身材魁梧*，*步伐威严*，边走边查看每家商户的门窗，警棍在他手里*不停地*翻转，*灵巧地挥舞出各种复杂*动作，目光还*时不时警觉地*扫过*宁静的*街道，那样子*完全就*是*一个和平守卫者*。这一带的商铺已*早早*歇业，只是你*还能偶尔*看见香烟店或*二十四小时营业的*便餐馆亮着灯，而绝大多数店铺*都*熄灯打烊了。

讲　评：

人际表达	类别	人际意义
many intricate and artful	形容词短语	该形容词短语属于态度系统中的判定系统，是对警察的个人判定，具有积极倾向。
now and then	副词短语	该副词短语属于情态系统中频率中的低值，同时属于态度系统中的判定系统，是对警察的个人判定，具有积极倾向。
watchful	形容词	该形容词属于态度系统中的判定系统，是对警察的个人判定，具有明显积极倾向。
pacific	形容词	该形容词属于态度系统中的鉴别系统，是对环境的鉴别，具有中性倾向。
stalwart form and slight swagger	名词联合短语	该名词短语属于态度系统中的判定系统，是对警察的个人判定，具有明显积极倾向。
fine	形容词	该形容词属于态度系统中的判定系统，是对警察的个人判定，具有明显积极倾向。
a guardian of the peace	名词短语	该名词短语属于态度系统中的判定系统，是对警察的个人判定，具有明显积极倾向。
early	形容词	该形容词属于态度系统中的鉴别系统，是对环境的鉴别，具有中性倾向。
now and then	副词短语	该副词短语属于情态系统中频率中的低值，是对环境的客观描写。
might	情态动词	该情态动词属于情态系统中概率中的低值，是对环境的客观描写。
all-night	形容词	该形容词属于态度系统中的鉴别系统，是对环境的鉴别，具有中性倾向。
long since	副词短语	该副词短语属于态度系统中的鉴别系统，是对环境的鉴别，具有中性倾向。

【例 161】

原　文：When about midway of a certain block the policeman *suddenly* slowed his walk. In the doorway of a *darkened* hardware store *a man leaned, with an unlighted cigar in his mouth*. As the policeman walked up to him the man spoke up *quickly*.

译　文：巡视到一段街区中间时，警察**突然**放慢了脚步。在一家五金店门前的**阴影**里，**一个男子斜倚大门站着，嘴里叼着一根尚未点燃的雪茄**。看见警察走过来，那人**迅速地**做出了解释。

第十一章 人际功能

讲　评：

人际表达	类别	人际意义
suddenly	副词	该词属于评价系统中的态度系统中的判定系统，是对警察行为的积极判定，体现出警察对环境敏锐的感觉。
darkened	形容词	该形容词属于评价系统中的态度系统中的鉴别系统，是对环境的鉴别，具有消极倾向，暗示着阴影之中可能潜藏着某种危机或不好的事情。
a man leaned, with an unlighted cigar in his mouth	小句	该小句属于评价系统中的态度系统中的判定系统，是对阴影中斜倚着大门站立的男子的消极判定。这种站立形象往往暗示此人不是犯罪分子，就是黑帮成员，总之不是好人。
quickly	副词	该词属于评价系统中的态度系统中的判定系统，是对该男子行为的消极判定，暗示着此人心里有鬼。

【例 162】

原　文："It's *all right*, *officer*," he said, *reassuringly*. "I'm *just* waiting for a friend. It's an appointment made twenty years ago. Sounds *a little funny* to you, doesn't it? Well, I'll explain if you'd like to make certain it's *all straight*. About that long ago there used to be a restaurant where this store stands—'Big Joe' Brady's restaurant."

译　文："**没事的**，**警官大人**，"他**信誓旦旦地**说道，"我**只是**在等一个老朋友，这是我们二十年前就定下的约会，今晚在这里重逢。听起来**有点滑稽**，是吧？要是你想知道，我愿意把事情的**来龙去脉**讲给你听。记得很多年前，这家店面所在的地方原是一家餐馆——'老乔·布雷迪餐馆'。"

讲　评：

人际表达	类别	人际意义
all right	形容词短语	该形容词短语属于评价系统中的态度系统中的鉴别系统，是对当时状况的积极鉴别，但却是对警官询问的敷衍。
officer	称谓语	该称谓属于代称系统中的称谓语中的常规表达，体现出警察的身份和地位，以及与该男子的关系。
reassuringly	副词	该副词属于评价系统中的态度系统中的判定系统，是对该男子说话方式的消极判定，表明此人明显心里有鬼。
just	副词	该词属于评价系统中的态度系统中的判定系统，是该男子对自身行为的中性判定。
a little funny	形容词短语	该形容词短语属于评价系统中的态度系统中的鉴别系统，是对赴约事件的消极鉴别，也是该男子自我解嘲的体现。
all straight	形容词短语	该形容词短语属于评价系统中的态度系统中的鉴别系统，是该男子对赴约事件的中性鉴别。

几段人际功能分析之后，有几点说明：第一，对于人际表达类别的确定，通常会以词性、短语为主要分析对象，有时候也以小句为分析对象。总之，只要该人际表达的意义较为独立，适合单独分析，就可以拿出来分析它的人际意义。第二，上面的例子中并没有分析语气系统，只是因为那些句子基本上都是在给予读者信息，并没有出现有标记的现象，故而没有分析语气。通常来说，小句语气可以不分析，除非有值得分析之处。第三，对于评价系统中的态度系统的分析，我们增加了中性倾向的说法，毕竟世界上的很多观点和说法并不总是要么积极，要么消极，也确实有一些中性倾向的说法。第四，上面的分析之所以那么繁复，是为了让大家知道此处的分析是基于何种理论，实际翻译时并不需要这样麻烦，但是应该有这样的意识和能力，至少能说清楚人际意义到底是什么。第五，无论人际功能分析理论的解释力多么强大，也需要大家不断通过理论与实践相结合才能较好掌握。因此，大家需要多多练习。

本章小结

作为三大元功能之一，人际功能与文学翻译的关系最为直接。虽然人际功能的理论框架比较清晰，但由于人际功能表达的是人们的身份、地位、情感、态度、动机、推测、判断和评价等内容，因而其所表达的意义具有强烈的主观色彩，因此也就最不容易把握。如果没有明确的理论框架做支撑，读者往往仁者见仁、智者见智，于是乎便形成了"一千个读者有一千个哈姆雷特"的局面。其实，只要译者时刻具有人际功能转换意识，能从语气系统、代称系统、情态系统和评价系统四个维度去全面审读小句，那么语篇内所建构的对说话人和受话人之间的角色关系的理解和翻译便有了比较坚实的基础，小句的人际功能就可以被客观地呈现给读者。如果说小句的人际功能是为人们所经历的世界涂抹上几许主观色彩，那么最后要学习的概念功能就是对人们所经历和体验的外部世界和内心世界的某种形式的描绘。

第十二章 概念功能
Ideational Metafunction

本章的核心观点是：译者应该始终具有概念功能转换的意识。本章分为三大部分：一、概念功能的定义；二、概念功能的体现；三、概念功能的翻译策略；第二部分又包括以下两部分：（一）经验功能；（二）逻辑功能。其中，经验功能又包括及物性系统、语态和小句经验功能之案例分析三个部分，而及物性系统是本章学习的重点和难点。

第一部分 概念功能的定义

胡壮麟等（2017: 71）指出，韩礼德所说的概念功能包括经验功能（experiential metafunction）和逻辑功能（logical metafunction）两个部分。经验功能指的是语言对人们在现实世界（包括内心世界）中的各种经历的表达。换言之，就是反映客观世界和主观世界中所发生的事、所牵涉的人和物以及与之有关的时间、地点等环境因素。逻辑功能指的则是语言对两个或两个以上的意义单位之间逻辑关系的表达。

汤普森（2004/2008: 30）认为，我们用语言来谈论对世界的经验，包括我们内心世界的经验，以此去描绘事件、情形和牵涉其中的对象。汤普森（2004/2008: 86）还认为，从经验功能角度看，语言由一系列用于指代世间事物的言语资源和事物间彼此影响和关联的表达方式组成。简单点说，语言反映了我们对世界的看法，它包括过程（体现为动词），这些过程所涉及的事物（体现为名词），这些事物可能拥有的某些特征（体现为形容词），并且依托哪些背景细节，例如地点、时间、方式等（体现为副词性表达）。汤普森（2004/2008: 38）还提出了一个问题：当小句与小句结合成小句复合体的时候，会发生什么？通过这个问题，对小句之间关系的思考进入了人们的视野，也就是第四个元功能：逻辑功能。正是有了系统功能语法的逻辑功能，才能显示出一组小句之间的相似点和不同点。

第二部分　概念功能的体现

一、经验功能（Experiential Metafunction）

（一）及物性系统（Transitivity）

汤普森（2004/2008: 88-89）特别提示读者，及物性这个术语很可能会被理解为动词后面是否接宾语。然而，这里该术语被用于更广泛的意义。特别是用于指代描述整个小句的系统，而不仅仅是动词和它的宾语。

根据汤普森（1996/2000: 79）和韩礼德与迈西森（2004/2008: 175-177），对小句及物性结构的理解就是在分析小句的三个方面：对动词过程的选择：(the selection of a process)；对参与者的数量和角色的选择：(the selection of participants)；对环境角色表达的选择：(the selection of circumstances)。

根据韩礼德与迈西森（2004/2008: 177），小句经验功能（这里指及物性系统）的实现由下列词汇类型来体现：

小句成分类型	具体体现为
过程（process）	动词词组（verbal group）
参与者（participant）	名词词组（nominal group）
环境（circumstance）	副词词组或介词短语（adverbial group or prepositional phrase）

及物性系统可以体现为下面这个树形结构图，而本章的及物性系统理论主要是基于何伟等（2017a/b）的研究。

第十二章 概念功能

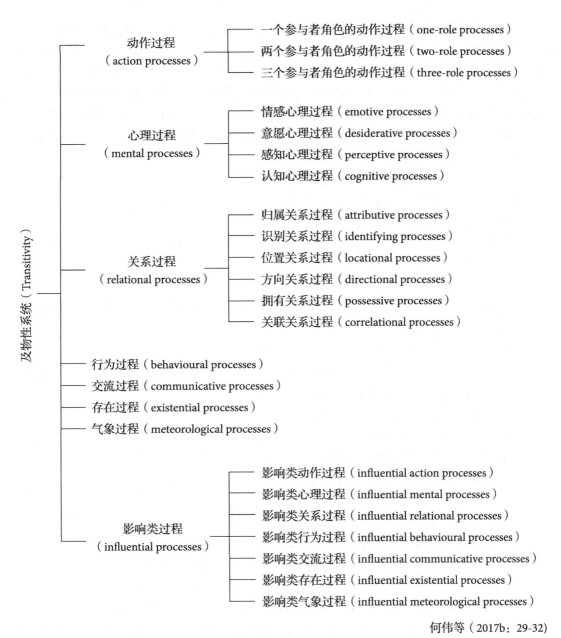

何伟等（2017b：29-32）

1. 动作过程（Action Processes）

动作过程用于描述做某件事的过程（doing）或者某件事发生的过程（happening）。韩礼德（1994/2000: 110; Halliday & Matthiessen, 2004/2008:179）将此类过程称为物质过程（material process）。系统功能语言学加的夫大学派代表学者福赛特使用的是"动作过程"（action process）这个术语。鉴于此类过程既表示具体的物理动作，也反映抽象行为，而"物质过程"可能会带来误解，故采用"动作过程"这一说法。

根据汤普森（2004/2008: 91），动作过程是及物性系统中涉及动词词汇最多、多样性最鲜明的类别。作为表征外部世界各类事件和活动的过程类型，动作过程可以根据动词本身是否反映了动作发出者（即施事，Agent）的意图，区分为"刻意性的"（intentional）和"意外性的"（involuntary）两大类。另外，还可以根据是倾向于反映客观实体世界还是社会交际领域，将动作过程动词分为"偏具体的"（specific）和"偏抽象的"（abstract）两大类。根据何伟等（2017a: 32-64），动作过程小句涉及 1-3 个参与者，包括施事、受事、创造物、范围、方式、程度、方向以及复合参与者角色等，并由此分成"单参与者角色动作过程""双参与者角色动作过程""三参与者角色动作过程"以及影响类动作过程。

1）单参与者动作过程（One-role Processes）

（1）单参与者，且为施事（Agent only）

[1] 施事 + 动作过程（Ag+Pro），例如：

① *We* [Ag] can *relax* [Pro].

② *Many wearing hoodies* [Ag] *marched* [Pro] during rush hour.

③ *The injured* [Ag] will soon *recover* [Pro].

④ *Those satellite businesses* [Ag] will *operate* [Pro] eventually.

（注：鉴于小句及物性分析使用的术语缩写较多，而且纷繁复杂，故将这些术语缩写及对应翻译统一放在附录中，以方便学习者查阅。）

[2] 施事 + 动作过程 + 过程延长成分（Ag+Pro+PrEx），例如：

① *My mom* [Ag] *did* [Pro] *some shopping* [PrEx] this weekend. (PrEx: Process Extension)

② *He* [Ag] actually *went* [Pro] *for a walk* [PrEx].

③ *The train* [Ag] *slid* [Pro] *in* [PrEx].

④ *Bunny* [Ag] *kept* [Pro] *talking* [PrEx] as he drove.

（2）单参与者，且为受事（Affected only）

[1] 受事 + 动作过程（Af+Pro），例如：

① *Anything* [Af] would *happen* [Pro].

② *The match* [Af] *ended* [Pro] two days later.

③ *The glass* [Af] *broke* [Pro] with a loud noise.

④ *The bowls and spoons* [Af] *washed* [Pro] easily with a dip in hot water.

[2] It+ 动作过程 + 受事（It+Pro+Af）（此种类型数量稀少），例如：

① It *happened* [Pro] *that on that same night Sam had invited Rose to supper* [Af].

② But it *came* [Pro] *about* [PrEx] *that this business was dropped just as soon as we Labor got into power* [Af].

（3）单参与者，且为创造物（Created only），例如：

① *Their baby Charlie* [Cre] *was* [Pro] *born* [PrEx] in 1989.

② *The new school* [Cre] *came* [Pro] *into being* [PrEx] later.

③ *His problems* [Cre] *began* [Pro] after only two days of training.

④ If nothing were done, *violence* [Cre] would *erupt* [Pro].

2）双参与者动作过程（Two-role Processes）

（1）施事 + 动作过程 + 受事（Ag+Pro+Af），例如：

① *They* [Ag] would *attack* [Pro] *someone else* [Af].
② Will *we* [Ag] *mend* [Pro] *the fence* [Af]?
③ *We* [Ag] ought to *split* [Pro] *the schools* [Af].
④ *He* [Ag] *raised* [Pro] *his hand* [Af], but his passion was so great that he could not speak.

（2）施事 + 动作过程 + 创造物（Ag+Pro+Cre），例如：
① *You* [Ag] can *build* [Pro] *a house* [Cre] from limestone in three ways.
② *Make* [Pro] *a dough* [Cre] with the plain flour and a little water.
③ *Charlie* [Ag] *began* [Pro] *his journey to London* [Cre].
④ *Combined adminstration of the two drugs* [Ag] *caused* [Pro] *a further decrease of insulin release* [Cre].

（3）施事 + 动作过程 + 范围（Ag+Pro+Ra），例如：
① *He* [Ag] can *climb* [Pro] *a high peak of the mountain* [Ra].
② Somehow *he* [Ag] had *traversed* [Pro] *the latest scorching zone* [Ra].
③ *I*'ve [Ag] got to *play* [Pro] *some flamenco* [Ra] tonight.
④ How can *you* [Ag] *play* [Pro] *football* [Ra] and not go to school then?

（4）施事 + 动作过程 + 方式（Ag+Pro+Ma），例如：
① *They* [Ag] *behave* [Pro] *naturally* [Ma] at home.
② *She* [Ag] *behaved* [Pro] *very well* [Ma] in public.
③ *She* [Ag] *acted* [Pro] *in a very calm manner* [Ma]—remarkably so considering the trauma she was being put through.
④ *He* [Ag] could *act* [Pro] *naturally* [Ma] when with a friend or when with a few friend, and he could perform easily behind a podium.

（5）施事 – 载体 + 动作过程 + 方向（Ag-Ca+Pro+Dir），例如：
① *She* [Ag-Ca] had *reached* [Pro] *London* [Dir: Des] at the height of the rush. (Des: destination)
② So *where* [Dir: Des] do *we* [Ag-Ca] *go* [Pro] *from here* [Dir: So]? (So: source)
③ *She*'d [Ag-Ca] *crossed* [Pro] *Afghanistan* [Dir: Pa] alone. (Pa: path)
④ *The government* [Ag-Ca], he says, must *go* [Pro] *back* [PrEx] *to those old days* [Dir: Des].

（6）受事 – 载体 + 动作过程 + 方向（Af-Ca+Pro+Dir），例如：
① *All the luggage* [Af-Ca] has *gone* [Pro] *to the hospital* [Dir: Des].
② *More than twenty thousand containers* [Af-Ca] *pass* [Pro] *through the ports of L.A. and Long Beach* [Dir: Pa] everyday.
③ On average, *the electrons* [Af-Ca] *travel* [Pro] *from the cathode* [Dir: So] *to the anode* [Dir: Des].
④ *How much money* [Af-Ca], has *gone* [Pro] *to that company* [Dir: Des]?

3）三参与者动作过程（Three-role Processes）
（1）施事 + 动作过程 + 受事 + 方式（Ag+Pro+Af+Ma），例如：

① If *the teacher* [Ag] does not *handle* [Pro] *them* [Af] *indirectly* [Ma], the class will hastily protect themselves by opting out, fooling around, etc.

② You get the best out of people if *you* [Ag] *treat* [Pro] *them* [Af] *in a certain way* [Ma].

③ *Bill* [Ag] *behaved* [Pro] *himself* [Af] *almost perfectly* [Ma] the first time round the field.

（2）施事＋动作过程＋受事－载体＋方向（Ag+Pro+Af-Ca+Dir），例如：

① *They*'ll [Ag] *send* [Pro] *ambassadors* [Af-Ca] *from England* [Dir: So].

② So *I* [Ag] *brought* [Pro] *her* [Af-Ca] *to the valley* [Dir: Des].

③ *You* [Ag] can *push* [Pro] *a screwdriver* [Af-Ca] *through some of the walls* [Dir: Pa].

④ *River boats* [Ag] *brought* [Pro] *wool* [Af-Ca] *to Rawcliffe* [Dir: Des] *from the West Riding* [Dir: So].

（3）施事＋动作过程＋受事－感知者＋受事-现象（Ag+Pro+Af-Perc+Af-Ph），例如：

① *He* [Ag] *showed* [Pro] *me* [Af-Perc] *the scars* [Af-Ph].

② *Show* [Pro] *us* [Af-Perc] *what you've been doing* [Af-Ph].

③ *He* [Ag] *demonstrated* [Pro] *to* [PrEx] *me* [Af-Perc] *an Ergoline 35-tube sunbed in which a man lies full length* [Af-Ph].

（4）施事＋动作过程＋受事－现象＋受事－感知者（Ag+Pro+Af-Ph+Af-Perc），例如：

① *He* [Ag] *revealed* [Pro] *this* [Af-Ph] *to* [PrEx] *a group of Irish journalists* [Af-Perc].

② We ordered Jerez wine and *he* [Ag] *presented* [Pro] *me* [Af-Ph] *to* [PrEx] *his wife* [Af-Perc].

③ It was a marble ball. *They* [Ag] *showed* [Pro] *it* [Af-Ph] *to* [PrEx] *me* [Af-Perc] later.

（5）施事＋动作过程＋受事－拥有者＋受事－拥有物（Ag+Pro+Af-Posr+Af-Posd），例如：

① And *she* [Ag] *gave* [Pro] *her* [Af-Posr] *a packet of sunflower seeds* [Af-Posd].

② *He* [Ag] had *lent* [Pro] *him* [Af-Posr] *a chauffeur-driven car and expensive office equipment* [Af-Posd] during the General Election.

③ *We* [Ag] *robbed* [Pro] *them* [Af-Posr] *of* [PrEx] *their land* [Af-Posd].

（6）施事＋动作过程＋受事－拥有物＋受事－拥有者（Ag+Pro+Af-Posd+Af-Posr），例如：

① *You* [Ag] should *give* [Pro] *it* [Af-Posd] *to* [PrEx] *a solicitor* [Af-Posr] after my funeral.

② Well, *Lloyd's of London* [Ag] can *buy* [Pro] *it* [Af-Posd] *for* [PrEx] *me* [Af-Posr].

③ "*He* [Ag] *stole* [Pro] *it* [Af-Posd] *from* [PrEx] *a girl* [Af-Posr]", she explained quickly, before she could feel intimidated.

（7）施事＋动作过程＋受事－载体＋受事－目的地／来源（Ag+Pro+Af-Ca+Af-Des/Af-So），例如：

① *The men* [Ag] *loaded* [Pro] *parts* [Af-Ca] *onto a system of fixtures* [Af-Dir: Af-Des].

② *He* [Ag] *sprinkled* [Pro] *water* [Af-Ca] *over the towel* [Af-Dir: Af-Des].

③ At one side of the room, *he* [Ag] *cleared* [Pro] *dust* [Af-Ca] *from sloping shelves* [Af-Dir:

Af-So].

（8）施事 + 动作过程 + 受事 – 目的地 / 来源 + 受事 – 载体（Ag+Pro+Af-Des/Af-So+Af-Ca），例如：

① *She* [Ag] *sprayed* [Pro] *it* [Af-Dir: Af-Des] *with* [PrEx] *her perfume* [Af-Ca].

② *Claudette* [Ag] *packed* [Pro] *it* [Af-Dir: Af-Des] *with* [PrEx] *her treasured possessions* [Af-Ca].

③ *He* [Ag] *cleared* [Pro] *it* [Af-Dir: Af-So] *of* [PrEx] *leaves* [Af-Ca].

（9）影响类动作过程（Influential Action Processes），例如：

① *We* [Ag] don't *force* [Pro] [[*people* [Ag] to *work* [Pro] here]], you know.

② *Administrators* [Ag] may *force* [Pro] [[*psychologists* [Ag] to *act* [Pro] *unethically* [Ma]]].

③ *He* [Ag] *made* [Pro] [[*me* [Ag] *give* [Pro] *him* [Af-Posr] *Celia's address* [Af-Posd]]].

④ *They* [Ag] can't *make* [Pro] [[*us* [Ag] *send* [Pro] *him* [Af-Ca] *to school* [Dir: Des]]], can they?

⑤ *The release of ice from Antarctica* [Ag] will also *cause* [Pro] [[*sea-levels* [Af] to *rise* [Pro]]].

⑥ *I* [Ag] *forbid* [Pro] [[*you* [Ag] to *go* [Pro] *to the woods* [Dir: Des] again]].

⑦ *We* [Ag] cannot *let* [Pro] [[*him* [Af] *die* [Pro]]].

⑧ *You*'ll [Ag] *let* [Pro] [[*me* [Ag] *make* [Pro] *the cakes* [Cre]]]?

⑨ Perhaps one day *you* [Ag] will *allow* [Pro] [[*me* [Ag] to *show* [Pro] *you* [Af-Perc] *my department in the university* [Af-Ph]]].

⑩ *The war* [Ag] has *enabled* [Pro] [[*farmers* [Ag] to *expand* [Pro] *their output* [Af] by taking marginal areas of land into cultivation]].

动作过程语义配置结构现用图表小结如下：

1）单参与者动作过程	
（1）施事 + 动作过程	Ag+Pro
（2）施事 + 动作过程 + 过程延长成分	Ag+Pro+PrEx
（3）受事 + 动作过程	Af+Pro
（4）It+ 动作过程 + 受事	It+Pro+Af
（5）创造物 + 动作过程 + （过程延长成分）	Cre+Pro+(PrEx)
2）双参与者动作过程	
（1）施事 + 动作过程 + 受事	Ag+Pro+Af
（2）施事 + 动作过程 + 创造物	Ag+Pro+Cre
（3）施事 + 动作过程 + 范围	Ag+Pro+Ra
（4）施事 + 动作过程 + 方式	Ag+Pro+Ma
（5）施事 – 载体 + 动作过程 + 方向	Ag-Ca+Pro+Dir

	续表
（6）受事 – 载体 + 动作过程 + 方向	Af-Ca+Pro+Dir
3）三参与者动作过程	
（1）施事 + 动作过程 + 受事 + 方式	Ag+Pro+Af+Ma
（2）施事 + 动作过程 + 受事 – 载体 + 方向	Ag+Pro+Af-Ca+Dir
（3）施事 + 动作过程 + 受事 – 感知者 + 受事 – 现象	Ag+Pro+Af-Perc+Af-Ph
（4）施事 + 动作过程 + 受事 – 现象 + 受事 – 感知者	Ag+Pro+Af-Ph+Af-Perc
（5）施事 + 动作过程 + 受事 – 拥有者 + 受事 – 拥有物	Ag+Pro+Af-Posr+Af-Posd
（6）施事 + 动作过程 + 受事 – 拥有物 + 受事 – 拥有者	Ag+Pro+Af-Posd+Af-Posr
（7）施事 + 动作过程 + 受事 – 载体 + 受事 – 目的地 / 来源	Ag+Pro+Af-Ca+Af-Des/Af-So
（8）施事 + 动作过程 + 受事 – 目的地 / 来源 + 受事 – 载体	Ag+Pro+Af-Des/Af-So+Af-Ca
4）影响类动作过程	

2. 心理过程（Mental Processes）

心理过程是人脑对外部世界的反映，描述的是人们的心理活动发生、发展的过程。韩礼德和迈西森（Halliday & Matthiessen, 2004/2008: 197-210）将心理过程分为四种类型：情感类（emotive）、意愿类（desiderative）、感知类（perceptive）和认知类（cognitive）。根据福赛特（2010: 89）和何伟等（2017b: 68），心理过程主要涉及两个参与者："感受者"和"现象"。前者（senser）指参与心理体验的人或人格化的物，后者（phenomenon）指被感知的对象。鉴于心理过程有不同类型，"感受者"可分别称为"情感表现者"（Emoter）、"意愿表现者"（Desiderator）、"感知者"（Perceiver）和"认知者"（Cognizant）。心理过程基本语义配置结构为："感受者 + 心理过程 + 现象。"具体说来，情感心理过程描述人们在看待客观事物时产生的或好或坏的各种主观体验；意愿心理过程描述人或人格化的物期待实现的或一般或强烈的想法；感知心理过程体现了人通过感知器官从外部世界获得各种反应；认知心理过程描述的是人们通过形成概念、知觉、判断或想象等心理活动而形成的对客体或主体的比较客观的认识。韩礼德和迈西森（2004/2008: 210）将这四种心理过程类型常见动词列表如下：

Mental Processes	"like" type （动作由主体发出）	"please" type （动作由客体发出）
Cognitive （认知类）	think, believe, suppose, expect, consider, know; understand, realize, appreciate; imagine, dream, pretend; guess, reckon, conjecture, hypothesize; wonder, doubt; remember, recall, forget; fear (think fearfully)	strike, occur to, convince; remind, escape; puzzle, intrigue, surprise
Perceptive （感知类）	perceive, sense; see, notice, glimpse; hear, overhear; feel; taste; smell	assail

续表

Desiderative（意愿类）	want, wish, would like, desire; hope (for), yearn for; intend, plan; decide, resolve, determine; agree, comply, refuse	tempt
Emotive（情感类）	like, fancy, love, adore, dislike, hate, detest, despise, loathe, abhor; rejoice, exult, grieve, mourn, bemoan, bewail, regret, deplore; fear, dread; enjoy, relish, marvel	allure, attract, please, displease, disgust, offend, repel, revolt; gladden, delight, gratify, sadden, depress, pain; alarm, startle, frighten, scare, horrify, shock, comfort, reassure, encourage; amuse, entertain, divert, interest, fascinate, bore, weary, worry

1）情感心理过程（Emotive Processes）

（1）情感表现者+心理过程+现象（Em+Pro+Ph），例如：

① *I* [Em] *like/love/fancy/adore* [Pro] *you* [Ph].

② *Both parties* [Em] *regret* [Pro] *that this is the case* [Ph].

③ (*You* [Em]) Don't *despise* [Pro] *yourself* [Ph].

④ *They* [Em] *were annoyed* [Pro] by *the final version of the video* [Ph].

⑤ *The jury* [Em] *were* [Pro] not *satisfied* [PrEx1] *about* [PrEx2] *that alleged representation* [Ph].

（2）现象+心理过程+情感表现者（Ph+Pro+Em），例如：

① *Her response* [Ph] *astonished* [Pro] *me* [Em].

② *Their odor* [Ph] *pleases/displeases* [Pro] *the sense of smell* [Em].

③ *Your insistence on a name* [Ph] *amuses* [Pro] *me* [Em].

④ *It* [Ph] might *cheer* [Pro] *her* [Em] *up* [PrEx].

⑤ *That he quitted the school* [Ph] *shocked* [Pro] *his mother* [Em] greatly.

（3）It+心理过程+情感表现者+现象（It+Pro+Em+Ph），例如：

① It still *shocks* [Pro] *you* [Em] *to see them* [Ph].

② It *annoys* [Pro] *him* [Em] *that none of his fans has been moved to rave over it* [Ph].

③ It really *pissed* [Pro] *me* [Em] *off* [PrEx] *that someone could do this* [Ph].

④ It *matters* [Pro] (*to* [PrEx] *my coach* [Em]) *that every day I'm here right when I said I would be* [Ph].

（4）受事–情感表现者+心理过程+现象（Af-Em+Pro+Ph），例如：

① *I* [Af-Em] *fell* [Pro] *for* [PrEx] *him* [Ph] not just as a man, but as a father.

② *She* [Af-Em] did *have* [Pro] *a crush* [PrEx1] *on* [PrEx2] *Dr. Russell* [Ph], of course.

③ *He* [Af-Em] never *fell* [Pro] *out* [PrEx1] *of* [PrEx2] *love* [PrEx3] *with* [PrEx4] *me* [Ph] because he wasn't ever in love with me!

"Af-Em"表示情感表现者在执行心理过程时一定程度上受到影响。

（5）情感表现者+心理过程+现象+相关方（Em+Pro+Ph+Cor），例如：

① *We* [Em] *prefer* [Pro] *short stories* [Ph] *to* [PrEx] *long novels* [Cor].

② *Aunt Janice* [Em] *prefers* [Pro] *staying here with Gavin* [Ph] *to* [PrEx] *traveling out* [Cor].

③ *The Bangor version of bigot* [Em] *prefers* [Pro] *an individual approach* [Ph] (*to* [PrEx] *some other approaches* [Cor]).

2）意愿心理过程（Desiderative Processes）

（1）意愿表现者+心理过程+现象（Desr+Pro+Ph），例如：

① *I* [Desr] *want* [Pro] *an apple* [Ph].

② *I* [Desr] was *longing* [Pro] *for* [PrEx] *the sight of something other than water and trees* [Ph].

③ *I* [Desr] *was*n't [Pro] *too keen* [PrEx1] *on* [PrEx2] *going to the party* [Ph].

④ *He* [Desr] *was* [Pro] *optimistic* [PrEx1] *about* [PrEx2] *resuming peace talks suspended since last December* [Ph].

3）感知心理过程（Perceptive Processes）

（1）感知者+心理过程+现象（Perc+Pro+Ph），例如：

① *I* [Perc] *heard* [Pro] *the news on my late wife's brithday* [Ph].

② I came, *I* [Perc] *saw* [Pro] ([Ph]), I conquered.

③ I had barely taken a sip, when *I* [Perc] *tasted* [Pro] *something bad in the juice* [Ph].

④ *He* [Perc] *smelled* [Pro] *frying bacon* [Ph] and *heard* [Pro] *the chatter of women* [Ph] as he walked across the tiled hall.

该过程强调重点在于现象本身，不突出感知者是否有目的。

（2）施事-感知者+心理过程+现象（Ag-Perc+Pro+Ph），例如：

① *I* [Ag-Perc] hadn't actually *tasted* [Pro] *whisky* [Ph] before.

② (*You* [Ag-Perc]) *Feel* [Pro] ([Ph]) with your heart.

③ I didn't own a pair of binoculars, so *I* [Ag-Perc] couldn't *observe* [Pro] *the birds* [Ph] as closely as I'd have wished.

④ Let's assume they waited around so that *you* [Ag-Perc] could *overhear* [Pro] *them talking* [Ph].

"Ag-Perc"表示感知者同时也是施事，对事物的感知具有主动性。

4）认知心理过程（Cognitive Processes）

（1）认知者+心理过程+现象（Cog+Pro+Ph），例如：

① *I* [Cog] *understand* [Pro] *these kids* [Ph].

② *You* [Cog] *know* [Pro] *how much I love you* [Ph].

③ Now *scientists* [Cog] *believe* [Pro] *they have found their remains* [Ph].

④ *I* [Cog] *'m* [Pro] *very positive* [PrEx] *that Natalie will be cured* [Ph].

⑤ But in those days *few* [Cog] *dreamed* [Pro] *of* [PrEx] *being a professional artist* [Ph].

该类型强调重点在于现象本身，不突出认知者是否有目的。

（2）It+ 心理过程 + 认知者 + 现象（It+Pro+Cog+Ph），例如：

① It *seems* [Pro] (*to* [PrEx] *somebody* [Cog]) *that it is apparent in some way* [Ph].

② It *seems* [Pro] *to* [PrEx] *me* [Cog] *that there is very little control of that expenditure* [Ph].

③ It *sounds* [Pro] (*to* [PrEx] *somebody* [Cog]) *as though it's going to go on forever then* [Ph].

④ It *appears* [Pro] *to* [PrEx] *the Prime Minister* [Cog] *that publication would be prejudicial to national security* [Ph].

（3）受事 – 认知者 + 心理过程 + 现象（Af-Cog+Pro+Ph），例如：

① *David* [Af-Cog] last night *discovered* [Pro] *that it's tough at the very top* [Ph].

② *I* [Af-Cog] have *learned* [Pro] *that I just have to take things easy* [Ph].

③ *I* [Af-Cog] *detected* [Pro] *that some doubts still remain* [Ph].

该类型中的认知者在执行心理过程时状态渐渐改变，开始认识或了解，而这是事先并不知道的。

（4）It+ 心理过程 + 受事 – 认知者 + 现象（It+Pro+Af-Cog+Ph），例如：

① It *strikes* [Pro] *me* [Af-Cog] *that this erring is a starting point* [Ph].

② It *occurred* [Pro] *to* [PrEx] *me* [Af-Cog] *that he might well have heard me and decided not to answer* [Ph].

③ It *came* [Pro] *to* [PrEx] *me* [Af-Cog] *that my mother was proud of her friendship with this high-spirited outcast* [Ph].

（5）施事 – 认知者 + 心理过程 + 现象（Ag-Cog+Pro+Ph），例如：

① *He* [Ag-Cog] *studied* [Pro] *the different aspects of the novel* [Ph] in detail.

② *We* [Ag-Cog] will now *consider* [Pro] *if there is potential for a civil claim* [Ph].

③ *She* [Ag-Cog] has *thought* [Pro] *about* [PrEx] *quitting acting* [Ph] several times.

"Ag-Cog" 表示强调重点在于认知心理过程，并且突出认知者有明确目的。

（6）施事 – 认知者 + 心理过程 + 创造物 – 现象（Ag-Cog+Pro+Cre-Ph），例如：

① *He* [Ag-Cog] *projected* [Pro] *the idea of the national leader* [Cre-Ph].

② *The kid* [Ag-Cog] *thought* [Pro] *up* [PrEx] *some justification of his silliness* [Cre-Ph].

③ *We* [Ag-Cog] *put* [Pro] *forward* [PrEx] *several possible uses for the old hospital, including re-siting of the library* [Cre-Ph].

（7）施事 – 认知者 + 心理过程 + 现象 + 相关方（Ag-Cog+Pro+Ph+Cor），例如：

① *We* [Ag-Cog] *compared* [Pro] *our design fees* [Ph] *with/to* [PrEx] *the scaled fees* [Cor].

② *He* [Ag-Cog] *contrasted* [Pro] *private charitable bodies* [Ph] *with* [PrEx] *public corporations* [Cor].

③ *A number of writers* [Ag-Cog] have *distinguished* [Pro] *such a procedural challenge* [Ph] *from* [PrEx] *the substantive challenge* [Cor].

5）影响类心理过程（Influential Mental Processes）

（1）施事+影响类动词+[[情感表现者+心理过程+现象]]（Ag+Pro+[[Em+Pro+Ph]]），

例如：

① *Nothing* [Ag] could *make* [Pro] [[*a mother* [Em] *hate* [Pro] *her child* [Ph]]].

② *Art criticism* [Ag] will *enable* [Pro] [[*the reader* [Em] to *enjoy* [Pro] *an exhibition better* [Ph]]].

③ (*You* [Ag]) *Let* [Pro] [[*them* [Em] *fear* [Pro] ([Ph])]]!

（2）施事＋影响类动词＋[[意愿表现者＋心理过程＋现象]]（Ag+Pro+[[Desr+Pro+Ph]]），例如：

① *You* [Ag] *make* [Pro] [[*me* [Desr] *want* [Pro] *to throw up* [Ph]]]!

② And certainly *nothing* [Ag] would *stop* [Pro] [[*him* [Desr] *from hoping that something was still significant* [Ph]]].

③ *This loving feeling* [Ag] *makes* [Pro] [[*me* [Desr] *long* [Pro] *for* [PrEx] *your kiss* [Ph]]].

（3）施事＋影响类动词＋[[感知者＋心理过程＋现象]]（Ag+Pro+[[Perc+Pro+Ph]]），例如：

① *A rabbit's large ears* [Ag] *enable* [Pro] [[*it* [Perc] to *hear* [Pro] *the slightest sound* [Ph]]].

② (*You* [Ag]) *Let* [Pro] [[*him* [Perc] *see* [Pro] *the image of her that everyone else saw* [Ph]]].

③ *This* [Ag] should *make* [Pro] it *possible* [PrEx] [[(for *somebody* [Perc]) to *see* [Pro] at last *what the key influences are* [Ph]]].

（4）施事＋影响类动词＋[[认知者＋心理过程＋现象]]（Ag+Pro+[[Cog+Pro+Ph]]），例如：

① *Modern techniques* [Ag] *allow* [Pro] [[*you* [Cog] to *realize* [Pro] *your dreams* [Ph]]].

② (*You* [Ag]) Don't *make* [Pro] [[*me* [Cog] *think* [Pro] *of* [PrEx] *you* [Ph]]].

③ *We* [Ag] *enable* [Pro] [[*customers* [Perc] to *plan* [Pro] *their trip in just 15 minutes* [Ph]]].

心理过程语义配置结构现用图表小结如下：

1）情感心理过程	
（1）情感表现者＋心理过程＋现象	Em+Pro+Ph
（2）现象＋心理过程＋情感表现者	Ph+Pro+Em
（3）It+心理过程＋情感表现者＋现象	It+Pro+Em+Ph
（4）受事－情感表现者＋心理过程＋现象	Af-Em+Pro+Ph
（5）情感表现者＋心理过程＋现象＋相关方	Em+Pro+Ph+Cor
2）意愿心理过程	
（1）意愿表现者＋心理过程＋现象	Desr+Pro+Ph
3）感知心理过程	
（1）感知者＋心理过程＋现象	Perc+Pro+Ph
（2）施事－感知者＋心理过程＋现象	Ag-Perc+Pro+Ph

续表

4）认知心理过程	
（1）认知者 + 心理过程 + 现象	Cog+Pro+Ph
（2）It+ 心理过程 + 认知者 + 现象	It+Pro+Cog+Ph
（3）受事 – 认知者 + 心理过程 + 现象	Af-Cog+Pro+Ph
（4）It+ 心理过程 + 受事 – 认知者 + 现象	It+Pro+Af-Cog+Ph
（5）施事 – 认知者 + 心理过程 + 现象	Ag-Cog+Pro+Ph
（6）施事 – 认知者 + 心理过程 + 创造物 - 现象	Ag-Cog+Pro+Cre-Ph
（7）施事 – 认知者 + 心理过程 + 现象 + 相关方	Ag-Cog+Pro+Ph+Cor
5）影响类心理过程	
（1）施事 + 影响类动词 +[[情感表现者 + 心理过程 + 现象]]	Ag+Pro+[[Em+Pro+Ph]]
（2）施事 + 影响类动词 +[[意愿表现者 + 心理过程 + 现象]]	Ag+Pro+[[Desr+Pro+Ph]]
（3）施事 + 影响类动词 +[[感知者 + 心理过程 + 现象]]	Ag+Pro+[[Perc+Pro+Ph]]
（4）施事 + 影响类动词 +[[认知者 + 心理过程 + 现象]]	Ag+Pro+[[Cog+Pro+Ph]]

3. 关系过程（Relational Processes）

关系过程反映了两个事物之间具有怎样的逻辑关系，是关于"什么是什么、什么像什么、什么在哪里、什么从哪里来或到哪里去、什么拥有什么、什么与什么相关"的过程类型。不同学者对关系过程的划分不尽相同，这里采用何伟等学者（2017a: 95-126）提出的较为简明易懂且具有较强操作性的六类划分，即关系过程分为归属过程、识别过程、位置过程、方向过程、拥有过程和关联过程。另外，还有一类贯穿于各过程中的影响类关系过程，表示一个实体引起另一个实体在属性、性状、方位等方面发生某些变化，或产生某些倾向。

1）归属关系过程（Attributive Processes）

归属关系过程描述的是某个实体是某个群体的一员，或者负载着某种特征。这个实体称为载体（Carrier），可以是人、物、情形等。实体所具有的特点或特征称为属性（Attribute）。属性是对实体的具体描述。任何一个实体总有许多特征，这些特征构成了它的属性。具有相同属性的实体构成一个类别。在归属关系过程小句中，属性也被视为参与者角色，表示载体的某些特征。载体和属性的位置一般不可调换。归属关系过程的典型动词有"be、appear、become、feel、get、keep、look、make、resemble、represent、sound、smell、seem、taste"。

（1）载体 + 关系过程 + 属性（Ca+Pro+At），例如：

① *I* [Ca] *am* [Pro] *a good swimmer* [At].
② *Your supper* [Ca] *smells* [Pro] *good* [At].
③ *That* [Ca] will *look* [Pro] *nice* [At].

④ *Such actions* [Ca] also *represent* [Pro] *considerable cost* [At].
⑤ *It* [Ca] *costs* [Pro] *fifty five pounds* [At].
⑥ *The mountain goat hunting season* [Ca] *lasts* [Pro] *11 weeks* [At].

（2）载体 + 关系过程（Ca+Pro），例如：
① *Her beautiful hair* [Ca] *shines* [Pro].
② *His eyes* [Ca] *glitter* [Pro] with delight.
③ *His brown eyes* [Ca] *twinkled* [Pro].
④ *Threads of light* [Ca] *gleamed* [Pro].
⑤ *The lamp* [Ca] *glows* [Pro] with a very feeble purple radiance.
⑥ *The sea* [Ca] *glimmered* [Pro] in the March evening.

在该类型中，属性表面上看消失了，但其实是与过程融为一体。

（3）It+ 关系过程 + 属性 + 载体（It+Pro+At+Ca），例如：
① It *is* [Pro] *so difficult* [At] *to get business leaders to come and help* [Ca].
② It *seems* [Pro] *likely* [At] *that the deal will go ahead pretty soon* [Ca].
③ It *is* [Pro] *a criminal offence* [At] *to sell or supply intoxicating liquor* [Ca].

（4）受事 – 载体 + 关系过程 + 属性（Af-Ca+Pro+At），例如：
① *Johnson* [Af-Ca] *had become* [Pro] *a travel writer* [At].
② *Potatoes* [Af-Ca] *turn* [Pro] *green* [At] when exposed to light.
③ At the same time *the surviving companies* [Af-Ca] *will grow* [Pro] *larger* [At].
④ *Its veins* [Af-Ca] *run* [Pro] *cold* [At] within my hand.

（5）施事 – 载体 + 关系过程 + 属性（Ag-Ca+Pro+At），例如：
Instead, *we* [Ag-Ca] *keep* [Pro] *calm* [At].

在现实语篇中，这种类型的小句数量稀少。

2）识别关系过程（Identifying Processes）

识别关系过程体现的是一个参与者（即标记，token）身份的识别是由另一个参与者（即价值，value）来体现。标记和价值都含有抽象语义，其中标记相对具体一些，价值则更抽象一些。标记和价值揭示了我们所在社会的文化意识形态。识别关系过程经常用于描述定义，解释现象等，在科技材料、商业文本、政府报告中比较常用。典型动词和词组有"play、act as、function as、serve as；mean、indicate、suggest、imply、show、betoken、mark、reflect；equal、add up to、make；comprise、feature、include；exemplify、illustrate；express、signify、realize、spell、stand for、mean；be、become、remain"。

（1）标记 + 关系过程 + 价值（Tk+Pro+Vl），例如：
① *I* [Tk] *am* [Pro] *the most miserable creature* [Vl].
② *She* [Tk] is *named* [Pro] *as* [PrEx] *the Chief Executive* [Vl].
③ *They* [Tk] *became* [Pro] *the object of public outrage and loathing* [Vl].
④ *One color* [Tk] *stands* [Pro] *for* [PrEx] *Jamaica's natural resources and sunshine* [Vl].

⑤ *That* [Tk] *is* [Pro] *what I would like to do when the time is right* [Vl].

（2）价值 + 关系过程 + 标记（Vl+Pro+Tk），例如：

① *What one misses most* [Vl] *is* [Pro] *jokes* [Tk].
② *What you do* [Vl] *is* [Pro] *to fix a line of battens across the wall* [Tk].
③ *What I see* [Vl] *is* [Pro] *to offend you* [Tk].
④ *In good business, what you do* [Vl] *is* [Pro] *to raise the money and then start the project* [Tk].
⑤ *The largest city* [Vl] *is* [Pro] *Miami* [Tk].

3）位置关系过程（Locational Processes）

位置关系过程体现的是某个实体参与者所处的方位（location）。该实体参与者即为载体，可以是人，也可以是物。方位即位置，可以是时间上的，也可以是空间上的。方位不是过程的对象，只是对载体的位置进行描述，但也依然被视为是小句的参与者，因为一旦缺失，语义便会被严重破坏，从而导致话语完全不能被理解。典型动词就是"be"，后面经常接的介词有"at、in、on、for、with、about、along"。

（1）载体 + 关系过程 + 位置（Ca+Pro+Loc），例如：

① *He* [Ca] *is* [Pro] *beside the bed* [Loc].
② *The book* [Ca] *is* [Pro] *on/under/beside/the desk* [Loc].
③ *That* [Ca] *is* [Pro] *in God's hands* [Loc].
④ *Everything* [Ca] *is* [Pro] *in its place* [Loc].
⑤ *Training* [Ca] *is* [Pro] *on Tuesday evenings* [Loc] for enthusiasts in the London area.

（2）施事－载体 + 关系过程 + 位置（Ag-Ca+Pro+Loc），例如：

① *He* [Ag-Ca] *lives* [Pro] *in an airplane* [Loc] because being made homeless.
② *He* [Ag-Ca] should *reside* [Pro] *at a probation hostel* [Loc].
③ *Most applicants* [Ag-Ca] *remain* [Pro] *in the United Kingdom* [Loc] for economic reasons.
④ *We* [Ag-Ca] *inhabit* [Pro] *the same planet* [Loc].
⑤ *They* [Ag-Ca] *work* [Pro] *in the central and usually wealthy areas* [Loc].

（3）受事－载体 + 关系过程 + 位置（Af-Ca+Pro+Loc），例如：

A few coins [Af-Ca] *remained* [Pro] *in my pocket* [Loc].

此种类型实例数量稀少。

4）方向关系过程（Directional Processes）

方向关系过程描述的是某个实体参与者所处的静态方向（direction）。根据福赛特（2010: 57），方向一共有三种：来源（source）、路径（path）和目的地（destination）。来源指方向的源头，使用"from"；路径指从源头到目的地的途径，使用"by"；目的地是过程的指向，使用"to"，在方向关系过程中最为常见。无论是来源、路径还是源头，都被视为小句的参与者。若缺少了它们，小句意义便会被严重损害。

载体 + 关系过程 + 来源和 / 或路径和 / 或目的地（Ca+Pro+So and/or Pa and/or

Des），例如：

① *One idea* [Ca] *leads* [Pro] *to another* [Des].
② *Rights* [Ca] *derive* [Pro] *from duties* [So].
③ *A pair of wide tracks* [Ca] *led* [Pro] *through the slush and mud* [Pa].
④ *The deadline for tenders* [Ca] was *postponed* [Pro] *to February 24* [Des].
⑤ *The breeding season* [Ca] *lasts* [Pro] *from late spring* [So] *until late summer* [Des].

5）拥有关系过程（Possessive Processes）

拥有关系过程描述了一个实体参与者与另一个实体参与者之间拥有和被拥有的关系。前者称为拥有者（Possessor），后者称为拥有物（Possessed）。福赛特（2010：82）认为，拥有关系不仅包括狭义上的拥有、持有关系，还包括广义上的参与、包含乃至缺失或缺少关系。典型动词和词组有"have、own、possess、include、involve、contain、comprise、consist of、provide"。

（1）拥有者 + 关系过程 + 拥有物（Posr+Pro+Posd），例如：

① *Those Eskimos* [Posr] must *have* [Pro] *a quiet life* [Posd].
② Today *we* [Posr] *own* [Pro] *the luxuries of life* [Posd].
③ *Few of us* [Posr] *possess* [Pro] *universal skills* [Posd].
④ *The Oral Test* [Posr] will *consist* [Pro] *of* [PrEx] *a conversation (7-8 minutes) with the examiner* [Posd].

（2）拥有物 + 关系过程 + 拥有者（Posd+Pro+Posr），例如：

① *The house* [Posd] *is* [Pro] *mine* [Posr].
② *We* [Posd] all *belong* [Pro] *to* [PrEx] *the human race* [Posr].
③ *The vast majority of our land* [Posd] is *owned* [Pro] *by* [PrEx] *a handful of individuals, private and public companies, trusts and associations* [Posr].

6）关联关系过程（Correlational Processes）

关联关系过程描述了一个参与者角色与另一个参与者角色之间的关系。两个参与者体现了匹配关系，通过关联过程而联系在一起。何伟等（2017b: 117）认为，两个参与者之间的地位往往是平等的，而且这种过程不仅包括互相匹配关系，还包括连接关系、结合关系等，并将这两个参与者角色命名为"相关方1"和"相关方2"。两个相关方（correlator）虽然密切相关，但却是不同的实体。另外，两个相关方之间也没有抽象程度方面的突出差异或区别。关联关系过程的典型动词有："add up、blend、compare、conflate、contrast、combine (with)、conjoin、connect、correlate、distinguish、differ from、equate、entwine、fit、fuse、go with、integrate、interlink、interlock、intertwine、interweave、join (to)、juxtapose、liken、link (up)、marry (to)、match (with)、mismatch、mix (up)、muddle、merge、overlap、reconcile、relate、separate (from)、touch、tie、unify、wed"。（Neale, 2002: 162）

（1）相关方1 + 关系过程 + 相关方2（Cor1+Pro+Cor2），例如：

① *Liz* [Cor1] *marries* [Pro] *David* [Cor2].

② *Their colors* [Cor1] *blend* [Pro] *with* [PrEx] *the mountains* [Cor2].
（2）施事 + 关系过程 + 相关方1+ 相关方2（Ag+Pro+Cor1+Cor2），例如：
① *We* [Ag] *combine* [Pro] *exercise* [Cor1] *with* [PrEx] *a healthy diet* [Cor2].
② *He* [Ag] *linked* [Pro] *the counselor's comment* [Cor1] *to* [PrEx] *his experiences* [Cor2].
③ *These options* [Ag] *tie* [Pro] *the artist* [Cor1] *to* [PrEx] *the record company* [Cor2].
7）影响类关系过程（Influential Relational Processes）
（1）施事 + 影响类动词 +[[载体 + 属性]]（Ag+Pro+[[Ca+At]]），例如：
① *You* [Ag] *make* [Pro] [[*me* [Ca] *a brand new woman* [At]]].
② *Harsh chemicals* [Ag] can *leave* [Pro] [[*hair* [Ca] *dry and dull* [At]]].
③ Perhaps *you* [Ag] *have* [Pro] [[*shelves* [Ca] *full of books* [At] *all over the house* [Ca]]].
（2）施事 + 影响类动词 +[[标记 + 关系过程 + 价值]]（Ag+Pro+[[Tk+Pro+Vl]]），例如：
① *I* [Ag] would *let* [Pro] [[*you* [Tk] *be* [Pro] *the judge of it* [Vl]]].
② *She* [Ag] *forced* [Pro] [[*him* [Tk] to *be* [Pro] *a specter at the back of her mind* [Vl]]].
（3）施事 + 影响类动词 +[[载体 + 关系过程 + 位置]]（Ag+Pro+[[Ca+Pro+Loc]]），例如：
① *She* [Ag] *required* [Pro] [[*him* [Ca] to *stay* [Pro] *at home* [Loc]]].
② *She* [Ag] *let* [Pro] [[*him* [Ca] *stay* [Pro] *at home* [Loc] yesterday]].
③ *I* [Ag] won't *have* [Pro] [[*her* [Ca] *stay* [Pro] *in my house* [Loc]]].
（4）施事 + 影响类动词 +[[载体 + 关系过程 + 方向：来源和/或路径和/或目的地]]（Ag+Pro+[[Ca+Pro+Dir: So and/or Pa and/or Des]]），例如：
① *The court* [Ag] can *make* [Pro] [[*it* [Ca] to be *extended* [Pro] *to the child's eighteenth birthday* [Des]]] if the circumstances of the case are exceptional.
（5）施事 + 影响类动词 +[[拥有者 + 关系过程 + 拥有物]]（Ag+Pro+[[Posr+Pro+Posd]]），例如：
① *They* [Ag] might *permit* [Pro] [[*the Dogers* [Posr] to *retain* [Pro] *a greater percentage of their TV rights than other clubs* [Posd]]].
② How did *they* [Ag] *make* [Pro] [[*the stuff* [Posr] *hold* [Pro] *all that water* [Posd]]].
（6）施事 + 影响类动词 +[[相关方1+ 关系过程 + 相关方2]]（Ag+Pro+[[Cor1+Pro+Cor2]]），例如：
His mother [Ag] *made* [Pro] [[*him* [Cor1] *marry* [Pro] *that girl in Durham* [Cor2]]].
关系过程语义配置结构现以图表小结如下：

1）归属关系过程	
（1）载体 + 关系过程 + 属性	Ca+Pro+At
（2）载体 + 关系过程	Ca+Pro
（3）It+ 关系过程 + 属性 + 载体	It+Pro+At+Ca

续表

（4）受事 – 载体 + 关系过程 + 属性	Af-Ca+Pro+At
（5）施事 – 载体 + 关系过程 + 属性	Ag-Ca+Pro+At
2）识别关系过程	
（1）标记 + 关系过程 + 价值	Tk+Pro+Vl
（2）价值 + 关系过程 + 标记	Vl+Pro+Tk
3）位置关系过程	
（1）载体 + 关系过程 + 位置	Ca+Pro+Loc
（2）施事 – 载体 + 关系过程 + 位置	Ag-Ca+Pro+Loc
（3）受事 – 载体 + 关系过程 + 位置	Af-Ca+Pro+Loc
4）方向关系过程	
（1）载体 + 关系过程 + 来源和 / 或路径和 / 或目的地	Ca+Pro+So and/or Pa and/or Des
5）拥有关系过程	
（1）拥有者 + 关系过程 + 拥有物	Posr+Pro+Posd
（2）拥有物 + 关系过程 + 拥有者	Posd+Pro+Posr
6）关联关系过程	
（1）相关方 1+ 关系过程 + 相关方 2	Cor1+Pro+Cor2
（2）施事 + 关系过程 + 相关方 1+ 相关方 2	Ag+Pro+Cor1+Cor2
7）影响类关系过程	
（1）施事 + 影响类动词 +[[载体 + 属性]]	Ag+Pro+[[Ca+At]]
（2）施事 + 影响类动词 +[[标记 + 关系过程 + 价值]]	Ag+Pro+[[Tk+Pro+Vl]]
（3）施事 + 影响类动词 +[[载体 + 关系过程 + 位置]]	Ag+Pro+[[Ca+Pro+Loc]]
（4）施事 + 影响类动词 +[[载体 + 关系过程 + 方向：来源和 / 或路径和 / 或目的地]]	Ag+Pro+[[Ca+Pro+Dir: So and/or Pa and/or Des]]
（5）施事 + 影响类动词 +[[拥有者 + 关系过程 + 拥有物]]	Ag+Pro+[[Posr+Pro+Posd]]
（6）施事 + 影响类动词 +[[相关方 1+ 关系过程 + 相关方 2]]	Ag+Pro+[[Cor1+Pro+Cor2]]

4. 行为过程（Behavioral Processes）

系统功能语言学研究者们（Halliday, 1994/2000: 107; Halliday & Matthiessen, 2004/2008: 248；胡壮麟等，2005: 82）指出，在动作、心理和关系三大主要经验过程之外，还有三个位于其间的经验过程。它们是行为过程、交流过程和存在过程。行为过程位于动作过程和心理过程之间，交流过程位于心理过程和关系过程之间，存在过程位于关系过程和动作过程之间。这种在一定程度上交叉和重叠的特点从侧面反映了及物性系统中动词过程之间的界限具有模糊性和重叠性（Thompson, 2004/2008: 104）。韩礼德（1994/2000: 107）和迈西森（2013: 215）认为，行为过程是人体内在机能的外部表现，是意识和生

第十二章 概念功能

理显性化的结果。简单点说，行为过程就是指"诸如呼吸、咳嗽、叹息、做梦、哭泣、大笑等生理活动的表现"。行为过程虽然也体现出人们做某事的过程，但这种过程基本都是人体条件反射类的生理活动，通常都是自然而然发生的，因此人们在经历行为过程时往往都是下意识的。行为过程中的动作并非完全不能控制，但往往要付出较大努力。典型英语动词有"cough、sneeze、burp、yawn、frown、breathe、nod、shudder、sigh、grin、smile、laugh、cry、weep、sob、chatter、mumble、mutter、hiss、shine、vomit、sweat、faint、twitch、hiccup、gasp、shake、shiver、sleep、grumble、gossip、stammer、stutter、moan"。

（1）行为者+行为过程（Behr+Pro），例如：

① *Marx* [Behr] *coughed* [Pro] again.
② *The man* [Behr] is *breathing* [Pro] very hard.
③ *He* [Behr] *sighed* [Pro] tiredly.
④ *He* [Behr] was *smiling* [Pro].
⑤ *He* [Behr] *yawned* [Pro], closed his eyes again and turned on his side.
⑥ *She* [Behr] was *shuddering* [Pro] uncontrollably.
⑦ *A police dog* [Behr] is *whining* [Pro] in the room.
⑧ *It* [Behr] would still *hiss* [Pro] and make noise, but the energy and power were gone.

（2）行为者+行为过程+范围（Behr+Pro+Ra），例如：

① *I* [Behr] *had* [Pro] *a funny dream* [PrEx1] *about* [PrEx2] *you* [Ra].
② *I* [Behr] *laughed* [Pro] *at* [PrEx] *Ann* [Ra] last night.
③ *You*'ve [Behr] been *mumbling* [Pro] *about* [PrEx] *cherry cheese coffee cake* [Ra] in your sleep.
④ When *I*'m [Behr] *watching* [Pro] *TV* [Ra], I'm thinking I'm learning about myself.
⑤ *She* [Behr] *laughed* [Pro] *a little tinkling laugh* [Ra] again.

（3）施事+影响类动词+[[行为者+行为过程(+范围)]]（Ag+Pro+[[Behr+Pro(+Ra)]]），例如：

① *The two boys* [Ag] *kept* [Pro] [[*me*[Behr] *laughing* [Pro] so much]].
② *The man* [Ag] was able to *let* [Pro] [[*her* [Behr] *weep* [Pro]]].
③ *The very mention of his name* [Ag] *caused* [Pro] [[*her* [Behr] to *tremble* [Pro]]].
④ *His grey eyes* [Ag] *made* [Pro] [[*her* [Behr] *smile* [Pro] *at* [PrEx] *the gleam of amusement she saw there* [Ra]]].

行为过程语义配置结构现以图表小结如下：

1）行为者+行为过程	Behr+Pro
2）行为者+行为过程+范围	Behr+Pro+Ra
3）施事+影响类动词+[[行为者+行为过程(+范围)]]	Ag+Pro+[[Behr+Pro(+Ra)]]

5. 交流过程（Communicative Processes）

交流过程是指通过语言进行信息交换的经验过程。韩礼德等（Halliday & Matthiessen, 2004/2008: 171; 胡壮麟等, 2005: 83）学者把这类过程称为"言语过程"，何伟等（2017a: 135; 2017b: 128）学者把这个过程称为"交流过程"。"言语过程"这一术语只侧重于体现说话类经验过程，而"交流过程"的表述既包括了说话类经验过程，又包括了意指类的经验过程，故而这里认同交流过程的说法。典型动词有"say、read、warn、report、state、tell、advise、ask、explain、convince、persuade、insult、abuse、talk、discuss、praise、speak、express、introduce、claim"。

（1）交流方 + 交流过程 + 交流内容（Comr+Pro+Comd），例如：

① *My watch* [Comr] *says* [Pro] *7:03* [Comd].
② *The sign* [Comr] *reads* [Pro] *LAS VEGAS, 30 MILES* [Comd].
③ *The paper* [Comr] *reported* [Pro] *the White House knew of the levees' failure on the night of the storm* [Comd].
④ *The notice* [Comr] *warned* [Pro] *that if they failed to pay, the county would start cation that could lead to the loss of their property* [Comd].

（2）交流方 + 交流过程（+ 交流对象）+ 交流内容（Comr+Pro(+Comee)+Comd），例如：

① *He* [Comr] may be able to *tell* [Pro] *us* [Comee] *something about his passenger* [Comd].
② In the interview *they* [Comr] *asked* [Pro] *me* [Comee] *about* [PrEx] *my future plans* [Comd].
③ *I* [Comr] *said* [Pro], *"What is it?"* [Comd].
④ *I* [Comr] can *tell* [Pro] *you* [Comee] *what goes down* [Comd].
⑤ *I* [Comr] *insulted* [Pro] *him* [Comd] at the time.

（3）交流方 + 交流过程 + 交流内容 + 交流对象（Comr+Pro+Comd+Comee），例如：

① *North* [Comr] *told* [Pro] *the story* [Comd] *to* [PrEx] *Bob Earl* [Comee].
② *They* [Comr-Comee] *discussed* [Pro] *the new turkey farms* [Comd].
③ *They* [Comr-Comee] *talked* [Pro] *about* [PrEx] *their plans* [Comd] for a few minutes.
④ But *he* [Comr] frequently *praised* [Pro] *her* [Comd] *to* [PrEx] *Mother* [Comee].

（4）施事 + 影响类动词 +[[交流方 + 交流过程 + 交流内容 (+ 交流对象)]]（Ag+Pro+[[Comr+Pro+Comd(+Comee)]]），例如：

① *I* [Ag] *forced* [Pro] [[*him* [Comr] to *tell* [Pro] *the truth* [Comd]]].
② *Allow* [Pro] [[*me* [Comr] to *introduce* [Pro] *myself* [Comd]]].
③ If *you* [Ag] will *permit* [Pro] [[*me* [Comr] to *ask* [Pro] *you* [Comee] *a few questions* [Comd]]]?
④ *That all is in flux* [Ag] seems to *prevent* [Pro] [[*us* [Comr] from *expressing* [Pro] *the truth* [Comd]]].

交流过程语义配置结构现以图表小结如下：

1）交流方 + 交流过程 + 交流内容	Comr+Pro+Comd
2）交流方 + 交流过程（+ 交流对象）+ 交流内容	Comr+Pro(+Comee)+Comd
3）交流方 + 交流过程 + 交流内容 + 交流对象	Comr+Pro+Comd+Comee
4）施事 + 影响类动词 +[[交流方 + 交流过程 + 交流内容 (+ 交流对象)]]	Ag+Pro+[[Comr+Pro+Comd (+Comee)]]

6. 存在过程（Existential Processes）

韩礼德和迈西森（2004/2008, 2013）、汤普森（2004/2008）和马丁等（2010）学者指出，英语中的"There be"句型由于具有独特的句法特征，应被视为一种独立的过程类型。"There be"句型中的某物自然会存在于某个地方或某个时间段内。某物可以被理解为东西、行动或事件（Halliday, 1994/2000: 142），术语上被称为"存在方"，是句中的新信息所在。典型英语动词和词组有"be、exist、remain、arise、occur、happen、come about、take place、follow、ensue、sit、stand、lie、hang、rise、stretch、emerge、grow、erupt、flourish、prevail"。

（1）There+ 存在过程 + 存在方 + 位置（There+Pro+Ext+Loc），例如：

① There *was* [Pro] *a school* [Ext] *about three miles away, at Mulindry* [Loc].

② There *remain* [Pro] *some domains of research which are disinterested* [Ext].

③ There *exist* [Pro] *within each nation* [Loc] *classes with antagonistic interests and "rights"* [Ext].

④ There, *in the yard below* [Loc], *was* [Pro] *Miss hardbroom wreathed in thick purple smoke* [Ext].

（2）位置（方向）+there+ 交流过程 + 施事 – 存在方（Loc(Dir)+there+Pro+Ag-Ext），例如：

① *From the prementum* [Dir: So] there *run* [Pro] *the levator and depressor muscles of the palps* [Ag-Ext].

② *Through the hall* [Dir: Pa], there *goes* [Pro] *a man with a guilty secret* [Ag-Ext].

③ There *arises* [Pro] *out of the couplet* [Dir: So] *a sense of the nobility of man* [Ext].

④ There *follow* [Pro] *three corporals, and two drummers, Kelley and Nicholson* [Ext].

（3）位置（方向）+there+ 交流过程 + 受事 – 存在方（Loc(Dir)+there+Pro+Af-Ext），例如：

① *On Eva's walls* [Loc] there *hang* [Pro] *posters of exotic place* [Af-Ext].

② *From husband and children* [Dir: So] there *rises* [Pro] *a rolling moan that thickens to something dirge-like* [Af-Ext].

③ There *ensues* [Pro] *a hilarious debate* [Af-Ext] *in the parking lot* [Loc].

④ There *follow* [Pro] *six essays on spirituality, pastoral ministry and preaching* [Af-Ext].

（4）施事 + 影响类动词 +[[there+ 交流过程 + 存在方 + 位置]]（Ag+Pro+[[there+Pro+Ext+Loc]]），例如：

① God said "*Let* [Pro] [[there *be* [Pro] *light* [Ext]]]".
② *Let* [Pro] [[there *be* [Pro] *a tree* [Ext]]]—and there will be one.
③ *Let* [Pro] [[there *be* [Pro] *no hostility* [Ext]]], except to those who practice oppression.

存在过程语义配置结构现以图表小结如下：

1）There+ 存在过程 + 存在方 + 位置	There+Pro+Ext+Loc
2）位置（方向）+there+ 交流过程 + 施事 – 存在方	Loc(Dir)+there+Pro+Ag-Ext
3）位置（方向）+there+ 交流过程 + 受事 – 存在方	Loc(Dir)+there+Pro+Af-Ext
4）施事 + 影响类动词 +[[there+ 交流过程 + 存在方 + 位置]]	Ag+Pro+[[there+Pro+Ext+Loc]]

7. 气象过程（Meteorological Processes）

根据迈西森（2013: 213-216）对过程类型的划分，气象过程小句可以定义为仅通过过程来表达天气意义的小句类型。本质上来讲，天气现象并不是一种动作，而是一种自然发生的事情，不需要任何参与者角色出现，因此气象过程只有过程类型，而没有参与者角色。英语气象过程小句的基本句式为：It+ 气象过程。这里的"It"并不是参与者，也不能理解为"天"，更不是"施事"，只是一种语言习惯罢了。实际上，这个句式想表达的意思是某种气象自天上而来。

（1）It+ 气象过程（It+Pro），例如：

① It's *blowing* [Pro] from the east now.
② It never *rains* [Pro] but it *pours* [Pro].
③ I will do it even when it *snows* [Pro] and when it *rains* [Pro].
④ It's *raining / snowing / hailing / freezing / drizzling / thundering / pouring / lightening / blowing* [Pro] *outside* [Cir: Loc] / *hardly* [Cir: De].

（2）It+ 气象过程 + 过程延长成分（It+Pro+PrEx），例如：

① It'*s* [Pro] *sunny/cloudy/windy/chilly* [PrEx] outside today.
② It's *getting* [Pro] *hot* [PrEx].
③ It'*s* [Pro] *freezing cold* [PrEx] today.
④ It *got* [Pro] *hot and dry* [PrEx] and the sun hammered the land.
⑤ It *stopped/started* [Pro] *raining* [PrEx]
⑥ It *grew* [Pro] *colder than it was before* [PrEx], which energized us.

（3）施事 + 影响类动词 +[[It+ 气象过程]]（Ag+Pro+[[It+Pro]]），例如：

① *She* [Ag] *made* [Pro] [[it *rain* [Pro]]] with her magic weather-control scarf.
② *I* [Ag] *made* [Pro] [[it *rain* [Pro] *cats and dogs* [PrEx]]] a while ago, but that was quite an accident.
③ ([Ag]) *Let* [Pro] [[it *rain* [Pro]]].

气象过程语义配置结构现以图表小结如下：

1）It+ 气象过程	It+Pro
2）It+ 气象过程 + 过程延长成分	It+Pro+PrEx
3）施事 + 影响类动词 +[[It+ 气象过程]]	Ag+Pro+[[It+Pro]]

（二）语态（Voice）

语态是语法范畴，是动词的形态体现，表示主语和谓语动词是主动关系还是被动关系。英语动词有两种语态：主动形式语态（active voice）和被动形式语态（passive voice）。主动形式语态用在主动句中，通常都用来表达主语是谓语动词的施动者，也有少量主动语态的句子表达被动含义。被动形式语态用在被动句中，表示主语是动作承受者。英语被动语态的基本结构为："be+ 过去分词"。一般来说，主动语态句式是无标记的，使用频率较高，而被动语态句式是有标记的，使用频率较低。

根据章振邦（2012：147）的理论，小句中被动语态的形式一共有 6 种，请见下表。

六种有被动语态的时体	被动语态表达形式（以 I ask 为例）
一般现在时	I am asked
一般过去时	I was asked
现在进行体	I am being asked
过去进行体	I was being asked
现在完成体	I have been asked
过去完成体	I had been asked

1. 被动语态的使用条件（The Conditions of Using the Passive Voice）

被动语态的结构可以分为两种：句尾加 "by sb/sth" 词组型，句尾不加 "by sb/sth" 词组型。后者是无标记的，强调事情发生本身，前者是有标记的，强调谁要对此负责。通常说来，句尾不加 "by sb/sth" 词组型被动语态句的使用要满足以下条件：首先，施事未知，只为凸显动作或事件本身；其次，施事已知，但为突显动作或事件本身；最后，施事已知，但又不想承担相关责任，或者想责备对方，于是采用被动句式，只说发生了什么事情，并隐藏施事。

结尾不加 "by sb/sth" 词组型 被动句式	例　子
1) 施事未知，只为凸显动作或事件本身。	① He *was killed* in the war. ② On his way home from the bank, the old man *was robbed*. ③ The injured *were allowed* home after treatment at the local hospital, but one of the firemen *was detained* for observation.

续表

2) 施事已知，但为凸显动作或事件本身。	① She *has been sacked*. ② The book *was first published* in 2000. ③ The drowning man was clinging to the rope which *was thrown* to him.
3) 施事已知，但又不想承担相关责任，或者想责备对方，于是采用被动句式，只说发生了什么事情，并隐藏施事。	① Tell your boss, the deed *was done*. ② Oh dear, look, the washing-up *hasn't been done*. ③ Don't blame me. Nothing can *be done* about it. ④ He *is said* to be a smuggler. ⑤ San Diego *is described* as the most beautiful place in South California.

句尾加"by sb/sth"词组型被动语态句的使用要满足以下条件：首先，施事成为小句焦点，放在句尾利于强调；其次，施事太长，不得不放在句尾以保持全句平衡。

结尾加"by sb/sth"词组型被动句式	例　子
1) 施事成为小句焦点，放在句尾利于强调。	① This picture was painted *by Picasso* in 1937. ② *Madame Bovery* was written *by Flaubert*. ③ Tea drinking is considered one of the pleasures of life *by the Chinese*.
2) 施事太长，不得不放在句尾以保持全句平衡。	① She was delighted *by the huge orange sun sinking slowly below the horizon*. ② The president was mistrusted *by the leaders of the two most powerful parties in the country*. ③ At least 150,000 people were killed *by the tsunami unleashed on December 26, 2004 by an extremely powerful earthquake off the coast of Indonesia*.

2. 常用被动语态的文体（The Genres That Commonly Use the Passive Voice）

不管被动句式是长是短，有没有突出施事，都常用在新闻报道、学术文章和科技文章等正式文体中，以彰显客观、理性，或者给人留下客观、公正的印象。

（1）新闻报道，例如：

① It was apparent to everyone in the ruling circles that Japan's fortune could not *be reversed*, that the war *was lost*.

② Negotiating an end to the war *was* first formally *raised* in an official discussion at the Imperial Conference on June 22, 1945.

③ Yesterday, December 7, 1941—a date which will live in infamy—the United States of America *was* suddenly and deliberately *attacked* by naval and air forces of the Empire of Japan.

（2）学术文章，例如：

① The word "plastic" comes from the Greek word "plastikos" and *is used* to describe something which can *be* easily *shaped*.

② Early fires on the earth *were* certainly *caused* by nature, not by man. Some *were caused* by lightning in a storm; others, perhaps, by hot material which came out of a volcano.

③ The framework we outline, then, *is directed* towards providing a systematic account of how such positionings *are achieved* linguistically.

（3）科技文章，例如：

① The mixture *is placed* in a crucible and *is heated* to a temperature of 300℃. It *is* then *allowed* to cool before it can *be analysed*.

② Some kinds of plastics can *be forced* through machines which separate them into long, thin strings, called "fibres", and these fibres can *be made* into cloth.

③ If a well *is sunk* near the middle of the oil-field, gas will *be obtained*. This may blow out of the well with great force if it *is not controlled*.

3. 部分主动语态表达特殊被动意义（Special Passive Meaning by Using Part of the Active Voice Expressions）

当主语具有某种内在品质，可导致、妨碍或阻止谓语表示的概念得以实现时，要使用主动形式语态。在这种句式中，常用来表达被动意义的动词有"carry、clean、fill、fire、grind、handle、kill、iron、light、lock、pack、read、scan、stain、tear"，例如：

① The middle house *won't let*（租不出去）。
The middle house *will not be let*（不出租）。
② His novels *don't sell*（销路不好）。
His novels *are not sold*（尚未销售）。
③ Her plays *won't act*（不适宜上演）。
Her plays *will not be acted*（不上演）。
④ The door *won't lock*（门锁不上）。
The door *will not be locked*（不会被锁上）。

注意，上述四组例子中，每一组两两对照的句子的含义都有明显的区别。

（三）小句经验功能分析（Case Analysis to Experiential Metafunction）

The Two Roads
John Ruskin

【例163】

原　文：It was New Year's Night. An aged man was standing at a window. He raised his mournful eyes towards the deep blue sky, where the stars were floating like white lilies on the surface of a clear calm lake. Then he cast them on the earth, where few more hopeless people than him now moved towards their certain goal—the tomb. He had already passed sixty of the stages leading to it, and he had brought from his journey nothing but errors and remorse. Now his health was poor, his mind vacant, his heart sorrowful, and his old age short of comforts.

译　文：那是个新年之夜，一位老人伫立在窗前。他忧伤地抬起头，仰望深蓝的夜空，那满天繁星就像朵朵白色睡莲，漂浮在清澈静谧的湖面上。他又忧伤地看了看大地，那里虽有芸芸众生与自己一道走向必然的终点——坟墓，但是却很少有人比他更为绝望。老人已经在旅途中度过了六十载春秋，而最终收获的只有过失和悔恨。如今他的身体大不如前，他的思绪一片茫然，他的心里满是悲伤，他的晚年缺少慰藉。

讲评：

原文小句		(1) It was New Year's Night.
及物性系统	过程类型	识别关系过程
	结构分析	It [Tk] was [Pro] New Year's Night [Vl].（标记＋识别关系过程＋价值）
语态		主动语态
意义解读		该小句交代了故事发生的时间。

原文小句		(2) An aged man was standing at a window.
及物性系统	过程类型	双参与者动作过程
	结构分析	An aged man [Ag] was standing [Pro] at a window [Loc].（施事＋动作过程＋位置）
语态		主动语态
意义解读		该小句交代了一位老人当时的动作和状态。

原文小句		(3) He raised his mournful eyes towards the deep blue sky,
及物性系统	过程类型	双参与者动作过程
	结构分析	He [Ag] raised [Pro] his mournful eyes [Af] towards the deep blue sky,（施事＋动作过程＋受事）
语态		主动语态
意义解读		该小句交代了老人当时的动作。

原文小句		(4) where the stars were floating like white lilies on the surface of a clear calm lake.
及物性系统	过程类型	单参与者动作过程
	结构分析	where the stars [Ag] were floating [Pro] like white lilies on the surface of a clear calm lake.（施事＋动作过程）
语态		主动语态
意义解读		该小句描绘了当时的夜空美景。

原文小句		(5) Then he cast them on the earth,
及物性系统	过程类型	三参与者动作过程
	结构分析	Then he [Ag] cast [Pro] them [Af-Ca] on the earth [Dir: Des],（施事＋动作过程＋受事－载体＋方向）
语态		主动语态
意义解读		该小句描绘了老人的一个具体动作——遥望大地。

原文小句		(6) where few more hopeless people than him now moved towards their certain goal—the tomb.
及物性系统	过程类型	双参与者动作过程
	结构分析	where *few more hopeless people than him* [Ag] now *moved* [Pro] *towards their certain goal—the tomb* [Dir: Des]. （施事＋动作过程＋方向）
语态		主动语态
意义解读		该小句描绘了老人当时看到的景象——自己成为最绝望的人。

原文小句		(7) He had already passed sixty of the stages leading to it,
及物性系统	过程类型	双参与者动作过程
	结构分析	*He* [Ag] had already *passed* [Pro] *sixty of the stages* [Dir: Pa] [[([Ca]) *leading* [Pro] *to* [PrEx] *it* [Des](关系过程)]], （施事＋动作过程＋路径）
语态		主动语态
意义解读		该小句描绘了老人当时已有六十岁的年纪。

原文小句		(8) and he had brought from his journey nothing but errors and remorse.
及物性系统	过程类型	双参与者动作过程
	结构分析	and *he* [Ag] had *brought* [Pro] from his journey *nothing but errors and remorse* [Cre]. （施事＋动作过程＋创造物）
语态		主动语态
意义解读		该小句强调了老人一生的收获唯有过失和悔恨。

原文小句		(9) Now his health was poor, his mind vacant, his heart sorrowful, and his old age short of comforts.
及物性系统	过程类型	归属关系过程
	结构分析	Now *his health* [Ca] *was* [Pro] *poor* [At], *his mind* [Ca] ([Pro]) *vacant* [At], *his heart* [Ca] ([Pro]) *sorrowful* [At], and *his old age* [Ca] ([Pro]) *short of comforts* [At]. （载体＋关系过程＋属性）
语态		主动语态
意义解读		该小句描绘了老人凄凉的晚景——身体糟糕，思绪空白，心里悲伤，缺少慰藉。

【例 164】

原　文：The days of his youth appeared like dreams before him, and he recalled the serious moment when his father placed him at the entrance of the two roads—one leading to a peaceful, sunny place, covered with flowers, fruits and resounding with soft, sweet songs; the other leading to a deep, dark cave, which was endless, where poison flowed instead of water and where devils and poisonous snakes hissed and crawled.

译　文：青春岁月梦幻般地浮现在他眼前，他回想起那庄严的时刻，父亲把他领到了两条路的分岔处———一条路通向和平安宁、阳光明媚的世界，那里有遍地鲜花，满园果实，处处回荡着柔和悦耳的歌声；另一条路则通向黑暗的深渊，那里流淌的是毒液而非清泉，而且恶魔在张牙舞爪，毒蛇在嘶嘶蠕动。

讲　评：

原文小句		(1) The days of his youth appeared like dreams before him.
及物性系统	过程类型	归属关系过程
	结构分析	*The days of his youth* [Ca] *appeared* [Pro] *like dreams* [At] before him.（载体 + 关系过程 + 属性）
语态		主动语态
意义解读		该小句叙述了老人开始回忆自己的青春岁月。

原文小句		(2) and he recalled the serious moment.
及物性系统	过程类型	认知心理过程
	结构分析	and *he* [Cog] *recalled* [Pro] *the serious moment* [Ph].（认知者 + 心理过程 + 现象）
语态		主动语态
意义解读		该小句突出了老人青春岁月的庄严性。

原文小句		(3) when his father placed him at the entrance of the two roads
及物性系统	过程类型	三参与者动作过程
	结构分析	when *his father* [Ag] *placed* [Pro] *him* [Af-Ca] *at the entrance of the two roads* [Af-Des]（施事 + 动作过程 + 受事 – 载体 + 受事 – 目的地）
语态		主动语态
意义解读		该小句描述了父亲引领孩子选择人生道路的情景。

原文小句		(4)—one leading to a peaceful, sunny place, covered with flowers, fruits and resounding with soft, sweet songs;
及物性系统	过程类型	方向关系过程
	结构分析	— *one* [Ca] *leading* [Pro] *to* [PrEx] *a peaceful, sunny place* [Des], covered with flowers, fruits and resounding with soft, sweet songs;（载体 + 关系过程 + 目的地）

第十二章 概念功能

续表

语态		主动语态
意义解读		该小句描绘了其中一条路所指向的美好图景。

原文小句		(5) the other leading to a deep, dark cave
及物性系统	过程类型	方向关系过程
	结构分析	*the other* [Ca] *leading* [Pro] *to* [PrEx] *a deep, dark cave* [Des]（载体 + 关系过程 + 目的地）
语态		主动语态
意义解读		该小句描绘了另一条路所指向的可怕图景。

原文小句		(6) which was endless,
及物性系统	过程类型	归属关系过程
	结构分析	*which* [Ca] *was* [Pro] *endless* [At]，（载体 + 关系过程 + 属性）
语态		主动语态
意义解读		该小句描绘了洞穴具有深不见底的特征。

原文小句		(7) where poison flowed instead of water
及物性系统	过程类型	单参与者动作过程
	结构分析	where *poison* [Ag] *flowed* [Pro] instead of water （施事 + 动作过程）
语态		主动语态
意义解读		该小句描绘了洞穴内部毒液横流的可怕景象。

原文小句		(8) and where devils and poisonous snakes hissed and crawled.
及物性系统	过程类型	行为过程
	结构分析	and where *devils and poisonous snakes* [Behr] *hissed* [Pro] and ([Behr]) *crawled* [Pro].（行为者 + 行为过程）
语态		主动语态
意义解读		该小句描绘了洞穴内恶魔与毒蛇横行的可怕景象。

这里特别说明一下：首先，上述表格是对两个段落中的小句经验功能的分析，其意义解读也仅限于对经验意义的理解，并没有结合全部语境。换言之，考虑语境之后，小

句的意义理解会有更多内容加入。其次，这两个段落小句的语态均为主动语态，也就是无标记语态表达，所以就没有特别分析其意义或内涵。但若是被动语态，往往需要指出作者使用被动句式的目的。再次，小句经验功能的分析对于译者难度极大，需要经过很多练习才能基本掌握。最后，对于翻译研究者而言，小句经验功能分析称得上是一个有益而强大的研究视角和方法。

二、逻辑功能（Logical Metafunction）

逻辑功能与语篇功能中的衔接有直接关联，但并不相同，请看它的定义：

One if the two modes of construing experience within the ideational metafunction, the other being the experiential mode. In the logical mode, our experience of the world is construed serially as chains of phenomena related by logico-semantic relationships. The logical mode engenders complexes of units within semantics. The logical mode also engenders patterns of modification (and submodification) within groups.

(Key Terms in Systemic Functional Linguistics)

概念功能框架内构建经验的两种模式之一，另一个是经验模式。在逻辑模式下，我们对世界的感知按照顺序被理解为与逻辑和语义相关的现象链。逻辑模式在语义范围内制造出复合单位。逻辑模式也在词组范围内制造出修饰和次级修饰的表达方式。（《系统功能语言学核心术语》）

由上述定义，我们可知，逻辑功能指的是语言所具备的反映两个或两个以上语言单位之间逻辑语义关系的功能。韩礼德从相互依存关系（interdependency）和逻辑语义关系（logical-semantic relation）两个视角来研究逻辑关系。

1. 相互依存视角（Interdependent）

韩礼德和迈西森（2004/2008）认为，任何两个不同的语言单位之间都有某种依赖关系，即"相互依存关系"。他把"相互依存关系"分为两种：并列关系（parataxis）和主从关系（hypotaxis）。并列关系指前后两个语言单位同等重要，可以体现在词语层面，也可以体现在小句层面。主从关系指两个或两个以上语言单位在逻辑和语义层面地位不同，其中一个单位比其他单位更重要，是其他单位的依附对象。韩礼德把占据重要地位的单位称为支配成分（dominant element），把处于从属地位的单位称为依附成分（dependent element）。并列关系与主从关系可通过下表清晰地呈现：

逻辑功能的相互依存视角	举例
1）并列关系 （parataxis） 注：小句内画线词语之间为并列关系。	① *Tea* or *coffee*? ② She is an *intelligent* and *diligent* girl. ③ He came in with *a book under his arm* and *a smile on his face*. ④ *He is a teacher* and *I am a student*. ⑤ *John came by car*, and *Mary came by taxi*.

逻辑功能的相互依存视角	举 例
2）主从关系 （hypotaxis） 注：小句内画线词语为支配成分，斜体词语为依附成分。	① Mary is *very* clever. ② There is a *stone* bridge on the river. ③ John ran away *because he was scared*. ④ Nobody believed *that John ran away*.

2. 逻辑语义视角（Logical-semantic）

韩礼德和迈西森（2004/2008）认为，虽然语言单位之间的逻辑关系纷繁复杂，但基本可以分为两类：扩展关系（expansion）和投射关系（projection）。扩展关系指一个词或一个小句在语义上对另一个词或另一个小句进行扩充。扩充的方式有三种：详述、延伸和增强。详述（elaboration）就是改换一个说法，以进一步表述前面的语义，延伸（extension）就是在原有语义基础上增加新内容，增强（enhancement）就是增加时间、地点、因果和条件等环境角色成分，以对小句的语义进行说明。投射指通过一个小句引出另一个小句。被投射的小句可以是某人的话语（locution），也可以是某人的主意（idea），二者均可采用直接引语或间接引语的方式。扩展关系与投射关系可通过下表清晰地呈现：

逻辑功能的逻辑语义视角		举 例
扩展关系 （expansion）	1）详述 （elaboration）	① John ran away; he didn't wait. ② John ran away, which means he didn't wait.
	2）延伸 （extension）	① John ran away and Fred stayed behind. ② John ran away whereas Fred stayed behind.
	3）增强 （enhancement）	① John was scared so he ran away. ② John ran away because he was scared.
投射关系 （projection）	1）话语 （locution）	① John said: "I'm running away." ② John said that he was running away.
	2）主意 （idea）	① John thought to himself: "I'll run away." ② John thought he would run away.

韩礼德和迈西森之所以采取相互依存和逻辑语义两个视角，是为了更加全面准确地分析语言的逻辑功能。其实，这两个视角相互关联，它们的关系正如下表所示：

		(i) 并列（paratactic）	(ii) 主从（hypotactic）
扩展关系 （expansion）	(a) 详述 （elaboration）	John didn't wait; [1] he ran away. [=2]	John ran away, [α] which surprised everyone. [=β]
	b) 延伸 （extension）	John ran away, [1] and Fred stayed behind. [+2]	John ran away, [α] whereas Fred stayed behind. [+β]
	(c) 增强 （enhancement）	John was scared, [1] so he ran away. [x2]	John ran away, [α] because he was scared. [xβ]

续表

		(i) 并列（paratactic）	(ii) 主从（hypotactic）
投射关系 （projection）	(a) 话语 （locution）	John said: [1] "I'm running away" ["2]	John said [α] he was running away. [" β]
	(b) 主意 （idea）	John thought to himself: [1] "I'll run away" ['2]	John thought [α] he would run away. [' β]

(Halliday, 1994: 220)

注：表中的1、2等阿拉伯数字表示并列关系；α、β等希腊字母表示主从关系，其中 α 表示主句，其他字母表示从句；= 表示详述，+ 表示延伸，x 表示修饰；" 表示直接引语，' 表示间接引语。

第三部分　概念功能的翻译策略

基于前面详尽的论述，在翻译原文的概念功能时要牢牢遵守以下三点：

第一，原文小句及物性系统的性质不应该变化。原则上讲，原小句是什么过程，翻译后还是相同的过程；原小句有什么参与者，翻译后还有相同的参与者；原小句参与者扮演什么角色，翻译后参与者也扮演相同的角色；原小句有什么环境成分，翻译后也要保持相同的环境成分。在保证及物性系统基本不变的基础上，同时考虑译入语的使用习惯和社会文化因素，最大限度地实现相等效果的翻译。

第二，充分考虑原文小句特定主语用词这一因素，原则上保证小句语态不要改变。原小句表达主动意义，采用主动语态，翻译后必须表达主动意义，同时最好也是主动语态；原小句表达被动意义，采用被动语态，翻译后必须表达被动意义，同时最好也是被动语态；原小句表达被动意义，但采用主动语态，翻译后必须表达被动意义，同时采用合适的语态。

第三，原文小句间的逻辑功能应准确再现。原文逻辑功能是并列关系，译文逻辑功能也应是并列关系；原文逻辑功能是主从关系，译文逻辑功能也是主从关系，并让读者明显感觉到句子重心。原文逻辑功能是某种扩展关系，译文逻辑功能也应是对应的扩展关系，原文逻辑功能是某种投射关系，译文逻辑功能也应是对应的投射关系。总之，意义和功能原则上必须一致，但是形式上不强求一致。

本章小结

作为三大元功能之一，概念功能理解和掌握的难度最大。概念功能中的经验功能指

第十二章　概念功能

语言对人们在现实世界中的各种经历的表达。按理说，这种对客观世界和主观世界的反映应该比较客观，但其实并不是这样简单。经验意义的表达取决于主语用词、语态、过程类型、参与者角色以及环境角色的选择。换句话说，现实语篇中经验意义的传递可以由作者客观地呈现事件，也可以为读者戴上一副有色眼镜，让他们误以为看到了真实。概念功能中的逻辑功能指语言对两个或两个以上的意义单位之间逻辑关系的表达，多数情况下逻辑联系体现在小句之间，因此对于语篇意义的产生和理解至关重要。在现实语篇中，如果说经验功能是人的骨，那么逻辑功能就是人的筋，二者相辅相成，共同支撑起人体（语篇）的基本框架。语篇功能、人际功能和概念功能犹如一条绳子的三股麻线，共同编织出小句乃至语篇的意义。在做语篇翻译时，对意义的解读可以从这三个维度分别入手，再辅以上编和中编中的有关理论，这样捕捉到的意义必然是客观而真实的。

翻译实践

小说翻译

（一）短篇小说

The Ballet Dancer

By Jane Mayhall

I remember when I was eleven years old and attended a ballet for the first time. It was held at the Memorial Auditorium, a large building in the town where I lived.

During the first group of dances, I sat up very high in the balcony with my family and the stage seemed too far away. It was a pretty show at such a distance, but the dancers with their bright dots of costumes appeared as small and no more alive than marionettes.

When intermission came some friends of the family suggested that I sit down in the second row orchestra with them. This was probably because they considered me a "nice little girl" a, point of view to which I had no objection.

The world of second row orchestra was an immensely different one. The seats were softer and had slightly reclining backs. Here the members of the audience sat with much dignity, as if each had been appointed to a separate throne. A sweet flowery scent came from the ladies. As they settled into their places, one heard a faint sound of silk and fur.

Then the music began. Everyone leaned forward. The high arc of the curtain lifted as if moved by a hundred tiny unseen hands. The stage before us was forest, bathed in willowy green light. The backdrop was splotched with painted leaves and gawk-headed birds whose artificiality seemed, for some reason, particularly exciting.

The dancers stepped forward, the make-up sharp on their faces.

But how near, how human they were! Their eyes moved, their lips smiled. Rising together and beginning to twirl on the tips of their toes, they were much more admirable from here than from afar!

It was a warm night. The sky appeared to reflect a pleasant tropical heat. Men wearing sky blue jackets leapt to girls whose dresses ruffled like swans. Their smiles mingled, their arms embroidered the air with wonderful patterns. Several more dancers came forward, carrying garlands of green and yellow flowers into which they wove themselves. And all with such remarkable enjoyment! Surely something marvelous was going to happen.

And then it did.

Suddenly the music stopped. The only sound to be heard was a thin, somewhat unsteady tone of a violin. The gaily costumed characters moved back silently and made way for someone.

A little flap in the backdrop pulled opened. And a young man stepped forth.

The rest of the dancers departed and left him alone. The lights took on a white hue and one saw that the young man was very pale with dark-penciled eyes. He was dressed in a light blousing shirt and tight breeches of cream-colored stain.

Stepping forward, with causal grace, he began to dance.

At first, all I could realize of him was the delicate-footed motion, the coolness and lightness of the figure. He wore soft close-fitting slippers and the insteps of his feet were so beautiful and alive that I fell in love with them at once. He was small and perfectly formed, slender-hipped and probably quite typical of the ballet dancer. And perhaps there was something too mannered and too self-conscious in the face. His eyes were drawn to appear elongated, Oriental. The head was finely shaped, dark-haired. But the very self-conscious style of him seemed to add to the charm. What could equal the stance, the quick lightning movements of the body, or the severe control of its quietness?

But none of these features by themselves gave the full effect. The complete harmonious accord of the moment—there was no way to explain it.

When the ballet was over and the dancers were bowing outside the curtain, I felt a terrible childish sadness, the kind that is felt only after the accidental pleasure. It is a puzzling sensation, the regret for the loss of that which one had not—no, never—even hoped for in the first place!

The young man stood a little in front of the others, bowing. I noticed that his ears were beautifully pointed and his hair was sleek.

The lights in the Auditorium went up. The orchestra began to play. People put on their wraps and began to talk in matter-of-fact voices. But I was gravely occupied with the memory of the young man. Moving slowly in the large arena of the Auditorium, I felt that I would never forget him. I listened dreamily to the music and watched the audience make dignified parade to the rear exit. It seemed, to my impressionable mind, that everything existed only for the contemplation of him.

After Twenty Years

By O. Henry

The policeman on the beat moved up the avenue impressively. The impressiveness was habitual and not for show, for spectators were few. The time was barely 10 o'clock at night, but chilly gusts of wind with a taste of rain in them had well nigh depeopled the streets.

Trying doors as he went, twirling his club with many intricate and artful movements, turning now and then to cast his watchful eye adown the pacific thoroughfare, the officer, with his stalwart form and slight swagger, made a fine picture of a guardian of the peace. The vicinity was one that kept early hours. Now and then you might see the lights of a cigar store or of an all-night lunch counter; but the majority of the doors belonged to business places that had long since been closed.

When about midway of a certain block the policeman suddenly slowed his walk. In the doorway of a darkened hardware store a man leaned, with an unlighted cigar in his mouth. As the policeman walked up to him the man spoke up quickly.

"It's all right, officer," he said, reassuringly. "I'm just waiting for a friend. It's an appointment made twenty years ago. Sounds a little funny to you, doesn't it? Well, I'll explain if you'd like to make certain it's all straight. About that long ago there used to be a restaurant where this store stands—'Big Joe' Brady's restaurant."

"Until five years ago," said the policeman. "It was torn down then."

The man in the doorway struck a match and lit his cigar. The light showed a pale, square-jawed face with keen eyes, and a little white scar near his right eyebrow. His scarf pin was a large diamond, oddly set.

"Twenty years ago to-night," said the man, "I dined here at 'Big Joe' Brady's with Jimmy Wells, my best chum, and the finest chap in the world. He and I were raised here in New York, just like two brothers, together. I was eighteen and Jimmy was twenty. The next morning I was to start for the West to make my fortune. You couldn't have dragged Jimmy out of New York; he thought it was the only place on earth. Well, we agreed that night that we would meet here again exactly twenty years from that date and time, no matter what our conditions might be or from what distance we might have to come. We figured that in twenty years each of us ought to have our destiny worked out and our fortunes made, whatever they were going to be."

"It sounds pretty interesting," said the policeman. "Rather a long time between meets, though, it seems to me. Haven't you heard from your friend since you left?"

"Well, yes, for a time we corresponded," said the other. "But after a year or two we lost track of each other. You see, the West is a pretty big proposition, and I kept hustling around over it pretty lively. But I know Jimmy will meet me here if he's alive, for he always was the truest, stanchest old chap in the world. He'll never forget. I came a thousand miles to stand in this door to-night, and it's worth it if my old partner turns up."

The waiting man pulled out a handsome watch, the lids of it set with small diamonds.

"Three minutes to ten," he announced. "It was exactly ten o'clock when we parted here at the restaurant door."

"Did pretty well out West, didn't you?" asked the policeman.

"You bet! I hope Jimmy has done half as well. He was a kind of plodder, though, good fellow as he was. I've had to compete with some of the sharpest wits going to get my pile. A man gets in a groove in New York. It takes the West to put a razor-edge on him."

The policeman twirled his club and took a step or two.

"I'll be on my way. Hope your friend comes around all right. Going to call time on him sharp?"

"I should say not!" said the other. "I'll give him half an hour at least. If Jimmy is alive on earth he'll be here by that time. So long, officer."

"Good-night, sir," said the policeman, passing on along his beat, trying doors as he went.

There was now a fine, cold drizzle falling, and the wind had risen from its uncertain puffs into a steady blow. The few foot passengers astir in that quarter hurried dismally and silently along with coat collars turned high and pocketed hands. And in the door of the hardware store the man who had come a thousand miles to fill an appointment, uncertain almost to absurdity, with the friend of his youth, smoked his cigar and waited.

About twenty minutes he waited, and then a tall man in a long overcoat, with collar turned up to his ears, hurried across from the opposite side of the street. He went directly to the waiting man.

"Is that you, Bob?" he asked, doubtfully.

"Is that you, Jimmy Wells?" cried the man in the door.

"Bless my heart!" exclaimed the new arrival, grasping both the other's hands with his own. "It's Bob, sure as fate. I was certain I'd find you here if you were still in existence. Well, well, well!—twenty years is a long time. The old gone, Bob; I wish it had lasted, so we could have had another dinner there. How has the West treated you, old man?"

"Bully; it has given me everything I asked it for. You've changed lots, Jimmy. I never thought you were so tall by two or three inches."

"Oh, I grew a bit after I was twenty."

"Doing well in New York, Jimmy?"

"Moderately. I have a position in one of the city departments. Come on, Bob; we'll go around to a place I know of, and have a good long talk about old times."

The two men started up the street, arm in arm. The man from the West, his egotism enlarged by success, was beginning to outline the history of his career. The other, submerged in his overcoat, listened with interest.

At the corner stood a drug store, brilliant with electric lights. When they came into this glare each of them turned simultaneously to gaze upon the other's face.

The man from the West stopped suddenly and released his arm.

"You're not Jimmy Wells," he snapped. "Twenty years is a long time, but not long enough to change a man's nose from a Roman to a pug."

"It sometimes changes a good man into a bad one," said the tall man. "You've been under arrest for ten minutes, 'Silky' Bob. Chicago thinks you may have dropped over our way and wires us she wants to have a chat with you. Going quietly, are you? That's sensible. Now, before we go on to the station here's a note I was asked to hand you. You may read it here at the window. It's from Patrolman Wells."

The man from the West unfolded the little piece of paper handed him. His hand was steady when he began to read, but it trembled a little by the time he had finished. The note was rather short.

Bob: I was at the appointed place on time. When you struck the match to light your cigar I saw it was the face of the man wanted in Chicago. Somehow I couldn't do it myself, so I went around and got a plain clothes man to do the job. JIMMY.

（二）长篇小说节选

1. 对话类语篇

Pride and Prejudice
Chapter 5

...

Lady Lucas was a very good kind of woman, not too clever to be a valuable neighbour to Mrs. Bennet—They had several children. The eldest of them, a sensible, intelligent young woman, about twenty-seven, was Elizabeth's intimate friend.

That the Miss Lucases and the Miss Bennets should meet to talk over a ball was absolutely necessary; and the morning after the assembly brought the former to Longbourn to hear and to communicate.

"*You* began the evening well, Charlotte," said Mrs. Bennet with civil self-command to Miss Lucas. "*You* were Mr. Bingley's first choice."

"Yes;—but he seemed to like his second better."

"Oh!—you mean Jane, I suppose—because he danced with her twice. To be sure that *did* seem as if he admired her—indeed I rather believe he *did*—I heard something about it—but I hardly know what—something about Robinson."

"Perhaps you mean what I overheard between him and Mr. Robinson; did not I mention it to you? Mr. Robinson's asking him how he liked our Meryton assemblies, and whether he did not think there were a great many pretty women in the room, and *which* he thought the prettiest? and his answering immediately to the last question—Oh! the eldest Miss Bennet beyond a doubt, there cannot be two opinions on that point."

"Upon my word!—Well, that was very decided indeed—that does seem as if—but however, it may all come to nothing you know."

"*My* overhearings were more to the purpose than *yours*, Eliza," said Charlotte. "Mr. Darcy is not so well worth listening to as his friend, is he?—Poor Eliza!—to be only just *tolerable*."

"I beg you would not put it into Lizzy's head to be vexed by his ill-treatment; for he is such a disagreeable man that it would be quite a misfortune to be liked by him. Mrs. Long told me last night that he sat close to her for half an hour without once opening his lips."

"Are you quite sure, Ma'am?—is not there a little mistake?" said Jane.—"I certainly saw Mr. Darcy speaking to her."

"Aye—because she asked him at last how he liked Netherfield, and he could not help answering her;—but she said he seemed very angry at being spoke to."

"Miss Bingley told me," said Jane, "that he never speaks much unless among his intimate acquaintance. With *them* he is remarkably agreeable."

"I do not believe a word of it, my dear. If he had been so very agreeable he would have talked to Mrs. Long. But I can guess how it was; every body says that he is ate up with pride, and I dare say he had heard somehow that Mrs. Long does not keep a carriage, and had come to the ball in a hack chaise."

"I do not mind his not talking to Mrs. Long," said Miss Lucas, "but I wish he had danced with Eliza."

"Another time, Lizzy," said her mother, "I would not dance with *him*, if I were you."

"I believe, Ma'am, I may safely promise you *never* to dance with him."

"His pride," said Miss Lucas, "does not offend *me* so much as pride often does, because there is an excuse for it. One cannot wonder that so very fine a young man, with family, fortune, every thing in his favour, should think highly of himself. If I may so express it, he has a *right* to be proud."

"That is very true," replied Elizabeth, "and I could easily forgive *his* pride, if he had not mortified *mine*."

"Pride," observed Mary, who piqued herself upon the solidity of her reflections, "is a very common failing I believe. By all that I have ever read, I am convinced that it is very common indeed, that human nature is particularly prone to it, and that there are very few of us who do not cherish a feeling of self-complacency on the score of some quality or other, real or imaginary. Vanity and pride are different things, though the words are often used synonymously. A person may be proud without being vain. Pride relates more to our opinion of ourselves, vanity to what we would have others think of us."

"If I were as rich as Mr. Darcy," cried a young Lucas who came with his sisters, "I should not care how proud I was. I would keep a pack of foxhounds, and drink a bottle of wine every day."

"Then you would drink a great deal more than you ought," said Mrs. Bennet; "and if I were to see you at it I should take away your bottle directly."

The boy protested that she should not; she continued to declare that she would, and the argument ended only with the visit.

Jane Eyre

Chapter 3

...

"Come, Miss Jane, don't cry," said Bessie as she finished. She might as well have said to the fire, "don't burn!" but how could she divine the morbid suffering to which I was a prey? In the course of the morning Mr. Lloyd came again.

"What, already up!" said he, as he entered the nursery. "Well, nurse, how is she?"

Bessie answered that I was doing very well.

"Then she ought to look more cheerful. Come here, Miss Jane: your name is Jane, is it not?"

"Yes, sir, Jane Eyre."

"Well, you have been crying, Miss Jane Eyre; can you tell me what about? Have you any pain?"

"No, sir."

"Oh! I daresay she is crying because she could not go out with Missis in the carriage," interposed Bessie.

"Surely not! why, she is too old for such pettishness."

I thought so too; and my self-esteem being wounded by the false charge, I answered promptly, "I never cried for such a thing in my life: I hate going out in the carriage. I cry because I am miserable."

"Oh fie, Miss!" said Bessie.

The good apothecary appeared a little puzzled. I was standing before him; he fixed his eyes on me very steadily: his eyes were small and grey; not very bright, but I dare say I should think them shrewd now: he had a hard-featured yet good-natured looking face. Having considered me at leisure, he said—

"What made you ill yesterday?"

"She had a fall," said Bessie, again putting in her word.

"Fall! why, that is like a baby again! Can't she manage to walk at her age? She must be eight or nine years old."

"I was knocked down," was the blunt explanation, jerked out of me by another pang of mortified pride; "but that did not make me ill," I added; while Mr. Lloyd helped himself to a pinch of snuff.

As he was returning the box to his waistcoat pocket, a loud bell rang for the servants' dinner; he knew what it was. "That's for you, nurse," said he; "you can go down; I'll give Miss Jane a lecture till you come back."

Bessie would rather have stayed, but she was obliged to go, because punctuality at meals was rigidly enforced at Gateshead Hall.

"The fall did not make you ill; what did, then?" pursued Mr. Lloyd when Bessie was gone.

"I was shut up in a room where there is a ghost till after dark."

I saw Mr. Lloyd smile and frown at the same time.

"Ghost! What, you are a baby after all! You are afraid of ghosts?"

"Of Mr. Reed's ghost I am: he died in that room, and was laid out there. Neither Bessie nor any one else will go into it at night, if they can help it; and it was cruel to shut me up alone without a candle,—so cruel that I think I shall never forget it."

"Nonsense! And is it that makes you so miserable? Are you afraid now in daylight?"

"No: but night will come again before long: and besides—I am unhappy—very unhappy, for other things."

"What other things? Can you tell me some of them?"

How much I wished to reply fully to this question! How difficult it was to frame any answer! Children can feel, but they cannot analyse their feelings; and if the analysis is partially effected in thought, they know not how to express the result of the process in words. Fearful, however, of losing this first and only opportunity of relieving my grief by imparting it, I, after a disturbed pause, contrived to frame a meagre, though, as far as it went, true response.

"For one thing, I have no father or mother, brothers or sisters."

"You have a kind aunt and cousins."

Again I paused; then bunglingly enounced—

"But John Reed knocked me down, and my aunt shut me up in the red-room."

Mr. Lloyd a second time produced his snuff-box.

"Don't you think Gateshead Hall a very beautiful house?" asked he. "Are you not very thankful to have such a fine place to live at?"

"It is not my house, sir; and Abbot says I have less right to be here than a servant."

"Pooh! you can't be silly enough to wish to leave such a splendid place?"

"If I had anywhere else to go, I should be glad to leave it; but I can never get away from Gateshead till I am a woman."

"Perhaps you may—who knows? Have you any relations besides Mrs. Reed?"

"I think not, sir."

"None belonging to your father?"

"I don't know. I asked Aunt Reed once, and she said possibly I might have some poor, low relations called Eyre, but she knew nothing about them."

"If you had such, would you like to go to them?"

I reflected. Poverty looks grim to grown people; still more so to children: they have not much idea of industrious, working, respectable poverty; they think of the word only as connected with ragged clothes, scanty food, fireless grates, rude manners, and debasing vices: poverty for me was synonymous with degradation.

"No; I should not like to belong to poor people," was my reply.

"Not even if they were kind to you?"

I shook my head: I could not see how poor people had the means of being kind; and then to learn to speak like them, to adopt their manners, to be uneducated, to grow up like one of the poor women I saw sometimes nursing their children or washing their clothes at the cottage doors of the village of Gateshead: no, I was not heroic enough to purchase liberty at the price of caste.

"But are your relatives so very poor? Are they working people?"

"I cannot tell; Aunt. Reed says if I have any, they must be a beggarly set: I should not like to go a begging."

...

2. 记叙类语篇

Pride and Prejudice

Chapter 4

...

Elizabeth listened in silence, but was not convinced; their behaviour at the assembly had not been calculated to please in general; and with more quickness of observation and less pliancy of temper than her sister, and with a judgment too unassailed by any attention to herself, she was very little disposed to approve them. They were in fact very fine ladies; not deficient in good humour when they were pleased, nor in the power of being agreeable where they chose it; but proud and conceited. They were rather handsome, had been educated in one of the first private seminaries in town, had a fortune of twenty thousand pounds, were in the habit of spending more than they ought, and of associating with people of rank; and were therefore in every respect entitled to think well of themselves, and meanly of others. They were of a respectable family in the north of England; a circumstance more deeply impressed on their memories than that their brother's fortune and their own had been acquired by trade.

Mr. Bingley inherited property to the amount of nearly an hundred thousand pounds from his father, who had intended to purchase an estate, but did not live to do it. Mr. Bingley intended it likewise, and sometimes made choice of his county; but as he was now provided with a good house and the liberty of a manor, it was doubtful to many of those who best knew the easiness of his temper, whether he might not spend the remainder of his days at Netherfield, and leave the next generation to purchase.

His sisters were very anxious for his having an estate of his own; but though he was now established only as a tenant, Miss Bingley was by no means unwilling to preside at his table, nor was Mrs. Hurst, who had married a man of more fashion than fortune, less disposed to consider his house as her home when it suited her. Mr. Bingley had not been of age two years, when he was tempted by an accidental recommendation to look at Netherfield House. He did look at it and into it for half an hour, was pleased with the situation and the principal rooms, satisfied with what the owner said in its praise, and took it immediately.

Between him and Darcy there was a very steady friendship, in spite of a great opposition of character.—Bingley was endeared to Darcy by the easiness, openness, ductility of his temper, though no disposition could offer a greater contrast to his own, and though with his own he never appeared dissatisfied. On the strength of Darcy's regard Bingley had the firmest reliance, and of his judgment the highest opinion. In understanding Darcy was the superior. Bingley was by no means deficient, but Darcy was clever. He was at the same time haughty, reserved, and fastidious, and his manners, though well bred, were not inviting. In that respect his friend had greatly the advantage. Bingley was sure of being liked wherever he appeared, Darcy was continually giving offence.

The manner in which they spoke of the Meryton assembly was sufficiently characteristic. Bingley had never met with pleasanter people or prettier girls in his life; every body had been most kind and attentive to him, there had been no formality, no stiffness, he had soon felt acquainted with all the room; and as to Miss Bennet, he could not conceive an angel more beautiful. Darcy, on the contrary, had seen a collection of people in whom there was little beauty and no fashion, for none of whom he had felt the smallest interest, and from none received either attention or pleasure. Miss Bennet he acknowledged to be pretty, but she smiled too much.

Mrs. Hurst and her sister allowed it to be so—but still they admired her and liked her, and pronounced her to be a sweet girl, and one whom they should not object to know more of.

Miss Bennet was therefore established as a sweet girl, and their brother felt authorised by such commendation to think of her as he chose.

Chapter 7

Mr. Bennet's property consisted almost entirely in an estate of two thousand a year, which, unfortunately for his daughters, was entailed in default of heirs male, on a distant relation; and *their mother's fortune*, though ample for her situation in life, could but ill supply the deficiency of his. Her father had been an attorney in Meryton, and had left her four thousand pounds.

She had a sister married to a Mr. Philips, who had been a clerk to their father, and succeeded him in the business, and a brother settled in London in a respectable line of trade.

The village of Longbourn was only one mile from Meryton; a most convenient distance for the young ladies, who were usually tempted thither three or four times a week, to pay their duty to their aunt and to a milliner's shop just over the way. The two youngest of the family, Catherine and Lydia, were particularly frequent in these attentions; their minds were more vacant than their sisters', and when nothing better offered, a walk to Meryton was necessary to amuse their morning hours and furnish conversation for the evening; and however bare of news the country in general might be, they always contrived to learn some from their aunt. At present, indeed, they were well supplied both with news and happiness by the recent arrival of a militia regiment in the neighbourhood; it was to remain the whole winter, and Meryton was the head quarters.

Their visits to Mrs. Philips were now productive of the most interesting intelligence. Every day added something to their knowledge of the officers' names and connections. Their lodgings were not long a secret, and at length they began to know the officers themselves. Mr. Philips visited them all, and this opened to his nieces a source of felicity unknown before. They could talk of nothing but officers; and Mr. Bingley's large fortune, the mention of which gave animation to their mother, was worthless in their eyes when opposed to the regimentals of an ensign.

…

The Scarlet Letter

Chapter 2 The Market-Place

The grass-plot before the jail, in Prison Lane, on a certain summer morning, not less than two centuries ago, was occupied by a pretty large number of the inhabitants of Boston, all with their eyes intently fastened on the iron-clamped oaken door. Amongst any other population, or at a later period in the history of New England, the grim rigidity that petrified the bearded physiognomies of these good people would have augured some awful business in hand. It could have betokened nothing short of the anticipated execution of some rioted culprit, on whom the sentence of a legal tribunal had but confirmed the verdict of public sentiment. But, in that early severity of the Puritan character, an inference of this kind could not so indubitably be drawn. It might be that a sluggish bond-servant, or an undutiful child, whom his parents had given over to the civil authority, was to be corrected at the whipping-post. It might be that an Antinomian, a Quaker, or other heterodox religionist, was to be scourged out of the town, or an idle or vagrant Indian, whom the white man's firewater had made riotous about the streets, was to be driven with stripes into the shadow of the forest. It might be, too, that a witch, like old Mistress Hibbins, the bitter-tempered widow of the magistrate, was to die upon the gallows. In either case, there was very much the same solemnity of demeanour on the part of the spectators, as befitted a people among whom religion and law were almost identical, and in whose character both were so thoroughly interfused, that the mildest and severest acts of public discipline were alike made venerable and awful. Meagre, indeed, and cold, was the sympathy that a transgressor might look for, from such bystanders, at the scaffold. On the other hand, a penalty which, in our days, would infer a degree of mocking infamy and ridicule, might then be invested with almost as stern a dignity as the punishment of death itself.

It was a circumstance to be noted on the summer morning when our story begins its course, that the women, of whom there were several in the crowd, appeared to take a peculiar interest in whatever penal infliction might be expected to ensue. The age had not so much refinement, that any sense of impropriety restrained the wearers of petticoat and farthingale from stepping forth into the public ways, and wedging their not unsubstantial persons, if occasion were, into the throng nearest to the scaffold at an execution. Morally, as well as materially, there was a coarser fibre in those wives and maidens of old English birth and breeding than in their fair descendants, separated from them by a series of six or seven generations; for, throughout that chain of ancestry, every successive mother had transmitted to her child a fainter bloom, a more delicate and briefer beauty, and a slighter physical frame, if not character of less force and solidity than her own. The women who were now standing about the prison-door stood within less than half a century of the period when the man-like Elizabeth had been the not altogether unsuitable representative of the sex. They were her countrywomen: and the beef and ale of their native land, with a moral diet not a whit more refined, entered largely into their composition. The bright morning sun, therefore, shone on broad shoulders and well-developed busts, and on round and ruddy cheeks, that had ripened in the far-off island, and had hardly yet grown paler or thinner in the atmosphere of New England. There was, moreover, a boldness and rotundity of speech among these matrons, as most of them seemed to be, that would startle us at the present day, whether in respect to its purport or its volume of tone.

...

The door of the jail being flung open from within there appeared, in the first place, like a black shadow emerging into sunshine, the grim and gristly presence of the town-beadle, with a sword by his side, and his staff of office in his hand. This personage prefigured and represented in his aspect the whole dismal severity of the Puritanic code of law, which it was his business to administer in its final and closest application to the offender. Stretching forth the official staff in his left hand, he laid his right upon the shoulder of a young woman, whom he thus drew forward, until, on the threshold of the prison-door, she repelled him, by an action marked with natural dignity and force of character, and stepped into the open air as if by her own free will. She bore in her arms a child, a baby of some three months old, who winked and turned aside its little face from the too vivid light of day; because its existence, heretofore, had brought it acquaintance only with the grey twilight of a dungeon, or other darksome apartment of the prison.

When the young woman—the mother of this child—stood fully revealed before the crowd, it seemed to be her first impulse to clasp the infant closely to her bosom; not so much by an impulse of motherly affection, as that she might thereby conceal a certain token, which was wrought or fastened into her dress. In a moment, however, wisely judging that one token of her shame would but poorly serve to hide another, she took the baby on her arm, and with a burning blush, and yet a haughty smile, and a glance that would not be abashed, looked around at her townspeople and neighbours. On the breast of her gown, in fine red cloth, surrounded with an elaborate embroidery and fantastic flourishes of gold thread, appeared the letter A. It was so artistically done, and with so much fertility and gorgeous luxuriance of fancy, that it had all the effect of a last and fitting decoration to the apparel which she wore, and which was of a splendour in accordance with the taste of the age, but greatly beyond what was allowed by the sumptuary regulations of the colony.

The young woman was tall, with a figure of perfect elegance on a large scale. She had dark and abundant hair, so glossy that it threw off the sunshine with a gleam; and a face which, besides being beautiful from regularity of feature and richness of complexion, had the impressiveness belonging to a marked brow and deep black eyes. She was ladylike, too, after the manner of the feminine gentility of those days; characterised by a certain state and dignity, rather than by the delicate, evanescent, and indescribable grace which is now recognised as its indication. And never had Hester Prynne appeared more ladylike, in the antique interpretation of the term, than as she issued from the prison. Those who had before known her, and had expected to behold her dimmed and obscured by a disastrous cloud, were astonished, and even startled, to perceive how her beauty shone out, and made a halo of the misfortune and ignominy in which she was enveloped. It may be true that, to a sensitive observer, there was some thing exquisitely painful in it. Her attire, which indeed, she had wrought for the occasion in prison, and had modelled much after her own fancy, seemed to express the attitude of her spirit, the desperate recklessness of her mood, by its wild and picturesque peculiarity. But the point which drew all eyes, and, as it were, transfigured the wearer—so that both men and women who had been familiarly acquainted with Hester Prynne were now impressed as if they beheld her for the first time—was that SCARLET LETTER, so fantastically embroidered and illuminated upon her bosom. It had the effect of a spell, taking her out of the ordinary relations with humanity, and enclosing her in a sphere by herself.

…

3. 描写类语篇

The Great Gatsby

Chapter 3

There was music from my neighbor's house through the summer nights. In his blue gardens men and girls came and went like moths among the whisperings and the champagne and the stars. At high tide in the afternoon I watched his guests diving from the tower of his raft or taking the sun on the hot sand of his beach while his two motor-boats slit the waters of the Sound, drawing aquaplanes over cataracts of foam. On week-ends his Rolls-Royce became an omnibus, bearing parties to and from the city, between nine in the morning and long past midnight, while his station wagon scampered like a brisk yellow bug to meet all trains. And on Mondays eight servants including an extra gardener toiled all day with mops and scrubbing-brushes and hammers and garden-shears, repairing the ravages of the night before.

Every Friday five crates of oranges and lemons arrived from a fruiterer in New York—every Monday these same oranges and lemons left his back door in a pyramid of pulpless halves. There was a machine in the kitchen which could extract the juice of two hundred oranges in half an hour, if a little button was pressed two hundred times by a butler's thumb.

At least once a fortnight a corps of caterers came down with several hundred feet of canvas and enough colored lights to make a Christmas tree of Gatsby's enormous garden. On buffet tables, garnished with glistening horsd'oeuvre, spiced baked hams crowded against salads of harlequin designs and pastry pigs and turkeys bewitched to a dark gold. In the main hall a bar with a real brass rail was set up, and stocked with gins and liquors and with cordials so long forgotten that most of his female guests were too young to know one from another.

By seven o'clock the orchestra has arrived—no thin five-piece affair but a whole pitful of oboes and trombones and saxophones and viols and cornets and piccolos and low and high drums. The last swimmers have come in from the beach now and are dressing upstairs; the cars from New York are parked five deep in the drive, and already the halls and salons and verandas are gaudy with primary colors and hair shorn in strange new ways and shawls beyond the dreams of Castile. The bar is in full swing and floating rounds of cocktails permeate the garden outside until the air is alive with chatter and laughter and casual innuendo and introductions forgotten on the spot and enthusiastic meetings between women who never knew each other's names.

The lights grow brighter as the earth lurches away from the sun and now the orchestra is playing yellow cocktail music and the opera of voices pitches a key higher. Laughter is easier, minute by minute, spilled with prodigality, tipped out at a cheerful word. The groups change more swiftly, swell with new arrivals, dissolve and form in the same breath—already there are wanderers, confident girls who weave here and there among the stouter and more stable, become for a sharp, joyous moment the center of a group and then excited with triumph glide on through the sea-change of faces and voices and color under the constantly changing light.

Suddenly one of these gypsies in trembling opal, seizes a cocktail out of the air, dumps it down for courage and moving her hands like Frisco dances out alone on the canvas platform. A momentary hush; the orchestra leader varies his rhythm obligingly for her and there is a burst of chatter as the erroneous news goes around that she is Gilda Gray's understudy from the "Follies". The party has begun.

...

There was dancing now on the canvas in the garden, old men pushing young girls backward in eternal graceless circles, superior couples holding each other tortuously, fashionably and keeping in the corners—and a great number of single girls dancing individualistically or relieving the orchestra for a moment of the burden of the banjo or the traps. By midnight the hilarity had increased. A celebrated tenor had sung in Italian and a notorious contralto had sung in jazz and between the numbers people were doing "stunts" all over the garden, while happy vacuous bursts of laughter rose toward the summer sky. A pair of stage "twins"—who turned out to be the girls in yellow—did a baby act in costume and champagne was served in glasses bigger than finger bowls. The moon had risen higher, and floating in the Sound was a triangle of silver scales, trembling a little to the stiff, tinny drip of the banjoes on the lawn.

...

I began to like New York, the racy, adventurous feel of it at night and the satisfaction that the constant flicker of men and women and machines gives to the restless eye. I liked to walk up Fifth Avenue and pick out romantic women from the crowd and imagine that in a few minutes I was going to enter into their lives, and no one would ever know or disapprove. Sometimes, in my mind, I followed them to their apartments on the corners of hidden streets, and they turned and smiled back at me before they faded through a door into warm darkness. At the enchanted metropolitan twilight I felt a haunting loneliness sometimes, and felt it in others—poor young clerks who loitered in front of windows waiting until it was time for a solitary restaurant dinner—young clerks in the dusk, wasting the most poignant moments of night and life.

Again at eight o'clock, when the dark lanes of the Forties were five deep with throbbing taxi cabs, bound for the theatre district, I felt a sinking in my heart. Forms leaned together in the taxis as they waited, and voices sang, and there was laughter from unheard jokes, and lighted cigarettes outlined unintelligible gestures inside. Imagining that I, too, was hurrying toward gayety and sharing their intimate excitement, I wished them well.

...

Jane Eyre

Chapter 2

...

The red-room was a square chamber, very seldom slept in, I might say never, indeed, unless when a chance influx of visitors at Gateshead Hall rendered it necessary to turn to account all the accommodation it contained: yet it was one of the largest and stateliest chambers in the mansion. A bed supported on massive pillars of mahogany, hung with curtains of deep red damask, stood out like a tabernacle in the centre; the two large windows, with their blinds always drawn down, were half shrouded in festoons and falls of similar drapery; the carpet was red; the table at the foot of the bed was covered with a crimson cloth; the walls were a soft fawn colour with a blush of pink in it; the wardrobe, the toilettable, the chairs were of darkly polished old mahogany. Out of these deep surrounding shades rose high, and glared white, the piled-up mattresses and pillows of the bed, spread with a snowy Marseilles counterpane. Scarcely less prominent was an ample cushioned easy-chair near the head of the bed, also white, with a footstool before it; and looking, as I thought, like a pale throne.

This room was chill, because it seldom had a fire; it was silent, because remote from the nursery and kitchen; solemn, because it was known to be so seldom entered. The house-maid alone came here on Saturdays, to wipe from the mirrors and the furniture a week's quiet dust: and Mrs. Reed herself, at far intervals, visited it to review the contents of a certain secret drawer in the wardrobe, where were stored divers parchments, her jewel-casket, and a miniature of her deceased husband; and in those last words lies the secret of the red-room—the spell which kept it so lonely in spite of its grandeur.

Mr. Reed had been dead nine years: it was in this chamber he breathed his last; here he lay in state; hence his coffin was borne by the undertaker's men; and, since that day, a sense of dreary consecration had guarded it from frequent intrusion.

My seat, to which Bessie and the bitter Miss Abbot had left me riveted, was a low ottoman near the marble chimney-piece; the bed rose before me; to my right hand there was the high, dark wardrobe, with subdued, broken reflections varying the gloss of its panels; to my left were the muffled windows; a great looking-glass between them repeated the vacant majesty of the bed and room. I was not quite sure whether they had locked the door; and when I dared move, I got up and went to see. Alas! yes: no jail was ever more secure. Returning, I had to cross before the looking-glass; my fascinated glance involuntarily explored the depth it revealed. All looked colder and darker in that visionary hollow than in reality: and the strange little figure there gazing at me, with a white face and arms specking the gloom, and glittering eyes of fear moving where all else was still, had the effect of a real spirit: I thought it like one of the tiny phantoms, half fairy, half imp, Bessie's evening stories represented as coming out of lone, ferny dells in moors, and appearing before the eyes of belated travellers. I returned to my stool.

Superstition was with me at that moment; but it was not yet her hour for complete victory: my blood was still warm; the mood of the revolted slave was still bracing me with its bitter vigour; I had to stem a rapid rush of retrospective thought before I quailed to the dismal present.

All John Reed's violent tyrannies, all his sisters' proud indifference, all his mother's aversion, all the servants' partiality, turned up in my disturbed mind like a dark deposit in a turbid well. Why was I always suffering, always browbeaten, always accused, for ever condemned? Why could I never please? Why was it useless to try to win any one's favour? Eliza, who was headstrong and selfish, was respected. Georgiana, who had a spoiled temper, a very acrid spite, a captious and insolent carriage, was universally indulged. Her beauty, her pink cheeks and golden curls, seemed to give delight to all who looked at her, and to purchase indemnity for every fault. John no one thwarted, much less punished; though he twisted the necks of the pigeons, killed the little pea-chicks, set the dogs at the sheep, stripped the hothouse vines of their fruit, and broke the buds off the choicest plants in the conservatory: he called his mother "old girl," too; sometimes reviled her for her dark skin, similar to his own; bluntly disregarded her wishes; not unfrequently tore and spoiled her silk attire; and he was still "her own darling." I dared commit no fault: I strove to fulfil every duty; and I was termed naughty and tiresome, sullen and sneaking, from morning to noon, and from noon to night.

My head still ached and bled with the blow and fall I had received: no one had reproved John for wantonly striking me; and because I had turned against him to avert farther irrational violence, I was loaded with general opprobrium.

"Unjust!—unjust!" said my reason, forced by the agonizing stimulus into precocious though transitory power: and Resolve, equally wrought up, instigated some strange expedient to achieve escape from insupportable oppression—as running away, or, if that could not be effected, never eating or drinking more, and letting myself die.

What a consternation of soul was mine that dreary afternoon! How all my brain was in tumult, and all my heart in insurrection! Yet in what darkness, what dense ignorance, was the mental battle fought! I could not answer the ceaseless inward question—*why* I thus suffered; now, at the distance of—I will not say how many years, I see it clearly.

I was a discord in Gateshead Hall: I was like nobody there; I had nothing in harmony with Mrs. Reed or her children, or her chosen vassalage. If they did not love me, in fact, as little did I love them. They were not bound to regard with affection a thing that could not sympathise with one amongst them; a heterogeneous thing, opposed to them in temperament, in capacity, in propensities; a useless thing, incapable of serving their interest, or adding to their pleasure; a noxious thing, cherishing the germs of indignation at their treatment, of contempt of their judgment. I know that had I been a sanguine, brilliant, careless, exacting, handsome, romping child—though equally dependent and friendless—Mrs. Reed would have endured my presence more complacently; her children would have entertained for me more of the cordiality of fellow-feeling; the servants would have been less prone to make me the scapegoat of the nursery.

...

Chapter 12

The promise of a smooth career, which my first calm introduction to Thornfield Hall seemed to pledge, was not belied on a longer acquaintance with the place and its inmates. Mrs. Fairfax turned out to be what she appeared, a placid-tempered, kind-natured woman, of competent education and average intelligence. My pupil was a lively child, who had been spoilt and indulged, and therefore was sometimes wayward; but as she was committed entirely to my care, and no injudicious interference from any quarter ever thwarted my plans for her improvement, she soon forgot her little freaks, and became obedient and teachable. She had no great talents, no marked traits of character, no peculiar development of feeling or taste which raised her one inch above the ordinary level of childhood; but neither had she any deficiency or vice which sunk her below it. She made reasonable progress, entertained for me a vivacious, though perhaps not very profound, affection; and by her simplicity, gay prattle, and efforts to please, inspired me, in return, with a degree of attachment sufficient to make us both content in each other's society.

This, *par parenthèse,* will be thought cool language by persons who entertain solemn doctrines about the angelic nature of children, and the duty of those charged with their education to conceive for them an idolatrous devotion: but I am not writing to flatter parental egotism, to echo cant, or prop up humbug; I am merely telling the truth. I felt a conscientious solicitude for Adèle's welfare and progress, and a quiet liking for her little self: just as I cherished towards Mrs. Fairfax a thankfulness for her kindness, and a pleasure in her society proportionate to the tranquil regard she had for me, and the moderation of her mind and character.

Anybody may blame me who likes, when I add further, that, now and then, when I took a walk by myself in the grounds; when I went down to the gates and looked through them along the road; or when, while Adèle played with her nurse, and Mrs. Fairfax made jellies in the storeroom, I climbed the three staircases, raised the trap-door of the attic, and having reached the leads, looked out afar over sequestered field and hill, and along dim sky-line—that then I longed for a power of vision which might overpass that limit; which might reach the busy world, towns, regions full of life I had heard of but never seen—that then I desired more of practical experience than I possessed; more of intercourse with my kind, of acquaintance with variety of character, than was here within my reach. I valued what was good in Mrs. Fairfax, and what was good in Adèle; but I believed in the existence of other and more vivid kinds of goodness, and what I believed in I wished to behold.

Who blames me? Many, no doubt; and I shall be called discontented. I could not help it: the restlessness was in my nature; it agitated me to pain sometimes. Then my sole relief was to walk along the corridor of the third storey, backwards and forwards, safe in the silence and solitude of the spot, and allow my mind's eye to dwell on whatever bright visions rose before it—and, certainly, they were many and glowing; to let my heart be heaved by the exultant movement, which, while it swelled it in trouble, expanded it with life; and, best of all, to open my inward ear to a tale that was never ended—a tale my imagination created, and narrated continuously; quickened with all of incident, life, fire, feeling, that I desired and had not in my actual existence.

It is in vain to say human beings ought to be satisfied with tranquillity: they must have action; and they will make it if they cannot find it. Millions are condemned to a stiller doom than mine, and millions are in silent revolt against their lot. Nobody knows how many rebellions besides political rebellions ferment in the masses of life which people earth. Women are supposed to be very calm generally: but women feel just as men feel; they need exercise for their faculties, and a field for their efforts, as much as their brothers do; they suffer from too rigid a restraint, too absolute a stagnation, precisely as men would suffer; and it is narrow-minded in their more privileged fellow-creatures to say that they ought to confine themselves to making puddings and knitting stockings, to playing on the piano and embroidering bags. It is thoughtless to condemn them, or laugh at them, if they seek to do more or learn more than custom has pronounced necessary for their sex.

…

The ground was hard, the air was still, my road was lonely; I walked fast till I got warm, and then I walked slowly to enjoy and analyse the species of pleasure brooding for me in the hour and situation. It was three o'clock; the church bell tolled as I passed under the belfry: the charm of the hour lay in its approaching dimness, in the low-gliding and pale-beaming sun. I was a mile from Thornfield, in a lane noted for wild roses in summer, for nuts and blackberries in autumn, and even now possessing a few coral treasures in hips and haws, but whose best winter delight lay in its utter solitude and leafless repose. If a breath of air stirred, it made no sound here; for there was not a holly, not an evergreen to rustle, and the stripped hawthorn and hazel bushes were as still as the white, worn stones which causewayed the middle of the path. Far and wide, on each side, there were only fields, where no cattle now browsed; and the little brown birds, which stirred occasionally in the hedge, looked like single russet leaves that had forgotten to drop.

This lane inclined up-hill all the way to Hay; having reached the middle, I sat down on a stile which led thence into a field. Gathering my mantle about me, and sheltering my hands in my muff, I did not feel the cold, though it froze keenly; as was attested by a sheet of ice covering the causeway, where a little brooklet, now congealed, had overflowed after a rapid thaw some days since. From my seat I could look down on Thornfield: the grey and battlemented hall was the principal object in the vale below me; its woods and dark rookery rose against the west. I lingered till the sun went down amongst the trees, and sank crimson and clear behind them. I then turned eastward.

On the hill-top above me sat the rising moon; pale yet as a cloud, but brightening momentarily, she looked over Hay, which, half lost in trees, sent up a blue smoke from its few chimneys: it was yet a mile distant, but in the absolute hush I could hear plainly its thin murmurs of life. My ear, too, felt the flow of currents; in what dales and depths I could not tell: but there were many hills beyond Hay, and doubtless many becks threading their passes. That evening calm betrayed alike the tinkle of the nearest streams, the sough of the most remote.

…

Something of daylight still lingered, and the moon was waxing bright: I could see him plainly. His figure was enveloped in a riding cloak, fur collared and steel clasped; its details were not apparent, but I traced the general points of middle height and considerable breadth of chest. He had a dark face, with stern features and a heavy brow; his eyes and gathered eyebrows looked ireful and thwarted just now; he was past youth, but had not reached middle-age; perhaps he might be thirty-five. I felt no fear of him, and but little shyness. Had he been a handsome, heroic-looking young gentleman, I should not have dared to stand thus questioning him against his will, and offering my services unasked. I had hardly ever seen a handsome youth; never in my life spoken to one. I had a theoretical reverence and homage for beauty, elegance, gallantry, fascination; but had I met those qualities incarnate in masculine shape, I should have known instinctively that they neither had nor could have sympathy with anything in me, and should have shunned them as one would fire, lightning, or anything else that is bright but antipathetic.

...

Chapter 13

...

These pictures were in water-colours. The first represented clouds low and livid, rolling over a swollen sea: all the distance was in eclipse; so, too, was the foreground; or rather, the nearest billows, for there was no land. One gleam of light lifted into relief a half-submerged mast, on which sat a cormorant, dark and large, with wings flecked with foam; its beak held a gold bracelet set with gems, that I had touched with as brilliant tints as my palette could yield, and as glittering distinctness as my pencil could impart. Sinking below the bird and mast, a drowned corpse glanced through the green water; a fair arm was the only limb clearly visible, whence the bracelet had been washed or torn.

The second picture contained for foreground only the dim peak of a hill, with grass and some leaves slanting as if by a breeze. Beyond and above spread an expanse of sky, dark blue as at twilight: rising into the sky was a woman's shape to the bust, portrayed in tints as dusk and soft as I could combine. The dim forehead was crowned with a star; the lineaments below were seen as through the suffusion of vapour; the eyes shone dark and wild; the hair streamed shadowy, like a beamless cloud torn by storm or by electric travail. On the neck lay a pale reflection like moonlight; the same faint lustre touched the train of thin clouds from which rose and bowed this vision of the Evening Star.

The third showed the pinnacle of an iceberg piercing a polar winter sky: a muster of northern lights reared their dim lances, close serried, along the horizon. Throwing these into distance, rose, in the foreground, a head,—a colossal head, inclined towards the iceberg, and resting against it. Two thin hands, joined under the forehead, and supporting it, drew up before the lower features a sable veil, a brow quite bloodless, white as bone, and an eye hollow and fixed, blank of meaning but for the glassiness of despair, alone were visible. Above the temples, amidst wreathed turban folds of black drapery, vague in its character and consistency as cloud, gleamed a ring of white flame, gemmed with sparkles of a more lurid tinge. This pale crescent was "the likeness of a kingly crown;" what it diademed was "the shape which shape had none."

...

（三）长篇小说完整章节节选

Pride and Prejudice

Chapter 14

During dinner, Mr. Bennet scarcely spoke at all; but when the servants were withdrawn, he thought it time to have some conversation with his guest, and therefore started a subject in which he expected him to shine, by observing that he seemed very fortunate in his patroness. Lady Catherine de Bourgh's attention to his wishes, and consideration for his comfort, appeared very remarkable. Mr. Bennet could not have chosen better. Mr. Collins was eloquent in her praise. The subject elevated him to more than usual solemnity of manner, and with a most important aspect he protested that he had never in his life witnessed such behaviour in a person of rank—such affability and condescension, as he had himself experienced from Lady Catherine. She had been graciously pleased to approve of both the discourses, which he had already had the honour of preaching before her. She had also asked him twice to dine at Rosings, and had sent for him only the Saturday before, to make up her pool of quadrille in the evening. Lady Catherine was reckoned proud by many people he knew, but *he* had never seen any thing but affability in her. She had always spoken to him as she would to any other gentleman; she made not the smallest objection to his joining in the society of the neighbourhood, nor to his leaving his parish occasionally for a week or two, to visit his relations. She had even condescended to advise him to marry as soon as he could, provided he chose with discretion; and had once paid him a visit in his humble parsonage; where she had perfectly approved all the alterations he had been making, and had even vouchsafed to suggest some herself, some shelves in the closets up stairs."

"That is all very proper and civil, I am sure," said Mrs. Bennet, "and I dare say she is a very agreeable woman. It is a pity that great ladies in general are not more like her. Does she live near you, sir?"

"The garden in which stands my humble abode, is separated only by a lane from Rosings Park, her ladyship's residence."

"I think you said she was a widow, sir? has she any family?"

"She has one only daughter, the heiress of Rosings, and of very extensive property."

"Ah!" cried Mrs. Bennet, shaking her head, "then she is better off than many girls. And what sort of young lady is she? is she handsome?"

"She is a most charming young lady indeed. Lady Catherine herself says that in point of true beauty, Miss De Bourgh is far superior to the handsomest of her sex; because there is that in her features which marks the young woman of distinguished birth. She is unfortunately of a sickly constitution, which has prevented her making that progress in many accomplishments, which she could not otherwise have failed of; as I am informed by the lady who superintended her education, and who still resides with them. But she is perfectly amiable, and often condescends to drive by my humble abode in her little phaeton and ponies."

"Has she been presented? I do not remember her name among the ladies at court."

"Her indifferent state of health unhappily prevents her being in town; and by that means, as I told Lady Catherine myself one day, has deprived the British court of its brightest ornament. Her ladyship seemed pleased with the idea, and you may imagine that I am happy on every occasion to offer those little delicate compliments which are always acceptable to ladies. I have more than once observed to Lady Catherine, that her charming daughter seemed born to be a duchess, and that the most elevated rank, instead of giving her consequence, would be adorned by her—These are the kind of little things which please her ladyship, and it is a sort of attention which I conceive myself peculiarly bound to pay."

"You judge very properly," said Mr. Bennet, "and it is happy for you that you possess the talent of flattering with delicacy. May I ask whether these pleasing attentions proceed from the impulse of the moment, or are the result of previous study?"

"They arise chiefly from what is passing at the time, and though I sometimes amuse myself with suggesting and arranging such little elegant compliments as may be adapted to ordinary occasions, I always wish to give them as unstudied an air as possible."

Mr. Bennet's expectations were fully answered. His cousin was as absurd as he had hoped, and he listened to him with the keenest enjoyment, maintaining at the same time the most resolute composure of countenance, and except in an occasional glance at Elizabeth, requiring no partner in his pleasure.

By tea-time however the dose had been enough, and Mr. Bennet was glad to take his guest into the drawing-room again, and when tea was over, glad to invite him to read aloud to the ladies. Mr. Collins readily assented, and a book was produced; but on beholding it, (for every thing announced it to be from a circulating library,) he started back, and begging pardon, protested that he never read novels.—Kitty stared at him, and Lydia exclaimed.—Other books were produced, and after some deliberation he chose Fordyce's Sermons. Lydia gaped as he opened the volume, and before he had, with very monotonous solemnity, read three pages, she interrupted him with,

"Do you know, mama, that my uncle Philips talks of turning away Richard, and if he does, Colonel Forster will hire him. My aunt told me so herself on Saturday. I shall walk to Meryton tomorrow to hear more about it, and to ask when Mr. Denny comes back from town."

Lydia was bid by her two eldest sisters to hold her tongue; but Mr. Collins, much offended, laid aside his book, and said,

"I have often observed how little young ladies are interested by books of a serious stamp, though written solely for their benefit. It amazes me, I confess;—for certainly, there can be nothing so advantageous to them as instruction. But I will no longer importune my young cousin."

Then turning to Mr. Bennet, he offered himself as his antagonist at backgammon. Mr. Bennet accepted the challenge, observing that he acted very wisely in leaving the girls to their own trifling amusements. Mrs. Bennet and her daughters apologised most civilly for Lydia's interruption, and promised that it should not occur again, if he would resume his book; but Mr. Collins, after assuring them that he bore his young cousin no ill will, and should never resent her behaviour as any affront, seated himself at another table with Mr. Bennet, and prepared for backgammon.

Jane Eyre

Chapter 8

Ere the half-hour ended, five o'clock struck; school was dismissed, and all were gone into the refectory to tea. I now ventured to descend: it was deep dusk; I retired into a corner and sat down on the floor. The spell by which I had been so far supported began to dissolve; reaction took place, and soon, so overwhelming was the grief that seized me, I sank prostrate with my face to the ground. Now I wept: Helen Burns was not here; nothing sustained me; left to myself I abandoned myself, and my tears watered the boards. I had meant to be so good, and to do so much at Lowood: to make so many friends, to earn respect and win affection. Already I had made visible progress: that very morning I had reached the head of my class; Miss Miller had praised me warmly; Miss Temple had smiled approbation; she had promised to teach me drawing, and to let me learn French, if I continued to make similar improvement two months longer: and then I was well received by my fellow-pupils; treated as an equal by those of my own age, and not molested by any; now, here I lay again crushed and trodden on; and could I ever rise more?

"Never," I thought; and ardently I wished to die. While sobbing out this wish in broken accents, some one approached: I started up—again Helen Burns was near me; the fading fires just showed her coming up the long, vacant room; she brought my coffee and bread.

"Come, eat something," she said; but I put both away from me, feeling as if a drop or a crumb would have choked me in my present condition. Helen regarded me, probably with surprise: I could not now abate my agitation, though I tried hard; I continued to weep aloud. She sat down on the ground near me, embraced her knees with her arms, and rested her head upon them; in that attitude she remained silent as an Indian. I was the first who spoke—

"Helen, why do you stay with a girl whom everybody believes to be a liar?"

"Everybody, Jane? Why, there are only eighty people who have heard you called so, and the world contains hundreds of millions."

"But what have I to do with millions? The eighty, I know, despise me."

"Jane, you are mistaken: probably not one in the school either despises or dislikes you: many, I am sure, pity you much."

"How can they pity me after what Mr. Brocklehurst has said?"

"Mr. Brocklehurst is not a god: nor is he even a great and admired man: he is little liked here; he never took steps to make himself liked. Had he treated you as an especial favourite, you would have found enemies, declared or covert, all around you; as it is, the greater number would offer you sympathy if they dared. Teachers and pupils may look coldly on you for a day or two, but friendly feelings are concealed in their hearts; and if you persevere in doing well, these feelings will ere long appear so much the more evidently for their temporary suppression. Besides, Jane"—she paused.

"Well, Helen?" said I, putting my hand into hers: she chafed my fingers gently to warm them, and went on—

"If all the world hated you, and believed you wicked, while your own conscience approved you, and absolved you from guilt, you would not be without friends."

"No; I know I should think well of myself; but that is not enough: if others don't love me I would rather die than live—I cannot bear to be solitary and hated, Helen. Look here; to gain some real affection from you, or Miss Temple, or any other whom I truly love, I would willingly submit to have the bone of my arm broken, or to let a bull toss me, or to stand behind a kicking horse, and let it dash its hoof at my chest—"

"Hush, Jane! you think too much of the love of human beings; you are too impulsive, too vehement; the sovereign hand that created your frame, and put life into it, has provided you with other resources than your feeble self, or than creatures feeble as you. Besides this earth, and besides the race of men, there is an invisible world and a kingdom of spirits: that world is round us, for it is everywhere; and those spirits watch us, for they are commissioned to guard us; and if we were dying in pain and shame, if scorn smote us on all sides, and hatred crushed us, angels see our tortures, recognise our innocence (if innocent we be: as I know you are of this charge which Mr. Brocklehurst has weakly and pompously repeated at second-hand from Mrs. Reed; for I read a sincere nature in your ardent eyes and on your clear front), and God waits only the separation of spirit from flesh to crown us with a full reward. Why, then, should we ever sink overwhelmed with distress, when life is so soon over, and death is so certain an entrance to happiness—to glory?"

I was silent; Helen had calmed me; but in the tranquillity she imparted there was an alloy of inexpressible sadness. I felt the impression of woe as she spoke, but I could not tell whence it came; and when, having done speaking, she breathed a little fast and coughed a short cough, I momentarily forgot my own sorrows to yield to a vague concern for her.

Resting my head on Helen's shoulder, I put my arms round her waist; she drew me to her, and we reposed in silence. We had not sat long thus, when another person came in. Some heavy clouds, swept from the sky by a rising wind, had left the moon bare; and her light, streaming in through a window near, shone full both on us and on the approaching figure, which we at once recognised as Miss Temple.

"I came on purpose to find you, Jane Eyre," said she; "I want you in my room; and as Helen Burns is with you, she may come too."

We went; following the superintendent's guidance, we had to thread some intricate passages, and mount a staircase before we reached her apartment; it contained a good fire, and looked cheerful. Miss Temple told Helen Burns to be seated in a low armchair on one side of the hearth, and herself taking another, she called me to her side.

"Is it all over?" she asked, looking down at my face. "Have you cried your grief away?"

"I am afraid I never shall do that."

"Why?"

"Because I have been wrongly accused; and you, ma'am, and everybody else, will now think me wicked."

"We shall think you what you prove yourself to be, my child. Continue to act as a good girl, and you will satisfy us."

"Shall I, Miss Temple?"

"You will," said she, passing her arm round me. "And now tell me who is the lady whom Mr. Brocklehurst called your benefactress?"

"Mrs. Reed, my uncle's wife. My uncle is dead, and he left me to her care."

"Did she not, then, adopt you of her own accord?"

"No, ma'am; she was sorry to have to do it: but my uncle, as I have often heard the servants say, got her to promise before he died that she would always keep me."

"Well now, Jane, you know, or at least I will tell you, that when a criminal is accused, he is always allowed to speak in his own defence. You have been charged with falsehood; defend yourself to me as well as you can. Say whatever your memory suggests is true; but add nothing and exaggerate nothing."

I resolved, in the depth of my heart, that I would be most moderate—most correct; and, having reflected a few minutes in order to arrange coherently what I had to say, I told her all the story of my sad childhood. Exhausted by emotion, my language was more subdued than it generally was when it developed that sad theme; and mindful of Helen's warnings against the indulgence of resentment, I infused into the narrative far less of gall and wormwood than ordinary. Thus restrained and simplified, it sounded more credible: I felt as I went on that Miss Temple fully believed me.

In the course of the tale I had mentioned Mr. Lloyd as having come to see me after the fit: for I never forgot the, to me, frightful episode of the red-room: in detailing which, my excitement was sure, in some degree, to break bounds; for nothing could soften in my recollection the spasm of agony which clutched my heart when Mrs. Reed spurned my wild supplication for pardon, and locked me a second time in the dark and haunted chamber.

I had finished: Miss Temple regarded me a few minutes in silence; she then said—

"I know something of Mr. Lloyd; I shall write to him; if his reply agrees with your statement, you shall be publicly cleared from every imputation; to me, Jane, you are clear now."

She kissed me, and still keeping me at her side (where I was well contented to stand, for I derived a child's pleasure from the contemplation of her face, her dress, her one or two ornaments, her white forehead, her clustered and shining curls, and beaming dark eyes), she proceeded to address Helen Burns.

"How are you to-night, Helen? Have you coughed much today?"

"Not quite so much, I think, ma'am."

"And the pain in your chest?"

"It is a little better."

Miss Temple got up, took her hand and examined her pulse; then she returned to her own seat: as she resumed it, I heard her sigh low. She was pensive a few minutes, then rousing herself, she said cheerfully—

"But you two are my visitors to-night; I must treat you as such." She rang her bell.

"Barbara," she said to the servant who answered it, "I have not yet had tea; bring the tray and place cups for these two young ladies."

And a tray was soon brought. How pretty, to my eyes, did the china cups and bright teapot look, placed on the little round table near the fire! How fragrant was the steam of the beverage, and the scent of the toast! of which, however, I, to my dismay (for I was beginning to be hungry) discerned only a very small portion: Miss Temple discerned it too.

"Barbara," said she, "can you not bring a little more bread and butter? There is not enough for three."

Barbara went out: she returned soon—

"Madam, Mrs. Harden says she has sent up the usual quantity."

Mrs. Harden, be it observed, was the housekeeper: a woman after Mr. Brocklehurst's own heart, made up of equal parts of whalebone and iron.

"Oh, very well!" returned Miss Temple; "we must make it do, Barbara, I suppose." And as the girl withdrew she added, smiling, "Fortunately, I have it in my power to supply deficiencies for this once."

Having invited Helen and me to approach the table, and placed before each of us a cup of tea with one delicious but thin morsel of toast, she got up, unlocked a drawer, and taking from it a parcel wrapped in paper, disclosed presently to our eyes a good-sized seed-cake.

"I meant to give each of you some of this to take with you," said she, "but as there is so little toast, you must have it now," and she proceeded to cut slices with a generous hand.

We feasted that evening as on nectar and ambrosia; and not the least delight of the entertainment was the smile of gratification with which our hostess regarded us, as we satisfied our famished appetites on the delicate fare she liberally supplied.

Tea over and the tray removed, she again summoned us to the fire; we sat one on each side of her, and now a conversation followed between her and Helen, which it was indeed a privilege to be admitted to hear.

Miss Temple had always something of serenity in her air, of state in her mien, of refined propriety in her language, which precluded deviation into the ardent, the excited, the eager: something which chastened the pleasure of those who looked on her and listened to her, by a controlling sense of awe; and such was my feeling now: but as to Helen Burns, I was struck with wonder.

The refreshing meal, the brilliant fire, the presence and kindness of her beloved instructress, or, perhaps, more than all these, something in her own unique mind, had roused her powers within her. They woke, they kindled: first, they glowed in the bright tint of her cheek, which till this hour I had never seen but pale and bloodless; then they shone in the liquid lustre of her eyes, which had suddenly acquired a beauty more singular than that of Miss Temple's—a beauty neither of fine colour nor long eyelash, nor pencilled brow, but of meaning, of movement, of radiance. Then her soul sat on her lips, and language flowed, from what source I cannot tell. Has a girl of fourteen a heart large enough, vigorous enough, to hold the swelling spring of pure, full, fervid eloquence? Such was the characteristic of Helen's discourse on that, to me, memorable evening; her spirit seemed hastening to live within a very brief span as much as many live during a protracted existence.

They conversed of things I had never heard of; of nations and times past; of countries far away; of secrets of nature discovered or guessed at: they spoke of books: how many they had read! What stores of knowledge they possessed! Then they seemed so familiar with French names and French authors: but my amazement reached its climax when Miss Temple asked Helen if she sometimes snatched a moment to recall the Latin her father had taught her, and taking a book from a shelf, bade her read and construe a page of Virgil; and Helen obeyed, my organ of veneration expanding at every sounding line. She had scarcely finished ere the bell announced bedtime! no delay could be admitted; Miss Temple embraced us both, saying, as she drew us to her heart—

"God bless you, my children!"

Helen she held a little longer than me: she let her go more reluctantly; it was Helen her eye followed to the door; it was for her she a second time breathed a sad sigh; for her she wiped a tear from her cheek.

On reaching the bedroom, we heard the voice of Miss Scatcherd: she was examining drawers; she had just pulled out Helen Burns's, and when we entered Helen was greeted with a sharp reprimand, and told that to-morrow she should have half-a-dozen of untidily folded articles pinned to her shoulder.

"My things were indeed in shameful disorder," murmured Helen to me, in a low voice: "I intended to have arranged them, but I forgot."

Next morning, Miss Scatcherd wrote in conspicuous characters on a piece of pasteboard the word "Slattern," and bound it like a phylactery round Helen's large, mild, intelligent, and benign-looking forehead. She wore it till evening, patient, unresentful, regarding it as a deserved punishment. The moment Miss Scatcherd withdrew after afternoon school, I ran to Helen, tore it off, and thrust it into the fire: the fury of which she was incapable had been burning in my soul all day, and tears, hot and large, had continually been scalding my cheek; for the spectacle of her sad resignation gave me an intolerable pain at the heart.

About a week subsequently to the incidents above narrated, Miss Temple, who had written to Mr. Lloyd, received his answer: it appeared that what he said went to corroborate my account. Miss Temple, having assembled the whole school, announced that inquiry had been made into the charges alleged against Jane Eyre, and that she was most happy to be able to pronounce her completely cleared from every imputation. The teachers then shook hands with me and kissed me, and a murmur of pleasure ran through the ranks of my companions.

Thus relieved of a grievous load, I from that hour set to work afresh, resolved to pioneer my way through every difficulty: I toiled hard, and my success was proportionate to my efforts; my memory, not naturally tenacious, improved with practice; exercise sharpened my wits; in a few weeks I was promoted to a higher class; in less than two months I was allowed to commence French and drawing. I learned the first two tenses of the verb Etre, and sketched my first cottage (whose walls, by-the-bye, outrivalled in slope those of the leaning tower of Pisa), on the same day. That night, on going to bed, I forgot to prepare in imagination the Barmecide supper of hot roast potatoes, or white bread and new milk, with which I was wont to amuse my inward cravings: I feasted instead on the spectacle of ideal drawings, which I saw in the dark; all the work of my own hands: freely pencilled houses and trees, picturesque rocks and ruins, Cuyp-like groups of cattle, sweet paintings of butterflies hovering over unblown roses, of birds picking at ripe cherries, of wren's nests enclosing pearl-like eggs, wreathed about with young ivy sprays. I examined, too, in thought, the possibility of my ever being able to translate currently a certain little French story which Madame Pierrot had that day shown me; nor was that problem solved to my satisfaction ere I fell sweetly asleep.

Well has Solomon said—"Better is a dinner of herbs where love is, than a stalled ox and hatred therewith."

I would not now have exchanged Lowood with all its privations for Gateshead and its daily luxuries.

The Scarlet Letter

Chapter 12 The Minister's Vigil

Walking in the shadow of a dream, as it were, and perhaps actually under the influence of a species of somnambulism, Mr. Dimmesdale reached the spot where, now so long since, Hester Prynne had lived through her first hours of public ignominy. The same platform or scaffold, black and weather-stained with the storm or sunshine of seven long years, and foot-worn, too, with the tread of many culprits who had since ascended it, remained standing beneath the balcony of the meetinghouse. The minister went up the steps.

It was an obscure night in early May. An unwearied pall of cloud muffled the whole expanse of sky from zenith to horizon. If the same multitude which had stood as eye-witnesses while Hester Prynne sustained her punishment could now have been summoned forth, they would have discerned no face above the platform nor hardly the outline of a human shape, in the dark grey of the midnight. But the town was all asleep. There was no peril of discovery. The minister might stand there, if it so pleased him, until morning should redden in the east, without other risk than that the dank and chill night air would creep into his frame, and stiffen his joints with rheumatism, and clog his throat with catarrh and cough; thereby defrauding the expectant audience of tomorrow's prayer and sermon. No eye could see him, save that everwakeful one which had seen him in his closet, wielding the bloody scourge. Why, then, had he come hither? Was it but the mockery of penitence? A mockery, indeed, but in which his soul trifled with itself! A mockery at which angels blushed and wept, while fiends rejoiced with jeering laughter! He had been driven hither by the impulse of that Remorse which dogged him everywhere, and whose own sister and closely linked companion was that Cowardice which invariably drew him back, with her tremulous gripe, just when the other impulse had hurried him to the verge of a disclosure. Poor, miserable man! what right had infirmity like his to burden itself with crime? Crime is for the iron-nerved, who have their choice either to endure it, or, if it press too hard, to exert their fierce and savage strength for a good purpose, and fling it off at once! This feeble and most sensitive of spirits could do neither, yet continually did one thing or another, which intertwined, in the same inextricable knot, the agony of heaven-defying guilt and vain repentance.

And thus, while standing on the scaffold, in this vain show of expiation, Mr. Dimmesdale was overcome with a great horror of mind, as if the universe were gazing at a scarlet token on his naked breast, right over his heart. On that spot, in very truth, there was, and there had long been, the gnawing and poisonous tooth of bodily pain. Without any effort of his will, or power to restrain himself, he shrieked aloud: an outcry that went pealing through the night, and was beaten back from one house to another, and reverberated from the hills in the background; as if a company of devils, detecting so much misery and terror in it, had made a plaything of the sound, and were bandying it to and fro.

"It is done!" muttered the minister, covering his face with his hands. "The whole town will awake and hurry forth, and find me here!" But it was not so. The shriek had perhaps sounded with a far greater power, to his own startled ears, than it actually possessed. The town did not awake; or, if it did, the drowsy slumberers mistook the cry either for something frightful in a dream, or for the noise of witches, whose voices, at that period, were often heard to pass over the settlements or lonely cottages, as they rode with Satan through the air. The clergyman, therefore, hearing no symptoms of disturbance, uncovered his eyes and looked about him. At one of the chamber-windows of Governor Bellingham's mansion, which stood at some distance, on the line of another street, he beheld the appearance of the old magistrate himself with a lamp in his hand a white night-cap on his head, and a long white gown enveloping his figure. He looked like a ghost evoked unseasonably from the grave. The cry had evidently startled him. At another window of the same house, moreover appeared old Mistress Hibbins, the Governor's sister, also with a lamp, which even thus far off revealed the expression of her sour and discontented face. She thrust forth her head from the lattice, and looked anxiously upward Beyond the shadow of a doubt, this venerable witch-lady had heard Mr. Dimmesdale's outcry, and interpreted it, with its multitudinous echoes and reverberations, as the clamour of the fiends and night-hags, with whom she was well known to make excursions in the forest.

Detecting the gleam of Governor Bellingham's lamp, the old lady quickly extinguished her own, and vanished. Possibly, she went up among the clouds. The minister saw nothing further of her motions. The magistrate, after a wary observation of the darkness—into which, nevertheless, he could see but little further than he might into a millstone—retired from the window.

The minister grew comparatively calm. His eyes, however, were soon greeted by a little glimmering light, which, at first a long way off was approaching up the street. It threw a gleam of recognition, on here a post, and there a garden fence, and here a latticed window-pane, and there a pump, with its full trough of water, and here again an arched door of oak, with an iron knocker, and a rough log for the door-step. The Reverend Mr. Dimmesdale noted all these minute particulars, even while firmly convinced that the doom of his existence was stealing onward, in the footsteps which he now heard; and that the gleam of the lantern would fall upon him in a few moments more, and reveal his long-hidden secret. As the light drew nearer, be beheld, within its illuminated circle, his brother clergyman—or, to speak more accurately, his professional father, as well as highly valued friend—the Reverend Mr. Wilson, who, as Mr. Dimmesdale now conjectured, had been praying at the bedside of some dying man. And so he had. The good old minister came freshly from the death-chamber of Governor Winthrop, who had passed from earth to heaven within that very hour. And now surrounded, like the saint-like personage of olden times, with a radiant halo, that glorified him amid this gloomy night of sin—as if the departed Governor had left him an inheritance of his glory, or as if he had caught upon himself the distant shine of the celestial city, while looking thitherward to see the triumphant pilgrim pass within its gates—now, in short, good Father Wilson was moving homeward, aiding his footsteps with a lighted lantern! The glimmer of this luminary suggested the above conceits to Mr. Dimmesdale, who smiled—nay, almost laughed at them—and then wondered if he was going mad.

As the Reverend Mr. Wilson passed beside the scaffold, closely muffling his Geneva cloak about him with one arm, and holding the lantern before his breast with the other, the minister could hardly restrain himself from speaking—

"A good evening to you, venerable Father Wilson. Come up hither, I pray you, and pass a pleasant hour with me!"

Good Heavens! Had Mr. Dimmesdale actually spoken? For one instant he believed that these words had passed his lips. But they were uttered only within his imagination. The venerable Father Wilson continued to step slowly onward, looking carefully at the muddy pathway before his feet, and never once turning his head towards the guilty platform. When the light of the glimmering lantern had faded quite away, the minister discovered, by the faintness which came over him, that the last few moments had been a crisis of terrible anxiety, although his mind had made an involuntary effort to relieve itself by a kind of lurid playfulness.

Shortly afterwards, the like grisly sense of the humorous again stole in among the solemn phantoms of his thought. He felt his limbs growing stiff with the unaccustomed chilliness of the night, and doubted whether he should be able to descend the steps of the scaffold. Morning would break and find him there The neighbourhood would begin to rouse itself. The earliest riser, coming forth in the dim twilight, would perceive a vaguely-defined figure aloft on the place of shame; and half-crazed betwixt alarm and curiosity, would go knocking from door to door, summoning all the people to behold the ghost—as he needs must think it—of some defunct transgressor. A dusky tumult would flap its wings from one house to another. Then—the morning light still waxing stronger—old patriarchs would rise up in great haste, each in his flannel gown, and matronly dames, without pausing to put off their night-gear. The whole tribe of decorous personages, who had never heretofore been seen with a single hair of their heads awry, would start into public view with the disorder of a nightmare in their aspects. Old Governor Bellingham would come grimly forth, with his King James' ruff fastened askew, and Mistress Hibbins, with some twigs of the forest clinging to her skirts, and looking sourer than ever, as having hardly got a wink of sleep after her night ride; and good Father Wilson too, after spending half the night at a death-bed, and liking ill to be disturbed, thus early, out of his dreams about the glorified saints. Hither, likewise, would come the elders and deacons of Mr. Dimmesdale's church, and the young virgins who so idolized their minister, and had made a shrine for him in their white bosoms, which now, by-the-bye, in their hurry and confusion, they would scantly have given themselves time to cover with their kerchiefs. All people, in a word, would come stumbling over their thresholds, and turning up their amazed and horror-stricken visages around the scaffold. Whom would they discern there, with the red eastern light upon his brow? Whom, but the Reverend Arthur Dimmesdale, half-frozen to death, overwhelmed with shame, and standing where Hester Prynne had stood!

Carried away by the grotesque horror of this picture, the minister, unawares, and to his own infinite alarm, burst into a great peal of laughter. It was immediately responded to by a light, airy, childish laugh, in which, with a thrill of the heart—but he knew not whether of exquisite pain, or pleasure as acute—he recognised the tones of little Pearl.

"Pearl! Little Pearl!" cried he, after a moment's pause; then, suppressing his voice—"Hester! Hester Prynne! Are you there?"

"Yes; it is Hester Prynne!" she replied, in a tone of surprise; and the minister heard her footsteps approaching from the side-walk, along which she had been passing. "It is I, and my little Pearl."

"Whence come you, Hester?" asked the minister. "What sent you hither?"

"I have been watching at a death-bed," answered Hester Prynne "at Governor Winthrop's death-bed, and have taken his measure for a robe, and am now going homeward to my dwelling."

"Come up hither, Hester, thou and Little Pearl," said the Reverend Mr. Dimmesdale. "Ye have both been here before, but I was not with you. Come up hither once again, and we will stand all three together."

She silently ascended the steps, and stood on the platform, holding little Pearl by the hand. The minister felt for the child's other hand, and took it. The moment that he did so, there came what seemed a tumultuous rush of new life, other life than his own pouring like a torrent into his heart, and hurrying through all his veins, as if the mother and the child were communicating their vital warmth to his half-torpid system. The three formed an electric chain.

"Minister!" whispered little Pearl.

"What wouldst thou say, child?" asked Mr. Dimmesdale.

"Wilt thou stand here with mother and me, to-morrow noontide?" inquired Pearl.

"Nay; not so, my little Pearl," answered the minister; for, with the new energy of the moment, all the dread of public exposure, that had so long been the anguish of his life, had returned upon him; and he was already trembling at the conjunction in which—with a strange joy, nevertheless—he now found himself—"not so, my child. I shall, indeed, stand with thy mother and thee one other day, but not to-morrow."

Pearl laughed, and attempted to pull away her hand. But the minister held it fast.

"A moment longer, my child!" said he.

"But wilt thou promise," asked Pearl, "to take my hand, and mother's hand, to-morrow noontide?"

"Not then, Pearl," said the minister; "but another time."

"And what other time?" persisted the child.

"At the great judgment day," whispered the minister; and, strangely enough, the sense that he was a professional teacher of the truth impelled him to answer the child so. "Then, and there, before the judgment-seat, thy mother, and thou, and I must stand together. But the daylight of this world shall not see our meeting!"

Pearl laughed again.

But before Mr. Dimmesdale had done speaking, a light gleamed far and wide over all the muffled sky. It was doubtless caused by one of those meteors, which the night-watcher may so often observe burning out to waste, in the vacant regions of the atmosphere. So powerful was its radiance, that it thoroughly illuminated the dense medium of cloud betwixt the sky and earth. The great vault brightened, like the dome of an immense lamp. It showed the familiar scene of the street with the distinctness of mid-day, but also with the awfulness that is always imparted to familiar objects by an unaccustomed light The wooden houses, with their jutting storeys and quaint gable-peaks; the doorsteps and thresholds with the early grass springing up about them; the gardenplots, black with freshly-turned earth; the wheel-track, little worn, and even in the market-place margined with green on either side—all were visible, but with a singularity of aspect that seemed to give another moral interpretation to the things of this world than they had ever borne before. And there stood the minister, with his hand over his heart; and Hester Prynne, with the embroidered letter glimmering on her bosom; and little Pearl, herself a symbol, and the connecting link between those two. They stood in the noon of that strange and solemn splendour, as if it were the light that is to reveal all secrets, and the daybreak that shall unite all who belong to one another.

There was witchcraft in little Pearl's eyes; and her face, as she glanced upward at the minister, wore that naughty smile which made its expression frequently so elvish. She withdrew her hand from Mr. Dimmesdale's, and pointed across the street. But he clasped both his hands over his breast, and cast his eyes towards the zenith.

Nothing was more common, in those days, than to interpret all meteoric appearances, and other natural phenomena that occured with less regularity than the rise and set of sun and moon, as so many revelations from a supernatural source. Thus, a blazing spear, a sword of flame, a bow, or a sheaf of arrows seen in the midnight sky, prefigured Indian warfare. Pestilence was known to have been foreboded by a shower of crimson light. We doubt whether any marked event, for good or evil, ever befell New England, from its settlement down to revolutionary times, of which the inhabitants had not been previously warned by some spectacle of its nature. Not seldom, it had been seen by multitudes. Oftener, however, its credibility rested on the faith of some lonely eyewitness, who beheld the wonder through the coloured, magnifying, and distorted medium of his imagination, and shaped it more distinctly in his after-thought. It was, indeed, a majestic idea that the destiny of nations should be revealed, in these awful hieroglyphics, on the cope of heaven. A scroll so wide might not be deemed too expensive for Providence to write a people's doom upon. The belief was a favourite one with our forefathers, as betokening that their infant commonwealth was under a celestial guardianship of peculiar intimacy and strictness. But what shall we say, when an individual discovers a revelation addressed to himself alone, on the same vast sheet of record. In such a case, it could only be the symptom of a highly disordered mental state, when a man, rendered morbidly self-contemplative by long, intense, and secret pain, had extended his egotism over the whole expanse of nature, until the firmament itself should appear no more than a fitting page for his soul's history and fate.

We impute it, therefore, solely to the disease in his own eye and heart that the minister, looking upward to the zenith, beheld there the appearance of an immense letter—the letter A—marked out in lines of dull red light. Not but the meteor may have shown itself at that point, burning duskily through a veil of cloud, but with no such shape as his guilty imagination gave it, or, at least, with so little definiteness, that another's guilt might have seen another symbol in it.

There was a singular circumstance that characterised Mr. Dimmesdale's psychological state at this moment. All the time that he gazed upward to the zenith, he was, nevertheless, perfectly aware that little Pearl was hinting her finger towards old Roger Chillingworth, who stood at no great distance from the scaffold. The minister appeared to see him, with the same glance that discerned the miraculous letter. To his feature as to all other objects, the meteoric light imparted a new expression; or it might well be that the physician was not careful then, as at all other times, to hide the malevolence with which he looked upon his victim. Certainly, if the meteor kindled up the sky, and disclosed the earth, with an awfulness that admonished Hester Prynne and the clergyman of the day of judgment, then might Roger Chillingworth have passed with them for the arch-fiend, standing there with a smile and scowl, to claim his own. So vivid was the expression, or so intense the minister's perception of it, that it seemed still to remain painted on the darkness after the meteor had vanished, with an effect as if the street and all things else were at once annihilated.

"Who is that man, Hester?" gasped Mr. Dimmesdale, overcome with terror. "I shiver at him! Dost thou know the man? I hate him, Hester!"

She remembered her oath, and was silent.

"I tell thee, my soul shivers at him!" muttered the minister again. "Who is he? Who is he? Canst thou do nothing for me? I have a nameless horror of the man!"

"Minister," said little Pearl, "I can tell thee who he is!"

"Quickly, then, child!" said the minister, bending his ear close to her lips. "Quickly, and as low as thou canst whisper."

Pearl mumbled something into his ear that sounded, indeed, like human language, but was only such gibberish as children may be heard amusing themselves with by the hour together. At all events, if it involved any secret information in regard to old Roger Chillingworth, it was in a tongue unknown to the erudite clergyman, and did but increase the bewilderment of his mind. The elvish child then laughed aloud.

"Dost thou mock me now?" said the minister.

"Thou wast not bold!—thou wast not true!" answered the child. "Thou wouldst not promise to take my hand, and mother's hand, to-morrow noon-tide!"

"Worthy sir," answered the physician, who had now advanced to the foot of the platform—"pious Master Dimmesdale! can this be you? Well, well, indeed! We men of study, whose heads are in our books, have need to be straitly looked after! We dream in our waking moments, and walk in our sleep. Come, good sir, and my dear friend, I pray you let me lead you home!"

"How knewest thou that I was here?" asked the minister, fearfully.

"Verily, and in good faith," answered Roger Chillingworth, "I knew nothing of the matter. I had spent the better part of the night at the bedside of the worshipful Governor Winthrop, doing what my poor skill might to give him ease. He, going home to a better world, I, likewise, was on my way homeward, when this light shone out. Come with me, I beseech you, Reverend sir, else you will be poorly able to do Sabbath duty to-morrow. Aha! see now how they trouble the brain—these books!—these books! You should study less, good sir, and take a little pastime, or these night whimsies will grow upon you."

"I will go home with you," said Mr. Dimmesdale.

With a chill despondency, like one awakening, all nerveless, from an ugly dream, he yielded himself to the physician, and was led away.

The next day, however, being the Sabbath, he preached a discourse which was held to be the richest and most powerful, and the most replete with heavenly influences, that had ever proceeded from his lips. Souls, it is said, more souls than one, were brought to the truth by the efficacy of that sermon, and vowed within themselves to cherish a holy gratitude towards Mr. Dimmesdale throughout the long hereafter. But as he came down the pulpit steps, the grey-bearded sexton met him, holding up a black glove, which the minister recognised as his own.

"It was found," said the Sexton, "this morning on the scaffold where evil-doers are set up to public shame. Satan dropped it there, I take it, intending a scurrilous jest against your reverence. But, indeed, he was blind and foolish, as he ever and always is. A pure hand needs no glove to cover it!"

"Thank you, my good friend," said the minister, gravely, but startled at heart; for so confused was his remembrance, that he had almost brought himself to look at the events of the past night as visionary.

"Yes, it seems to be my glove, indeed!"

"And, since Satan saw fit to steal it, your reverence must needs handle him without gloves henceforward," remarked the old sexton, grimly smiling. "But did your reverence hear of the portent that was seen last night? a great red letter in the sky—the letter A, which we interpret to stand for Angel. For, as our good Governor Winthrop was made an angel this past night, it was doubtless held fit that there should be some notice thereof!"

"No," answered the minister; "I had not heard of it."

散文翻译

1. My Mother's Desk

By Elizabeth Sherrill

I'm sitting at my mother's desk, a mahogany secretary with a writing leaf that folds down to reveal rows of cubbyholes and tiny drawers—even a sliding secret compartment. I've loved it since I was just tall enough to see above the leaf as Mother sat doing letters. Standing by her chair, staring at the ink bottle, pens, and smooth white paper, I decided that the act of writing must be the most delightful thing in the world.

Years later, during her final illness, Mother reserved various items for my sister and brother. "But the desk," she'd repeat, "is for Elizabeth." I sensed Mother communicating with this gift, a communication I'd craved for 50 years.

My mother was brought up in the Victorian belief that emotions were private. Nice people said only nice things. I never saw her angry, never saw her cry. I knew she loved me; she expressed it in action. But as a teenager I yearned for heart-to-heart talks between mother and daughter.

They never happened. And a gulf opened between us. I was "too emotional." She lived "on the surface." She was willing to accept the relationship on these terms. I was not.

As years passed and I raised my own family, I loved the equilibrium. I loved her and thanked her for our harmonious home. Forgive me, I wrote, for having been critical. In careful words, I asked her to let me know in any way she chose that she did forgive me.

I mailed the letter and waited eagerly for her reply. None came.

Eagerness turned to disappointment, then resignation and, finally, peace. I couldn't be sure that the letter had even got to Mother. I only knew that having written it, I could stop trying to make her into someone she was not. For the last 15 years of her life we enjoyed a relationship on her terms—light, affectionate, cheerful.

Now the gift of her desk told me, as she'd never been able to, that she was pleased that writing was my chosen work.

My sister stored the desk until we could pick it up. Then it stayed in our attic for nearly a year while we converted a bedroom into a study.

When at last I brought the desk down, it was dusty from months of storage. Lovingly, I polished the drawers and cubbyholes. Pulling out the secret compartment, I found papers inside. A photograph of my father. Family wedding announcements. And a one-page letter, folded and refolded many times.

Send me a reply, my letter asks, in any way you choose. Mother, you always chose the act that speaks louder than words.

2. A Room of His Own

By Mary E. Potter

Unmistakable noises are coming through my bedroom wall. Now a scuffling, now a bumping, a long, drawn-out scraping. "John, are you moving furniture in there? Again?" I call. The wall muffles his "yes" but does not filter out of his voice the tinge of excitement.

I am not upset by these impulsive rearrangements, just amused at their frequency. I remember my own feelings when I was 13 as he is—the startling, rapid evolution of body and mind and emotions, the need to invent and reinvent yourself through clothes, hairstyles and the arrangement and decor of your room.

Amid the smothered thuds I remember how much John longed for the privacy of his own domain, how he took me aside two years ago when he was sharing a room with his younger brother, Robert. "Mom," he said, "can I please have a room of my own? I could use Jeff's. He won't mind."

It was true that Jeff had graduated from college that past June and had flown from the nest. But would he mind if the place where he had spent countless hours growing up was yanked out from under him? Would he feel ousted from the family, barred from ever coming home again?

But beyond his feelings, would I mind? That room was so much a part of our lives over the many years that Jeff had been our only child. In it I taught him to read; we constructed architectural wonders out of blocks and set up elaborate desks. It was where Jeff perfected his artwork and struggled with college applications. It was the place where I told him a thousand stories and where we had a thousand talks.

As close as we were, though, the time came when Jeff needed a door between us, a space of his own to grow in. The door to that bedroom would be shut most of the evening, behind it the muffled sound of a radio or the clack of his secondhand manual typewriter as he banged out one of his marathon letters.

I knew those letters to friends must have been filled with thoughts and opinions Jeff did not share with me. His life was spreading into areas that had nothing to do with home and family. I no longer could—or should—know everything about him.

As conscientious parents, we strive to foster independence. But when it happens, when you pause outside that door and look at the blank panels it is always a little unsettling.

It turned out that getting Jeff's permission to change the room was easy. "Of course," he said. "It would be selfish of me to hold on to it." Then his voice softened. "Mom, I won't be living at home again—you know that." Behind his glasses, his eyes were lit with all the love that has passed between us over the years. There were no doors closed here—they had all opened up again.

Then John and I jumped into the task of cleaning out closets and drawers, dispatching all the things Jeff had left behind. Playbills, and snapshots, a withered boutonniere, old report cards that stung me with pride, a stack of homemade thank-you cards from the second-grade Spanish class Jeff volunteered to teach.

Suddenly, amid all the upheaval my throat caught. There, in a pile of assorted sketches, was a pencil drawing of T-Bird—Jeff's beagle, dead these many years—curled up asleep. Jeff's rendering was so evocative I could almost feel the dear old dog's satiny warm ears. And in that room, with Jeff's things heaped around me, I could almost touch the little boy I knew was gone forever.

But we accept—at least we say we do. All of parenting is a series of letting go by degrees. The child walks and runs and rides a bike; he is stricken with the pangs of first love that we are powerless to kiss away. Then he is driving a car, and we are falling asleep before he gets home, alert, even in our dreams, to the sound of his motor gearing down.

I looked at the room around me and, in my heart, I let it go. To hold on would be, as Jeff said, selfish. Now it was time for John, shouldering through the door with an armload of his things his eyes bright with the promise of independence, to disappear behind the door. It was time for the letting go to begin again.

3. A Valentine to One Who Cared Too Much

By Nancy J. Rigg

It's raining, again. As I lie awake in bed, listening to the sound of those razor-sharp drops pounding on the pavement, my mind goes reeling down dark corridors teeming with agonizing flashbacks, and a chill from within fills me with dread. It's raining, again.

It does this every year in Southern California; at least that's what they told me last year when I marveled at the relentless determination of the rain. There seem to be two seasons here. During the rainy season, sometimes the storms drench the area nonstop for days. Sometimes the storms come and go. Often property damage and disrupted lives result. It's hard to predict the intensity of the patterns from year to year. Then there is the fire season. That takes care of the property that managed to survive the deluge, again disrupting lives. The days connecting these seasons are monotonous, with some sun, some smog and some more sun. This is nothing like back home in Colorado.

We have rains there, too. Thunderstorms in spring and summer often come with intensity great enough to cause flash-flooding. Every child raised in the West knows about these dangers. At least that's what I used to think. I'm not so sure anymore. In second grade they showed us a terrifying film about flash-flooding. A man parked his 57 Chevy on a little bridge overlooking a picturesque, arid gully and took out his camera. It was starting to rain, but he really wanted to get that picture. The image of a sudden wall of dark water carrying the man and his car away in an instant is still imprinted on my mind. They used this kind of scare tactic when I was growing up. I wonder what they use today.

A year ago I would have sworn that children here are taught nothing about the dangerous powers of nature. My fiancé, Earl Higgins, and I had recently moved to Los Angeles from Colorado. It was a move we had made by choice, for career purposes. About a week and a half after we moved into an apartment in Atwater, a block from the Los Angeles River, the rains started in earnest. On Valentine's Day, I remember thinking what dismal weather it was for being in love, but after studying Earl's face I knew that the weather didn't matter much. At least that's what I thought. Because we were together, life was safe and secure. We talked of our plans to wed and start a family, once we were settled in Los Angeles, and we listened to the rain.

The Sunnynook footbridge connects Atwater with Griffith Park, spanning the Los Angeles River and the Golden State Freeway. Like the freeway, the river is fenced to keep people out. During several walks to the park, Earl and I had noticed many children who ignored the fences and found holes to allow them through in order to play in the dirt in the river bed and run up and down the sloping concrete banks. Most of the time parents probably have no worry about their kids playing in the concrete channel, because most of the time the river is dry. Habits form, however, and in a child's mind, most of the time becomes all of the time, and nobody gives it much thought. Then the rains come.

Each day we make choices that affect our lives and, sometimes, the lives of others. Last year, on a simple Sunday, three days after Valentine's Day, after many consecutive days of steady downpour, the sun came out. Earl and I decided to walk our dog. Somehow our path took us toward the park, across the footbridge high above the rolling waters of the Los Angeles River. It is like a dream to me now, floating through my mind in slow motion. Many children were playing close to the water, and we were stunned by their ignorance and daring.

Two little boys in particular caught our attention. They were riding their bikes up and down the far bank of the river, taunting the water, obviously fascinated by its power and its draw. One little boy on a bright-yellow bike dipped his wheels into the edge of the water. Just the edge, mind you. But, oh, water is powerful. In an instant his bike was ripped from under him and he went sprawling on the river bank. Then he made a choice. He jumped into the water to get his bike and was carried rapidly downstream, a look of panic and horror registering on his young face. In an instant, we had a choice to make.

Why did Earl run to rescue that little boy? Why did I support his decision, instead of stopping him? The greatest instinct, I believe, is to help a child in need. The little boy's face, his look of fear and desperation, his cries for help—the choice was made in our intrinsic love for children. In an instant Earl ran across the bridge, vaulted the fence and ran to the water's edge. Unable to reach the boy safely from the shore, Earl stepped into the water. Then the shock registered on Earl's face as the water grabbed him, too, and prevented him from completing his mission immediately. In Earl's expression, I could see that he had confronted much more than he could handle, even being as strong and athletic as he was. The little boy was just slightly ahead of Earl, always just out of reach, like a tiny beacon lighting the way to death's door.

…

"People disappear in that river every year," one of the policemen said to me that afternoon, half in dismay, half in frustration. He did not seem very sympathetic when he took his report. But the whole city was falling apart. He implied that we had been wrong in attempting such a rescue in the first place. Was he really being critical, or was I projecting my own tremendous feelings of guilt onto him? Or was he simply stating the facts? And does that mean that this year, too, lives will be lost as a matter of course in the Los Angeles River and in other channels? Did any parents hear my pleas last year to warn their children of these dangers? Do we ever learn anything from the tragic experience of others?

I asked the policeman what we should have done. "Nothing. Call the police. Why lose two lives? That little kid was lucky to get out. There is no way to beat water like that—no way to survive it." Oh, but all the rules of self-preservation were broken when we saw that little face, filled with the terror of death, being sucked downstream. In an instant, both child and Earl were gone. The boy went home that night, but Earl never came back.

And now, it's raining, again.

4. The Two Roads

By John Ruskin

It was New Year's Night. An aged man was standing at a window. He raised his mournful eyes towards the deep blue sky, where the stars were floating like white lilies on the surface of a clear calm lake. Then he cast them on the earth, where few more hopeless people than him now moved towards their certain goal—the tomb. He had already passed sixty of the stages leading to it, and he had brought from his journey nothing but errors and remorse. Now his health was poor, his mind vacant, his heart sorrowful, and his old age short of comforts.

The days of his youth appeared like dreams before him, and he recalled the serious moment when his father placed him at the entrance of the two roads—one leading to a peaceful, sunny place, covered with flowers, fruits and resounding with soft, sweet songs; the other leading to a deep, dark cave, which was endless, where poison flowed instead of water and where devils and poisonous snakes hissed and crawled.

He looked towards the sky and cried painfully, "O youth, return! O my father, place me once more at the entrance to life, and I'll choose the better way!" But both his father and the days of his youth had passed away.

He saw the lights flowing away in the darkness. These were the days of his wasted life; he saw a star fall from the sky and disappeared, and this was the symbol of himself. His remorse, which was like a sharp arrow, struck deeply into his heart. Then he remembered his friends in his childhood, who entered on life together with him. But they had made their way to success and were now honoured and happy on this New Year's Night.

The clock in the high church tower struck and the sound made him remember his parents' early love for him. They had taught him and prayed to God for his good. But he chose the wrong way. With shame and grief he dared no longer look towards that heaven where his father lived. His darkened eyes were full of tears, and with a despairing effort, he burst out a cry: "Come back, my early days! Come back, my lost youth!"

And his youth did return, for all this was only a dream, which he had on New Year's Night. He was still young though his faults were real; he had not yet entered the deep, dark cave, and he was still free to walk on the road which leads to the peaceful and sunny land.

Those who still linger on the entrance of life, hesitating to choose the right road, remember that when years are passed and your feet stumble on the dark mountains, you will cry bitterly, but in vain: "O youth, return! Oh give me back my early days!"

5. First Snow

By Gilean Douglas

One evening I look out the window of my secluded cabin, and there are soft languid flakes falling in the golden lamplight. They fall all night, while the voice of the Teal River becomes more and more hushed and the noises of the forest die away. By dawn, the whole world of stream and wood and mountain has been kindled to a white flame of beauty.

I go out in the early morning and there is such silence that even breath is a profanation. The mountain to the north has a steel-blue light on it, and to the west the sky still holds something of the darkness of the night. To the east and the south a faint pink is spreading. I look up and see the morning star keeping white watch over a white world.

Soon the whole sky is azure and flaming. Every branch of every tree is weighted with cold and stillness; every stump is crowned with crystal; every fallen log is overlaid with silver. The wild berry bushes have puffballs of jeweler's cotton here and there along their branches, and the stark roots of hemlocks and cedars have become grottoes of quartz and chrysolite.

After heavy snowfalls, it is the evergreens that are the loveliest, with their great white branches weighted down until they are almost parallel with the trunks. They seem like giant birds with their wings folded against the cold.

But after a light fall, it is the deciduous trees that are the most beautiful. They are so fragile, so ethereal, that it seems even the sound of the rivers might shatter them as they appear to drift like crystal smoke along the banks. The bushes are silver filigree, so light, so much on tiptoe in this enchanted world. Even the slightest breeze sends the snow shimmering down from them, leaving the branches brown and bare and rather pitiful.

The sky is clear blue now and the sun has flung diamonds down on meadow and bank and wood. Beauty, the virgin, walks here quietly, no sign upon the immaculate snow. The silence is dense and deep. Even the squirrels have stopped their ribald chattering. And faint snowbird whisperings seems to emphasize the stillness.

Night comes, and the silence holds. There is a feeling about this season that is in no other— a sense of snugness, security and solitude. It is good to be out in the bracing cold, which cleans the mind and invigorates the heart. It is equally good to come in and feel the warmth wrap around the body like a soft fluffy blanket. Fire is a first-rate companion. The coffee is full-bodied and fragrant; shadows dance on the walls and the world outside my windows is very still. I am more than content to begin and end a day like this amid all the calm clarity of wintered earth.

Outside the moon is high with a dark-blue sky behind it and with mountains, plains, and forests of silver lying below. The trees, the bushes and the tall ferns are carved with alabaster. The river runs like quicksilver between the porcelain of its banks.

Earth and heavens glitter, and the sword-fern clumps are diamond sunbursts pinned to the silver-sequined ground. But it is all in silence. There are shadows from the stars. They are white, sharp lights in the midnight blue sky and appear literally to spark with coldness. I feel as though I can see every star in the universe.

It seems impossible for one human heart to contain all this loveliness without breaking. Perhaps the ache that is in mine comes from the knowledge that all this beauty is so ephemeral, that it will be gone almost before I have done more than touch it with my fingertips.

6. The Pleasures of Reading

By Bennett Cerf

All the wisdom of the ages, all the stories that have delighted mankind for centuries, are easily and cheaply available to all of us within the covers of books — but we must know how to avail ourselves of this treasure and how to get the most of it.

I am most interested in people, in meeting them and finding out about them. Some of the most remarkable people I've met existed only in a writer's imagination, then on the pages of his book, and then, again, in my imagination. I've found in books new friends, new societies, new worlds.

If I am interested in people, others are interested not so much in who as in how. Who in the books includes everybody from science fiction superman two hundred centuries in the future all the way back to the first figures in history. How covers everything from the ingenious explanations of Sherlock Holmes to the discoveries of science and ways of teaching manners to children.

Reading is a pleasure of the mind, which means that it is a little like a sport: your eagerness and knowledge and quickness make you a good reader. Reading is fun, not because the writer is telling you something, but because it makes your mind work. Your own imagination works along with the author's or even goes beyond his. Your experience, compared with his, brings you to the same or different conclusions, and your ideas develop as you understand his.

Every book stands by itself, like a one-family house, but books in a library are like houses in a city. Although they are separate, together they all add up to something, they are connected with each other and with other cities. The same ideas, or related ones, turn up in different places; the human problems that repeat themselves in life repeat themselves in literature, but with different solutions according to different writings at different times.

Reading can only be fun if you expect it to be. If you concentrate on books somebody tells you "ought" to read, you probably won't have fun. But if you put down a book you don't like and try another till you find one that means something to you, and then relax with it, you will almost certainly have a good time—and if you become, as a result of reading, better, wiser, kinder, or more gentle, you won't have suffered during the process.

7. My Mother's Gift

By Suzanne Chazin

I grew up in a small town where the elementary school was a ten-minute walk from my house and in an age, not so long ago, when children could go home for lunch and find their mothers waiting.

At the time, I did not consider this a luxury, although today it certainly would be. I took it for granted that mothers were the sandwich-makers, the finger-painting appreciators and the homework monitors. I never questioned that this ambitious, intelligent woman, who had had a career before I was born and would eventually return to a career, would spend almost every lunch hour throughout my elementary school years just with me.

I only knew that when the noon bell rang, I would race breathlessly home. My mother would be standing at the top of the stairs, smiling down at me with a look that suggested I was the only important thing she had on her mind. For this, I am forever grateful.

Some sounds bring it all back: the high-pitched squeal of my mother's teakettle, the rumble of the washing machine in the basement, the jangle of my dog's license tags as she bounded down the stairs to greet me. Our time together seemed devoid of the gerrymandered schedules that now pervade my life.

One lunch time when I was in the third grade will stay with me always. I had been picked to be the princess in the school play, and for weeks my mother had painstakingly rehearsed my lines with me. But no matter how easily I delivered them at home, as soon as I stepped onstage, every word disappeared from my head.

Finally, my teacher took me aside. She explained that she had written a narrator's part to the play, and asked me to switch roles. Her words, kindly delivered, still stung, especially when I saw my part to go to another girl.

I didn't tell my mother what had happened when I went home for lunch that day. But she sensed my unease, and instead of suggesting we practice my lines, she asked if I wanted to walk in the yard.

It was a lovely spring day and the rose vine on the trellis was turning green. Under the huge elm trees, we could see yellow dandelions popping through the grass in bunches, as if a painter had touched our landscape with dabs of gold.

I watched my mother casually bend down by one of the clumps. "I think I'm going to dig up all these weeds," she said, yanking a blossom up by its roots. "From now on, we'll have only roses in this garden."

"But I like dandelions, "I protested." All flowers are beautiful—even dandelions."

My mother looked at me seriously. "Yes, every flower gives pleasure in its own way, doesn't it?" she asked thoughtfully. I nodded, pleased that I had won her over. "And that is true of people too," she added. "Not everyone can be a princess, but there is no shame in that."

Relieved that she had guessed my pain, I started to cry as I told her what had happened. She listened and smiled reassuringly.

"But you will be a beautiful narrator," she said, reminding me of how much I loved to read stories aloud to her. "The narrator's part is every bit as important as the part of a princess."

Over the next few weeks, with her constant encouragement, I learned to take pride in the role. Lunchtimes were spent reading over my lines and talking about what I would wear.

Backstage the night of the performance, I felt nervous. A few minutes before the play, my teacher came over to me. "Your mother asked me to give this to you," she said, handing me a dandelion. Its edges were already beginning to curl and it flopped lazily from its stem. But just looking at it, knowing my mother was out there and thinking of our lunchtime talk, made me proud.

After the play, I took home the flower I had stuffed in the apron of my costume. My mother pressed it between two sheets of paper toweling in a dictionary, laughing as she did it that we were perhaps the only people who would press such a sorry-looking weed.

I often look back on our lunchtime together, bathed in the soft midday light. They were the commas in my childhood, the pauses that told me life is not savored in pre-measured increments, but in the sum of *daily rituals* and *small pleasures* we casually share with loved ones. Over peanut-butter sandwiches and chocolate-chip cookies, I learned that love, first and foremost, means being there for the little things.

A few months ago, my mother came to visit. I took off a day from work and treated her to lunch. The restaurant bustled with noontime activity as businesspeople made deals and glanced at their watches. In the middle of all this sat my mother, now retired, and I. From her face I could see she relished the pace of the work world.

"Mom, you must have been terribly bored staying at home when I was a child," I said.

"Bored? Housework is boring. But you were never boring."

I didn't believe her, so I pressed. "Surely children are not as stimulating as a career."

"A career is stimulating," She said, "I'm glad I had one. But a career is like an open balloon. It remains inflated only as long as you keep pumping. A child is a seed. You water it. You care for it the best you can. And then it grows all by itself into a beautiful flower. "

Just then, looking at her, I could picture us sitting at her kitchen table once again, and I understood why I kept that flaky brown dandelion in our old family dictionary pressed between two crumpled bits of paper towel.

8. Mystery of the White Gardenia

By Marsha Arons

Every year on my birthday, from the time I turned 12, a white gardenia was delivered to my house in Bethesda, Md. No card or note came with it. Calls to the florist were always in vain—it was a cash purchase. After a while I stopped trying to discover the sender's identity and just delighted in the beauty and heady perfume of that one magical, perfect white flower nestled in soft pink tissue paper.

But I never stopped imagining who the anonymous giver might be. Some of my happiest moments were spent daydreaming about someone wonderful and exciting but too shy or eccentric to make known his or her identity.

My mother contributed to these imaginings. She'd ask me if there was someone for whom I had done a special kindness who might be showing appreciation. Perhaps the neighbor I'd help when she was unloading a car full of groceries. Or maybe it was the old man across the street whose mail I retrieved during the winter so he wouldn't have to venture down his icy steps. As a teen-ager, though, I had more fun speculating that it might be a boy I had a crush on or one who had noticed me even though I didn't know him.

When I was 17, a boy broke my heart. The night he called for the last time, I cried myself to sleep. When I awoke in the morning, there was a message scribbled on my mirror in red lipstick: "Heartily know, when half-gods go, the gods arrive." I thought about that quotation from Emerson for a long time, and until my heart healed, I left it where my mother had written it. When I finally went to get the glass cleaner, my mother knew everything was all right again.

I don't remember ever slamming my door in anger at her and shouting, "You just don't understand!" because she did understand.

One month before my high-school graduation, my father died of a heart attack. My feelings ranged from grief to abandonment, fear and overwhelming anger that my dad was missing some of the most important events in my life. I became completely uninterested in my upcoming graduation, the senior-class play and the prom. But my mother, in the midst of her own grief, would not hear of my skipping any of those things.

The day before my father died, my mother and I had gone shopping for a prom dress. We'd found a spectacular one, with yards and yards of dotted swiss in red, white and blue, it made me feel like Scarlett O'Hara, but it was the wrong size. When my father died, I forgot about the dress.

My mother didn't. The day before the prom, I found that dress—in the right size—draped majestically over the living-room sofa. It wasn't just delivered, still in the box. It was presented to me—beautifully, artistically, lovingly. I didn't care if I had a new dress or not. But my mother did.

She wanted her children to feel loved and lovable, creative and imaginative, imbued with a sense that there was magic in the world and beauty even in the face of adversity. In truth, my mother wanted her children to see themselves much like the gardenia—lovely, strong and perfect—with an aura of magic and perhaps a bit of mystery.

My mother died ten days after I was married. I was 22. That was the year the gardenias stopped coming.

9. My Father's Music

By Wayne Kalyn

I remember the day Dad first lugged the heavy accordion up our front stoop, taxing his small frame. He gathered my mother and me in the living room and opened the case as if it were a treasure chest. "Here it is," he said. "Once—you learn to play, it'll stay with you for life."

If my thin smile didn't match his full-fledged grin, it was because I had prayed for a guitar or a piano. It was 1960, and I was glued to my AM radio, listening to Del Shannon and Chubby Checker. Accordions were nowhere in my hit parade. As I looked at the shiny white keys and cream-colored bellows, I could already hear my friend's squeezebox jokes.

For the next two weeks, the accordion was stored in the hall closet. Then one evening Dad announced that I would start lessons the *following week*. In *disbelief* I shot my eyes toward Mom for support. The firm set of her jaw told me I was out of luck.

Spending $300 for an accordion and $5 per lesson was out of character for my father. He was practical always—something he learned growing up on a Pennsylvania farm. Clothes, heat and sometimes even food were scarce.

Before I was born, he and my mother moved into her parents' two-story home in Jersey City, N. J. I grew up there on the second floor; my grandparents lived downstairs. Each weekday Dad made the three-hour commute to and from Long Island, where he was a supervisor in a company that serviced jet engines. Weekends, he tinkered in the cellar, turning scraps of plywood into a utility cabinet or fixing a broken toy with spare parts. Quiet and shy, he was never more comfortable than when at his workbench.

Only music carried Dad away from his world of tools and projects. On a Sunday drive, he turned the radio on immediately. At red lights, I'd notice his foot tapping in time. He seemed to hang on every note.

Still, I wasn't prepared when, rummaging in a closet, I found a case that looked to me like a tiny guitar's. Opening it, I saw the polished glow of a beautiful violin. "It's your father's," Mom said. "His parents bought it for him. I guess he got too busy on the farm to ever learn to play it." I tried to imagine Dad's rough hands on this delicate instrument—and couldn't.

Shortly after, my lessons began with Mr. Zelli at the Allegro Accordion School, tucked between an old movie theater and a pizza parlor. On my first day, with straps straining my shoulder, I felt clumsy in every way. "How did he do?" my father asked when it was over. "Fine for the first lesson," said Mr. Zelli. Dad glowed with hope.

I was ordered to practice half an hour every day, and every day I tried to get out of it. My future seemed to be outside playing ball, not in the house mastering songs I would soon forget, but my parents hounded me to practice.

Gradually, to my surprise, I was able to string notes together and coordinate my hands to play simple songs. Often, after supper, my father would request a tune or two. As he sat in his easy chair, I would fumble through "Lady of Spain" and "Beer Barrel Polka".

"Very nice, better than last week," he'd say. Then I would segue into a medley of his favorites, "Red River Valley" and "Home on the Range", and he would drift off to sleep, the newspaper folded on his lap. I took it as a compliment that he could relax under the spell of my playing.

One July evening I was giving an almost flawless rendition of "Come Back to Sorrento", and my parents called me to an open window. An elderly neighbor, rarely seen outside her house, was leaning against our car humming dreamily to the tune. When I finished, she smiled broadly and called out, "I remember that song as a child in Italy. Beautiful, just beautiful."

Throughout the summer, Mr. Zelli's lessons grew more difficult. It took me a week and a half to master them now. All the while I could hear my buddies outside playing heated games of stickball. I'd also hear an occasional taunt: "Hey, where's your monkey and cup?"

Such humiliation paled, though, beside the impending fall recital, I would have to play a solo on a local movie theater's stage. I wanted to skip the whole thing. Emotions boiled over in the car one Sunday afternoon.

"I don't want to play a solo," I said.

"You have to," replied my father.

"Why?" I shouted. "Because you didn't get to play your violin when you were a kid? Why should I have to play this stupid instrument when you never had to play yours?"

Dad pulled the car over and pointed at me.

"Because you can bring people joy. You can touch their hearts. That's gift I won't let you throw away," he added softly, "Someday you'll have the chance I never had: you'll play beautiful music for your family. And you'll understand why you've worked so hard."

I was speechless. I had rarely heard Dad speak with such feeling about anything, much less the accordion. From then on, I practiced without my parents' making me.

The evening of concert Mom wore glittery earrings and more makeup than I could remember. Dad got out of work early, put on a suit and tie, and slicked down his hair with Vitalis. They were an hour early, so we sat in the living room chatting nervously. I got the unspoken message that playing this one song was a dream come true for them.

At the theater nervousness overtook me as I realized how much I wanted to make my parents proud. Finally, it was my turn. I walked to the lone chair on stage and performed "Are You Lonesome Tonight?" without a mistake. The applause spilled out, with a few hands still clapping after others had stopped. I was lightheaded, glad my ordeal was over.

After the concert Mom and Dad came backstage. The way they walked—heads high, faces flushed—I knew they were pleased. My mother gave me a big hug; Dad slipped an arm around me and held me close. "You were just great," he said. Then he shook my hand and was slow to let it go.

As the years went by, the accordion drifted to the background of my life. Dad asked me to play at family occasions, but the lessons stopped. When I went to college, the accordion stayed behind in the hall closet next to my father's violin.

A year after my graduation, my parents moved to a house in a nearby town. Dad, at 51, finally owned his own home. On moving day, I didn't have the heart to tell him he could dispose of the accordion, so I brought it to my own home and put it in the attic.

There it remained, a dusty memory, until one afternoon several years later when my two children discovered it by accident. Scott thought it was a secret treasure; Holly thought a ghost lived inside. They were both right.

When I opened the case, they laughed and said, "Play it, play it." Reluctantly, I strapped on the accordion and played some simple songs. I was surprised my *skills* hadn't rusted away. Soon the kids were dancing in circles and giggling. Even my wife, Terri, was laughing and clapping to the beat. I was amazed at their unbridled glee.

My father's words came back to me: "Someday you'll have the chance I never had. Then you'll understand."

I finally knew what it meant to work hard and sacrifice for others. Dad had been right all along: the most precious gift is to touch the hearts of those you love.

Later I phoned Dad to let him know that, at long last, I understood. Fumbling for the right words, I thanked him for the legacy it took almost 30 years to discover. "You're welcome," he said, his voice choked with emotion.

Dad never learned to coax sweet sounds from his violin. Yet he was wrong to think he would never for his family. On that wonderful evening, as my wife and children laughed and danced, they heard my accordion. But it was my father's music.

10. Life in a Violin Case

By Alexander Bloch

In order to tell what I believe, I must briefly sketch something of my personal history.

The turning point of my life was my decision to give up a promising business career and study music. My parents, although sympathetic, and sharing my love of music, disapproved of it as a profession. This was understandable in view of the family background. My grandfather had taught music for nearly forty years at Springhill College in Mobile and, though much beloved and respected in the community, earned barely enough to provide for his large family. My father often said it was only the hardheaded thriftiness of my grandmother that kept the wolf at bay. As a consequence of this example in the family, the very mention of music as a profession carried with it a picture of a precarious existence with uncertain financial rewards. My parents insisted upon college instead of a conservatory of music, and to college I went—quite happily, as I remember, for although I loved my violin and spent most of my spare time practicing, I had many other interests.

Before my graduation from Columbia, the family met with severe financial reverses and

I felt it my duty to leave college and take a job. Thus was I launched upon a business career—which I always think of as the wasted years.

Now I do not for a moment mean to disparage business. My whole point is that it was not for me. I went into it for money, and aside from the satisfaction of being able to help the family, money is all l got out of it. It was not enough. I felt that life was passing me by. From being merely discontented I became acutely miserable. My one ambition was to save enough to quit and go to Europe to study music. I used to get up at dawn to practice before I left for "downtown", distracting my poor mother by bolting a hasty breakfast at the last minute. Instead of lunching with my business associates, I would seek out some cheap cafe, order a meager meal and scribble my harmony exercises. I continued to make money, and finally, bit by bit, accumulated enough to enable me to go abroad. The family being once more solvent, and my help no longer necessary, I resigned from my position and, feeling like a man released from jail, sailed for Europe. I stayed four years, worked harder than I had ever dreamed of working before and enjoyed every minute of it.

"Enjoyed" is too mild a word. I walked on air. I really lived. I was a freeman and I was doing what I loved to do and what I was meant to do.

If I had stayed in business I might be a comparatively wealthy man today, but I do not believe I would have made a success of living. I would have given up all those intangibles, those inner satisfactions that money can never buy, and that are too often sacrificed when a man's primary goal is financial success.

When I broke away from business it was against the advice of practically all my friends and family. So conditioned are most of us to the association of success with money that the thought of giving up a good salary for an idea seemed little short of insane. If so, all I can say is "Gee! It's great to be crazy."

Money is a wonderful thing, but it is possible to pay too high a price for it.

参考文献

奥斯汀 . 1993. 傲慢与偏见 . 张玲，张扬译 . 北京：人民文学出版社 .
奥斯汀 . 2009. 傲慢与偏见 . 张经浩译 . 北京：中国对外翻译出版 .
奥斯汀 . 2010. 傲慢与偏见 . 孙致礼译 . 南京：译林出版社 .
奥斯汀 . 2016. 傲慢与偏见 . 陈伯雨译 . 北京：中国华侨出版社 .
勃朗特 . 1990. 简·爱 . 吴钧燮译 . 北京：人民文学出版社 .
勃朗特 . 2010. 简·爱 . 黄源深译 . 南京：译林出版社 .
勃朗特 . 2016. 简·爱 . 陈伯雨译 . 北京：北京联合出版公司 .
曹明伦 . 2007. 英汉翻译实践与评析 . 成都：四川人民出版社 .
方梦之 . 2004. 译学辞典 . 上海：上海外语教育出版社 .
菲茨杰拉德 . 2004. 了不起的盖茨比 . 姚乃强译 . 北京：人民文学出版社 .
菲茨杰拉德 . 2012. 了不起的盖茨比 . 邓若虚译 . 海口：南海出版公司 .
菲茨杰拉德 . 2013. 了不起的盖茨比 . 巫宁坤译 . 南京：译林出版社 .
菲茨杰拉德 . 2018. 了不起的盖茨比 . 陈伯雨译 . 北京：中国华侨出版社 .
古今明 . 1997. 英汉翻译基础 . 上海：上海外语教育出版社 .
何伟等 . 2017a. 英语功能语义分析 . 北京：外语教学与研究出版社 .
何伟等 . 2017b. 汉语功能语义分析 . 北京：外语教学与研究出版社 .
何兆熊 . 2000. 新编语用学概要 . 上海：上海外语教育出版社 .
胡壮麟 . 1994. 语篇的衔接与连贯 . 上海：上海外语教育出版社 .
胡壮麟 . 2018. 新编语篇的衔接与连贯 . 上海：华东师范大学出版社 .
胡壮麟等 . 2001. 语言学教程（修订版）. 北京：北京大学出版社 .
胡壮麟等 . 2005. 系统功能语言学概论 . 北京：北京大学出版社 .
胡壮麟等 . 2017. 系统功能语言学概论（第三版）. 北京：北京大学出版社 .
霍桑 . 1991. 红字 . 胡允桓译 . 北京：人民文学出版社 .
霍桑 . 2011. 红字 . 苏福忠译 . 上海：上海译文出版社 .
霍桑 . 2012. 红字 . 王元媛译 . 武汉：长江文艺出版社 .
黎洪 . 2012. 汉语偏正副句句序变异研究 . 合肥：安徽大学出版社 .
李鑫华 . 2000. 英语修辞格详论 . 上海：上海外语教育出版社 .
连淑能 . 2010. 英汉对比研究（增订本）. 北京：高等教育出版社 .

林六辰，姚乃强. 2012. 英语短篇小说品鉴（上）. 上海：上海外语教育出版社.
林六辰，姚乃强. 2012. 英语短篇小说品鉴（下）. 上海：上海外语教育出版社.
欧·亨利. 2018. 欧·亨利短篇小说精选. 陈伯雨，党清译. 北京：中国华侨出版社.
释赞宁. 1987. 高僧传（上）. 北京：中华书局.
孙致礼. 2003. 新编英汉翻译教程. 上海：上海外语教育出版社.
申雨平，戴宁. 2002. 实用英汉翻译教程. 北京：外语教学与研究出版社.
束定芳. 2000. 隐喻学研究. 上海：上海外语教育出版社.
王东风. 2009. 语言学与翻译：概念与方法. 上海：上海外语教育出版社.
杨平等. 2004. 名作精译——《中国翻译》英译汉选萃. 青岛：青岛出版社.
叶子南. 2013. 认知隐喻与翻译实用教程. 北京：北京大学出版社.
章振邦等. 2012. 新编高级英语语法. 上海：上海外语教育出版社.
赵一凡等. 2006. 西方文论关键词. 北京：外语教学与研究出版社.
朱立元等. 2014. 当代西方文艺理论（第三版）. 上海：华东师范大学出版社.
庄绎传. 1999. 英汉翻译教程. 北京：外语教学与研究出版社.

Baker, M. (2011). *In Other Words: A Coursebook on Translation.* London and New York: Routledge.

Baker, P. & Ellece, S. (2016). *Key Terms in Discourse Analysis.* Beijing: Foreign Language Teaching and Research Press.

Brown, G. & Yule, G. (2000). *Discourse Analysis.* Beijing: Foreign Language Teaching and Research Press.

Diessel, H. (2001). *The Ordering Distribution of Main and Adverbial Clauses: A Typological Study. Language,* 77, 343-365.

Fawcett, R. P. (2010). *How to Analyze Participant Roles and So Processes in English.* USTB Handbook.

Grice, H. P. (1975). Logic and Conversation. In Cole, P. & Morgan, J. L. (eds.), *Syntax and Semantics, Vol. 3: Speech Acts,* 41-58. New York: Academic Press.

Halliday, M. A. K. (1966). Notes on Transitivity and Theme in English. *Journal of Linguistics,* 2(1), 57-67.

Halliday, M. A. K. (1967/1968). Notes on Transitivity and Theme in English: Parts 1, 2 & 3. *Journal of Linguistics,* 3(1), 3(2), 4(2).

Halliday, M. A. K. & Hasan, R. (1976). *Cohesion in English.* London: Longman.

Halliday, M. A. K. & Hasan, R. (1985). *Language, Context and Text.* Victoria: Deakin University Press.

Halliday, M. A. K. (2000). *An Introduction to Functional Grammar (Second Edition).* Beijing: Foreign Language Teaching and Research Press.

Halliday, M. A. K. & Matthiessen, C. (2008). *An Introduction to Functional Grammar (Third Edition).* Beijing: Foreign Language Teaching and Research Press.

参考文献

Jakobson, R. (1987). *Language in Literature.* Cambridge, MA: The Belknap Press of Harvard University Press.

Julie Rivkin, et al. eds. (2004). *Literary Theory: An Anthology (Second Edition).* Malden, Massachusetts: Blackwell Publishing.

Kövecses, Z. (2002). *Metaphor: A Practical Introduction.* Oxford: Oxford University Press.

Lakoff, G. (1992). *The Contemporary Theory of Metaphor.* Cambridge: Cambridge University Press.

Lakoff, G. & Johnson, M. (2003). *Metaphors We live By (With a New Afterword).* Chicago: The University of Chicago Press.

Leech, G. N. (1981). *Semantics (Second Edition).* Harmondsworth: Penguin.

Leech, G. N. & M. H. Short. (1981). *Style in Fiction: A Linguistic Introduction to English Fictional Prose.* London and New York: Longman.

Leech, G. N. (1983). *Semantics.* London: Longman.

Lyons, John. (1977). *Semantics,* 2 vols. London and New York: Cambridge University Press.

Martin, B. & Ringham, F. (2016). *Key Terms in Semiotics.* Beijing: Foreign Language Teaching and Research Press.

Martin, J. R., Matthiessen, C. M. I. M. & Painter, C. (2010). *Deploying Functional Grammar.* Beijing: The Commercial Press.

Martin, J. R. & White, P. R. R. (2005). *The Language of Evaluation: Appraisal in English.* New York: Palgrave MacMillan.

Malinowski, B. (1923). *The Problem of Meaning in Primitive Language.* In Ogdan C. K, Richards I. A (eds.) (pp.296-336) *The Meaning of Meaning.* London: Routledge.

Malinowski, B. (1935). *Coral Gardens and Their Magic* (Vol. 2). London: Routledge.

Munday, J. (2012). *Introducing Translation Studies: Theories and Applications (Third Edition).* London and New York: Routledge.

Munday, J. (2016). *Introducing Translation Studies: Theories and Applications (Fourth Edition).* London and New York: Routledge.

Matthiessen, C. M. I. M. (2013). *Halliday's Introduction to Functional Grammar (Fourth Edition).* London and New York: Routledge.

Matthiessen, C. M. I. M. & Teruya, K. (2016). *Key Terms in Systemic Functional Linguistics.* Beijing: Foreign Language Teaching and Research Press.

Neale, A. (2002). *More Delicate TRANSITIVITY: Extending the PROCESS TYPE System Networks for English to Include Full Semantic Classifications.* Welsh: Cardiff University.

Newmark, P. (2001). *Approaches to Translation.* Shanghai: Shanghai Foreign Language Education Press.

Nord, C. (2005/2006). *Text Analysis in Translation: Theory, Methodology, and Didactic Application of a Model for Translation-oriented Text Analysis (Second Edition).* Beijing:

Foreign Language Teaching and Research Press.

Norgaard, N. et al. eds. (2017). *Key Terms in Stylistics.* Beijing: Foreign Language Teaching and Research Press.

Palmer, F. R. (1981). *Semantics.* Cambridge: Cambridge University Press.

Reiss, K. (2004). *Translation Criticism: The Potentials & Limitations.* Shanghai: Shanghai Foreign Language Education Press.

Richards, J. C. et al. eds. (2000). *Longman Dictionary of Language Teaching & Applied Linguistics.* Beijing: Foreign Language Teaching and Research Press.

Robins, A. (1980) *The Writer's Practical Rhetoric.* New York: John Wiley & Sons.

Saussure, F. (2001). *Course in General Linguistics.* Beijing: Foreign Language Teaching and Research Press.

Thompson, G. (2000). *Introducing Functional Grammar.* Beijing: Foreign Language Teaching and Research Press.

Thompson, G. (2004). *Introducing Functional Grammar (Second Edition).* London: Hodder Arnold.

William Morris & Mary Morris. (1975). *Harper Dictionary of Contemporary Usage.* New York: Harper & Row Publishers.

附　　录

及物性系统术语缩写表

动作过程		
PR	=Participant Role	参与者角色
Ag	=Agent	施事
Pro	=Process	过程
PrEx	=Process Extension	过程延长成分
Af	=Affected	受事
Cre	=Created	创造物
Ra	=Range	范围
Ma	=Manner	方式
Dir	=Direction	方向
So	=Source	来源
Pa	=Path	路径
Des	=Destination	目的地
Loc	=Location	位置
Ag-Ca	=Agent-Carrier	施事－载体
Af-Ca	=Affected-Carrier	受事－载体
Af-Perc	=Affected-Perceiver	受事－感知者
Af-Ph	=Affected-Phenomenon	受事－现象
Af-Posr	=Affected-Possessor	受事－拥有者
Af-Posd	=Affected-Possessed	受事－拥有物
Af-Dir	=Affected-Direction	受事－方向
Af-So	=Affected-Source	受事－来源
Af-Pa	=Affected-Path	受事－路径
Af-Des	=Affected-Destination	受事－目的地

心理过程		
Em	=Emoter	情感表现者
Desr	=Desiderator	意愿表现者
Perc	=Perceiver	感知者
Cog	=Cognizant	认知者
Ag-Perc	=Agent-Perceiver	施事－感知者
Ag-Cog	=Agent-Cognizant	施事－认知者
Af-Em	=Affected-Emoter	受事－情感表现者
Af-Desr	=Affected-Desiderator	受事－意愿表现者
Af-Perc	=Affected-Perceiver	受事－感知者
Af-Cog	=Affected-Cognizant	受事－认知者
Ph	=Phenomenon	现象
Cre-Ph	=Created-Phenomenon	创造物－现象
Cor	=Correlator	相关方
关系过程		
Ca	=Carrier	载体
At	=Attribute	属性
Tk	=Token	标记
Vl	=Value	价值
Ir	=Identifier	识别者
Id	=Identified	被识别者
Posr	=Possessor	拥有者
Posd	=Possessed	拥有物
行为过程		
Behr	=Behaver	行为方
交流过程		
Comr	=Communicator	交流方
Comd	=Communicated	交流内容
Comee	=Communicatee	交流对象
Comr-Comee	=Communicator-Communicatee	交流方－交流对象
存在过程		
Ext	=Existent	存在方
Ag-Ext	=Agent-Existent	施事－存在方
Af-Ext	=Affected-Existent	受事－存在方

何伟等（2017a: xi-xii）